Creativity in PRIMARY EDUCATION

In memory of Anna Craft 1961–2014

3rd Edition

Creativity
in PRIMARY
EDUCATION

Edited by
Anthony Wilson

SAGE | LearningMatters

Los Angeles | London | New Delhi
Singapore | Washington DC

Learning Matters
An imprint of SAGE Publications Ltd
1 Oliver's Yard
55 City Road
London EC1Y 1SP

SAGE Publications Inc.
2455 Teller Road
Thousand Oaks, California 91320

SAGE Publications India Pvt Ltd
B 1/I 1 Mohan Cooperative Industrial Area
Mathura Road
New Delhi 110 044

SAGE Publications Asia-Pacific Pte Ltd
3 Church Street
#10–04 Samsung Hub
Singapore 049483

Editor: Amy Thornton
Development editor: Geoff Barker
Production controller: Chris Marke
Project management: Deer Park Productions,
Tavistock
Marketing manager: Lorna Patkai
Cover design: Wendy Scott
Typeset by: C&M Digitals (P) Ltd, Chennai, India
Printed by: CPI Group (UK) td, Croydon, CR0 4YY

First published in 2007 by Learning Matters Ltd
Second edition published in 2009
Reprinted in 2009, 2010 and 2011
Third edition 2015

Library of Congress Control Number: 2014952505

British Library Cataloguing in Publication Data

A catalogue record for this book is available
from the British Library

ISBN 978-1-4462-8064-5
ISBN 978-1-4462-8065-2 (pbk)

MIX
Paper from
responsible sources
FSC
www.fsc.org   FSC® C013604

Contents

Contributors

Anthony Wilson is subject leader for PGCE Primary English and a Senior Lecturer at the University of Exeter. His research is in the field of creative writing and creative literacy pedagogies in education. He is co-convener of the ESRC Seminar Series Poetry Matters and was lead researcher for Bath Festivals' The Write Team project, on the impact of creative writers in schools. He is co-editor of *Making Poetry Happen* (Bloomsbury, 2015), *Making Poetry Matter* (Bloomsbury, 2013*)*, and *The Poetry Book for Primary Schools* (1998). He is author of *Riddance* (Worple Press, 2012) and a prose memoir *Love for Now* (Impress Books). He blogs at www.anthonywilsonpoetry.com

Rob Bowker is subject leader from Primary PGCE Science at the University of Exeter. His research interests are children's learning in informal environments such as museums, botanical gardens and environmental centres. He continues to work in partnership with the Eden Project, Cornwall.

Mary Briggs is a Principal Lecturer and Programme Lead for ITE Early years and Primary in the School of Education at Oxford Brookes University. She is a teacher and researcher who has worked across the early years and primary age range in special and mainstream schools. Mary has written a number of books focusing on mathematics education, assessment and leadership.

Simon Catling is Emeritus Professor of Primary Education at Oxford Brookes University. Before moving into teacher education he taught in London primary schools. He is a Past-President of the Geographical Association. His research and professional interests are in primary children's geographical learning, teachers' geographical understanding and their teaching practices. He has published extensively for children, teachers and teacher educators, including *Teaching Primary Geography for Australian Schools* (with Tessa Willy and John Butler, HawkerBrownlow, 2013).

Liz Chamberlain is a Senior Lecturer for Primary English, teaching both undergraduates and postgraduate education students. Her main area of expertise is in working with and mentoring teaching students, with a focus on children's reading and writing. She was a primary teacher for over 20 years and regularly spends time in school, hosting Writers' Workshop sessions. Liz's research interests are linked to the field of English and, in particular, her doctorate focuses on children's home writing practices. For four years she was the Strategic Consultant for the 'Everybody Writes' national writing project and continues to use this work to reflect on effective literacy practices.

Sue Chedzoy is an Honorary University Fellow at the University of Exeter. During her academic career she was responsible for the initial training of Early Years, Primary, Middle School and Secondary School trainee teachers, as well as being Programme Director of Primary / Key Stage 2/3 and the Master's Programme in Teaching and Learning. Sue is a recipient of the Ling Award by the Physical Education Association of the United Kingdom in recognition of outstanding contribution to the Physical Education profession. She currently works as a Consultant/Evaluator for the Cognitive Education Development Unit within the Centre for Teaching Thinking and Dialogue.

Hilary Claire taught history and citizenship in ITE at London Metropolitan University. She published extensively in both primary history and citizenship education and was the national co-ordinator of the Primary Educators Network for the Advancement of Citizenship (PENAC).

Hilary Cooper is Professor of History and Pedagogy at the University of Cumbria. Previously she taught at Goldsmiths' College, London University, and in a variety of London primary schools. Her doctoral research on 'Young Children's Thinking in History' was undertaken as a class teacher. She has published widely.

Anna Craft was Professor of Education at Exeter University and The Open University where she co-ordinated research groups in the twin areas of creativity in educa-tion and learning futures. She was Principal Investigator at the Open University and Exeter University respectively for two new European projects funded by the European Commission, exploring how Possibility Thinking can fuel quiet revolutions. Anna wrote and edited over twenty books, including *Creativity and Education Futures* (2011, Trentham Books), *Reflective Practice in the Early Years* (two editions, with Alice Paige-Smith, 2008 and 2011, Open University Press), *Close Encounters* (with Kerry Chappell, Veronica Jobbins, Linda Rolfe, Trentham 2011), *Creativity in schools* (2005, Routledge), *Creativity in the Early Years* (2002, Continuum) and *Creativity across the Primary Curriculum* (2000, Routledge). Anna was founding Co-Editor of the jour-nal, *Thinking Skills and Creativity* and founding Co-Convenor of *British Educational Research Association Special Interest Group, Creativity in Education*.

Teresa Cremin is a Professor of Education (Literacy) at The Open University. She is a joint coordinator of the British Educational Research Association (BERA) Special Interest Group on Creativity, an Academician of the Academy of Social Sciences, a Fellow of the English Association, a Trustee of UKLA and the Society for Educational Studies, and a Board Member of Booktrust and The Poetry Archive. Teresa's research, her teaching and consultancy focuses mainly on teachers' literate identities and practices, the pedagogies of reading and writing for pleasure and creativity in teaching and learning from the early years through to Higher Education. Additionally, working with teachers as co-participant researchers she has explored the everyday reading practices of young people in the 21st century. Most recently her projects have involved exploring contemporary enactments of Vivian Gussin Paley's work with young children scribing and enacting their own narra-tives, and the literary discussions of extracurricular reading groups who were shadowing the Carnegie, Kate Greenaway Awards. Teresa has written and edited over 25 books and numerous papers and professional texts, most recently publishing *Building Engaged Communities of Readers: Reading for Pleasure*, and Researching literacy Lives: Building Home school communities and *Teaching English Creatively* (2nd edition) (all Routledge).

Dan Davies is Professor of Science and Technology Education and Head of Research in the School of Education at Bath Spa University. After teaching in London primary schools he worked as an education officer for the Design Council and as Lecturer in Primary Science Education at Goldsmiths' University of London before moving to Bath Spa University in 1998. He has written extensively on creativity in both science and design & technology education.

Tony Eaude was the headteacher of a multi-cultural first school in Oxford. He works as an independent research consultant and is a Research Fellow at the Department of Education, University of Oxford. He is the author of *Children's Spiritual, Moral, Social and Cultural Development- Primary and Early Years*, *Thinking Through Pedagogy for*

Primary and Early Years and *How do expert primary classteachers really work?* More details of his work can be seen on www.edperspectives.org.uk

Emese Hall is Subject Leader for PGCE Primary Art at the University of Exeter. She is a member of DfE Expert Advisory Group for Art and Design Education, a member of NSEAD Publications Board, and South West Regional Network Co-ordinator for the Cambridge Primary Review Trust. Her research interests encompass drawing, reflective practice and creativity.

Sarah Hennessy is a Senior Lecturer in Music Education at the University of Exeter, where she teaches both specialist and generalist primary music courses. She also undertakes research into music teacher education and children's musical creativity. She is author of *Music 7–11: Developing Primary Teaching Skills* (Routledge, 1995) and *Coordinating Music Across the Primary School* (RoutledgeFarmer, 1998). She is editor of *Music Education Research*, director of the International Conference for Research in Music Education (RIME) and Chair of the Orff Society.

Alan Howe is Head of the Department of Education Studies in the School of Education at Bath Spa University. He taught in primary schools in Bath and Bristol before moving into higher education, and has written extensively on creativity in both science and design & technology education, including *Design and Technology for the Future: Creativity Culture and Citizenship* (with Dan Davies and Ron Ritchie, 2001).

Jane Johnston is a recently retired Reader in Education, who has contributed to the development of early years and primary science education both nationally and internationally. She has many publications in the field, is the editor of the Journal of Emergent Science, helped to set up the Early Years research group for the European Science Education Research Association, and was one of the first five science teachers to achieve Chartered Science Teacher (CSci Teach).

Paul Key is a Senior Lecturer at the University of Winchester, specialising in art and design education, and is currently the joint Programme Leader for the Primary PGCE programme. His research interests have included the exploration of landscapes and artistry as 'images' through which to investigate teachers and teaching, and he co-authored, with Jayne Stillman, *Teaching Primary Art and Design* (Learning Matters, 2009).

Avril Loveless is a Professor of Education at the University of Brighton. Her professional life of being a teacher, teacher educator and researcher spans over 30 years. Her current research interests are in the narratives of the learning lives of creative educators, and digital 'tools of the trade' for educators in times of reform. The key research themes in her work are creativity and learning; pedagogy and professional knowledge; and digital tools and pedagogy.

Alison Peacock is Headteacher of The Wroxham Teaching School, one of the first to be included in the DfE's Teaching School initiative. She was a member of the Cambridge Primary Review team and was instrumental in establishing a national network to disseminate the outcomes of the final report and to empower teachers towards excellence. Additionally, she was a founding member of the Cambridge Primary Review Trust from which she resigned as a Director in April 2013, although she remains as a consultant advisor. In addition to school leadership she provides advice and consultancy to a range of educational organisations, including Cambridge Assessment Colloquium, Headteacher groups, Hertfordshire Development Trust, Local Authorities and Teach First. Alison is co-author of *Creating Learning without Limits*, Member of the Royal Society Vision Committee, Member of the Commission for The Royal College of Teaching, Trustee of The Teacher Development Trust and a National Leader of Education. In the 2014 New Year's Honours list, Alison was awarded the rank of Dame Commander of the Order of the British Empire (DBE) for services to education.

Dr Elizabeth Wood is Professor of Education at the University of Sheffield. She specialises in early childhood and primary education, and has conducted research into teachers' professional knowledge and beliefs; progression and continuity; play and pedagogy; children's choices during free play; critical perspectives on early childhood policy and practice.

Dr Richard Woolley is Head of Centre for Education and Inclusion and Associate Head (Research) in the Institute of Education at the University of Worcester, UK. His interests include personal, social and health education, religious education, children's well-being, and how teachers are prepared to explore sensitive and controversial issues with children.

Acknowledgements

Teresa Cremin would like to acknowledge the work of her colleagues Jonathon Barnes and Stephen Scoffham in the Kent Creative Partnerships funded research upon which Chapter 3 draws.

Richard Woolley wishes to thank final year Education Studies students at the University of Worcester for their support and insights during the preparation of this chapter.

Every effort has been made to trace the copyright holders and to obtain their permission for the use of copyright material. The publisher and author will gladly receive any information enabling them to rectify any error or omission in subsequent editions.

Introduction
Anthony Wilson

Large numbers leave school with the bitter taste of defeat in them, not having mas-
tered even moderately well those basic skills which society demands, much less
having become people who rejoice in the exercise of creative intelligence.

Margaret Donaldson, *Children's Minds*

Two aspects of educational reform have occupied the policy discourse in Anglophone countries in the last 20 years. First, in a context of dwindling natural resources, there is an imperative placed on education systems to create a workforce that can compete in the global marketplace. At the same time, these systems have seen an increase of high-stakes accountability which shows no sign of abating. The tension arising from this has resulted in 'barriers' to creativity in schools (Sahlberg, 2011), not least the pressure upon teachers to conform (*ibid*). It is not surprising, therefore, that teachers' views of crea-tivity are variable (Kampylis, Berki and Saariluoma, 2009). For example, some research shows that teachers self-report as setting great store by creativity at the same time as disliking some of the characteristics associated with it such as risk-taking, independence and spontaneity (Westby and Dawson, 1995). In some cases this results in what Alencar (2002) calls 'inhibiting practices' in the classroom. These include: emphasising the need for 'correct' responses; on reproducing information; and underestimating students' capacity for divergent thinking (Kampylis, Berki and Saariluoma, 2009). Csikszentmihalyi (2011) describes this situation in the following way thus: he notes that teachers are hun-gry for creativity but that they often lack vision, in the form of models and leadership, for implementing it in practice. He identifies the lack of a clear theoretical framing of creativ-ity as a fundamental issue facing the profession.

For teachers, this unease is compounded by the feeling that we should be planning for creativity and bringing to bear all of our energies on teaching towards it, including the implications this might have for planning, assessment and progression. These feelings can be complicated even further when we take into consideration the demands of curriculum orders and recommendations which teachers need to engage with, interpret and 'deliver'.

The last word of the previous paragraph is freighted with different expectations in our context of targets and accountability. As the late Ted Wragg stated in an interview in the first edition of this book, many teachers enter into teaching not because they are passionate about 'delivery', but because they see it as a profession where they can develop their own creativity as well as those of their pupils. Conversely, when we detect its absence, in curricular documentation, schemes of work, or in our own practice, we can be quick to label that as negative. There has, perhaps, never been a a more pivotal moment to address issues of individual and collective creativity within the profession. The late Anna Craft and Emese Hall remind us that we are most likely to feel creative about our practice when we have ownership of it. The implications of this 'learner inclu-sive' pedagogy (Jeffrey and Craft, 2004; Jeffrey and Woods, 2003) are not easily assimi-lated, for it involves trust, self-examination, honesty, risk-taking and the possibility that we may encounter failure.

How to use this book

This book is an attempt to illuminate and discuss what this view of creativity means for us as primary practitioners, and how it might be put into practice across the curriculum (DfE, 2013). Far from being an 'instruction manual', however, the aim of the book is to prompt you to reconsider any preconceived notions of what creativity might be, and to ask that you reconceptualise your own responses to different subjects by trying out the suggested activities in each chapter.

You will also encounter 'Reflective Task' sections within each chapter. Please use these to reflect on the challenge to think about concepts within each subject in ways which you might not have considered before. Recording for yourself how your responses change as you read the book might be a good way of developing the four modes of creativity noted by Guy Claxton (1999) referred to in Chapter 10 by Avril Loveless: Resilience, Reflection, Resourcefulness and Relationship.

Intended audience

It is hoped that this book will be of direct interest to primary trainee teachers on all courses of initial teacher training and education in England and other parts of the UK. One of the themes running through the book is that creativity is not the preserve of the arts alone. While visual, performing and literary arts are tackled explicitly within it, the book is aimed at generalists as well as specialists on PGCE courses. The book will also be of interest to those studying creativity within educational and/or childhood and youth studies on undergraduate programmes and all primary teachers looking to reconsider the place of creativity in their practice.

Chapter details

The book is divided into three parts. Part 1 contextualises the concept of creativity and how it has come to be such an important term in educational discourse. In 'Changes in the landscape for creativity in education', Anna Craft and Emese Hall present an overview of how creativity came to be represented in educational thinking in the UK in three distinct 'waves'. As well as providing a historical overview, the chapter contains a summary of different models of how creativity develops, and a critique of the tensions inherent in teaching in a fast-changing world. They warn that the coalition government's response (2012) to the Henley Review (2012), while positive, implicitly privileges the notion of culture as 'the main priority, with creativity now regarded as an aspect of culture'.

There follows two new chapters to this edition of the book. In 'The art of the possible', Alison Peacock takes us on a tour of The Wroxham School, where she is Headteacher. Hers is a vision of 'trust, co-agency and inclusion'. She reminds us that children only get the chance to be five, or seven, once. With that in mind she and her staff have designed an environment where learners are encouraged to pursue challenges rather than dwell on their failures; and where assessment is used to inform teaching rather than as a system for judging performance.

In another new chapter, Rob Bowker reminds us that not all learning takes place in the formal setting of the classroom. He argues that informal learning has an important part to play in terms of children's creative development. He questions the false 'dichotomy' of pupil-led informal learning on the one hand, and teacher-led formal learning on the other; and argues that both formal and informal learning need to be 'consciously blended' by teachers wanting to provide 'real world' experiences for their pupils. Placing children at the centre of decisions about their learning is not without risks, he says, but the concomitant rise in self-motivation and delight is more than worth it.

Creativity in the core primary curriculum

Parts 2 and 3 of this book present practical ideas for creative practice in the core and foundation subjects respectively. In Chapter 7 Liz Chamberlain reports on schools who have taken part in the action research project 'Everybody Writes', where the key attitude of teachers was that they remained flexible in their determination to offer children real-life opportunities for writing which were practised across the whole school.

Mary Briggs' chapter 'Creative mathematics' is critical of recent curricular recommendations and challenges the reader to re-evaluate mathematics as a creative subject. The chapter argues that children need to be given open-ended and problem-solving tasks which cater for a variety of learning styles in order for their interest and development in mathematics to be sustained.

In Chapter 9 Jane Johnston asks 'What is creativity in science education?'. Creative science teaching, she says, involves teachers adapting their pedagogy to suit the learning objectives, children and context they find themselves in. Promoting a view of science teaching which develops curiosity, motivation and self-esteem, the chapter also reminds us that interaction with peers and supportive adults in the undertaking of exploratory and investigatory tasks are key to successful learning.

Creativity in the foundation primary curriculum

Avril Loveless' chapter 'Thinking about creativity' is an extremely useful summary of different models of creativity, including in the subject of computing. The chapter locates its discussion of creativity much more explicitly on personal responses to questions such as: What wider role do teachers play in both being creative themselves and encouraging creativity in others? One of the central tenets of the chapter is that creative people do not work in isolation, directly challenging the myth of creativity to be found in Western cultures, that of 'special' individuals operating alone. How schools and teachers take up the challenge to draw upon local and global knowledge is exemplified by a case study showing how trainee teachers came to further their own understanding of creativity through working with children and ICT.

Paul Key's chapter, 'Creativity and primary art and design education' warns that while art and design is a subject traditionally associated with creativity, opportunities for developing ideas and experimenting with different techniques are sometimes missed within it. He argues that the benefits outweigh such lapses, and can provide learners with creative 'habits of mind', as well as the chance to learn a new language of visual, spatial and tactile responses (Gentle, 1985).

In chapter 12, Richard Woolley adapts the work of the late Hilary Claire to ask: 'What has creativity got to do with citizenship education?' As in previous chapters, this question requires individual teachers to place their own sense of self-esteem, confidence and identity at the core of their citizenship education. Only when we value ourselves, they argue, can we begin to value the 'worth' of others. Using the metaphor of 'journey' to describe citizenship education, teachers are encouraged to set small achievable goals on a road towards greater collaboration, responsibility and autonomy in response to global and societal issues. Teaching the acquisition of values is at the heart of this approach: 'When we ask children to consider creative solutions to social issues we must make sure that they constantly measure them against values which we debate in terms of principles and consequences. When we ask them to judge other people's creative proposals they must also refer to values. This is because creativity can be the handmaid of evil as well as benign change.'

In 'Creativity in primary design and technology', Dan Davies and Alan Howe challenge us to conceptualise design and technology as both 'hands-on' and 'minds-on'. Creating and evaluating the efficacy of objects which by definition do not yet exist teaches children that creativity is not alien to evaluation. The key, they argue, is not to set children artificial problems, but to support them in developing strategies that will help them to make new connections between different disciplines in the midst of designing and making. Synthesising the work of Csikszentmihalyi (2011) with good classroom practice, they advocate a style of teaching design and technology which is centred on building on children's interests, identifying real opportunities and using relevant contexts for learning.

Simon Catling's chapter 'Creative primary geography' argues that creativity involves 'understanding the world about us as much as [...] something fictional or imagined'. Geography is an active subject which integrates both skills (e.g. fieldwork) and knowledge (e.g. of place and human activity). New curriculum orders do not, however, promote 'an enquiry approach to teaching and learning', nor do they 'refer to sustainability in our places and environments and to our futures'. He challenges us to use children's perspectives about their own geographies; to 'problematise' the topic; and question the 'accepted', always bearing in mind how 'they might go about things differently in their use of and/or attitude to the environment, places and other peoples (Hicks, 2002)'.

Hilary Cooper puts it slightly differently. Learning history, she says, requires us to develop and defend arguments, to listen to others and to recognise that there may be no single 'right answer' to the questions we pose in the classroom.

In 'Creativity in the music curriculum' Sarah Hennessy develops further the idea of the teacher as artist, a role which involves risk-taking, confidence, imagination and the mutual handing over of responsibility between teacher and pupils: 'Good practice in music teaching always aspires to an integration of listening, composing and performing'. Drawing on a model of creativity developed by Wallas (1926), she presents practical ideas for music teaching based on four stages of the creative process: preparation, incubation, illumination and verification.

The book closes with Sue Chedzoy's 'Children, creativity and physical education'. Her overview of how PE teaching has changed in the postwar period will resonate with many readers. Being 'expert', she argues, is not as important as feeling secure in setting up safe environments for children and having a basic understanding of how children learn and develop through PE. Her definition of how children learn, with enjoyment and 'flow', summarises what all teachers seek for those in their care: 'They are not afraid to show others what they can do; they volunteer questions and answers, ask for help and talk positively about their achievements, whatever their level of attainment. They explore and experiment with new activities without worrying about failing.' These behaviours facilitate and complement progress and academic knowledge in all the subjects covered here. They are the outward signs that we have provided the entitlement of all children in our care: to be safe, valued, trusted in an environment which delights in their social, emotional as well as cognitive growth. Can the goal of education be any more important? And can the need for creative pedagogy which promotes these be any more urgent than it is now?

REFERENCES REFERENCES **REFERENCES** REFERENCES REFERENCES REFERENCES

Alencar, EMLS (2002) Mastering creativity for education in the 21st century. In Proceedings of the 13th biennial world conference of the world council for gifted and talented children Istanbul, Turkey.

Csikszentmihalyi, M (2011) A systems perspective on creativity and its implications for measurement. In R. Schenkel and O. Quintin (Eds.), *Measuring Creativity* (407–414). The European Commission: Brussels.

Claxton, G (1999) *Wise up.* London: Bloomsbury.

DfE (2013) *The National Curriculum in England: Key stages 1 and 2 framework document.* London: Department for Education.

Gentle, K (1985) *Children and art teaching.* Beckenham: Croom Helm.

Hicks, D (2002) *Lessons for the future.* Abingdon: Routledge.

Kampylis, P, Berki, E, and Saariluoma, P (2009) *In-service and prospective teachers' conceptions of creativity, Thinking Skills and Creativity*, 4, 15–29.

Sahlberg, P (2011) The role of education in promoting creativity: potential barriers and enabling factors. In R Schenkel and O Quintin (Eds.), *Measuring Creativity* (pp.337–344). The European Commission: Brussels.

Wallas, B (1926) *The art of thought.* New York: Harcourt Brace & World.

Westby, EL and Dawson, VL (1995) Creativity: Asset of burden in the classroom? *Creativity Research Journal*, 8 (1), 1–11.

PART 1
SETTING THE SCENE

1
Changes in the landscape for creativity in education
Anna Craft and Emese Hall

Chapter objectives

By the end of this chapter you should have:

- understood that creativity is no longer the preserve of arts education;
- explored how creative teaching focuses on the teacher;
- seen how creativity is critical for individuals to thrive in a rapidly changing world.

This chapter addresses the following Teachers' Standards (DfE, 2012a):

- establish a safe and stimulating environment for pupils, rooted in mutual respect;
- have a secure knowledge of the relevant subject(s) and curriculum areas, foster and maintain pupils' interest in the subject, and address misunderstandings;
- promote a love of learning and children's intellectual curiosity;
- fulfil wider professional responsibilities.

Introduction

In the last part of the twentieth century and the start of the twenty-first, creativity in education has increasingly become a focus in curriculum and pedagogy. It is now embedded in the Early Years Foundation Stage Curriculum and the National Curriculum for schools (England). There has been a substantial investment in staff development and the creation of teaching resources for school teachers.

This chapter explores why the landscape has altered so radically from the policy context which immediately preceded it. It also explores current concepts of creativity in use in education, and strategies used to enhance opportunity for pupils to be creative.

Finally it raises some fundamental tensions and dilemmas that face teachers fostering creativity in education.

What has changed?

The last twenty-five or so years have seen a global revolution so that in many places creativity has moved from the fringes of education and/or from the arts to being seen as a core aspect of educating. No longer seen as an optional extra, nor as primarily to do with self-expression through the arts, early twenty-first century creativity is seen as generative problem-identification and problem-solving, across life (Craft, 2000, 2001, 2002, 2005).

Three waves of creativity in education

We can describe the change in creativity policy as occurring in three 'waves'.

- The 'first wave' of creativity in education was perhaps in the 1960s, codified by Plowden (CACE, 1967), drawing on child-centred philosophy, policy and practice.
- The second wave began in the late 1990s, about ten years after the introduction of the National Curriculum.
- And the third is well under way in the early years of the twenty-first century.

The first wave: Plowden and beyond

The recommendations of the Central Advisory Council in Education in 1967 (which became known as the Plowden Report), formed thinking about creativity in education for the generation which followed it (CACE, 1967). Drawing on a large body of so-called liberal thinking on the education of children, it recommended that children learn by discovery, taking an active role in both the definition of their curriculum and the exploration of it. Active and individualised learning was strongly encouraged, as well as learning through first-hand experience of the natural, social and constructed world beyond the classroom. A core role was given to play.

Plowden made a significant contribution to the way in which creativity in education was understood. It influenced the early years of education but had an impact on the later primary years and secondary education, too. It provided an early foundation for the more recent move in creativity research towards emphasising social systems rather than personality, cognition or psychodynamics.

Through Plowden, creativity became associated with a range of other approaches: discovery learning, child-centred pedagogy, an integrated curriculum and self- rather than norm-referencing.

However, within the Plowden 'take' on creativity, there are several problems.

The first is the role of knowledge. For while we cannot exercise imagination or creativity in any domain without knowledge if we are to go beyond the given or assumed, Plowden nevertheless implies that a child may be let loose to discover and learn without any prior knowledge.

Secondly, there is a lack of context implied in the rationale for 'self-expression'. Plowden appears to conceive of the child's growth and expression in a moral and ethical vacuum. It has been argued more recently that encouraging children and young people to have ideas and express them should be set in a moral and ethical context within the classroom (Craft, 2000, 2006; Fischmann et al., 2004; Gardner, 2004).

Thirdly, Plowden suggests that play provides the foundation for a variety of other forms of knowledge and expression and in doing so appears to connect play creativity within the arts only and not with creativity across the whole curriculum.

Related to the third point is a further problem, which is that play and creativity are not the same as one another, for not all play is creative.

Such conceptual and practical problems, it has been argued (NACCCE, 1999), were in part responsible for creativity being pushed to the back of policy-makers' priorities in curriculum development. Until, that is, the late 1990s, which saw a revival of official recognition of creativity in education: the second wave (Craft, 2002, 2003a, 2004).

The second wave of creativity in education

During the late 1990s, there was a resurgence of interest in psychology and education research. This accompanied policy shifts reintroducing creativity into education.

Three major curriculum-based initiatives occurred.

The National Advisory Committee on Creative and Cultural Education Report

The report linked the fostering of pupil creativity with the development of culture, in that original ideas and action are developed in a shifting cultural context. It suggested that the fostering of pupil creativity would contribute to the cultural development of society, since creativity rarely occurs without some form of interrogation of what has gone before or is occurring synchronously. The Report proposed the idea of democratic creativity, i.e. 'all people are capable of creative achievement in some area of activity, provided the conditions are right and they have acquired the relevant knowledge and skills' (paragraph 25). This notion has some connection with Plowden, in that children's self-expression is valued and all people are seen as capable of creativity. But it *contrasts* with the Plowden approach too. First, it argues for the acquisition of knowledge and skills as the necessary foundation to creativity – reflecting the wider research context in the 'situating' of knowledge. Secondly, it has a great deal more to say on creativity than Plowden since that was its main focus. Criticisms of the NACCCE Report are very few. Since its publication, it has increasingly informed the way that creativity is being developed in the codified curriculum for Foundation Stage and beyond.

'Creative development' in Foundation Stage and Early Years Foundation Stage

The codifying of this part of the Early Years curriculum for children up to the age of five in 2000, reinforced in 2007, meshed closely with the existing norms and discourse about early education. 'Creative development' in both sets of policy guidance encompasses art, craft and design, imaginative play, music and dance, all of which have traditionally formed a core part of Early Years provision. It emphasises the role of imagination and of children developing and deepening a range of ways of responding to experiences and expressing and communicating ideas and feelings through a wide range of media and materials. In the 2007 guidance, creativity and critical thinking is seen as a core aspect of provision, allowing children to make connections, transform understanding and develop sustained, shared thinking. It involves valuing creativity and critical thinking right across the curriculum and balancing freedom with structure. In addition, creative development continued to be named as one of the six areas of learning and development and comprised being creative (responding to experiences, communicating and expressing ideas), exploring materials and media, creating music and dance, and developing imagination and imaginative play. It emphasised the need to support children in exploratory risk-taking, absorption in their activities, initiating ideas, choices and decisions, and recognising novelty in children's explorations. It includes, very significantly, offering children opportunities to 'work alongside artists and other creative adults' (DfES, 2007, card Creative Development, side 2).

In the 2012 update of the Early Years Foundation Stage (DfE, 2012b), there was some re-naming of the areas of learning and development, with 'Expressive Arts and Design' replacing what was 'Creative Development'. In essence, the learning content did not change a great deal – other than condensing the statutory requirements – and a desire for children's creative learning is still evident. However, this new name can be seen to reflect the top-down influence of the coalition Government's educational vision; in this case, there is a clear link to the primary National Curriculum, with its distinct subject areas.

Codifying creativity within the early learning curriculum has been a significant landmark: particularly in the 2007 and 2012 versions which acknowledge that problem-finding and problem-solving using imagination and posing 'what if?' questions occur within a whole range of domains. On the other hand there are at least two difficulties with seeing creativity in terms of 'development'.

Firstly, conceiving of creativity as something which may be 'developed' implies that there is a ceiling, or a static end-state, and that, given the appropriate immediate learning environment, children will 'develop'. Both presuppositions are problematic.

Secondly, the implication is that play and creativity are the same. As already suggested, they are not. Play may be, but is not necessarily, creative. For example, 'Snakes and Ladders', being dependent upon a mix of chance and a set structure, is not creative, but 'Hide and Seek' may well be. Similarly, imaginative play may be imitative but it may equally be highly creative.

'Creative thinking' named as a key skill in the National Curriculum – for a short time

This contrasts with the Early Years formulation in seeing a cross-curricular role for creativity in the aims of the school curriculum, suggesting that creativity is not the preserve of the arts alone but that it arises in all domains of human endeavour.

Criticisms of the National Curriculum focused on the lack of exploration of how this skill was manifest in different curriculum areas. At the time of writing the third edition of this text (Summer, 2014), the new primary National Curriculum (DfE, 2013b) has been published and will become statutory from September 2014. Contrary to earlier predictions, the new formulation does not reflect the 2007 formulation of the KS3 curriculum (DfES, 2007), which was implemented from September 2008. This included six personal learning and thinking skills (PTLS), one of which was creative thinking, reflecting the NACCCE definition.

When the coalition Government's proposals for education were set out in their white paper (DfE, 2010), it was stated that the old National Curriculum was constraining creativity. However, despite this argument, there was no indication of how creativity was going to be conceptualised or supported in any new policies, perhaps other than lessening the content of the programmes of study for the foundation subjects to allow teachers to exercise more autonomy. Fortunately, the period between the review of the National Curriculum in late 2011 and the implementation of the new policy in 2014 presented opportunities. Although it seemed that the emphasis on creativity that had been so visible for the past decade had come to an end, schools were free to explore creative pedagogies on their own terms (Craft *et al.*, 2013).

It is encouraging that the new National Curriculum framework for primary schools (DfE, 2013b) specifically mentions creativity in connection to a wide range of subject areas, including: mathematics, science, art and design, computing, design and technology, and music. Indeed, one of the document's opening statements encourages 'an appreciation of human creativity and achievement' (*ibid*, p3). It thus appears that both Big C (major impact) and little c (everyday) creativity (Craft, 2001) have been recognised, albeit to varying degrees, in this new curriculum.

All kinds of other policy initiatives have flowed from these major developments in the second wave. These include the following:

- *Excellence in Cities*, a scheme to replace Education Action Zones and designed to raise achievement particularly in the inner city, was launched in 1999. Targeted to start with secondary schools and then introduced to primary schools too, this programme was believed to have led to higher attainment in both GCSEs and vocational equivalents for pupils whose schools were in the scheme. Some schools and action zones focused on creativity (DfES, 2005a; OFSTED, 2004).
- For several years at the end of the 1990s and start of the 2000s, DfES Best Practice Research Scholarships and Professional Bursaries for teachers enabled teachers to research creativity in their classrooms (DfES, 2005b). From 2004 the theme was continued through the Creativity Action Research Awards offered by Creative Partnerships and DfES (Creative Partnerships, 2004).
- OFSTED took a positive and encouraging perspective on creativity through two reports published in August 03: *Improving City Schools*: How the Arts Can Help (OFSTED, 2003b) and Raising Achievement Through the Arts (OFSTED, 2003b).
- DfES published *Excellence and Improvement* in May 2003 (DfES, 2003), exhorting primary schools to take creative and innovative approaches to the curriculum and to place creativity high on their agendas following this in 2004 with materials.
- DfES established the Innovation Unit with the brief to foster and nurture creative and innovative approaches to teaching and learning.
- DfES funded research, development and CPD initiatives including the Creative Action Research Awards (Craft *et al.*, 2007).
- The Arts Council and DCMS became integrally bound into the delivery of Creative Partnerships and associated activities (Creative Partnerships, 2005).
- A creativity strand was established within the DTI from the end of the 1990s (DTI, 2005).
- The National College for School Leadership developed the notion of Creative Leadership for fostering creativity in pupils (NCSL, 2005).
- DfES introduced 'personalised learning' (DfES, 2004a, 2004b, 2004c).
- QCA developed creativity CPD materials for Foundation Stage through to KS2 (QCA, 2005a, 2005b).

The work of the QCA in this second wave is particularly significant as a landmark. It attempted to both describe and promote creativity in schools, through its creativity curriculum development and research project launched in 2000, Creativity: Find it! Promote it! Drawing on the NACCCE definition of creativity, QCA added an emphasis on purposeful shaping of imagination, producing original and valuable outcomes. It aimed to exemplify creativity across the curriculum, through a framework providing early years and school settings with both a lens and strategies for finding and promoting creativity. Specifically, the QCA suggest that creativity involves pupils in thinking or behaviour involving:

- questioning and challenging;
- making connections, seeing relationships;
- envisaging what might be;
- exploring ideas, keeping options open;
- reflecting critically on ideas, actions, outcomes.

(QCA, 2005a, 2005b)

There are many other aspects to the framework, including suggestions for pedagogical strategies and ways in which whole schools might develop their creativity.

The model of learning which underpins the QCA framework, is found commonly in what might be called second-to-third-wave work in creativity, including that which focuses on creative partnerships of a variety of kinds. For it assumes, perhaps unsurprisingly, that creativity is situated in a social and cultural context. A situated perspective, then, it emphasises the practical, social, intellectual and values-based practices and approaches involved in creative activities. From this perspective, 'creative learning' is seen as an apprenticeship into these, a central role being given to the expert adult, offering induction to the relative novice.

Aspects of apprenticeship include:

- *modelling expertise and approaches*
  When the adults taking a lead role in stimulating young people to work creatively are creative practitioners in their own fields, they offer novices ways into their own artistic practices. This model of teaching and learning could be seen as quite different to that of the traditional classroom teacher in a school (Craft *et al.*, 2004).

- *authenticity of task*
  The more closely the activities generated by the adult expert correspond to those that form part of their normal professional life, the greater the likelihood that pupils will be able to effectively integrate propositional and procedural knowledge, and the greater the chances of learners finding personal relevance and meaning in them too. This is sometimes referred to as 'cultural authenticity'.

- *locus of control*
  It is very important that the locus of control rests with the young person (Jeffrey, 2001a, 2001b, 2003a, 2003b, 2004; Jeffrey and Woods, 2003; Woods 1990, 1993, 1995, 2002). Connected with this, the quality of interactions between adults and pupils determines, in large part, the decision-making authority.

- genuine risk-taking
  If the locus of control resides with the pupils, this can facilitate greater and more authentic risk-taking than might otherwise have been undertaken.

When creative practitioners lead the apprenticeship, children can see work created as part of the leader's own artistic or commercial practices, and are therefore engaged in coming to understand the artist's own ways of working.

The model of creative learning as apprenticeship implies ownership by children of ideas, processes and directions, together with engagement in and motivation toward, their own creative journey. But an apprenticeship is finite. Ultimately the novice becomes a newly fledged expert, taking off without the scaffolding, travelling alone or with others, making their own map. Griffiths and Woolf (2004) document the ways in which skilful creative practitioners are sensitised to when it is appropriate to encourage young people to move to the edge of, and then beyond, the scaffolding.

There are two other issues touched on but perhaps not yet adequately explored, by the QCA framework in this particular incarnation.

- *What is the relationship between individual and collective work?*
  How do the two interact? Although this question has been examined by researchers over some twenty years at least (Amabile, 1983, 1988, 1996, 1997; Craft, 1997; John-Steiner, 2000; Miell and Littleton, 2004; Sonnenburg, 2004; Wegerif, 2004), it is still not well understood.
  One aspect of the individual/collective negotiation is negotiating the balance between the creative needs of the individual and the collective creative needs of a group. Nourishment and support for the individual occurs in a wider social context. Seeing how ideas are responded to is a part of this, and therefore so is evaluative two-way feedback in written, dramatic, symbol-based and other forms. The creator should be able to negotiate meaning and possible implications with evaluators.

- *Models of how creativity can be fostered*
  It may not be fruitful to consider creativity as being 'triggered' in any simple or direct way. As with all social science, it is very hard to be sure of cause-effect relationships. But we do have some working hypotheses implied in some key terms: teaching for creativity, creative teaching and creative learning.

Creative teaching is focused on the teacher. Studies suggest that teachers feel creative when they control and take ownership of their practice, are innovative and ensure that learning is relevant to learners, envisaging possibilities and differences, seeing these through into action (Jeffrey and Woods, 2003; Woods and Jeffrey, 1996).

Teaching for creativity by contrast focuses on the child and is often 'learner inclusive' (Jeffrey and Craft, 2004; Jeffrey and Woods, 2003). A learner inclusive pedagogy involves giving the child many choices and a great deal of control over what is explored and how. It is, essentially, learner-centred (Jeffrey and Craft, 2004; Craft *et al.*, 2013).

Research suggests that a teacher who is successful in stimulating children's creativity does some or all of the following:

- encourages development of purposeful outcomes across the curriculum;
- develops children's motivation to be creative;
- fosters the study of any discipline in depth, developing children's knowledge of it, to enable them to go beyond their own immediate experiences and observations;
- offers a clear curriculum and time structure to children but involves them in the creation of new routines when appropriate;
- provides an environment where children are rewarded for going beyond what is expected;
- uses language to both stimulate and assess imaginativeness;
- helps children to find personal relevance in learning activities;
- models the existence of alternatives while also helping children to learn about and understand existing conventions;
- encourages additional and alternative ways of being and doing, celebrating, where appropriate to do so;

- their courage to be different;
- gives children enough time to incubate their ideas.

(Sources: Balke, 1997; Beetlestone, 1998; Craft, 2000; Edwards and Springate,1995; Fryer, 1996; Halliwell, 1993; Hubbard, 1996; Jeffrey and Woods, 2003; Kessler, 2000; Shallcross, 1981; Torrance, 1984; Woods, 1990, 1993, 1995; Woods and Jeffrey, 1996.)

OFSTED (2003a, 2003b) would add to this the significance of:

- partnership;
- authentic relationships with the social, economic, cultural and physical environment.

The middle ground between creative teaching and teaching for creativity has been gradually expanded to include a relatively new term in the discourse: 'creative learning', which has been described as a 'middle ground' between teaching for creativity and creative teaching, emphasising the learner's experience (Jeffrey and Craft, 2006). So what does this term mean? European work (Jeffrey and Craft, 2006) suggests that it involves learners in using their imagination and experience to develop learning, that it involves them strategically collaborating over tasks and contributing to the classroom pedagogy and to the curriculum, and it also involves them critically evaluating their own learning practices and teachers' performance. It offers them, in many ways, a form of apprenticeship.

Nevertheless, the teaching profession and other collaborative partners still have a long way to go in characterising creative learning as distinct from other kinds of learning (Cochrane *et al.*, 2008).

During the second wave of creativity, then, there were common themes to many of the policy initiatives, for example:

- role of the arts;
- social inclusion;
- raising achievement;
- exploration of leadership;
- place of partnerships.

Within the research community both prior to and during the second wave, there was a matched growth. After a relatively fallow period from the 1970s until the late 1980s, the last part of the twentieth century saw greatly increased activity in creativity research as applied to education.

Research foci included the conceptualising of creativity (Craft, 1997, 2001, 2002; Fryer, 1996), exploring how creativity could be fostered and maintained (Jeffrey, 2001a, 2001b), investigation of creativity in specific domains such as information and communications technology (Leach, 2001), documenting creative teaching (Woods and Jeffrey, 1996) and exploring creative leadership (Imison, 2001; NCSL, 2005).

In common with other educational and social science research a significant direction of research into creativity, both within education and beyond it, has been to situate within it a social psychological framework which recognises the role of social structures and collaborative practices in fostering individual creativity (Jeffrey and Craft, 2001; Miell and Littleton, 2004; Rhyammar and Brolin, 1999).

Since the 1990s, research into creativity has focused more on the creativity of ordinary people within aspects of education, what Boden calls 'p' creativity (Boden, 2001). The methodology for investigating creativity in education has also shifted, from large-scale studies aiming to measure creativity toward ethnographic, qualitative approaches to research focusing on the actual site of operations and practice, again contextualising creativity in the social and cultural values and practices of both the underlying disciplines and the particular setting. There has also been a move toward philosophical discussions around the nature of creativity (Craft, 2002).

This was – and is – quite distinct from the earlier climate, in its changed emphasis on:

- characterising, rather than measuring;
- ordinary creativity rather than genius;
- complexity rather than simplicity;
- encompassing views of creativity which include products but do not see these as necessary;
- emphasis on the social system rather than the individual;
- recognition of creativity as situated, not 'universalised'.

The third wave: a tsunami?

The first years of the twenty-first century have, then, seen a gradual move from a second to a third wave, which goes beyond seeing creativity as universalised, to characterising it as everyday (Craft, 2001, 2002, 2005; Feldman, 1999) – seeing creativity as necessary for all at a critical period for our species and for our planet. For the children in our schools will help to shape the world in which they grow up and in which we grow old. Their ability to find solutions to the problems they inherit from us and to grow beyond the restrictions we have placed upon our own world-view will, more than in any other generation, define the future of our species and our planet.

The third wave can be viewed as a 'tsunami', or tidal wave, of change, reflecting underpinning seismic shifts that now see creativity as fundamental to 21st century learning and living. The third wave policies all have their foundations in the second wave, and include:

- The Roberts Review (2006)
- Select Committee (2007)
- Creative Economy Strategy (2008)
- The Henley Review (2012)

The Roberts Review (2006) and the Government's response (2006)

The Roberts Review was perhaps the most significant of the third wave policies, in further codifying creativity in the curriculum and channelling the tsunami of change into an economic position and one which would also enhance learner engagement and inclusion. The review was established in late 2005 by the Department for Culture, Media and Sport (DCMS) and Department for Education and Skills (DfES). Led by Paul Roberts, a civil servant, it was established to consider initiatives under way to support the creative and cultural development of young people and creativity in schools since the 1999 NACCCE Report, as well as considering how creativity as a set of skills could be poised to feed the creative and cultural industries, helping to establish Britain as the world's 'Creative Hub' (Purnell, 2005).

The Roberts Review (DfES, 2006a) mapped out a framework for creativity, including provision in the early years, extended schools, building schools for the future, leadership in creative teaming, initial teacher education, professional development, partnerships, frameworks of regulation and support, and introduced the idea of the individual creative portfolio, arguing creativity is a key part of the development of young citizens.

The Government's response, in late 2006, committed to the recommendations made in the Roberts Review. It emphasised the cross-curricular approach to creativity as broader than the arts, and indicated the need to retain high standards alongside creative engagement. This should include opportunities across the curriculum, some of these involving creative partnership, and creativity should be nurtured through teacher development and school leadership; support for developing these priorities was to come from both DfES and DCMS. It confirmed the QCA version of the NACCCE definition of creativity, stating:

We believe, as QCA makes clear, that:

- Creativity involves thinking or behaving – imaginatively;
- This imaginative activity is purposeful: that is, it is directed to achieving an objective;
- These processes must generate something original;
- The outcome must be of value in relation to the objective.

(DCMS/DfES, 2006b, p4)

The eight areas of commitment made by Government at this point were:

- the development of a Creative Portfolio, in a wide range of settings and reflecting creative industries-related activities;
- a commitment to the Early Years, ensuring that creativity remains at the heart of the Foundation Stage, and that creative practice is encouraged and rewarded;
- development of creativity within Extended Schools, paying attention to supporting schools to mirror this within formal provision;
- closer attention to the development of the Building Schools for the Future (BSF) programme to provide inspirationally designed built environments to nurture creative engagement, involving young people in this process;
- developing further support for Leading Creative Learning through head teachers and other school leaders, to regard 'every subject as a creative subject', considering how both initial teacher education and continuing professional development may contribute to this;
- fostering appropriate and systemic Practitioner Partnerships between schools and creative industries and partnerships with particular attention to the future of the Creative Partnerships programme;
- mapping access and progression routes of Pathways to Creative Industries, through apprenticeship frameworks and diplomas;
- further development of Frameworks and Regulation such that the holistic, enquiry-based approaches of the Primary and Secondary National Strategies are supported through development of the Ofsted subject surveys and other regulatory frameworks.

A Board (The Cultural and Creative Education Board – CCEAB) was established in late 2006 to progress the recommendations of the Roberts Review and over the year of its existence, laid increasing emphasis on 'cultural learning' rather than 'creative learning'. It was perhaps unsurprising, then, that the McMaster eport (2008), commissioned by the Secretary of State for Culture, Media and Sport, to explore how the public sector might encourage innovation, risk-taking and excellence, describes it as a 'cultural' rather than 'creative' learning programme, and that in February, 2008, Government launched the 'Cultural Offer', ten regional pilots for which were to sit within the Youth Culture Trust, within a slimmed-down Creative Partnerships organisation (DCMS, Feb 2008).

The Education Select Committee report (2007) and the Government's response (2008)

The House of Commons Education and Skills Select Committee (2007), was focused on creative partnership in particular. Entitled Creative Partnerships and the Curriculum, it argued creativity was a set of skills relevant across the curriculum, broader than the arts, and suggested there was an 'urgent' need to prioritise 'developing new methods of assessing incremental progress' stating that 'existing measures of progress which focus on the attainment of Key Stages, are unlikely to capture small but steady improvements, or progress in areas such as self-confidence, and team-working' (*ibid*, para 28, p17).

The Government response to this report, recognised that 'creativity is not just about the arts . . . it applies across all subjects.' (House of Commons Children, Schools and Families Committee, January, 2008, Appendix, page 1), also stated that 'both Departments consider that Creative Partnerships' principal focus should remain on the arts and culture' (*ibid*, p3).

Creative Economy Strategy (2008)

This document, published by the Government in February 2008, shortly after the response to the Select Committee on Creative Partnerships brought together a number of aspects of creativity in relation to the economy, initiated in 2005. It focused on creativity as a set of skills to be developed in relation to careers and progression into the creative and cultural industries. As Cochrane *et al*., (2008) argue, two clear narratives were evident from it. The first focuses on 'nurturing talent' to enable young people to progress into careers and further education in the arts, cultural and creative industries. The second focuses on broader support for 'cultural learning' embedded in the Cultural Offer (Creative Partnerships, 2008).

Taken together, these three initiatives alone provide a powerful recognition of creativity and culture as embedded in education for children and young people of all ages. They emerged, too, in the context of a developing framework for ensuring that Every Child Matters, which has led to interprofessional practices to ensure that children and young people thrive. The DCSF's 2007 Children's Plan identified creativity as important (albeit in terms of the economy), and the DfES Manifesto to Learning Outside the Classroom (DfES, 2006) also urged the need to respond to children's curiosity and to nurture creativity. At the time of writing this third edition it is disappointing to note that the widely praised Creative Partnerships programme, launched in 2002, ceased existence in late 2011, due to funding cuts. However, in these times of austerity there still exists Government commitment to investment in creativity and culture.

The Henley Review (2012) and the Government's response (2012)

The Henley Review, an independent review into cultural education in England, was initiated by the Secretary of State for Education and the Minister for Culture,

Communications and Creative Industries in 2011. Darren Henley, the Managing Director of Classic FM, had previously been commissioned to carry out an independent review of Music Education, which was published in 2010. In common with the Robert's Review, the Henley Review (DCMS/DfE, 2012a) again emphasised the central role of cultural education in developing the nation's economy, stating 'It is vitally important that there is continued investment in giving the next generation of creative practitioners the tools and training necessary for the UK to continue its position of pre-eminence.' (*ibid*, p3). The review's recommendations – twenty-four in total – not surprisingly, were closely tied to those made in the earlier music education review. For example, there was attention placed on the value of partnership work, and professional development opportunities for teachers and artists.

The Government's response, published shortly after, was very positive. This positivity was supported by a financial commitment to cultural education of £15 million until 2015, to fund inspirational enrichment programmes, with the ultimate aim of supporting and expanding the cultural arts industries. Given that these industries are worth £8 million an hour to the UK economy (DCMS, 2014) this investment seems rather modest, but is nonetheless welcome. In summary, the response highlighted ten key areas that were deemed worthy of further attention on a national level:

- New joint Ministerial Board
  - A National Plan for Cultural Education together with the sponsored bodies
  - Work with Teaching Schools and sponsored bodies to improve the quality of cultural education in schools
  - A new National Youth Dance Company
  - National Art & Design Saturday Clubs
  - Heritage Schools – providing access to local history and cultural heritage
  - Cultural education passport – so that all children and young people can have a rich variety of cultural education
  - Museums education – to encourage and facilitate more school visits to museums and art galleries
  - Film education – to inspire and train the next generation of British filmmakers
  - The Bridge Network bringing heritage and film as well as arts, museums and libraries closer to every school.

(DCMS/DfE, 2012b, p2/3)

In sharp contrast to the wording of the Government's response to the Roberts Review in 2006, it is notable, that the word 'creativity' does not appear in any of these headline areas. Indeed, in the Henley Review itself 'creativity' only appears 15 times over 84 pages.

The shift toward cultural development seems significant; at the time of writing the third edition of this book, it seems that, in popular ideology, culture is the main priority, with creativity now regarded as an aspect of culture. For example, in 2011 the Cultural Learning Alliance published Imagination Nation: The Case for Cultural Learning, advocating for 'the transformative role played by the arts and heritage in the lives of children and young people' (CLA, 2011, p2). In 2013, following on from the Henley Review, a Cultural Education Plan was produced by the Government (DCMS/DfE). This sets out, in considerable detail, programmes and opportunities aimed at schools and teachers. However, in the appendix, only the draft National Curriculum programmes of study for art and design, and music are included; a somewhat slim choice, given the broad definition of culture evident elsewhere in the Plan.

While the most recent shifts in England have been toward cultural development, the European Union named 2009 as the European Year of Creativity and Innovation and the European Commission recently launched the €1.46 billion Creative Europe programme (2014–2020) to support Europe's cultural and creative sectors, which brought back an emphasis on creativity. Additionally, in 2013 the United Nations published a Creative Economy Report exploring 'local development pathways' in developing countries. What seems undisputable is that this is a period in which creativity, culture and innovation are highly valued, particularly in relation to the 'creative economy'.

Why the changing landscape?

The reasons for this resurrection of interest and the shift from a first to a second and then to a third wave of change to the landscape of creativity emerge from a mix of political, economic and social change.

The globalisation of economic activity has brought with it increased competitiveness for markets, driving the need for nation states to raise the levels of educational achievement of their potential labour forces (Jeffrey and Craft, 2001). Changes in our economy mean an increased proportion of small businesses or organisations, employing less than five people and with a turnover of less than £500,000 (Carter *et al.*, 2004). Employment in no organisation is for life. We have shifted our core business from manufacturing to a situation where 'knowledge is the primary source of economic productivity' (Seltzer and Bentley, 1999, p9).

Education has, of course, a dynamic relationship with this shifting world of employment and the wider economy. In response to changes in these domains, what is considered significant in terms of educational achievement is changing.

It is no longer merely sufficient to have excellence in depth and grasp of knowledge. Critical to surviving and thriving is, instead, creativity. For it is creativity which enables a person to identify appropriate problems and to solve them. It is creativity that identifies possibilities and opportunities that may not have been noticed by others. And it is argued that creativity forms the backbone of the economy based on knowledge (Robinson, 2001).

In the wider social environment, certitudes are in many ways on the decrease. Roles and relationships in family and community structures, unchanging for centuries, are shifting fast; a young person growing up in the twenty-first century has a much more active role than perhaps ever before in making sense of their experiences and making choices about their own life (Craft, 2001).

And alongside all this, information and communication technology plays an increasing role, both offering potential for creativity and demanding it.

All this change in the economic, political, social and technological context means that our conceptualisations of creativity, how to investigate and foster it, are changing. An aspect of the third wave in creativity is that the notion of creativity as 'universalised' is now common-place, i.e. the perspective that everybody is capable of being creative given the right environment (Jeffrey and Craft, 2001).

But the third wave also problematises creativity. It has brought with it exploration of the tensions and dilemmas encapsulated in fostering it.

Tensions and dilemmas

There are some fundamental tensions and dilemmas inherent in developing creativity. They are rather more than mere tensions between policy and practice although these too pose serious challenges in perspective, disconnected curricula and curriculum organisation to name a few.

There are at least four much more fundamental challenges, bearing in mind that in this third wave the education of children must nurture the creativity which will determine their ability to survive and flourish in a chaotic world.

Culture and creativity

There is growing evidence (for example, Ng, 2003; Nisbett, 2003; Saad *et al.*, 2013) that creativity is manifested and defined in different cultural contexts. To what extent can and should we take account of this in a multicultural learning environment? It has been argued that it is imperative that we do address these possible differences in the ways that we foster creativity in the classroom (Craft, 2005). And yet, in these times when teachers and creative partners are still celebrating the relative freedoms afforded by increased policy support for creativity, and therefore not perhaps critically scrutinising their practices in ways that they might later do, there is little sign of this occurring at present.

Creativity and the environment

How does creativity impact on the wider environment? For the creativity we are experiencing is anchored in a global marketplace that has a powerful influence on values. It is heavily marketised, so that wants are substituted for needs, convenience lifestyles and image are increasingly seen as significant and form part of a 'throw-away' culture where make-do-and-mend are oldspeak, and short shelf-life and built-in obsolescence are seen to be positive. In this marketised context, the drive to innovate ever further perhaps becomes an end in itself. And this occurs against a rising global population and an increasing imbalance between nations in the consumption of reducing world resources. How appropriate is this? What significance do we accord the evaluation of the impact of our ideas on others or on our wider environment? For to do so might mean seeing creativity in perhaps a more spiritual way in terms of fulfilment, individual or collective. And so it could also mean taking a different kind of existential slant on life (Craft, 2006).

Ethics

This is of course related to the environmental point. We want to encourage children's choices, but in a wider social and ethical context. What kind of world do we create where the market is seen as God? And how can we see creativity divorced from its ends? For the human imagination is capable of immense destruction as well as infinitely constructive possibilities. How do we balance these? An aspect of the teacher's role is to encourage children to examine the possible wider effects of their own ideas and those of others and to determine worth in the light of these. This, of course, means the balancing of conflicting perspectives and values – which may themselves be irreconcilable, particularly where they stem from fundamentalist beliefs (Craft, 2005).

Such fundamental challenges clearly leave us with pedagogical challenges. For example, if creativity is culturally specific how do we foster it in a multicultural classroom? And how do we rise to the direct and indirect challenges posed by creativity linked to the market? How far does creativity in the classroom reflect or challenge the status quo?

Wise creativity

Stemming from all three of the previous challenges, is the question of how creativity is fostered with wisdom in schools, since the development of policy can be seen as underpinned by Western individualism, in relation to a globalised market economy which brings with 'blindness' to diversity in culture and values (Craft, 2008), a dissipation of trust and responsibility (Gardner, 2008) and a reluctance to consider what 'good' or 'wise' creativity might involve (Claxton, 2008). The time has perhaps come to explore how responsibility is equal to self-realisation, to recognise the intuitive and other resonances between our own actions and those of others; to recognise dispositions which may enable us to foster in the classroom creativity which dares to consider a moral role for creativity beyond current, economy-bound and habitual horizons (Craft *et al.*, 2008; Craft, 2010; Craft, 2013).

We have a challenging agenda ahead of us in education, but an exciting one.

REFLECTIVE TASK

- How familiar are the three creativity waves in your own experience of fostering creativity in education?
- How can you go about using the QCA framework to help you identify and promote creativity in learning?
- To what extent do partnership and apprenticeship form a part of your own pedagogy?
- How can you document children's perspectives about creative learning experiences?
- Which of the fundamental tensions and dilemmas could you begin to address in your own practice, and how?

A SUMMARY OF KEY POINTS

Changes in the landscape for creativity in education:

- ➢ No longer the preserve of the arts or arts education, creativity has moved from the fringes of educational concern to being seen as a core aspect of educating, which pertains to all aspects of human endeavour.
- ➢ Creative teaching focuses on the teacher. Studies suggest that teachers feel creative when they are in control and take ownership of their practice. Teaching for creativity focuses on the learner and includes giving the child many choices over what is explored and how.
- ➢ 'Creative learning' is a phrase which explores the middle ground between creative teaching and teaching for creativity. This involves learners using their imagination and experience to develop learning while strategically collaborating over tasks, critically evaluating their own teachers' practices. This mode of teaching often involves an 'apprenticeship' approach.
- ➢ In a world of rapid economic and social change it is no longer sufficient to have excellence in depth and grasp of knowledge. Wise creativity is critical for individuals to thrive and survive in the twenty-first century. This is because wise creativity enables a person to identify appropriate problems, possibilities and opportunities and to solve them in ways which others may not notice.

MOVING *ON* > > > > > > MOVING *ON* > > > > > > MOVING *ON*

In developing your own practice in fostering children's creativity, keep in mind three key questions.

What am I trying to nurture? Familiarise yourself with the NACCCE definition developed by QCA: creativity as imagination that is purposeful, leading to original and valuable outcomes. Try to be specific about how you can foster this in children you work with.

How can I do this? Consider resources, including people within and beyond school that you could work with to nurture children's creativity, enabling children in navigating choices and possibilities.

Why am I trying to develop children's creativity? How does your practice relate to the creative and cultural agenda? How far does it reflect the themes of creativity and innovation? How can you encourage children to develop 'wise' creativity in your classroom?

REFERENCES REFERENCES **REFERENCES** REFERENCES REFERENCES REFERENCES

Amabile, TM (1983) *The social psychology of creativity*. New York: Springer Verlag.

Amabile, TM (1988) A model of creativity and innovation in organizations, in Staw, BM and Cunnings, LL (eds) *Research in organizational behavior*. Greenwich, CT: JAI Press.

Amabile, TM (1996) *Creativity in context (update to The social psychology of creativity)*. Boulder, CO: Westview Press.

Amabile, TM (1997) Motivating creativity in organisations: on doing what you love and loving what you do. *California Management Review*, 40:1.

Balke, E (1997) Play and the arts: the importance of the 'unimportant'. *Childhood Education*, 73:6, 353–60.

Beetlestone,F (1998) *Creative children, imaginative teaching*. Buckingham: Open University Press.

Boden, MA (2001) Creativity and knowledge, in Craft, A, Jeffrey, B., and Liebling, M. (eds) *Creativity in Education*. London: Continuum.

Carter, S, Mason, C and Tagg, S (2004) *Lifting the barriers to growth in UK small businesses: the FSB biennial membership survey*. Report to the Federation of Small Businesses. London: Federation of Small Businesses.

Central Advisory Council for Education in England (CACE) (1967) *Children and their primary schools, Report of the Central Advisory Council for Education in England (The Plowden Report)*. London: HMSO.

Claxton, G (2008) Wisdom: Advanced Creativity?, in Craft, A, Gardner, H, Claxton, G, et al. *Creativity, wisdom and trusteeship: exploring the role of education*. Thousand Oaks, CA: Corwin Press.

Cochrane, P, Craft, A and Jeffery, G (2008) *Mixed messages or permissions and opportunities? Reflections on current policy perspectives on creativity in education*. Paper produced for Creative Partnerships Seminar 13 February 2008 (revised for publication April 2008).

Craft, A (1997) Identity and creativity: education for post-modernism? *Teacher Development: International Journal of Teachers' Professional Development*, 1:1, 83–96.

Craft, A (2000) *Creativity across the primary curriculum: framing and developing practice*. Abingdon: RoutledgeFalmer.

Craft, A (2001) Little c creativity, in Craft, A, Jeffrey, B and Leibling, M (eds), *Creativity in education*. London: Continuum.

Craft, A (2002) *Creativity and Early Years education*. London: Continuum.

Craft, A (2003a) Early Years education in England and little c creativity: the third wave? *Korean Journal of Thinking and Problem Solving*, 13:1, 49–57.

Craft, A (2004) *Creative thinking in the Early Years of education*, in Fryer, M (ed.), *Creativity and cultural diversity*. Leeds: Creativity Centre Educational Trust.

Craft, A (2005) *Creativity in schools: tensions and dilemmas*. Abingdon: RoutledgeFalmer.

Craft, AR (2006). Fostering creativity with wisdom. *Cambridge Journal of Education*, 36(3), 337–350

Craft, A (2008) Tensions in Creativity and Education: Enter Wisdom and Trusteeship?, in Craft, A, Gardner, H and Claxton, G (2008) *Creativity, wisdom and trusteeship: exploring the role of education*. Thousand Oaks, CA: Corwin Press.

Craft, AR (2010). Possibility Thinking and Fostering Creativity with Wisdom: opportunities and constraints in an English context. In Bhegetto R ,Kaufman ,J (eds.) *Creativity in the Classroom*, Cambridge: Cambridge University Press.

Craft, AR (2013). Childhood, Possibility Thinking and Wise, Humanising Educational Futures. *International Journal of Educational Research*, 61, 126–134.

Craft, AR, Cremin, T., Clack, J. and Hay, P. (2013). Creative Primary Schools: Developing and maintaining pedagogy for creativity. *Ethnography and Education*, 9(1), 16–34.

Craft, A, Chappell, K and Best, P (2007) *Analysis of the Creativity Action Research Awards Two (CARA2) Programme*. Final Report, October 2007. Available at: http://education.exeter.ac.uk/ projects. php?id=100

Craft, A, Gardner, H and Claxton, G (2008) *Creativity, wisdom and trusteeship: exploring the role of education*. Thousand Oaks, CA: Corwin Press.

Creative Partnerships (2005) Available at: **www.creative-partnerships.com** accessed 8/8/14.

Cultural Learning Alliance (CLA) (2011) *Imagination nation: The case for cultural learning*. London: Cultural Learning Alliance.

Department for Children, Schools and Families (DCSF) (2007) *The children's plan*. London: The Stationery Office. Available at: **https://www.gov.uk/government/publications/the-childrens-plan** accessed 8/8/14.

Department for Culture, Media and Sport (DCMS) (2014) *Creative Industries worth £8million an hour to UK economy*. Available at: **https://www.gov.uk/government/news/creative-industries-worth-8million-an-hour-to-uk-economy** accessed 8/8/14.

Department for Culture, Media and Sport (DCMS) and Department for Education (DfE) (2012a) *Cultural education in England: An independent review by Darren Henley for the Department for Culture, Media and Sport and the Department for Education*. Available at: **http://media.education.gov.uk/assets/files/pdf/h/henley%20review%20of%20cultural%20education%20in%20england.pdf** accessed 8/8/14.

Department for Culture, Media and Sport (DCMS) and Department for Education (DfE) (2012b) *Cultural education in England: The Government response to Darren Henley's Review of Cultural Education*. Available at: **https://www.gov.uk/government/uploads/system/uploads/attachment_data/file/260727/Cultural_Education_Govt_response.pdf** accessed 8/8/14.

Department for Culture, Media and Sport (DCMS) and Department for Education and Skills (DfES) (2006a) *Nurturing creativity and young people*. London: HMSO.

Department for Culture, Media (DCMS) and Sport and Department for Education and Skills (DfES) (2006b) *Government response to nurturing creativity and young people*. London: HMSO.

Department for Culture, Media and Sport (DCMS) (2008) Joint DCMS/DCSF Press Release on the Cultural Offer, 13 February.

Department for Culture, Media and Sport (DCMS) Department for Business, Enterprise and Regulatory Reform (BERR) and Department for Innovation, Universities and Skills (DIUS) (2008) *Creative Britain: new talents for the creative economy*. London: DCMS.

Department for Education (DfE) (2010) *The importance of teaching: The schools white paper 2010*. Available at: **https://www.gov.uk/government/publications/the-importance-of-teaching-the-schools-white-paper-2010** accessed 8/8/14.

DfE (2012a) Teachers' Standards available at **https://www.gov.uk/government/publications/teachers-standards** accessed 7/9/14.

Department for Education (DfE) (2012) *Statutory framework for the early years foundation stage: Setting the standards for learning, development and care for children from birth to five*. Available at: **https://www.gov.uk/government/uploads/system/uploads/attachment_data/file/271631/eyfs_statutory_framework_march_2012.pdf** accessed 8/8/14.

Department for Education (DfE) (2013a) *Cultural education: A summary of programmes and opportunities*. Available at: **https://www.gov.uk/government/uploads/system/uploads/attachment_data/file/226569/Cultural-Education.pdf** accessed 8/8/14.

Department for Education (DfE) (2013b) *The national curriculum in England: Key stages 1 and 2 framework document*. Available at: **https://www.gov.uk/government/uploads/system/uploads/attachment_data/file/335133/PRIMARY_national_curriculum_220714.pdf** accessed 8/8/14.

Department for Education and Employment (DfEE) (1999a) *All our futures: creativity, culture and education. The National Advisory Committee's Report on Creative and Cultural Education*. London: HMSO.

Department for Education and Skills (DfES) (2003) *Excellence and enjoyment*. London: HMSO.

Department for Education and Skills (DfES) (2004a) *A national conversation about personalised learning*. Nottingham: DfES Publications.

Department for Education and Skills (DfES) (2004b) *High quality PE and sport for young people: a guide to recognising and achieving high quality PE and sport in schools*. London: DfES.

Department for Education and Skills (DfES) (2004c) *Personalised learning for every child, personalised contact for every teacher*. London: DfES.

Department for Education and Skills (DfES) (2005a) See website: www.standards.dfee.gov.uk/

Department for Education and Skills (DfES) (2005b) See website: www.teachernet.gov.uk/professional development/resourcesandresearch/bprs/search/

Department for Education and Skills (DfES) (2006) *Learning outside the classroom manifesto*. London: DfES

Department for Education and Skills (DfES) (2007) *The Early Years Foundation Stage*. London: DfES.

Department for Trade and Industry (DTI) (2005) *DTI economics paper no. 15. Creativity, design and business performance*. Available at: http://www.ifacca.org/publications/2005/11/01/dti-economics-paper-no-15-creativity/

Edwards, CP and Springate, KW (1995) *Encouraging creativity in early childhood classrooms*. ERIC

Digest. Washington, DC: ERIC Clearing House on Elementary and Early Childhood Education.

Feldman, DH (1999) The development of creativity, in Sternberg, RJ (ed.), *Handbook of creativity*. Cambridge: Cambridge University Press.

Fischmann, W, Solomon, B, Greenspan, D and Gardner, H (2004) *Making good: how young people cope with moral dilemmas at work*. Cambridge, MA: Harvard University Press.

Fryer, M (1996) *Creative teaching and learning*. London: Paul Chapman Publishing.

Gardner, H (2004) *Can there be societal trustees in America today?* Working paper, Harvard Graduate School of Education.

Gardner, H (2008) Creativity, wisdom and trusteeship, in Craft, A, Gardner, H, Claxton, G, *et al.* (2008) *Creativity, wisdom and trusteeship: exploring the role of education*. Thousand Oaks, CA: Corwin Press.

Griffiths, M and Woolf, W (2004) *Report on creative partnerships Nottingham action research*. Nottingham: Nottingham Trust University.

Halliwell, S (1993) Teacher creativity and teacher education, in Bridges, D and Kerry, T, *Developing teachers professionally*. Abingdon: Routledge.

House of Commons Education and Skills Committee (2007) Creative partnerships and the curriculum. *Eleventh Report of Session 2006–07. Report, together with formal minutes, oral and written evidence*. London: The Stationery Office Limited.

House of Commons Children, Schools and Families Committee (2008). *Creative partnerships and the curriculum: government response to the eleventh report from the Education and Skills Committee, Session 2006–07*. London: The Stationery Office Limited.

Hubbard, RS (1996) *A workshop of the possible: nurturing children's creative development*. York, ME: Stenhouse Publishers.

Imison, T (2001) Creative leadership: innovative practices in a secondary school, in Craft, A, Jeffrey, B and Leibling, M (eds), *Creativity in education*. London: Continuum.

Jeffrey, B (2001a) Challenging prescription in ideology and practice: the case of Sunny first school, in Collins, J, Insley, K and Soler, J (eds), *Developing pedagogy: researching practice*. London: Paul Chapman Publishing.

Jeffrey, B (2001b) Primary pupils' perspectives and creative learning, *Encyclopaideia 9*, Spring (Italian journal).

Jeffrey, B (2003a) Countering student instrumentalism: a creative response. *British Educational Research Journal*, 29:4, 489–503.

Jeffrey, B (2003b) *Creative learning and student perspectives*. CLASP Report. Swindon: ESRC.

Jeffrey, B (2004a) End of award report: creative learning and student perspectives (CLASP) Project, submitted to ESRC, November 2004.

Jeffrey, B (2004b) Meaningful creative learning: learners' perspectives. Paper given at the ECER conference, Crete.

Jeffrey, B and Craft, A (2001) The universalization of creativity in education, in Craft, A, Jeffrey, B and Leibling, M (eds), *Creativity in education*. London: Continuum.

Jeffrey, B and Craft, A (2004) Teaching creatively and teaching for creativity: distinctions and relationships. *Educational Studies*, 30:1, 77–87.

Jeffrey, B and Craft, A (2006) Creative learning and possibility thinking. In Jeffrey, B (ed) *Creative learning practices: European experiences*. London: Tuffnell Press.

Jeffrey, B and Woods, P (2003) *The creative school: a framework for success, quality and effectiveness*. Abingdon and New York: Routledge Falmer.

John-Steiner, V (2000) *Creative collaboration*. New York: Oxford University Press.

Kessler, R (2000) *The soul of education: helping students find connection, compassion and character at school*. Alexandria, VA: Association for Supervision and Curriculum Development.

Leach, J (2001) A hundred possibilities: creativity, community and ICT, in Craft, A, Jeffrey, B and Leibling, M (eds), *Creativity in education*. London: Continuum.

McMaster, Sir B (2008) *Supporting excellence in the arts: from measurement to judgement*. London: Department for Culture, Media and Sport.

Miell, D and Littleton, K (2004) *Collaborative creativity*. London: Free Association Books.

National Advisory Committee on Creative and Cultural Education (NACCCE) (1999) *All our futures: creativity, culture and education (The Roberts Report)*. London: DfEE.

National College for School Leadership (NCSL) (2005) See website: **www.ncsl.org.uk** accessed 7/9/14.

Ng, AK (2003) A cultural model of creative and conforming behaviour. *Creativity Research Journal*, 15:2 and 3, 223–33.

Nisbett, RE (2003) *The geography of thought*. New York: Free Press.

Office for Standards in Education (OFSTED) (2003) *Improving city schools – How the arts can help*. Available at: http://www.ofsted.gov.uk/resources/improving-city-schools-how-arts-can-help

Office for Standards in Education (OFSTED) (2004) *Excellence in cities' primary extension: real stories*, document reference HM12394. See website: **www.ofsted.gov.uk** accessed 8/8/14.

Purnell, P (2005) *Making Britain the world's creative hub*. Available at http://www.gov-news.org/gov/uk/news/quotmaking_britain_world39s_creative_hubquot/18221.html

Qualifications and Curriculum Authority (QCA) (2005a) *Creativity: Find It! Promote It! – promoting pupils' creative thinking and behaviour across the curriculum at Key Stages 1, 2 and 3 – practical materials for schools*. London: Qualifications and Curriculum Authority.

Qualifications and Curriculum Authority (QCA) (2005b)

Robinson, K (2003) *Out of our minds: learning to be creative.* Chichester: Capstone.

Ryhammar, L and Brolin, C (1999) Creativity research: historical considerations and main lines of development. *Scandanavian Journal of Educational Research*, 43:3, 259–73.

Saad,CS, Damian, RI, Benet-Martinez, V, Moons, WG and Robins, RW (2013) Multiculturalism and creativity: Effects of cultural context, bicultural identity, and ideational fluency. *Social Psychological and Personality Science*, 4:3, 369–75.

Seltzer, K and Bentley, T (1999) *The creative age: knowledge and skills for the new economy*. London: Demos.

Shallcross, DJ (1981) *Teaching creative behavior: how to teach creativity to children of all ages*. Englewood Cliffs, NJ: Prentice-Hall.

Sonnenburg, S (2004) Creativity in communication: a theoretical framework for collaborative product creation. *Creativity and Innovation Management*, 13:4, 254–62.

Torrance, EP (1984) *Mentor relationships: how they aid creative achievement, endure, change and die*. Buffalo, NY: Bearly.

United Nations (2013) Creative economy report – 2013 special edition: Widening local development pathways. Available at: **www.unesco.org/new/en/culture/themes/creativity/creative-economy-report-2013-special-edition** accessed 8/8/14.

Wegerif, R (2004) *Reason and creativity in classroom dialogues*. Unpublished paper based on seminar given at The Open Creativity Centre Seminar Series, Milton Keynes, UK, March 2003.

Woods, F (1990) *Teacher skills and strategies*. Abingdon: Falmer Press.

Woods, P (1993) *Critical events in teaching and learning*. Abingdon: Falmer Press.

Woods, P (1995) *Creative teachers in primary schools*. Buckingham: Open University Press.

Woods, F and Jeffrey, B (1996) *Teachable moments: the art of teaching in primary schools*. Buckingham: Open University Press.

Woods, P (2002) Teaching and learning in the new millennium, in Sugrue, C and Day, D (eds), *Developing teachers and teaching practice: international research perspectives*. Abingdon and New York: RoutledgeFalmer.

2

The art of the possible: creative principled leadership

Alison Peacock

Chapter objectives

By the end of this chapter you should have:

- recognised the challenges of creating a curriculum which maintains a vision of education which seeks to inspire as well as raise standards;
- considered your own beliefs and values regarding the grouping of children according to ability;
- reflected on how to encourage pupils to take agency in their learning, and examined the implications of this for your own practice.

This chapter addresses the following Teachers' Standards (DfE, 2012):

- establish a safe and stimulating environment for pupils, rooted in mutual respect;
- encourage pupils to take a responsible and conscientious attitude to their own work and study;
- have a secure knowledge of the relevant subject(s) and curriculum areas, foster and maintain pupils' interest in the subject, and address misunderstandings;
- promote a love of learning and children's intellectual curiosity;
- have a secure understanding of how a range of factors can inhibit pupils' ability to learn, and how best to overcome these;
- make use of formative and summative assessment to secure pupils' progress.

Introduction

How is it possible to offer a stimulating curriculum in an era of high-stakes account-ability? This chapter tells the story of one school's journey towards creating a learn-ing environment which demonstrates that belief in the enjoyment of learning need not be sacrificed in place of raising achievement. As future leaders of education policy and practice, I want you to reflect on how you will wield the power that you have, both in and out of the classroom, so that you can make decisions which will enable children and teachers to empower each other as collaborators in learning rather than units of numerical value.

Charting success instead of documenting failure

The Wroxham School is a one-form entry primary school in Hertfordshire. I joined the school as headteacher in January 2003. The school had been categorised as requiring special measures in May 2001 and almost two years later, although termly inspections had taken place, Her Majesty's Inspectorate (HMI) judged that only minimal progress had been achieved. I had a strong vision for the school built on the belief that every learner should be given the opportunity to develop the capacity to surprise us (Hart *et al.*, 2004). I was interviewed about my leadership by a research team in 2005:

> *Let's make this wonderful because you only get the chance to be five once. You only get the chance to be seven once. If you're going to be a teacher, then you know, I don't think I've met a teacher yet who came into the profession for any other reason than that they wanted to work with young people ... if you're going to be working with our youngsters whether you're working in the kitchen or whether you're the site manager or whether you're the deputy head you know that it's about respect, about values, about not wasting people's time and opportunities really... I hope that comes through in what we're trying to do. It's about values and relationships and then you're celebrating success and when you start to chart the successes it's great because everybody feels good and they go on to the next [challenge] rather than documenting their failures.*

Transformational teaching and learning inspired by the core principles of trust, co-agency and inclusion enabled the school to achieve rapid and sustained success. Children in this school are not grouped or limited by so called 'ability': there is no gifted and talented register, and individuals are described in terms of their increasing learning capacity instead of by test results and targets. The school was removed from special measures ten months after my arrival. The school was subsequently inspected by Ofsted in 2006, 2009 and 2013 and judged to be 'outstanding'. The crucial difference in our approach is that assessment is used to inform teaching rather than as a system for judging performance. This frees the assessment process to be used powerfully throughout the school as a means of informing both learners and teachers about next steps, instead of grades. The curriculum we offer – and our approach to teaching – ensures that every individual (child and adult) achieves excellent progress.

An imaginary school tour – ordinary yet different

In the following pages we take a tour of The Wroxham School. The school is a vibrant, ever-changing community. I have tried to capture the essence of what it feels like to visit. We shall look into classrooms and meet children and teachers and we shall also observe some of the rigorous systems and structures that enable both freedom and innovation.

The Wroxham School has two hundred and forty children on roll: it is a one-form entry primary school with nursery. The school is oversubscribed and mobility is very low. Family income varies but, on average, only 8 per cent of children receive free school meals.

The school was built forty years ago and originally was of open-plan design. Various building alterations over the years, including the addition of a large new classroom, mean that the building now has separate classrooms with interconnecting glass doors and one central area that houses the library and café. There is a large hall, two courtyard areas and a small additional detached room that is used for instrumental music lessons and the after-school 'Kids' Club'. The smallest courtyard has a domed roof and provides a linked area between the Lower Foundation and Upper Foundation classrooms, providing an area that is used daily for a variety of messy play. The larger courtyard is adjacent to the Year Six classroom, cloakroom and café. This is where our guinea pigs, Ant and Rupert live.

The extensive grounds incorporate a field bordered by trees, a pond, vegetable garden and playgrounds. Recent additions include a double-decker bus library, an outdoor music garden, a log cabin and a Celtic roundhouse with fire-pit.

Arriving at the school we see a single-storey, flat-roofed building. The entrance brings the visitor into a reception area with the school office to our right, the Lower Foundation room on our left and the Rainbow room straight ahead. The Rainbow room is a small room used for medical attention but is also an area where children can take 'time out' during lessons or playtimes if they need a quiet space to think or calm down. A large, brightly-painted flying bird hangs from the ceiling, with the mission statement *'Working together, aiming high'* painted in the background. The first impression once inside the building is one of colour and vibrancy. Art displays decorate the school office and all around, display boards invite you to take a closer look.

The Foundation Stage

A visit to the Foundation Stage is an opportunity to see how the children's independence is fostered from the earliest days. All families host a home visit prior to starting in nursery and children and parents or carers visit us prior to starting. When the placement begins, parents and carers are encouraged to stay and play until the child is happy to be left. The morning begins with indoor play and families are welcomed to come into Foundation Stage rooms for early morning routines such as hanging up coats and putting special belongings in the 'treasure box' for safe keeping. Families self-register by reading together the question of the day and placing the child's name card under the 'yes' or 'no' heading on the velcro board. The question of the day might be something like *'Do you like splashing in puddles?'*

On our tour we meet a group making fruit kebabs, see children embarking on a trip into outer space in a rocket, dancing to music in the big brick area, or creating swirly patterns in a tray of shaving foam. Outside, the garden is set up for wheeled toys, spades are ready for planting willow in the new wild garden, a large white board and pens have been provided to keep score in a ball game and capes are ready for dressing up. Children are encouraged to develop their imaginative play and to bring items outside as long as they remember where to put them back afterwards. Two adult-led activities have been planned for the outdoors: one is planting in the wild garden and the other is creating footprint patterns on a long roll of wallpaper.

The Foundation Unit incorporates two large classrooms, a connecting covered courtyard and a shared outdoor play area with canopy. There are three staff in nursery and two staff in reception. This ratio is regularly supplemented with trainee staff, volunteers and parent helpers.

Small-group time in nursery takes place each session for approximately twenty minutes. Two small-group times are organised each day in reception. These groups are organised around friendships and are never ability based. Aspects of the Foundation Stage curriculum, such as phonics, are taught within these groups, supported by puppet Peter Parrot. Initially for some children, group time is not meaningful: if this is the case, the child may play alongside an adult in another space within the room and gradually learn to take part in the group. This process may take weeks, or even months, but children are never forced to participate if they are unhappy to do so. The children spend at least 75 per cent of their time engaged in child-initiated play. The Foundation team scaffold play, offer structured activities such as gardening or cooking, and engage in detailed observations. The children eat lunch in the Wroxham Café and return to play in the Foundation Stage.

Key Stage One

Double glass doors and windows in the reception room look onto the Year One classroom. This room was added in the 1990s as part of the grant-maintained expenditure. It is a very large bright room with pitched ceiling, velux windows and exposed timbered beams. We see children busy in the role-play area, painting cardboard models, using sand and water, exploring puzzle programs at computers and building with large wooden bricks. A small group are writing with the teacher. The teaching assistant moves around the room talking with children and helping to facilitate the wide range of activities on offer. There is a reading area with colour-coded books used by children across the key stage. The role-play area is a 'bear cave' made from screens, stage blocks and drapes that can only be entered only by crawling through tunnels. It is dark inside and the children are seen excitedly exploring with torches. Photographs on the display board illustrate the 'school night walk' that had taken place a week earlier when families returned to school in the early evening to explore the playground by torch light.

Throughout the school, from Year One upwards, children who need more help with reading, writing or maths are offered additional time with an adult. The opportunity to have a sense of agency in your own learning is very important at Wroxham. The idea that children as young as five or six are given the opportunity to express their preferences around learning support is surprisingly radical and yet it is very much a part of what this school is all about. Children are encouraged to self-assess their readiness to take home reading scheme materials at the next level of difficulty. This works surprisingly well and avoids the sense that to begin the process of learning to read is akin to revving up the engine on a race track. Parents are welcomed into the classroom to help their child choose a new book as often as they wish to. Children are not grouped according to ability and are not pitched against each other. This message communicates itself very clearly in all areas of learning encountered in the school and almost eliminates competitive ranking of performance among families on the playground.

Glass doors lead from the Year One classroom into Year Two. This classroom is a large room with double doors out onto the playground. On one of the display boards there is a planning map drawn together with the children exploring all the possible things they could learn and do with Roald Dahl's stories as their inspiration. There are Big Friendly Giant dream bottles on the wall and all that we can see of Mrs Twit are her legs, as she has apparently shot through the ceiling surrounded by balloons. In the corner of the classroom is a 'writing hut' inspired by the one used daily by the author. Children can go there to write and play and dress up. A letter on the classroom door reminds families that there will be a Roald Dahl day next week where everyone is invited to arrive at school in role as a story character. As we walk into this room there is a tremendous atmosphere of noise and excitement as each table is following their own group recipe to create George's Marvellous Medicine. All kinds of ingredients are carefully measured and added to each concoction.

Within the Year Two classroom children are offered a range of learning tasks and are encouraged to self-assess how much challenge they need. Homework is offered in many classes at three levels of challenge or is open-ended. This allows children to set their own pace and never to feel held back. Parents are clear that the school helps children learn to value themselves, doing the best they can instead of comparing and ranking performance.

The Wroxham café

School dinners have become much more civilised since the children decided that the dining area should be reinvented as The Wroxham Café. Each table now has a small checked tablecloth, vase of flowers and a menu stand where children can read about their choices for the week. An LCD screen display reminds everyone which lunch clubs are on that day, who has a music lesson, where indoor quiet club will be and any news for the day. On the walls there are brightly-coloured photographs of the children, with reminders such as *'We listen to friends in the playground'*. There is a constant modelling of the behaviours that enable the school ethos to be so powerful.

Whole school democracy

Whole school decisions and discussions take place at Wroxham on a weekly basis. The idea of reinventing the school dining-room came during Circle Meetings. These meetings take place every Tuesday for 15 minutes before playtime. The circle meetings enable children and adults to achieve shared decisions about issues that occur week by week. The groups are led by Year Six children and the agenda is shared across the school. Some decisions are agreed upon following a 'blind' vote, others are achieved after several weeks of discussion and reflection. Each group has a notebook and meetings to share ideas and results take place among Year Six in preparation for the following meeting. Groups are held on the bus and in the log cabin, as well as each classroom. This enables each meeting to comprise on average 26 children of mixed age between five and 11. Adults join in the circle meetings as equal members. Each meeting begins with a game and is then followed by discussion and closing game. The atmosphere is very supportive and good humoured. Children leading the groups model the respectful way that they themselves are treated by adults in school: giving little ones time to articulate their ideas and supporting less-confident children by encouraging them or offering to return to them later for suggestions they may wish to make. Decisions are taken on a wide range of issues.

Lower Key Stage Two

As we enter the year Three classroom, it is difficult to see where the teacher is. The room is very busy with children in an Ancient Egyptian role-play area; others are reading or writing individually, others are busy constructing a sarcophagus from cardboard. The teacher can now be seen sitting on the floor laughing with children around her as they try to thread a needle for embroidery. Children grow to love this teacher and make excellent emotional and academic progress throughout the year, often exceeding their own expectations. As we look round this apparently chaotic room, we notice that every child is highly motivated and sure of themselves as learners.

A glass partition forms one third of the wall. This looks into the Year Four classroom, which we shall visit next. As we enter the room, children are busy writing. Around the room are displays about the Tudors and a 'magpie wall' has a collection of phrases and vocabulary. A bow and arrow is propped up in one corner and a Robin Hood hat and jerkin are pinned to a notice board. As we enter the room, children look up excitedly. They are writing a Robin Hood story and as nine-year-old Abbie is keen to inform us, they are 'experts' about Robin Hood as they had dressed up the day before and spent all day on the field experiencing what it would be like to live in the woods. On the occasion of our visit, we can see that most children have a collective sense of purpose in their writing and are very keen to share their efforts with us. The class teacher is sitting with a group of children who have chosen to write with his support. They are deep in conversation about what the camp fire smelt like and he helps them find a simile to describe this.

We emerge from Year Four onto the playground. To our right is a small building with *'Welcome to Kids' Club'* written on the door in several languages. This room houses the after school club from 3.15 to 6.00pm each day. As we approach, we can hear the sounds of a trumpet being played. Peripatetic music lessons take place in this room throughout the week. The school has a dedicated team of musicians, some of whom are parents, who voluntarily give time each week to run a choir, wind band and recorder groups. The room is furnished with a sofa, art tables and sink. There is a piano with a television screen above it and a carpeted area where Christopher is sitting with his teacher learning how to play a piece for his Grade Two exam.

Behaviour – from 'unteachable' to 'outstanding'

The playground is shared by all the children with the Year Six children trained as play-leaders. The mixed age circle meetings ensure that all children know and understand each other. When the school was first placed in the Ofsted category of special measures (May 2001 – October 2003), behaviour on the playground and around the school was poor. Children were described as 'unteachable' by an inspector during the 2001 Ofsted visit. Incidents of bullying and intimidation have become increasingly rare as the school has improved. The school reports any behaviour issues on incident forms that record events from the adult's perspective. Children involved also complete a form ensuring that their opinions are equally listened to. This positive approach to behaviour management ensures that everyone can tell their story in an effort to resolve the conflict. I collate every incident form onto a central document for termly review. This enables patterns of behaviour to be easily identified and ensures that any child subject to bullying is identified rapidly. Children interviewed during the recent inspection were very clear that personal safety allows risk taking in learning. As behaviour has improved throughout the school, opportunities to try new things have become available. Anna, interviewed at the end of Year Six, reflected:

If teachers trust their children more, like you trust us to do things ... we have sort of our own free space, we can use the woods, we can make dens and we can do cooking and lots of things like that, but other schools can't because they can't be trusted.

As we visit the playground on our virtual tour, we see children running across the field. Others are rolling in the long grass. A kwik-cricket match is taking place refereed by our sports coach. Ball games and skipping organised by Year Six children involves a wide range of children. Others are sitting eating their packed lunch in the Quiet Garden. The forest school woods are not open today as the circle groups have agreed to 'rest' this area for several weeks to allow it to regenerate. Looking around the playground, we see that there are many more adults than usual. Today is Year Five's 'Bring a Parent to School' day. There are 14 mums, dads and older brothers visiting the school at the invitation of children from Year Five.

Upper Key Stage Two

We enter the Year 5 classroom from the playground and see a room filled with advice about learning to learn. There is a display entitled *'Our learning toolbox'* and another board filled with photographs of the children who have brought special treasures into school to share *'What makes me, me'*.

Families have come to join children for the morning to understand what is taught at school. Throughout the school, children are offered a range of choices of challenge instead of being told which level of task to undertake. This is particularly the case in mathematics, where children self-select from a range of tasks of increasing difficulty. Children routinely talk about challenging themselves in their learning as this is part of their daily experience. On this occasion we find children explaining to their families why they have made a particular choice before working with them to begin a problem-solving activity with dominoes.

The final classroom on our tour is the Year Six room. This is a classroom where self-esteem and self-belief are viewed by the teacher as the most important assets that she can help to build. Throughout the year, the English and maths skills needed for successful assessment in national tests are taught through a wide range of activities that the children find highly engaging. Specialist teaching of grammar is offered each week by one staff member who is passionate about this aspect of English. Standards in writing have improved dramatically since children have taken on the role of 'editors' using a green pen.

As we enter the room, children are busy working in small groups to plan activities for the Year One children at a small local museum. The museum education officer has come to visit and together with the teacher is helping groups in turn to decide what they can realistically plan to do. Each group has a teacher's lesson plan format and is busily discussing the materials that they will need, the timing of each part of their activity and the roles of each group member during their teaching. This project aims for children to plan exciting learning opportunities at a local museum, Mill Green, in Hatfield. Having visited the museum and water mill and experienced the activities currently on offer, the children have talked with museum staff and are now planning a range of activities for younger children that they will subsequently teach on a carousel basis for a whole day. As we walk around the groups, we see that some children are planning to bake bread with added ingredients such as chocolate, one group plans to use percussion instruments to make music to accompany the sounds of the water mill, others aim to make Roman tiles, others wish to dress as Victorians and wash and hang out clothes using soapy water in an antique tub with washing dolly, while others are planning a herb trail linked to the traditional 'Little Red Hen' story.

Learning Review Days

Children are encouraged to make choices in many areas of their learning and to offer their views on all aspects of school life. Learning Review Days are organised for Year Five and Year Six. Appointments with families take place during the day or after school. I attend all meetings and listen while the child presents his challenges and successes often using a short powerpoint presentation. The meeting is attended by the class teacher and parents but the emphasis is on listening to the child and responding to their views. This is similar to a traditional parents' evening and yet profoundly different in that the child is the most important participant in the conversation and blame does not play a part. The aim is for all those who care about the child's learning to engage in a supportive and meaningful discussion about how best to help, by listening and responding to what the child says he needs. I prepare a record sheet for every child, which includes their recent and predicted assessment, the child's comments from their annual report, and any feedback from parents when reports are sent home. This is not a target-setting meeting, and levels of attainment are not discussed. What is important is that the child feels motivated, challenged and supported. Suggestions offered during the meeting are recorded and followed up. This is another example of the rigorous systems in process that enable learning priorities to be supported by management decisions such as allocation of staffing and resources.

Anything feels possible …

The Wroxham School recognises the importance of offering irresistible learning. Actions such as the purchase of an old bus from e-bay to create a new library, and a project to work with local craftsmen to build a Celtic roundhouse, capture the imagination of the entire community. The underlying ethos of the school invites learning to be a life-long process where limits are overcome and hope thrives. There is a palpable sense that through working together, anything feels possible. When we combine imagination with skilled, dedicated teaching, amazing things happen.

REFERENCES REFERENCES **REFERENCES** REFERENCES REFERENCES REFERENCES

DfE (2012) Teachers' Standards available at **https://www.gov.uk/government/publications/teachers-standards** accessed 7/9/14.

Hart, S, Dixon, A, Drummond, MJ, McIntryre, D (2004) *Learning without Limits* Maidenhead: Open University Press.

Swann, M Peacock, A, Hart, S, Drummond, MJ (2012) *Creating Learning without Limits* Maidenhead: Open University Press.

3
Creative teachers and creative teaching
Teresa Cremin

Chapter objectives

By the end of this chapter you should have:

- widened your knowledge of theory and practice about creative teachers and creative teaching;
- considered your own personal qualities and emerging pedagogic practice in relation to creativity;
- reflected upon specific features of creative pedagogic practice and identified ways forward in the context of the new National Curriculum in England.

This chapter addresses the following Teachers' Standards (DfE, 2012):

- set high expectations which inspire, motivate and challenge pupils;
- adapt teaching to respond to the strengths and needs of all pupils.

Introduction

What are the key features of creative teachers' pedagogical practice and just how do teachers teach creatively and teach for creativity, thus fostering children's creative learning in the 21st century? This chapter seeks to respond to these questions, putting forward a three-dimensional model in which creative practice is seen as a product of the dynamic interplay between the teacher's personal qualities, the pedagogy they adopt and the ethos developed in the primary class and school. A number of key features of creative practice are highlighted including: curiosity, making connections, autonomy and ownership, as well as originality. The research underpinning these is explored and the difference between good teaching and creative teaching is examined in the light of the new NC.

Exploring creative teaching

In the late 1990s, the literacy and numeracy strategies in England (DfEE, 1998; DfEE,1999) heralded a move towards increasingly centralised conceptions of classroom pedagogy, yet many teachers (after an initial period of tunnel vision) exercised their professional artistry and sought to teach more creatively and nurture children's creativity (Jeffrey and Woods, 2003; Grainger, Goouch and Lambirth, 2005; Craft, Cremin and Burnard, 2007). At the time these professionals were encouraged in their endeavours by numerous government reports and recommendations (DfES, 2003; OFSTED, 2003) as well as support materials (QCA, 2005a, 2005b). The new National Curriculum (DfE, 2013) pays scant attention to creativity, although borrowing HMI Matthew Arnold's words (without accrediting these), it does state that the NC 'introduces pupils to the best that has been thought and said; and helps engender an appreciation of human creativity and achievement'(DfE, 2013:5). In order to sustain such human creativity in the young of tomorrow, teachers will need to adopt creative approaches to this new curriculum and teach for creativity as well as teach creatively.

Distinctions between creative teaching and teaching for creativity tend to highlight the teacher orientation of the former and the learner orientation of the latter. Creative teaching is seen to involve teachers in making learning more interesting and effective and using imaginative approaches in the classroom. Teaching for creativity by contrast is seen to involve teachers in identifying children's creative strengths and fostering their creativity.

The National Advisory Committee on Creative and Cultural Education suggests that the first task in teaching for creativity is 'to encourage young people to believe in their creative potential, to engage their sense of possibility and to give them the confidence to try' (NACCCE, 1999, p90). The same challenge might well be set by your education department lecturers and school mentors who need to help new entrants to the profession like you to recognise and believe in your own creative potential and enable you to take risks as you learn to teach creatively and teach for creativity. In the process they will be developing your professional awareness, understanding and capacity for making connections between your own creativity and that of the children you teach.

There has been considerable research into creative teaching, some of which focuses on people's perceptions of creative educators, and tends to result in long lists of particular character traits and propensities which such teachers possess (e.g. Fryer, 1996; Beetlestone, 1998). Other research makes use of close observation and analysis of creative teachers, resulting in case study accounts of individuals' classroom practice (e.g. Jeffrey and Woods, 2003; Grainger, Barnes and Scoffham, 2004, 2006; Cremin, Burnard, and Craft, 2006; Craft, Cremin, Hay and Clack, 2013). The research of Woods and Jeffrey has been particularly influential in this area in documenting the creative response of primary professionals to the changing face of education (Woods, 1995; Woods and Jeffrey, 1996; Jeffrey and Woods, 2003; Jeffrey, 2006) and in identifying core features of creative teaching, namely relevance, ownership, control and innovation.

In seeking to become a creative teacher you will want to widen your understanding of your own creativity, and the imaginative approaches and repertoire of engaging activities that you can employ in order to develop the children's capacity for original ideas and action. You will also want to exert your professional autonomy, learning to be flexible and responsive to different learners and diverse learning contexts. For as Joubert (2001, p21) observes:

> *Creative teaching is an art. One cannot teach teachers didactically how to be creative; there is no fail-safe recipe or routine. Some strategies may help to promote creative thinking, but teachers need to develop a full repertoire of skills which they can adapt to different situations.*

In a study of creative teachers, funded by Creative Partnerships Kent, the university-based team sought to investigate the presence of commonalities between teachers who were identified as highly creative professionals in both primary and secondary schools (Grainger, Barnes and Scoffham, 2006). This case study research, acknowledging the close relationship between teacher and learner creativity, focused on the nature of creative practice. It proposed an emergent creative teaching framework, highlighting three interrelated dimensions of creative practice: namely teachers' personal characteristics, their pedagogy and the class/school ethos (see Figure 3.1). Research in the field of creative teaching has highlighted different aspects of these dimensions and this is now explored, before a closer examination is made of the core features of creative teachers' practice.

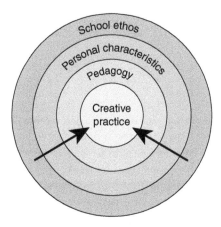

Figure 3.1 Diagram to represent a framework for creative teaching

Personal qualities

It is extremely difficult to identify the personality characteristics of creative individuals, although some researchers have sought to list features, including for example: curiosity, independence in judgement and thinking, intuition, idealism, risk taking and a capacity to become preoccupied with tasks (Torrance, 1965). In drawing together the findings from a number of studies, Stein (1974) again notes curiosity, independence, the capacity to become preoccupied, persistence and assertiveness, as well as domain expertise and unconventional tendencies.

Research in educational contexts reveals that confidence, enthusiasm and commitment are common qualities in creative teachers (Beetlestone 1998; Jones and Wyse, 2004; Grainger *et al.*, 2004) and that a sense of the self as a creative being is an important aspect of this (Sternberg, 1997). There is also some agreement that a key source of teacher self-confidence is secure subject knowledge (Gardner, 1999; QCA, 2003).The current government's White Paper on *The Importance of Teaching* (DfE, 2010) highlights the role of subject knowledge and the new National Curriculum (DfE, 2013) also foregrounds such knowledge, with a focused breakdown of the content to be 'covered' across the curriculum. To be a creative teacher within this new curriculum, it will be essential for practitioners to have the confidence to take risks and explore ways of combining curriculum content areas in order to foster creative learning through creative teaching.

Creative teachers are noted by many writers to be comfortable with risk-taking in both their private and professional lives (Boden, 2001; Craft, 2001; Ofsted, 2003). Arguably they are at ease with demonstrating their own creative engagement and exposing the ambiguity and uncertainty inherent in creative endeavour (Halpin, 2003), and are likely to perceive failure as a learning opportunity. Several writers also emphasise the combination of childlike play and exploration with adult-like self-awareness, and stress that such teachers are individuals who are curious (QCA, 2005a; Richhart, 2002). In addition, Woods and Jeffrey (1996) highlight the humanist approach of creative teachers, their openness to emotions and feelings, and their strong moral and political investment in their work.

In noting personal creative characteristics from the research literature, however, we must remember that creativity can also be collaborative since ideas emerge from joint thinking and interaction (John-Steiner, 2000; Littleton and Mercer, 2013).

REFLECTIVE TASK

In order to foster creativity in the children you will want to model and share a range of creative experiences from your life, during which you engaged in using your imagination and developed ideas with others. Consider what insights you have learnt from problem-solving contexts for example, when you had to find and shape unexpected solutions. How might you share these? Bear in mind children need to know that creativity can involve challenge and even discomfort as well as pleasure and play, and that perseverance plays a part. In this way you will be modelling creativity and demonstrating its everyday 'little c' nature.

Pedagogic practice

Creative teachers' pedagogic practice is seen to be most effective when they help children find relevance in their work either through practical application or by making emotional and personal connections (Abbs, 2002; Woods and Jeffrey, 1996). Although it might be argued emotional engagement is a requirement of all good teaching, creative teaching depends upon it more because creativity is, as Csikszentmihalyi (2002) observes, a 'central source of meaning in our lives'. Identifying the purpose and relevance of work may help prompt 'flow', which Csikszentmihalyi notes is a common characteristic of creative people.

Practice which fosters children's self-direction and agency as learners is also recognised as central (Grainger *et al.*, 2006; Jeffrey and Woods, 2003; Craft *et al.*, 2013), this arguably arises most effectively from a pedagogy which seeks to involve them as a co-participants, offering work that is of personal significance and ensuring there is time and space to experiment. Such an inclusive approach (Jeffrey and Craft, 2004) expects and fosters independence from the very earliest years of schooling (Cremin *et al.*, 2006).

Flexibility of style and pace is another recorded characteristic of a creative pedagogy (Grainger *et al*., 2004; Halpin, 2003; Nickerson, 1999). Varying the tempo, allowing time for students to have their say, a willingness to be spontaneous and the desire to give each child an opportunity to excel, mark out those who are called creative (Grainger *et al*, 2006). Research into possibility thinking as the engine of creativity suggests that teachers pausing to stand back and observe learner engagement is another potent pedagogical tool (Cremin *et al*., 2006; Craft, McConnon and Matthews, 2012;Craft, Cremin, Burnard, Drajovic and Chappell, 2012).

Another strategy seen as common is the frequent use of open-ended questions, the promotion of speculation and the generation of possibilities (Chappell *et al*., 2008; Robertson, 2002). It is suggested that teachers who reflect back questions asked of them will be developing a more generative and open stance in children (Cremin et *al*., 2006). Fostering persistence and resourcefulness is also seen as important (Claxton, 1997), as is providing time for reflection and refinement, and helping children make connections. There are many ways in which creative teachers use metaphor, anecdote and analogy to promote connection making (Jensen, 1996).

REFLECTIVE TASK

Can you identify a recent curriculum activity which you believe led to learner creativity, prompting the children to offer more unusual or innovative ideas and connections or ask questions and generate possibilities to pursue? How relevant was the task to them personally and/or emotionally? What degree of control did the children have over the activity? Was time and space offered for open exploration? What was it about the pedagogy that supported their creativity?

Ethos

While ethos is central to a consideration of what makes a creative teacher, the dividing line between creative pedagogy and ethos is inevitably blurred, because of the links between creative teaching and learning and emotional security (Halpin, 2003; Jeffrey and Woods, 2003). Positive, trusting relationships and a high degree of emotional safety are seen as necessary to ensure a creative ethos (Shayer and Adey, 2002). Such relationships are likely also to be mirrored among staff (Barnes, 2003) since the institutional ethos will affect the ethos created by each teacher (Amabile, 1988). In terms of the physical and social environment, creative professionals appear to provide children with a range of resources, and the space and time to experiment with these purposefully (Cremin *et al*., 2006).

The core features of creative teachers' practice

Research into the three major dimensions of creative practice suggests a diverse range of personal qualities and pedagogical strategies as well as different kinds of ethos are present in the classrooms of creative teachers. But attempting to encompass all of these is unrealistic, so what are the core features of such practice which as a trainee teacher you will want to adopt and develop more explicitly in order to teach the NC creatively engendering commitment and creativity on the part of younger learners?

In examining the personal qualities, pedagogy and ethos of the classrooms of creative teachers, recent research with teachers of 4–16 year olds, revealed that five core characteristics were in evidence in each of these three dimensions of creative practice (Grainger *et al.*, 2006). These included: curiosity and a questioning stance, connection making, originality, autonomy and ownership, and a developing sense of themselves as creative people and creative educators, educators who consciously use their own creative capacity in the classroom context. It is clear that creative teachers in both their planning and teaching are alert to the potential mental connections between imagination and personal/professional experience and attribute high value to curiosity and risk taking, to ownership and autonomy and to the development of imaginative and unusual ideas in both themselves and in their children.

So to become a creative teacher, pedagogically conscious of trying to teach for creativity, you will want to work to attend to these core features (detailed further below) and become more creatively involved yourself. For as Sternberg (1997) points out, those who work most creatively, identify and reward creativity in others and in addition, young people's creative abilities are 'most likely to be developed in an atmosphere in which the teacher's creative abilities are properly engaged' (NACCCE, 1999, p90). You will find considerable pleasure and satisfaction in being creatively engaged as a role model in the classroom as you seek to promote creativity in the children. Developing your awareness of yourself as a creative being is therefore an important first step, for with a flexible and creative mindset you will be able to teach creatively and foster creativity in the young.

PRACTICAL TASK   PRACTICAL TASK   PRACTICAL TASK

Seize the opportunity to become better acquainted with your own creativity in various ways. Perhaps you already engage at your own level as a creative artist (a writer, web-designer, musician, dancer, etc.) and could connect this to your work in school (Cremin, 2006), or you could seek to work in institutions with a creative frameset or instigate partnerships with the cultural/creative sector or research your own creative practice as you train. Plan a way forward to harness and enrich your creativity.

Curiosity and a questioning stance

Personal qualities: Creative teachers demonstrate curiosity and genuine desire to learn. Such individuals are likely to have a wide range of personal interests and passions and knowledge of the wider world and are likely to share their enquiring stance with the learners, pondering aloud and reflecting on issues in classroom conversations in a genuinely open and interested manner. They are also interested in and curious about the children as people and as learners.

Pedagogically: Creative teachers make extensive use of large framing questions and employ a speculative stance in the classroom regardless of the subject domain or the age of the learners (Chappell *et al.*, 2008; Cremin, Chappell and Craft, 2013).Their questioning perspective demonstrates that the formulation of a problem is as important as the resolution of one, and they make use of generative questions, creating further interest, enquiry and thinking. Such teachers explicitly encourage children to identify and share their own questions, through brainstorms, partner work on puzzlements and recording questions on sticky notes for example, as well as by providing opportunities for the learners to take responsibility for undertaking research based on their own enquiries in small groups. When invited to respond to children's problems, such teachers frequently employ reverse questioning passing back the responsibility for resolving difficulties to the learners, enquiring for example 'What can you do about this problem?'

Ethos: Being able and willing to express partial knowledge and show a genuine interest in issues through asking questions and generating possibilities involves taking risks, and is only possible in safe and affirmative environments (in which individuals feel supported and do not expect to be judged). It is evident that the ethos created by creative teachers tends to be positive, secure and inclusive, encouraging the articulation of tentative and reflective questions in whole-class and small-group conversational contexts. Furthermore, creative teachers appear to profile and give status to children's speculations, affirming these and expressing genuine interest in them.

For example, in a project on ancient Egyptians, a class of eight-to-nine year-olds grouped into research teams, each generated and selected a theme (food, daily life, clothes) to investigate, later presenting their findings to the class. Teams began by sharing their provisional knowledge and brainstorming questions and issues to research. Over time they used a range of resources (books, artefacts, internet sites and photographs) to respond to their enquiries. The focus on *identifying open, interesting and unusual questions* and the challenge to *dazzle us with your new knowledge* resulted in a buzz of research activity, which was sustained and developed through feedback and their teacher's genuine interest in their insights. As new enquiries and possibilities emerged, their most intriguing questions were highlighted and celebrated. At one point the teacher observed: *you've become researchers just like me – I wonder if you too will find questions you just can't really answer – we'll have to wait and see...*

Making connections

Personal qualities: Creative teachers perceive making connections as central both to the craft of teaching and to themselves as individuals. They are often committed to personalising teaching and model the process of sense-making through making multiple imaginative connections in whole-class and small-group contexts. For example, in a poetry session, one teacher read aloud from a personal AA Milne collection and showed the children an old holiday photograph of herself in East Sussex at 'Pooh Sticks' bridge. They later brought in favourite first books and recalled when and where they had read them, or who had read them. Creative teachers know a great deal about their children's interests and passions and see this as essential knowledge in order to make connections.

Pedagogically: Creative teachers seek to avoid the limiting nature of subject boundaries, and make frequent references to and integration with other subjects and to the world beyond the school gate. They provide time to revisit prior knowledge, make links and offer multiple opportunities for children to work collaboratively in order to widen their perspectives. Such teachers encourage children to link their learning between subjects and within subjects and often prompt connections with the children's lives outside school. This appears to increase the relevance of the curriculum to the learners. As one teacher observed: *If they can't connect to what we're learning – can't make it personal – or relate it to what they know already, then they'll never retain it.*

Ethos: Creative teachers, although aware of the requirements of the NC, often appear to give precedence to children's social and personal learning intentions over subject outcomes, and strongly defend their right to shape the curriculum in response to the learners. As a consequence the classroom ethos reflects considerable respect for the children whose emotional comfort and engagement is planned for, thus enabling them perhaps to perceive themselves as individuals first and pupils second, making connections to their lives as well as their learning.

Autonomy and ownership

Personal qualities: Creative teachers show a considerable degree of ownership with regard to planning, teaching and assessment. They exert a strong sense of professional autonomy in the classroom and demonstrate both flexibility and confidence, asserting their desire to create a co-constructed curriculum which builds on the learners' interests and their social/cultural capital, as well as curriculum requirements.

Pedagogically: Creative professionals focus explicitly on the development of children's autonomy. They seek to share ownership of the educational agenda and expect the youngsters to identify areas for enquiry and possibilities to investigate and review, co-constructing the curriculum with young learners (Craft, Cremin, Hay and Clack, 2013). They demonstrate considerable trust, interest and respect for children's ideas and set group tasks which the children have to organise for themselves, engendering both self-direction and offering scope for collaborative creativity. Creative teachers thus provide freedom and frame challenges so that, as one teacher noted: *they make their own decisions, get organised and take ownership of their learning*.

Ethos: The classroom ethos of creative professionals also reflects this sense of autonomy as children are expected to take shared responsibility for shaping their own learning. They are trusted and viewed as co-participants who have to make decisions for themselves, use of available resources and complete their work in the time available. In viewing classrooms as the children's spaces, creative teachers share responsibility for the environment, and encourage voting on the role-play area or the organisation of the reading corner for example.

Fostering originality

Personal qualities: We are all creative in different ways in our personal lives, although you may not be used to thinking of yourself as creative. Creative teachers are prepared to take risks, and remain open to new ideas, sharing any particularly inventive practices they trial or develop. Through involvement in the creative process of generating and evaluating ideas, creative teachers seek to develop their creative dispositions and enhance their ability to be inventive educators.

Pedagogically: Creative teachers model creativity and take part as learners in the classrooms; they experiment with resources, engage in problem-solving, take up different roles, and generate and critique their ideas. Such teachers demonstrate considerable flexibility and model creativity by being innovative, acting spontaneously, and shifting the focus of sessions in response to children's interests and questions, thus tempering the planned with the lived. In perceiving children as creative thinkers, they leave space for uncertainty and the unknown and show considerable creative assurance in building on unexpected contributions or enquiries, fostering the autonomy of the learners in the process.

Ethos: Creative teachers pay attention to unusual ideas or novel elements evident in children's work and celebrate and affirm these in order to help them appreciate the development of their creative thinking. Such teachers also seek to profile and make public the children's original and alternative work in displays, presentations and assemblies.

Creative and autonomous teachers

Professionally independent and curious, creative teachers are aware of themselves as creative beings, although for some this may be a relatively new insight. They model, demonstrate and foster a questioning stance and the making of connections, and a marked degree of autonomy and ownership; in the process they value and nurture originality and the generation/evaluation of ideas. Through such practice they seek to develop the creative dispositions of their students.

Recognising and exercising personal creativity appears to be an important part of creative teachers' professional and personal meaning-making. So perhaps the difference between being a good teacher and being a creative one is one of emphasis and

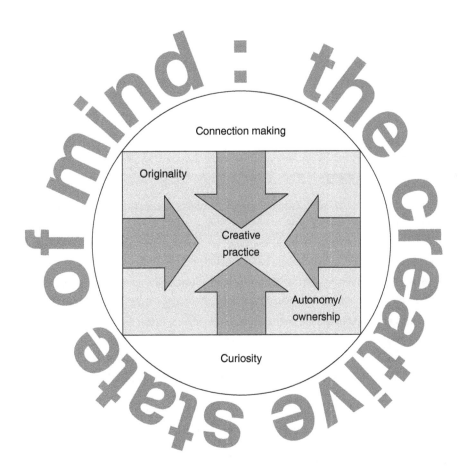

Figure 3.2 A model of creative practice and a creative state of mind

intention. Although good teachers recognise the importance of inventiveness, creative teachers see the development of creativity and originality as the distinguishing mark of their teaching. They recognise their own creativity and seek to develop such a creative mindset in the children.

The creative teacher, it is suggested, is one who is aware of, and values, the human attribute of creativity in themselves and seeks to promote it in others. The creative teacher has a creative state of mind which is actively exercised and developed in practice through the four core features of creative practice (see Figure 3.2). These features are closely interrelated and are fostered in schools which profile creativity, expect the unexpected and encourage the professional autonomy of the teaching staff, enabling them to take supported risks as they collaborate with one another and the children on their learning journeys. In the light of the White Paper on the *Importance of Teaching* (DfE, 2010), which highlights the autonomy of the profession, exercising this professional autonomy for the benefit of the children of tomorrow, who need creativity to cope in an ever more uncertain world, is crucial and requires a creative state of mind.

PRACTICAL TASK　　　　　PRACTICAL TASK　　　　　　　　PRACTICAL TASK

To widen your confidence and efficacy as a creative professional, consider the core features of creative pedagogical practice and identify one which you wish to develop further. Plan how you might nurture this capacity in yourself as well as in your teaching and learning; how might you make it more explicit in your pedagogy and classroom ethos? Discuss your plan with other trainees, and decide how you will profile this element of creative teaching on placement.

A SUMMARY OF **KEY POINTS**

➤ **Creative teachers are aware of and value the human attribute of creativity in themselves and seek to foster such a mindset in the young.**

➤ **Creative practice is multi-layered: it encompasses the three dimensions, namely personal qualities, pedagogy and ethos, each of which has a distinctly creative orientation.**

➤ **Creative teachers personally, pedagogically and in their classroom ethos, both demonstrate and develop children's curiosity, their connection making, autonomy, ownership and originality.**

➤ **Creative teachers are autonomous professionals, who actively model their own creative engagement in the classroom and seek to nurture this in children.**

➤ **While all good teachers reward originality, creative ones depend on it to enhance their well-being and that of their pupils; they see the development of creativity and originality as the distinguishing mark of their teaching.**

MOVING *ON* > > > **>** **>** **>** MOVING *ON* > > > **>** **>** **>** MOVING *ON*

In order to develop and sustain your own creative state of mind, your flexibility, collaborative capacity, optimistic and creative disposition as an individual and as creative practitioner you should seek to:

- prize a questioning stance and foster children's curiosity through offering them the chance to undertake their own enquiries;
- make personal and professional connections;
- exert your professional autonomy and co-construct the NC with the children, thus increasing their owner-ship and autonomy;
- encourage, profile and celebrate originality in both yourself and the children;
- continue to read and reflect upon your growth as a creative professional and research your own and the children's creative learning within and beyond the classroom.

REFERENCES REFERENCES **REFERENCES** REFERENCES **REFERENCES** REFERENCES

Abbs, P (2002) *Against the flow*. Abingdon: Routledge.

Amabile, TM (1988) A model of creativity and innovation in organizations, in Staw, BM and Cunnings, LL (eds) *Research in organizational behaviour.* Greenwich, CT: JAI.

Barnes, J (2003) Teachers' emotions, teachers' creativity. *Improving Schools*, 6:1, 39–43.

Beetlestone, F (1998) *Creative children, imaginative teaching.* Buckingham: Open University Press.

Boden, M (2001) Creativity and knowledge, in Craft, A, Jeffrey, B and Liebling, M (eds) *Creativity in education.* London: Continuum.

Chappell, K, Craft, A, Burnard, P and Cremin, T (2008) Question posing and question respond-ing: the heart of possibility thinking in the early years. *Early Years: An International Journal of Research and Development,* 28:3, 267–86.

Claxton, G (1997) *Hare brain, tortoise mind: why intelligence increases when you think less.* London: Fourth Estate.

Craft, A (2001) Little c Creativity, in Craft, A, Jeffrey, B, and Leibling, M (eds) *Creativity in education*. London: Continuum, pp45–61.

Craft, A, Cremin, T and Burnard, P (2007) (eds) *Creative learning 3–11.* Stoke-on-Trent: Trentham

Craft, A, Cremin, T, Burnard, P, Dragovic, T, Chappell, K (2012). "Possibility thinking". *Education 3–13*

Craft, A, Cremin, T, Chappell, K and Burnard, P (2007) Possibility thinking and creative learning in Craft, A, Cremin, T and Burnard, P (eds) *Creative learning 3–11.* Stoke-on-Trent: Trentham.Craft, A, Cremin, T , Hay, P and Clack, J (2013) Creative Primary Schools: developing and maintaining peda-gogy for creativity, *Ethnography and education* **http://dx.doi.org/10.1080/17457823.2013.828474** accessed 8/8/14.

Craft, A. McConnon, L. and Matthews, A. 2012. "Creativity and child-initiated play". *Thinking Skills and Creativity 7*(1): 48–61

Cremin, T, Burnard, P and Craft, A (2006) Pedagogies of possibility thinking. *International Journal of Thinking Skills and Creativity,* 1:2, 108–19.

Cremin, T (2006) Creativity, uncertainty and discomfort: teachers as writers. *Cambridge Journal of Education,* 36:3, 415–33.

Cremin, T, Chappell, K, Craft, A (2013). Reciprocity between narrative, questioning and imagina-tion in the early and primary years. *Thinking Skills and Creativity.* **http://dx.doi.org/10.1016/j. tsc.2012.11.003** accessed 8/8/14.

Czikszentmihalyi, M (2002) *Flow: the classic work on how to achieve happiness.* London: Rider.

Department for Education and Employment (1998) *The National Literacy Strategy framework for teaching.* London: DfEE.

Department for Education (2010) *The Importance of Teaching: The Schools White Paper, 2010.* London: The Stationery Office

Department for Education (DfE, 2012) Teachers' Standards available at **https://www.gov.uk/ government/publications/teachers-standards** accessed 7/9/14.

Department for Education (2013) *The National Curriculum Framework document* London DFE.

Department for Education and Employment (1999) *The National Curriculum: handbook for primary teachers in England.* London: HMSO.

Department for Education and Skills (2003) *Excellence and enjoyment: a strategy for primary schools.* Nottingham: DfES Publications.

Fryer, M (1996) *Creative teaching and learning.* London: Paul Chapman Publishing.

Gardner, H (1999) *The disciplined mind: beyond facts and standardized tests, the K-12 education that every child deserves.* New York: Simon & Schuster; New York: Penguin Putnam.

Grainger, T, Barnes, J and Scoffman, S (2004) A creative cocktail: creative teaching in initial teacher education. *Journal of Education and Teaching,* 38:3, 243–53.

Grainger, T, Barnes, J and Scoffham, S (2006) *Creative teaching for tomorrow.* Research report for creative partnerships.

Grainger, T, Goouch, K and Lambirth, A (2005) *Creativity and writing: developing voice and verve in the classroom.* Abingdon: Routledge.

Halpin, D (2003) *Hope and education.* Abingdon: Routledge.

Jeffrey, B (ed.) (2006) *Creative learning practices: European experiences.* London: Tufnell Press.

Jeffrey, B and Craft, A (2004) Teaching creatively and teaching for creativity: distinctions and relationships. *Educational Studies*, 30:1, March.

Jeffrey, B and Woods, P (2003) *The creative school: a framework for success, quality and effectiveness.* Abingdon: RoutledgeFalmer.

Jensen, E (1996) *Brain-based learning.* Del Mar: Turning Point.

John-Steiner, V (2000) *Creative collaboration.* New York: Oxford University Press.

Jones, R and Wyse, D (eds) (2004) *Creativity in the primary curriculum.* London: David Fulton.

Joubert, MM (2001) The art of creative teaching: NACCCE and beyond, in Craft, A, Jeffrey, B and Liebling, M (eds) *Creativity in education,* London: Continuum.

Littleton, K and Mercer, N (2013) *Interthinking: Putting talk to work* London: Routledge

NACCCE (1999) *All our futures: creativity, culture and education.* Report of the National Advisory Committee on Creative and Cultural Education. Sudbury: DfEE.

Nickerson, RS (1999) Enhancing creativity, in Sternberg, R (ed.) *Handbook of creativity.* Cambridge: Sternberg.

Office for Standards in Education (OfSTED) (2003) *Expecting the unexpected: developing creativity in primary and secondary schools,* HMI 1612. E-publication, available at **www.ofsted.gov.uk** accessed 8/8/14.

Qualifications and Curriculum Authority (2003) *New directions in spoken English: discussion papers.* London: Qualifications and Curriculum Authority.

Qualifications and Curriculum Authority (QCA) (2005a) *Creativity: Find it! Promote It! – promoting pupils' creative thinking and behaviour across the curriculum at Key Stages 1, 2 and 3 – practical materials for schools*. London: Qualifications and Curriculum Authority.

Qualifications and Curriculum Authority (QCA) (2005b)

Richhart, R (2002) *Intellectual character: what it is and how to get it.* NY: Basic Books.

Robertson, I (2002) *The mind's eye.* London: Bantam.

Shayer, M and Adey, P (2002) *Learning intelligence: cognitive acceleration across the curriculum from 5–15.* Buckingham: Open University Press.

Stein, M (1974) *Stimulating creativity*, vol. 1. New York: Academic.

Sternberg, RJ (1997) *Successful intelligence*. New York: Plume.

Torrance, EP (1965) *Rewarding creative behaviour.* Englewood Cliffs: NJ Hall.

Woods, P (1995) *Creative teachers in primary schools*. Buckingham: Open University Press.

Woods, P and Jeffrey, B (1996) *Teachable moments: the art of creative teaching in primary schools.* Buckingham: Open University Press.

4

Play and playfulness in the Early Years Foundation Stage
Elizabeth Wood

Chapter objectives

By the end of this chapter you should have:

- understood the role of play in early learning;
- explored the pedagogical approaches to play in the Early Years Foundation Stage;
- recognised the importance of creative and playful approaches to teaching and learning.

This chapter addresses the following Teachers' Standards (DfE, 2012a):

- promote good progress and outcomes by children;
- demonstrate good subject and curriculum knowledge.

Introduction

The aims of this chapter are to consider how teachers can develop playful approaches towards teaching and learning, and to understand how play activities contribute towards many aspects of children's learning: emotional, social, cognitive, physical, spiritual and creative. Play is considered to be a natural activity for children to the extent that play is sometimes privileged as *the* way in which children learn. Indeed the absence of play, and the inability to play, are considered to be harmful to children's development (Wood, 2008). This has led to the assumption that all children play and, being the natural activity of childhood, play is easy, fun and enjoyable. These assumptions have, over many years, been aligned with a substantial body of research that indicates the ways in which play activities enable children to learn new skills and knowledge, adapt to their cultures and environments, create and solve problems and build a sense of their identities as individuals and as members of different communities (Broadhead and Burt, 2012; Frost, Wortham and Reifel, 2012; Wood, 2013a). It is not surprising, therefore, that the qualities of play have been captured within early childhood education, and have been used to construct distinctly educational versions of play in preschool and school settings. But, as Kuschner (2012, p244) has argued, attempts to integrate play into the curriculum have been beset with problems which, he suggests, *may be a case of an irresistible force (play) meeting and immovable object (school)*. Similarly, Kane, Ljusberg and Larsson (2013) problematise the regulation of play, and how adults facilitate play in Swedish early childhood settings. They use the metaphors of *making magic soup* and *Lego time* to contrast free, open-ended play with regulating children through *inflexible blocks of time stacked one on top of the other* (2013, p15). These metaphors highlight ongoing tensions in how teachers, and other practitioners, manage their own roles in and out of play. As Rose and Rogers (2012, p45) argue, these tensions are particularly salient for student teachers as they struggle to reconcile the dissonance between the theories and principles obtained from their training, and the pedagogic practices observed and experienced in teaching practice classrooms. Some of these tensions will be examined in this chapter, so that you begin to develop a critical understanding of how adult-directed and child-initiated activities can be integrated in the curriculum.

The first two sections explore definitions and justifications for play, and the research that has been used to support play-based learning. Section three sets out the main approaches to educational play in the Early Years Foundation Stage (DfE, 2012b). In Section four, the Model of Integrated Pedagogical Approaches (Wood, 2010) is presented as a means of enabling you to develop your own approaches, and responding to the challenges in policy frameworks.

Defining play

It is perhaps not surprising that there is no agreed definition of play given the wide variety of activities that are typically labelled as play, including:

- free play;
- structured play;
- organised games with rules;
- theatrical performances such as plays, films, pantomimes and comedy acts;
- leisure activities (ranging from street football and cricket to extreme sports and Olympic contexts);
- rough and tumble play;
- community events such as carnivals and festivals.

Play is full of contradictions: it can be ephemeral and transitory, or can reveal the ways in which children build themes and interests over time. Play can be an act of rebellion, a space for taking risks and challenging rules. Or children can learn important cultural routines and behaviours, and create spaces for safety, for example, building cubbies and dens. One of the main challenges of play for teachers is identifying the immediate or measurable outcomes demanded by early childhood curricula. However, the benefits of play transcend curriculum boundaries, and may only become evident over time, through careful observation. A further challenge is that imagination and pretence are often seen as less important and less valuable than work. This view neglects the importance of a well-informed imagination to the immediate needs of the playing child, and to their subsequent leaning in, for example, history, geography, the sciences and the arts. In their role play activities, children often demonstrate funds of knowledge that they bring from different parts of their lives, including their knowledge of popular culture, media, home-based interests and hobbies, and play repertoires, as well as everyday activities such as shopping, cooking, gardening and participating in festivals and celebrations. As they progress into Key Stages 1 and 2, structured play and drama can, for example, involve acting out events from history, which involves using and applying their historical knowledge, or exploring concepts such as empathy, change, and social justice (see the Case Study of Year 4 children developing role play and writing).

In policy-centred educational discourses, progression involves making the transition from play/informal learning to work/formal learning, and ensuring that children are ready for these changes. However, an alternative perspective is that children should be able to progress to more complex forms of play as means of developing their creativity, imagination, and playfulness. In reality the distinctions between play and work, or play and not play, are not clearly delineated, because many aspects of our lives can be infused with playfulness, including how we interact with people and everyday events, the activities that we plan for children, and the ways in which we respond to children's playfulness.

There is some agreement (Wood, 2013a) about the characteristics of play, which make the connections between *what play is* and *what play does* for the playing child.

- Play is chosen by children, based on their ongoing ideas, interests, hobbies, and personal dispositions.
- Play is personally motivated by the satisfaction that is gained from playing.
- Play is invented by children and enables them to explore ideas, materials, roles and events that are new or unfamiliar to them. They transform reality according to their own wishes and intentions.
- Play is free from outside rules, but children may create and modify their own internal rules.
- Play enables children to develop and express an inner sense of self, which has moral, spiritual and ethical dimensions.
- Play is pretend (non-literal), but is done 'as if' the activity were real: children weave between real and pretend actions, making cognitive and symbolic transformations (making one thing stand for another).
- Children attach their own meanings in play (a piece of material can be a blanket, a magic cape, a surfboard). Imagination is more complex than pretence (which is often dismissed as merely making things up), for it involves image-making – calling images and events into mind, and transforming them into meaning and activity.
- Play is fun and enjoyable: it is done for its own sake, and for the satisfaction of the players. The process is more important than outcomes, although children may produce an outcome if they so wish, such as performing a play or dance, making props, creating artefacts.
- Play requires active involvement, engagement and participation of the players, including minds, bodies and spirits.

These characteristics relate predominantly to free, imaginative play. However, children may also choose structured play activities such as games with rules (snakes and ladders, ludo, chess) or create their own games with rules (skipping and clapping games, role play). Children also move seamlessly between 'traditional' and digital forms of play, often integrating favourite characters from popular culture, myths and folklore (Marsh, 2012).

REFLECTIVE TASK

What forms of play did you engage in as a child? Who did you play with? How much freedom did you have from adult control? What do you think are some of the main differences between your own play lives, and those of young people today?

Justifying play

Inevitably, teachers may be asked to justify their approaches to play to parents, colleagues, inspectors, and students. Although play is often justified according to the developmental needs of young children there is no definitive research that demonstrates the efficacy of play as *the* way of learning. Play is one of *many* ways in which children learn, and can offer qualitatively different ways of thinking, acting and being in the world. Research indicates that there are cultural and gender variations in children's play, so charting a 'typical' developmental or educational pathway for all children is unrealistic

(Wood, 2013a). Some of the evidence regarding the value of play is summarized below, drawing on contrasting disciplinary perspectives.

In the psychoanalytical and therapeutic traditions, play is important for healthy social and emotional development. Children's patterns of play activity can reveal how they experience themselves as individuals, how they build and manage their identities, how they experience others in relation to themselves, and how they adapt and manage their internal and external realities. Play enables children to develop strategies for coping with and adapting to life, especially as they can play with powerful emotions such as anger, anxiety, jealousy, fear, shame, indifference, dread, aggression, protest, humiliation, loss and abandonment. It is normal (and desirable) for children to feel positive as well as negative emotions: imaginative play helps children to understand that such feelings can be experienced, managed and accepted. Resilience and coping abilities stem from the capacity to develop a coherent narrative of the experience, to create meaning, and to make sense of traumatic events, transitions and dislocations. Children also learn to express sympathy and empathy in imaginative contexts, and to transfer those insights into other social contexts and relationships, thereby contributing to social affiliation and competence (Broadhead and Burt, 2012).

In the area of cognitive development, play involves lateral thinking, adaptability, problem-creating and problem-solving, symbolic activity, creativity, transformational capabilities, fantasy and imagination, curiousity, and investigation, metacognition.

Through imagination and fantasy, play activities enable children to reach beyond everyday realities, and to create potential spaces, potential selves and different possibilities for action. Thus play has a transcendental quality because children are able to play in and with real/not real boundaries. Within the flow of play, children transform themselves and their co-players, along with materials and resources, to their immediate needs, wants and desires. Cognitive flexibility can be seen in these transformational processes, especially their use of everyday resources and tools, and the symbolic meanings they convey: a cardboard tube becomes the microphone for the X-Factor contestants; a length of fabric becomes a Roman toga; a box of counters becomes the pirates' golden treasure. It is in children's play and self-initiated activities that they demonstrate meta-cognitive and meta-communicative skills – talking about their learning, thinking and actions, and representing their inner and outer worlds (Robson, 2010; Whitebread and O' Sullivan, 2012).

Research evidence shows that play integrates children's discipline-based knowledge. Carruthers and Worthington (2011) present a fascinating study of children's mathematical graphics, and detail the ways in which the beginnings of mathematical understandings are evident in their play and multi-modal representations. They present evidence of the complexity of children's thinking as they integrate everyday mathematical knowledge into their play, progressing to the beginnings of mathematical notation. Key pedagogical implications are that children need varied opportunities to explore their thinking and understanding through play, and engage with real, everyday problems.

Research on the communicative potential of children's drawings Hall (2010) also values multi-modal representations. Hall argues that drawing is a means of creative expression in its own right, and not just a pre-writing skill. Through reflective dialogues with the children in her study, Hall uncovered the meanings that they attached to their drawings. She found evidence of children expressing their own identities through power, agency, control and transformation, where children could be inventors, explorers, adventurers, superheroes, and other fantasy characters. They drew themselves into scenarios and narratives that combined everyday knowledge and experiences with their families, with imagined events and interests.

The everyday worlds that children inhabit are becoming increasingly complex, increasingly virtual, and almost without borders in terms of their flexibility and potential. Many of children's literacy practices in the new media age are inherently playful, as they engage with popular culture, computer games, social networking sites, text-messaging via computers and mobile phones, as well as making their own movies, using interactive television and engaging in virtual worlds. The challenge to teachers is to integrate new media technologies into their practice in ways that are consistent with children's rapidly developing capabilities, and to see these as valuable tools for play and playful activity.

Much of the research evidence on play demonstrates its complexity, and challenges the idea that play is the natural activity of childhood (Broadhead and Burt, 2012). Play is socially constructed, and culturally influenced. Learning how to play is a major developmental achievement that is dependent on assembling a repertoire of play skills and knowledge that become more complex over time. Children's motivations for play may not be to develop their mathematical, scientific or literacy competences, but to extend their play in ways that enable them to experience peer affiliation, social status, inclusion, and leadership roles. They experience the pleasure (and challenges) of understanding that the world can be understood and managed differently from the perspective that 'this is play'. These contrasting perspectives pose a number of challenges to the ways in which teachers manage play in their settings, in relation to policy versions of 'educational play'.

REFLECTIVE TASK

Carry out some observations of children at play in different contexts (constructive play, water play, outdoor play, digital play). Observe a child or group of children for ten minutes each day for a week. Note down their actions and interactions. Try to include their spoken language, gestures, facial expressions (if you have permission, use a digital camera as an aide-mémoire). With your teaching team, review and discuss these episodes in terms of what they reveal about children's unique identities, their play skills, their choices and decisions.

Consider these questions:

- **Who leads or dominates the play?**
- **Which children play together?**
- **What are the patterns or themes in the play?**

Consider play in relation to dimensions of diversity: ethnicity, gender, ability/disability, religious affiliation, social class, special or additional needs, sexual orientations.

- Who is included or excluded, and why?
- How can you use this knowledge to inform your practice, provision, and the roles that you take in play?

Because play activities are difficult to accommodate within a school environment it is helpful to distinguish between truly free play and educational play. Those who take the view that only free play is real play contest the concept of educational play because it changes and distorts the essential nature of play. I take the pragmatic view that play in educational settings will always be structured by rules, routines, structures and cultures of learning. What typically distinguishes play is children's freedom to choose and control their activities without undue interference from adults (Broadhead, 2004). The need for some degree of freedom is understandable, given the extent to which children's lives are controlled and regulated in and out of school. However, such freedom poses challenges to teachers, because 'truly free play' can be messy, chaotic, exuberant, mischievous, wild, noisy, and subversive. Allowing children to make their own choices and rules often invites challenges to established rules, and may result in activities that are not approved, such as war games, superhero and rough and tumble play (Wood, 2013b). However, teachers need to take a pragmatic view of what is possible in their settings, because they have to justify play in the context of national policy frameworks (though this is not the only, or even the most appropriate justification for play).

A pragmatic approach to play is preferable to little or no play at all: teachers can provide diverse and imaginative spaces for play activities, and opportunities for collaborative play, which may otherwise not be available to children. Similarly, all adults can imbue their practice with a sense of playfulness, humour and fun in order to maintain the essence or spirit of play. So how can teachers integrate free and structured play within the context of national policy frameworks for early childhood education?

Play and policy frameworks

Successive attempts to capture play within policy frameworks have produced versions of 'educational play'. This can be seen in the four UK nations: England, Northern Ireland, Scotland and Wales, which have their own distinctive frameworks, but with some similarities in their support for *planned and purposeful play* (see Wood, 2013a, Chapter 3).

The Early Years Foundation Stage in England

The early years policy framework has undergone four changes between 1997 and 2012. The EYFS was introduced in 2008, and, following a review led by Dame Clare Tickell (DfE, 2011), a revised statutory framework (DfE, 2012b). The EYFS has been influenced by government-funded research on pre-school and school effectiveness (Sylva *et al.*, 2010; **www.ioe.ac.uk/projects/epppe**) in which play is seen as contributing to the overall quality of provision, as measured by children's learning outcomes. The findings of this longitudinal study are that effective pedagogy includes both 'teaching' and the provision of instructive learning and play environments and routines. Play-based learning activities are not seen as being more important than activities that involve teacher direction and direct instruction. Rather it is the mix of activities (child-initiated and teacher-directed) that contribute to pedagogical effectiveness and child outcomes.

Curriculum planning in the EYFS is organised around three *prime* areas, and four *specific* areas of learning:

Prime areas: Communication and languages; Physical development; Personal, social and emotional development.

Specific areas: Literacy; Mathematics; Understanding the world; Expressive arts and design.

The assessment and reporting arrangements are set out by the Standards and Testing agency (STA):

> *The revised EYFS Profile requires practitioners to assess children against a new set of 17 early learning goals (ELGs). Practitioners should use their judgement to decide whether children have met each ELG or whether their level of attainment is above or below the level described by the ELGs. This will result in a judgement of expected, emerging or exceeding, for each child.*
>
> (STA, 2012, p4)

So how are teachers expected to develop the curriculum to ensure that children are achieving these goals? The EYFS recognises play as one of three key characteristics of effective teaching and learning:

1. *Playing and exploring* – children investigate and experience things, and 'have a go'.
2. *Active learning* – children concentrate and keep on trying if they encounter difficulties, and enjoy achievements.
3. *Creating and thinking critically* – children have and develop their own ideas, make links between ideas, and develop strategies for doing things. (DfE, 2012b, p7)

The EYFS takes an instrumental view of play as *the route through which the areas of learning should be delivered* (DfE, 2011, p28):

> *Each area of learning and development must be implemented through planned, purposeful play and through a mix of adult-led and child-initiated activity. Play is essential for children's development, building their confidence as they learn to explore, to think about problems, and relate to others. Children learn by leading their own play, and by taking part in play which is guided by adults. There is an ongoing judgement to be made by practitioners about the balance between activities led by children, and activities led or guided by adults. Practitioners must respond to each child's emerging needs and interests, guiding their development through warm, positive interaction. As children grow older, and as their development allows, it is expected that the balance will gradually shift towards more activities led by adults, to help children prepare for more formal learning, ready for Year 1.*
>
> (DfE, 2012b, p6, para 1.9)

This statement requires careful consideration because the EYFS privileges planned and purposeful play, which implies that teachers must ensure that children can reach the learning goals through play activities. There are also clear expectations that the transition from play to formal learning will take place during the Reception year (age 4–5), as a means of ensuring school readiness, with a focus on children's performance in literacy and numeracy. As Rose and Rogers (2012) argue, these continued 'top-down' pressures (particularly for Reception class teachers) may further compromise the provision of appropriate contexts for children's learning and development.

So how do some of these influences impact on play, and can we recognise Kuschner's argument regarding the *irresistible force (play) meeting an immovable object (school)* (2012, p244)? As previously argued, play is not always the best means of achieving instrumental purposes because of its free flow nature. Given the policy environment, and the tensions identified above, it is perhaps not surprising that free play may be restricted in favour of play that is planned, structured and purposeful, in order to align with curriculum goals and outcomes. This pedagogical position is also validated in the international literature on 'educational play' because there is some consensus that play/learning environments (indoors and outdoors) can be planned intentionally to achieve curriculum goals (Frost, Wortham and Reifel, 2012). Even within demo-cratic pedagogical approaches (for example in Scandinavian countries) it is accepted that some structures are necessary to support and enhance learning through play (Sandberg and Ärlemalm-Hagsér, 2011). Johnson, Christie and Wardle (2004, p251) argue for a combination of curriculum-led play and play-led curriculum: practitioners can be involved in play organizing the environment; planning for play/learning activi-ties; playing alongside children; observing and assessing play. Play can incorporate specific areas of learning, for example by ensuring that role play areas include literacy-related resources, by teaching rhymes and songs that include counting, and telling sto-ries that may enrich children's imagination. However, as Wood (2013a) argues, a critical distinction is that practitioners cannot plan children's play, but can plan for play, and interpret the outcomes, including the ways in which children create their own spaces, meanings and purposes.

Developing integrated pedagogical approaches to play

Two persistent areas of debate are the role of adults and the balance or mix of child-initiated, free play with adult-directed, structured play – the *Magic Soup* and *Lego Time* dilemmas identified by Kane *et al.* (2013). Much research advocates that teachers adopt a proactive approach to creating play/learning environments, alongside responsiveness to children's agendas and interests. Teachers' plans and purposes can be part of the ped-agogical mix, but should not dominate play. Wood (2010, p21) has developed a model of integrated pedagogical approaches as a guide to combining activities in the following areas:

1. *Child-initiated/child-directed activities* incorporate freely chosen play and other activities, which reveal individual and collaborative engagement, interests and motivations. These activities are flexible, open-ended, and develop mainly under the control and direction of the children. Play activities may be spon-taneous, or may be planned by the children to build on previous themes and activities. They make the rules, choose the players and resources, and, if possible, where play will take place (indoors or outdoors). There may be no tangible 'outcomes' from these activities in relation to curriculum goals: children make their own decisions about products and outcomes (building a spaceship, creating a drama to present to the class).

2. *Child-initiated/adult-responsive activities* are initiated by children, and may provoke 'potentially instruc-tive' responses from teachers and adults in the setting. Adults observe play, and identify how children's interests, agendas and themes develop over time. They respond to children's prompts or requests for involvement (making resources and costumes to enhance play, using video and still images to record a performance). The key to being a sensitive co-player is the ability to realise the magical and transforma-tive power of play, and to avoid inappropriate interventions, which may destroy the flow. When adults do become involved in play, it should always be on the basis of discrete observation, leading to informed and intuitive actions, usually with the permission or invitation of the players.

3. *Adult-initiated/child-responsive activities* involve intentional teaching, structure or direction, and are linked to learning outcomes. Such activities incorporate playful orientations, with some flexibility for unplanned developments based on children's responses. For example, the teacher chooses a story (fact or fiction) to create a structured role play or drama. Children can respond with their own ideas and there is some flexibility to take the activity in unplanned directions. Children may choose how to express their

ideas through multi-modal representations such as modeling, sculpture, writing, drawing, painting, dance, constructions, collage.

4. *Teacher-initiated and -directed activities* are defined as non-play or work because they involve little choice or flexibility, and are linked to specific learning outcomes. There may be elements of imagination and fun in how the activity is presented in order to engage and interest the children. The adult maintains control and direction of the activity, including how children's thinking and learning are represented.

Exploring play and playfulness – some case studies

Throughout childhood, play activities typically become increasingly complex, more organized and industrious, more rule-bound, and more focused on ends as well as means. As children become skilled players they set their own challenges: their play becomes more sustained, with increased attention to structures, problem-solving, intentional activities and outcomes (Broadhead, 2004). They display many positive dispositions that are considered essential to lifelong learning, such as planning and organisation, taking risks, creating challenges, problem-creating and problem-solving, concentration, persistence on task, engagement, involvement, participation, and meta-cognitive capabilities. Therefore it can be argued that the model of integrated pedagogical approaches is equally relevant to children across the Early Years Foundation Stage, Key Stages 1 and 2 (and beyond).

The following section includes narrative descriptions of children's play to support the case for continuity and progression, and to reveal the development of complexity and challenge. The narratives can be used to stimulate discussions about the nature of play across childhood, and challenge how we think about play, including our own beliefs, values and practices. They also exemplify the importance of close observation of children at play in order to understand their meanings and intentions, and the knowledge that children bring into their play.

CASE STUDY

School play (Reception and Year 1)

Abigail is a creative and playful teacher, who believes in the importance of stimulating children's imagination, and allowing them to take her planned activities in their own directions. In her PGCE year she is prepared to take some risks with her teaching, and to explore her own ideas about the kind of teacher she wants to become. She uses stories in a playful way, encouraging children to go beyond the original and create their own characters, plotlines, and endings. In the traditional story of 'The Three Little Pigs', the children are visited by the local community police officer, who asks for a report of the wolf's bad behaviour, a description of him, and some ideas about where he might be hiding. The children collaborate in designing 'Wanted' posters, with some inventive ideas about the wolf's habits and characteristics. A teaching assistant presents the children with a report from the planning committee which identifies all the problems with illegal house construction, and sets out what they have to do to get planning permission for well-built houses. These stimuli result in many different ideas and activities, which the children are able to develop in groups. Abigail uses the integrated pedagogical model to balance teacher-led and child-initiated activities, ensuring that she makes time to respond to their ideas, provides appropriate resources, and allows free play for the children to develop roles and themes in their own ways.

CASE STUDY

Technological play Reception/Year 1

Amanda has resourced her classroom to include a range of digital resources, including computers, hand-held video cameras, voice recorders, programmable computers such as Beebots and Roamers. The children are allowed to use these resources indoors and outdoors during free-flow time for play and self-initiated activities. She is on hand to support the children's choices, teach them skills when needed, make suggestions, and record her observations of their learning. These are some of the activities recorded during a two-hour session of free choice activity.

Luca (Year 1) takes the voice recorder to the library area where he records himself telling a story. He plays it back to himself, then gathers together four children. He plays the story for them, and turns the pages of the book in the right place. He then asks the children some questions about the story, repeating some of the pedagogical techniques used by Amanda. Luca is beginning to see himself as a competent reader and demonstrates his understanding of literacy as a social practice. His confident use of the voice recorder is also seen in his enthusiasm for other digital technologies. His next choice of activity is making a short video of the book which he loads onto the computer. Aamina and Kai join Luca and they add special effects, including explosions, music and animations, exchanging knowledge about techniques and suggestions for the best effects. They show the video at review time and talk about the design processes and how they collaborated on the different tasks.

Outside, children are using Roamers to practice programming the directions, and to develop their expertise. Lizzie and John draw a trail on the playground with chalk and experiment with making the Roamer follow it. This leads to them talking about snail trails, and they ask Amanda to cut out a snail shape, which is then stuck over the Roamer. They decide that they want to measure the trails and this leads to much discussion about how they can measure straight and wavy lines. George decides to video the activity which is shown at review time, when they talk about how they solved the measurement problem using string and small and large rulers.

These episodes demonstrate the potential for creative approaches to teaching and learning, within an environment that supports the integration of child-and-adult-led activities, and enables different possibilities for learning to emerge and to be followed by the children. Review time is important for meta-cognitive processes – talking and thinking about learning, identifying the next possible steps, and planning further activities.

Developing play in Key Stage 2

Early years teachers may have the opportunity to take on the role of the school's play coordinator, which is likely to become an increasingly important role in light of the policy emphasis on play in extended provision. Therefore I have included two narratives of play in Key Stage 2 to exemplify progression and continuity. In response to developing the new Foundation Phase in Wales, the management team of a large primary school decided to implement an action research project to develop a whole school approach to play and playfulness. This diverse school community included children from a wide range of ethnic backgrounds, and with around 27 community languages (typically six or seven different languages in a class). I worked with the staff over one school year, visiting the school each term to discuss progress, and supporting their ideas. The following case studies report the action research projects for Year 4 and Year 6, and provide evidence that drama, structured play, and free play can support continuity and progression.

CASE STUDY

Developing drama and writing in Year 4

Miriam teaches a Year 4 class, and is concerned about the motivation and performance of some of the boys, who are underachieving and underperforming. She decides to explore role play and drama in the context of their History/English project on the Romans to see if she can stimulate their interest and engagement, and improve their literacy skills. The project develops over half a term and includes a wide range of activities.

The children research the Romans on the internet and in text books, with a focus on everyday life (for a slave girl, a gladiator, a centurion and a rich family). They begin to create stories about their chosen characters, thinking about what they would say and do, and taking care to use correct historical facts. Their scripts reveal empathy with the characters (putting themselves in someone else's life, thoughts and feelings) and include dramatic events such as being captured, flogged and starved as a slave, learning how to fight as a gladiator, being brave in adversity, and choosing clothes and jewellery.

Miriam gives the children video cameras to record their developing dramas. They use them responsibly and with great enthusiasm. Some of the children choose to rehearse during playtimes, recording on video, then writing and editing their scripts. They use lengths of fabric as costumes to help them get into their roles. When they are satisfied with their script, they rehearse formally, and then present their dramas during a whole-school assembly. At the end of the project, Miriam highlighted the improvement in the children's interest and motivation. The boys who were the focus of her concern showed improvements in the quality and creativity of their writing, and in their literacy levels.

CASE STUDY

Year 6 children as action researchers – improving playtime

Following an in-service session on action research methods, the Year 6 team decided to cascade these ideas to the children, and give them the choice of the research topic. A specific area of concern was the use of the playground (typically by boys) for football, which limited other activities. The children became the action researchers and were involved in each stage of the study, exploring a range of strategies and activities that would improve collaboration and interaction between children during playtimes.

Their research included interviews with children in Key Stages 1 and 2, identifying 'problem' areas, and generating solutions; researching games and playgrounds on the internet; designing their own PowerPoint presentations to feedback their research findings; making games; considering appropriate play spaces/activities for children with special educational needs. A half-day workshop was provided by the team to teach the children how to use/play the games they had either found on the internet, or made themselves. Children brought in ideas for play activities from their families and home cultures, which led to culturally diverse games.

The project was particularly beneficial for Sama, who felt excluded from play because of her visual impairment; she was afraid of being knocked over by the footballers, and there was nothing for her to do. Sama co-operated with her peers to make a sensory play box containing a range of games and activities that she could use on her own or with friends. When she transferred to secondary school, Sama insisted on leaving the box for other children to use. The teaching team found that active playtimes provided continuity of learning through purposeful activity, which led to exploration, experimentation, developing independence and collaboration, self-esteem, creativity, imagination, social relationships, language, cognitive and physical skills, and improved behaviour.

A SUMMARY OF **KEY POINTS**

The case studies also reveal how creative teachers can sustain creative approaches to teaching and learning. Play and playfulness incorporate many different processes that contribute to children's learning and development. Free and structured play can be integrated into the early childhood curriculum in ways that enable children to make choices and develop their own play themes. Close observation of play enables teachers to interpret and understand the intricacies of children's play lives, and the knowledge and skills that they bring to their activities. The model of integrated pedagogical approaches can guide teachers in their planning within and beyond the Foundation Stage. Constraining play may deny its many benefits, including opportunities for children to become master players, to develop well-being and emotional resilience, and to develop the flexibility and creativity needed in their immediate and future lives. A shared professional responsibility is maintaining a sense of what it means to be a playful teacher, and a playful learner.

MOVING *ON* > > > > > > MOVING *ON* > > > > > > MOVING *ON*

- What are your own beliefs and values regarding children's play? Discuss with colleagues your attitudes towards risky play (such as rough-and-tumble, play fighting).
- Discuss your definitions of playfulness with colleagues and members of the teaching team.
- In what ways do you create playful approaches to teaching and learning in your setting?
- Using the model of integrated pedagogical approaches, consider how you will aim to develop this in your practice. What are the main challenges for you in integrating child-initiated and adult-directed activities?
- What are the key messages about the value of play and playfulness that you would give to colleagues and parents?

REFERENCES REFERENCES **REFERENCES** REFERENCES REFERENCES REFERENCES

Broadhead, P (2004) *Early Years Play and Learning, Developing Social Skills and Co-operation*, London: RoutledgeFalmer.

Broadhead, P and Burt, A (2012) *Understanding Young Children's Learning Through Play: Building Playful Pedagogies*. Abingdon: Routledge.

Carruthers, E and Worthington, M (2011) *Understanding Children's Mathematics: Beginnings in Play*. Maidenhead: Open University Press.

DfE (Department for Education) (2011) *The Early Years: Foundations for Life, Health and Learning. An Independent Report on the Early Years Foundation Stage to Her Majesty's Government*.

DfE (Department for Education) (2012a) Teachers' Standards available at **https://www.gov.uk/government/publications/teachers-standards** accessed 7/9/14.

DfE (Department for Education) (2012b) *The Statutory Framework for the Early Years Foundation Stage. Setting the Standards for Learning, Development and Care for Children from Birth to Five.*

Department for Education and Skills (2007) The Early Years Foundation Stage. Nottingham: DfES Publications.

Effective Provision for Preschool and Primary Education (EPPPE) **http://eprints.ioe.ac.uk/5309/1/sylva2004EPPEfinal.pdf** accessed 8/8/14.

Frost, JL, Wortham, SC and Reifel, RS (2012) *Play and Child Development*. Prentice-Hall. 4th edition.

Hall, E 2010. Identity in Young Children's Drawings: Power, Agency, Control, and Transformation. In *Play and Learning in the Early Years: from Research to Practice,* in P Broadhead, J Howard and E Wood, (Eds) 95–112. London: SAGE.

Johnson, JE, Christie, J and Wardle, F (2004) *Play, Development and Early Education.* Oxford: Pearson.

Kane, E, Ljusberg, A, and Larsson, H (2013) Making Magic Soup – the facilitation of play in school-age childcare. *International Journal of Play*, 2:1, 7–21.

Kuschner, D (2012) Play is natural to childhood but school is not: The problem of integrating play into the curriculum. *International Journal of Play,* 1:3, 242–249.

Marsh, J (2012). Purposes for literacy in children's use of the online virtual world 'Club Penguin'. *Journal of Research in Reading*.

Robson, S. 2010. Self-regulation and metacognition in young children's self-initiated play and reflective dialogue. *International Journal of Early Years Education* 18/3: 227–241.

Rose, J and Rogers, S (2012) Principles under pressure: student teachers' perspectives on final teaching practice in early childhood classrooms. *International Journal of Early Years Education*, 29:1, 43–58. **http://dx.doi.org/10.1080/09669760.2012.664472** accessed 8/8/14.

Sandberg, A and Ärlemalm-Hagsér, E (2011) The Swedish National Curriculum: play and learning with fundamental values in focus, *Australian Journal of Early Childhood*, 36:1, 44–50.

Standards and Testing Agency (2012) 2013 Early Years Foundation Stage Assessment and Reporting Arrangements. **www.education.gov.uk/assessment** accessed 8/8/14.

Sylva, K, Melhuish, E, Sammons, P, Siraj-Blatchford, I and Taggart, B (2010) *Early Childhood Matters: Evidence from the Effective Pre-school and Primary Education Project*, London: Routledge.

Whitebread, D and O'Sullivan, L (2012) Preschool children's social pretend play: supporting the development of metacommunication, metacognition and self-regulation. *International Journal of Play 1*(2).

Wood, E (2008) Everyday play activities as therapeutic and pedagogical encounters, *European Journal of Psychotherapy and Counselling,* 10:2, 111–120

Wood, E (2010) Developing Integrated pedagogical approaches to play and learning, in P Broadhead, J Howard, and E Wood, (eds) *Play and learning in the early years: from research to practice,* London: SAGE, pp 9–26.

Wood, E. (2013a) *Play, Learning and the Early Childhood Curriculum*. London, Sage.

Wood, E. (2013b) Free choice and free play in early childhood: troubling the discourse. *International Journal of Early Years Education*.

5
Creativity and spiritual, moral, social and cultural development
Tony Eaude

Chapter objectives

By the end of this chapter, you should:

- understand more about spiritual, moral, social and cultural development and how these are linked to creativity;
- recognise the importance of the learning environment in enhancing both SMSC and creativity;
- have reflected on the importance of process rather than content in encouraging children's creativity across all subject areas.

This chapter addresses the following Teachers' Standards (DfE, 2012):

- set high expectations which inspire, motivate and challenge pupils;
- promote good progress and outcomes by pupils;
- adapt teaching to respond to the strengths and needs of all pupils;
- manage behaviour effectively to ensure a good and safe learning environment.

CASE STUDY

Leigh was a rather troubled and disorganised six year old, often late for school and with little self-belief. In a project on electricity, we made working models. He designed and built a lighthouse. The children checked at least once a day that the models still worked. And every day they were reminded to break the circuit. For some weeks afterwards, first thing, Leigh would dash into the classroom. Before anything else he would reconnect the wires to see that his lighthouse still worked. It was not just the light that shone. The beam on his face was even brighter.

Introducing creativity

This chapter considers the relationship between creativity and spiritual, moral, social and cultural development (SMSC). The word 'creativity' is used with different meanings. So is SMSC, without necessarily being associated closely with creativity. I start with a definition of creativity and then explore, in turn, spiritual, moral, social and cultural development and how these relate to creativity. Finally, I consider the features of a learning environment to encourage these and the implications for teachers.

All Our Futures, often called the Robinson report, defines creativity as *imaginative activity fashioned so as to produce outcomes that are both original and of value.* (NACCCE, 1999, p 29). Think about Leigh and his lighthouse. His work involved:

- imagination (planning the wiring);
- activity (making the model);
- an outcome (something tangible);
- originality (something different); and
- value (at least we thought so).

If you are wondering whether young children can be original, consider Robinson's (p30) distinction between *historic*, *relative* and *individual* originality. The first is confined to a few geniuses. Relative originality occurs when a child takes an approach or arrives at an outcome which is original compared to other children's. Individual originality relates to the child's previous work, so that a child trying out unfamiliar ways of applying paint or discovering a mathematical pattern for the first time can be seen as original. Relative and individual originality roughly correspond with what Craft (Craft *et al.*, 2001, pp45–62) calls 'little c creativity', with 'big C creativity' reserved for historic originality. So young children can be creative in making a discovery that is original – to themselves – but this requires a divergent approach, not just following someone else's ideas. To achieve a successful outcome requires knowledge and skills, but imagination and divergent thinking come first.

This definition, in my view, misses out one important aspect of most creative activity – that the exact outcome changes between the planning and the performance stages. A choreographer does not know quite how the dance will turn out. A website designer will experiment with the structure and the look of the site. Writers, starting out, are unsure what the final text will look like. Creativity involves imagining the outcome, without this being too definite at the outset.

REFLECTIVE TASK

What qualities do you, or a child, need to be creative? Add your own to my list:

flexibility				curiosity
		openness	imagination	

Figure 5.1 Creative qualities

Approaching spiritual, moral, social and cultural development

Spiritual, moral, social and cultural development (or a very similar list) occupies an important place in legislation, from the 1944 to the 1988, 1992, 2005 and 2010 Education Acts. A greater emphasis on SMSC recently is reflected in the Ofsted Inspection Handbook (2014) although in practice inspectors tend to focus heavily on measurable outcomes. To see how Ofsted defines SMSC, consider Paragraphs 131– 4:

131. Spiritual development:

- *ability to be reflective about their own beliefs, religious or otherwise, that inform their perspective on life and their interest in and respect for different people's faiths, feelings and values;*
- *sense of enjoyment and fascination in learning about themselves, others and the world around them;*
- *use of imagination and creativity in their learning;*
- *willingness to reflect on their experiences.*

132. Moral development:

- *ability to recognise the difference between right and wrong, readily apply this understanding in their own lives and, in so doing, respect the civil and criminal law of England;*
- *understanding of the consequences of their behaviour and actions;*
- *interest in investigating and offering reasoned views about moral and ethical issues, and being able to understand and appreciate the viewpoints of others on these issues.*

133. Social development

- *use of a range of social skills in different contexts, including working and socialising with pupils from different religious, ethnic and socio-economic backgrounds;*
- *willingness to participate in a variety of communities and social settings, including by volunteering, cooperating well with others and being able to resolve conflicts effectively;*
- *acceptance and engagement with the fundamental British values of democracy, the rule of law, individual liberty and mutual respect and tolerance of those with different faiths and beliefs; the pupils develop and demonstrate skills and attitudes that will allow them to participate fully in and contribute to life in modern Britain.*

134. Cultural development:

- *understanding and appreciation of the wide range of cultural influences that have shaped their own heritage and that of others;*
- *understanding and appreciation of the range of different cultures within school and further afield as an essential element of their preparation for life in modern Britain;*
- *knowledge of Britain's democratic parliamentary system and its central role in shaping our history and values, and in continuing to develop Britain;*
- *willingness to participate in and respond positively to artistic, sporting and cultural opportunities;*
- *interest in exploring, improving understanding of and showing respect for different faiths and cultural diversity, and the extent to which they understand, accept, respect and celebrate diversity, as shown by their tolerance and attitudes towards different religious, ethnic and socio-economic groups in the local, national and global communities.*

This list is a useful starting point, though one may wonder how much some of these apply to young children. Let us look at SMSC in greater depth. It may help to think of spiritual, moral, social and cultural as four facets or dimensions of personal development. Who we are has many other facets, such as emotional, intellectual, physical and mental. The emphasis on these four does not mean that others are not important – after all, each of us is one person, with different facets. An educated person, in my view, is one who integrates these.

The current emphasis of education is so strongly on cognitive and intellectual ability, where attainment can be measured, that personal development is seen as something separate – even having its own subject heading personal, social, health and citizenship education (PSHCE). However, attainment and personal development are like two strands of a rope intertwined and depending on each other. Too much attention to 'personal development' may lead to a lack of mental and intellectual challenge, while too little may result in children not learning life-skills and how to relate to other people. We all need both.

My perspective is similar to Pollard's (1985, p x) when he writes that

> *Individuals are thought to develop a concept of 'self' as they interpret the responses of other people to their own actions. Although the sense of self is first developed in childhood, ... it is continually refined in later life and... provides the basis for thought and behaviour.*

Children's spiritual, moral, social and cultural development involves children creating their own selves: being, in Goodman's phrase, world-makers, with *worldmaking... always start(ing) from worlds already on hand: the making is a remaking* (1978, p6).

My guess is that you may feel fairly comfortable with what social, and probably moral, development are all about, a bit less sure about cultural and fairly puzzled about, or perhaps hostile towards, spiritual development. I discuss each of them in more detail in Eaude (2007), but the next four sections explore what is distinctive about each and how they link to creativity. It will help to think of them as overlapping but with:

Spiritual		Meaning
Moral	*mainly related to*	Action
Social		Interaction
Cultural		Belonging

Figure 5.2 Four facets of personal development

Spiritual development and creativity

Spiritual development is an elusive idea, and hard to define. Your immediate response probably relates it to religion. Historically, this link has been very close, and many people still argue that spiritual development depends on involvement in a religious tradition. However, the view that 'spiritual' is wider than 'religious' is more common. Hyde (2008), for instance, identifies four aspects: the felt sense, integrating awareness, weaving the threads of meaning and spiritual questing; while Hay and Nye (1998) write of awareness sensing, mystery sensing, and value sensing.

REFLECTIVE TASK

Think (ideally with someone else) about other connotations of the word 'spiritual'. Add your own to these that teachers often mention:

		relationships to each other and/ or to God		beyond the ordinary
reflection/ prayer	evocative/ favourite places/ experiences		awe and wonder	

Figure 5.3 Reflecting on the word 'spiritual'

My research (see Eaude, 2007) sees spiritual development as primarily about questions related to meaning, such as:

- Who am I?
- Where do I fit in?
- Why am I here?

These are the sorts of question that religion tries to answer, but they are universal. They are asked repeatedly at any age, not necessarily frequently and never answered easily, quickly or finally. They require space and time and regular re-visiting. They involve making sense of puzzling and difficult experiences, as well as joyous ones; and realising that much of what gives meaning to our lives is intangible, rather than material possessions.

You may think that young children do not ask such questions. Of course, they may use different language, and are (often) more centred on themselves than adults are. However, they often wonder:

- who they are (think of their fascination with mirrors and puppets);
- whether they belong (think of the importance of their family and groups they are part of); and
- why things are as they are (think of how children ask questions about what they do not understand).

So, how is spiritual development linked to creativity? Music, poetry, drama, worship, the direct experience of nature may come to mind as routes into spiritual development; but these questions can occur in any subject area. Remember the importance of children making sense of the world and creating personal meaning, a process involving questions and space and time to explore these.

REFLECTIVE TASK

One remarkable thing about spiritual development, taught in many religious traditions, is that children have qualities that are lost, or at least inhibited, in adults: for example, openness, capacity for joy and an ability to live in the here and now. Can you think of others? Put the book down and spend a few minutes thinking about what children can teach us in this respect.

Moral development and creativity

Moral development is often seen as children learning the difference between right and wrong and behaving well. This seems to me too simple. The problem is not one of knowing but of acting appropriately and living what philosophers from Aristotle onwards have called 'a good life'; and internalising this, so that actions are based on positive dispositions and motives, rather than fear or reward. Moral development is something wider, and more profound, than behaviour management. To use an old-fashioned term, it is about building character – the sort of person one is or becomes.

Character consists of a range of qualities and dispositions, some intrapersonal, some interpersonal, which help in living the good life. Often, these are called values, though I prefer 'virtues', because 'values' is used about cultures and societies as well. Which virtues help us to lead the good life is not just a matter of individual choice, but reflect the different traditions and cultures we come from: the home and school, wider society and faith communities.

REFLECTIVE TASK

REFLECTIVE TASK

Think what qualities (or virtues) you value in a child – again I have started you off.

			Courage	
Tolerance				
	Honesty			Thoughtfulness

Figure 5.4 Valuable qualities/virtues in a child

While you may see these as universal, I believe that, while there is a lot of overlap, they vary between cultures. For example, compassion and respect appear to be fairly universal, but modesty, or humility, or patriotism are more contested. For each, one needs a balance – neither too much, nor too little – of each, and this requires individual judgement.

Consider how children learn these rather abstract qualities. The most important way is through example, and habituation; that is, by role modeling and by practice, with positive reinforcement. Talking about what such qualities 'look like' in themselves and other people is valuable, but internalising them requires a subtle mixture of example, habituation and conscious deliberation. Remember the importance of stories, an insight which religious traditions recognise in emphasising the stories of faith: because stories engage children of all ages and their open-endedness encourages them to think about characters' actions and motives. Such a process helps develop a sense of self – and what is sometimes called a coherent personal narrative (see Bruner, 1996).

You may worry that if children are not given clear rules they will not know how to act. But too didactic an approach or too limiting a structure discourages children's intrinsic motivation – doing something because it is right, rather than because of reward or punishment. Children need both guidance and the chance to internalise these virtues, to understand what they mean and to live them, to determine for themselves how to act and to be able to navigate a way through confusion that often results from mixed messages for instance from the media or peer group. So, adults who provide a good example and the opportunity to reflect on how they have acted, and how they should, help children to act appropriately and so to create the sort of person they become.

Social development and creativity

Social and emotional development are closely linked. Indeed, as Gerhardt (2004) indicates, babies learn to regulate their emotional impulses and responses through interaction and feedback. From the start, identity and sense of self are created by interacting with other people.

Anxiety leads to aggression or to withdrawal. Put simply, it is very hard to be creative if you are feeling unsafe. However, creativity also requires challenge and an element of risk-taking. So, the culture and the mood of the classroom has to offer the right balance of safety and challenge; for all children, but especially so those who find learning difficult because:

- the expectations at home clash with those at school; or
- previous experience, such as rejection, or their current situation, such as poverty or domestic responsibilities, make them too anxious.

Emotional intelligence involves learning to respond to, and regulate, the whole range of emotions – anger, grief and envy as well as calmness, joy and hope – and is learned in many contexts, not only in particular lessons. Just as personal development and attainment are interdependent, emotional development is interwoven with the whole range of learning.

Part of the challenge of learning is to build on what is familiar and to learn about similarity and difference. So, children benefit from a range of experiences which take them beyond their current state of knowledge, moving them away from being centred on themselves, by recognising the feelings and needs of others.

Learning is both an individual and a collective activity. Good learners can act both independently and interdependently. Of course, many learning activities require individuals to work on their own. But, think, for example, of how in activities like singing as a group or playing team sport, discussing a scientific experiment or being quiet together, a group experience creates more than the sum of its parts. By co-operating with others, children both learn the skills of interaction and extend the range of their learning. Social development involves more than children knowing how to get on with each other. It entails learning how to co-operate and negotiate, working with others, as well as on one's own. Our sense of self, or identity, is social as well as individual, because we become ourselves only as part of something bigger than ourselves.

Cultural development and creativity

In Eagleton's (2000, p 131) words, *culture is not only what we live by. It is, also, in great measure, what we live for. Affection, relationship, memory, kinship, place, community, emotional fulfilment, intellectual enjoyment, a sense of ultimate meaning*: areas where the four facets of SMSC overlap.

However, 'culture' is one of the most complicated words in English, with several different meanings. The section in *All Our Futures* (NACCCE, 1999, pp40–53) is excellent on this. Two relevant meanings relate to:

- cultural background, identity and belonging; and
- 'high' and 'low' culture.

Children come to school with what is often called 'cultural capital': expectations and beliefs influenced by their background and previous experience. These result from many factors, including family, social class, and ethnicity. Where these expectations and beliefs clash with those of the school, children may be confused or anxious, for instance about how to respond to other children or adults, or about dress or diet. Remember the importance of feeling safe. So, taking account of children's cultural capital helps them to belong, for example by valuing the knowledge brought from home and being sensitive to what they are encouraged (or forbidden) to do there. Where children feel that they do not belong, or feel excluded, their learning suffers.

Identity depends on belonging, being part of a whole range of different groups, each with its own culture: family, nursery, class, voluntary or sporting groups, and, for some, faith community; and in other ways such as supporting a football club or wearing a particular brand of clothes. These cultures may protect or challenge, guide or inhibit, at different stages of our lives, but all contribute to the 'narrative' that each of us tells of ourselves, which is always a mixture of different, often conflicting, stories about who we are.

The second meaning of culture relates to the arts, what is often called 'high' culture, and is often linked to creativity. Particular sorts of experience help us to understand ourselves better – and to improve ourselves (though this is a hotly debated area). The arts – music, drama, visual art, poetry – are wonderful ways of learning about different people and about ourselves. Visits to a concert, a museum or a farm, hearing a poet or working with an artist can help expand children's cultural horizons both in experiencing other people's creativity and developing their own.

Creative activity can help to create or reinforce our identity, as it did for Leigh (see *Case Study* at the beginning of the chapter). However, like SMSC, this depends on *how* children approach tasks and experiences, rather than *what* these are, as such. So, creativity is more like a way of learning than located within any particular experience or subject. And this is where you as a teacher can open up possibilities by the culture, the environment and the expectations that you create.

Creating environments to encourage creativity

Think back to the story of Leigh. Making the lighthouse was a creative activity, where his imagination and activity helped him complete the task. However, it appeared to be more than that. The lighthouse was *his,* almost a part of him. In re-creating it each day, he was, in a sense, re-creating himself and re-affirming the possibility of his own creativity.

Although the four facets of SMSC have been treated separately, they overlap and depend on an environment very similar to that which encourages children's creativity. In this section, I consider features of such an environment.

For children to be creative requires both *safety* and *challenge*. How much of each will differ according to background, experience, confidence, and task. It may change from day to day, or between subject areas. Think of your own strengths and weaknesses and how these depend on where you are and how you feel. Meeting new people, or performing in public, may energise or panic you. What you can do easily on your own may become next to impossible in a group – or vice versa. However, we all thrive on challenge as long as we remain in control. Too often, adults assume that children are not-capable, rather than creative learners and lateral thinkers; and in assuming this, we may help to make them so. Being in control helps to build children's growing sense of agency, in both their academic and personal development.

Creativity and SMSC both entail a mixture of *structure* and *freedom*. To be creative (at least in a focused way) children require both some guidance and the chance to:

- generate their own ideas;
- ask questions and pose and solve their own problems;
- try out new experiences and ways of working, including taking risks and making mistakes;
- engage in open-ended activities, adopting different approaches and making unusual connections.

A third feature is the chance *to play* and *to be playful*. Look at a young child playing (seriously) and consider Winnicott's words (1980, p63) *it is in playing and only in playing that the individual child or adult is able to be creative and to use the whole personality. It is only in being creative that the individual discovers the self.* Similar opportunities to be playful may occur most obviously in drama or dance, but also through literature, planning a presentation or solving a problem. These provide opportunities for children to explore their own, and other people's feelings and beliefs, involving qualities such as empathy, imagination and lateral thinking.

A fourth feature is *space*. At times, expecting children to work quickly is appropriate; but an environment to encourage creativity and SMSC requires space for thinking, imagining, planning, exploring and reflecting. This space may be physical and emotional, or both, sometimes individual, sometimes in a group. Remember how busy and cluttered many children's lives are and the pressure they are under. Space enables children (and adults) to reflect, slow down and allow the unconscious to work, as Claxton (1997) discusses, and so gives children the chance to make sense of, and to answer for themselves, life's more profound and difficult questions. What are often called 'awe and wonder' experiences may help children gain a sense of something beyond themselves, and of perspective. This can involve language but symbols, times of quiet and stillness and direct experience of nature offer alternative, often more accessible, opportunities for this.

PRACTICAL TASK   PRACTICAL TASK   PRACTICAL TASK

What other features of an environment to encourage creativity would you highlight? Think back to those areas where you are creative and what helps (or inhibits) your own creativity.

Teaching for creativity

Many of the implications for teachers follow directly from the sort of environment described. This section considers some less obvious implications.

All Our Futures (NACCCE, 1999, p89) distinguishes between teaching creatively and teaching for creativity. Nurturing and demonstrating your own creativity will enhance your children's creativity – as well as ensuring that you look after yourself. However, it is possible to teach creatively without encouraging creativity. What appears to be creative teaching may leave some children without enough structure. Teaching for creativity implies empowering, encouraging and enabling children to be in control of activities. Children's learning benefits from more opportunities to exercise creativity than they often receive, but no teacher can foster creativity all the time. Dictating what sort of picture, model or piece of writing is required, while not encouraging creativity, may at times be appropriate.

Other chapters in this book explore creativity within specific subject areas. Although 'the arts' may present more obvious opportunities than maths or geography, possibilities exist in every subject area. While circle time or PSHCE may help you focus on social and emotional development, this can happen in any situation.

You may be thinking that teaching for creativity presents a big challenge. It does, especially given the strong emphasis on content coverage, tightly defined learning objectives and measurable outcomes. But:

- think more about *how* children learn – by imagining, questioning and creating, for instance – than *what* they learn;
- plan carefully, but give some space for flexibility and exploration; and
- recognise that many important questions cannot be answered definitively and that adults who provide answers which are too-definite inhibit children's ability to live with uncertainty and mystery, ambiguity and paradox.

The culture of your school influences how you teach, just as the classroom culture you create affects how children learn. Many primary schools, especially in the early years, are very good at encouraging and enabling teaching for creativity. For example, the Foundation Stage Curriculum encourages creating and thinking critically as one of the three key characteristics of effective learning. Such a curriculum based on broad areas of learning rather than definite boundaries between subjects makes it easier to adopt an approach conducive to children's SMSC.

The stronger emphasis on curriculum content and what can be measured often evident in Key Stage 2 makes it harder, but hopeful signs include:

- the recognition, since *Excellence and Enjoyment* (2003), that creativity and enjoyment help children to learn better, two sides of one coin, or two strands of the same rope;
- the growing interest in formative assessment, asking open questions and expecting and helping children to be reflective, aspects widely recognised as good teaching by encouraging children's creativity; and
- the greater emphasis on SMSC in Ofsted inspections.

However, children's creativity and SMSC is enhanced more by what you do and who you are than by any government policy. You can make a huge difference by encouraging, rather than inhibiting, creativity and divergence and by having expectations which are high but realistic. Remember that children do not have one fixed, inherent level of ability but:

- bring tremendous experience of active, creative learning; and
- have a range of what Gardner (1993) calls multiple intelligences and (often untapped) gifts and talents.

Ofsted (2004, p4) were right to say that *most teachers would see (pupils' SMSC development) as the heart of what education is all about – helping pupils grow and develop as people*. Your most important contribution to this comes from who you are and the ways of acting and interacting you demonstrate. The relationships you make can ensure the right balance of reassurance and of challenge. By displaying qualities such as openness, courage and flexibility, you will encourage children to adopt these. And your ability to be reflective, to be curious and to address difficult questions thoughtfully will be an example for children who, very often, lack such a model. Your identity, as a learner and as a person, will help shape your children's identities.

In exercising their creativity, children – like Leigh – are not just making things, but are helping to shape themselves and their future; and teachers who enable this are engaged in one of the most exciting creative processes of all.

A SUMMARY OF **KEY POINTS**

➢ spiritual, moral, social and cultural development are four important, but elusive, facets of personal development;

➢ personal development and attainment are closely interlinked;

➢ an environment which enables SMSC is similar to one that encourages creativity;

➢ teaching for creativity depends more on process than content and can happen in all subject areas.

MOVING *ON* > > > > > > MOVING *ON* > > > > > > MOVING *ON*

Points to consider for practice

Think about how:

- the classroom environment where you teach can encourage children to be creative and questioning;
- you can plan and assess allowing for some flexibility to take account of children's responses and interests;
- the relationships you form can provide both security and challenge;
- your own (often natural) actions and responses set an example for children.

REFERENCES REFERENCES **REFERENCES** REFERENCES REFERENCES REFERENCES

Bruner, J (1996) *The Culture of Education* Cambridge, Mass.: Harvard University Press.

Claxton, G (1997) *Hare brain, tortoise mind: why intelligence increases when you think less* London: Fourth Estate.

Craft, A, Jeffrey, B and Leibling M (eds) (2001) *Creativity in Education* London: Continuum.

DfE (2012) Teachers' Standards available at **https://www.gov.uk/government/publications/teachers-standards** accessed 7/9/14.

DfES (2003) *Excellence and Enjoyment* Nottingham: DfES.

Eaude, T (2007) *Children's Spiritual, Moral, Social and Cultural Development: Primary and Early Years* Exeter: Learning Matters.

Eagleton, T (2000) *The Idea of Culture* Oxford: Blackwell.

Gardner, H (1993) *Frames of mind: the Theory of Multiple Intelligences* London: Fontana.

Gerhardt, S (2004) *Why love matters* Hove: Routledge.

Goodman, N (1978) *Ways of worldmaking* Hassocks: Harvester.

Hay, D with Nye, R (1998) *The Spirit of the Child* London: Fount.

Hyde, B (2008) *Children and Spirituality* London: Jessica Kingsley.

NACCCE (National Advisory Committee on Creative and Cultural Education) (1999) *All Our Futures: Creativity, Culture and Education* London: DfEE.

Ofsted (2004) *Promoting and evaluating pupils' spiritual, moral, social and cultural development.* **www.ofsted.gov.uk/resources/promoting-and-evaluating-pupils-spiritual-moral-social-and-cultural-development** accessed 7/9/14.

Ofsted (2014) *School Inspection Handbook* (from September 2014) **www.ofsted.gov.uk/resources/school-inspection-handbook** accessed 7/9/14.

Pollard, A (1985) *The Social World of the Primary School* London: Cassell.

Winnicott, D (1980) *Playing and Reality* Harmondsworth: Penguin.

6

The importance of informal learning to children's creative education
Rob Bowker

Chapter objectives

The aims of this chapter are to:

- define informal learning and creativity;
- better understand the relationship between informal learning, formal learning and creativity;
- gain a theoretical understanding of informal learning in children's creative development;
- be able to incorporate informal learning within your future practice to promote children's creativity.

This chapter addresses the following Teachers' Standards (DfE, 2012):

- set high expectations which inspire, motivate and challenge children;
- promote good progress and outcomes by pupils;
- plan and teach well-structured lessons;
- adapt teaching to respond to the strengths and needs of all pupils.

and Principle 8. Effective teaching and learning recognises the significance of informal learning Teaching and Learning Research Programme (James and Pollard, 2011).

Introduction

In this chapter I wish to briefly explore learning and in particular looking at learning in terms of informal and formal learning. Also, I will discuss the benefits of informal learning especially in terms of promoting children's creative development. I will look at the relationship between formal and informal learning and make the argument that both types of learning should be consciously blended for effective teaching. Finally, I will give some guidelines on how teachers can use this information to improve their practice.

Learning is contended to be a difficult concept to define (Braund and Reiss, 2004); a broad definition appropriate is outlined by the Campaign for Learning:

> *Learning is a process of active engagement with experience. It is what people do when they want to make sense of the world. It may involve the development or deepening of skills, knowledge, understanding, awareness, values, ideas and feelings or an increase in the capacity to reflect.*
>
> (The Campaign for Learning, 2014, p3)

Learning can also be considered in terms of formal and informal learning, often with polarised definitions of each (Malcolm *et al.*, 2003). Colley *et al.* (2003, p4) defines formal learning as *containing high status, propositional knowledge with learning processes centred upon teaching or instruction, and is located within specialist educational institutions such as schools, colleges or universities*. Conversely, informal learning is argued to be the antithesis of formal learning, taking place out of the formal classroom and not under direct control of the teacher. (Gerber *et al.*, 2001). In looking to give a definition of both formal and informal learning it is best to look at the features of both. These are outlined in Figure 6.1, taken from Wellington (1990, p248).

Informal learning	Formal learning
Voluntary	Compulsory
Haphazard, unstructured, un-sequenced	Structured and sequenced
Non-assessed, non-certified	Assessed, certificated
Open-ended	More closed
Learner-led, learner-centred	Teacher-led, teacher-centred
Outside of formal settings	Classroom and institution based
Unplanned	Planned
Many unintended outcomes (outcomes more difficult to measure)	Fewer unintended outcomes
Social aspect central, e.g. social interactions between visitors	Social aspect less central
Low 'currency'	High 'currency'
Undirected, not legislated for	Legislated and directed (controlled)

Figure 6.1 Formal and informal learning compared

One important distinction Wellington (1990) makes is that informal learning is often pupil led, and is a highly social activity, whereas formal learning is predominantly led by the teacher. Echoing this, Boekaerts and Minnaert (1999, p25) define informal learning as allowing control of learning to rest *primarily in the hands of the learner* whereas Nias (1988, p123), by compiling teachers own views that to teach formally is *to show, tell, instruct, direct, with a view to controlling what pupils learnt.*

Coffield (2000) gives the analogy of learning as an iceberg and suggests that the tip of ice above the water represents formal learning with the remaining submerged mass beneath conveying the much greater importance of informal learning. Falk and Dierking (2000) highlight that children are more likely to display different knowledge and understanding in informal settings as opposed to formal school ones. This is because an informal setting is not structured to relate in simple ways to the formal curriculum that children have experienced, and as such, prior learning of different kinds may become more relevant to the situation than it does in school.

However, some authors argue against the dichotomy of formal and informal learning and suggest informal and formal educations are on a fluid continuum, which can interchange even within an activity (Malcolm *et al.*, 2003). Later, in this chapter I hope to convince you of the importance for teachers to reflect on the implications of their formal and informal pedagogies and consciously plan to use both in their teaching to allow the time, space and environment for creative teaching.

The argument for informal learning and creativity

Prominent contemporary thinkers have been vocal in their belief that we need to be cultivating creativity through our education system (Claxton, cited in NESSE, 2008; Robinson, 2001). They believe that we should be adapting the to the demands of the modern world and educating our children for a fast changing work place.

The rapid change of the work place is not new. Dewey (1916) was greatly concerned with the changing world in which he found himself. The industrial revolution was changing the world and the education that children were receiving. Dewey believed that children were becoming 'isolated from the real world', and that good schooling takes place outdoors as this was where real-life took place (Rivkin, 1998). Dewey was considered revolutionary as he considered that children learn through doing, and that ideally this should occur in real life materials and experiences (Mooney, 2000). Dewey also considered that if children are involved in learning something that interests them, and is in some way related to their experience, then the process of learning will be an enjoyable one. Whilst Dewey believed that learning in the formal traditional sense, for example learning by rote, was ineffective, he also considered that it was equally ineffective to simply turn children loose in a learning environment without guidance (Mooney, 2000).

Wellington (1990) found that the science presented in schools bore little resemblance to the natural world, where science is ubiquitous. According to Wellington, there is enough science to investigate for a lifetime, on playgrounds, in kitchens, on sport fields, an in the back garden. In contrast he cites one of the main achievements of interactive science centres is their ability to relate science to everyday uses and experiences. This view is echoed by St John and Perry (1993) who see 'free-choice' learning environments, as helping people make links between the world of science and their daily lives. The benefits of an informal learning style are outlined by Tofield *et al.* (2003) in terms of school visits to zoos. They describe these as an opportunity to make a topic entertaining and enjoyable, and to forge links with everyday experiences and observations. This makes the learning experience more meaningful and therefore more memorable. Therefore, a more creative and informal approach could be adopted in schools using real life experiences.

REFLECTIVE TASK

Should schools therefore be focusing their curriculums more towards Wellington's and Dewey's more 'natural view', where children are able to learn in the real world and from their experiences in everyday life? This question in turn determines whether a greater proportion of school curriculum should be taking place outside the confines of the classroom.

Falk and Dierking (2000) created 'The Contextual Model of Learning', a model to show how learning takes place. In their model, learning is influenced by three different factors: personal, sociocultural and physical contexts. The personal context states that learning is affected by motivation and emotions. They recommended that museums should foster good experiences that motivate intrinsic learning. The socio-cultural context is significant as learning is often accumulated through communication with others. This is supported by Vygotsky's (1978) theory of social constructivism, where communication with knowledgeable others helps to scaffold learning. Uzzell (1993) describes how evaluation research at his institution has moved from behavioural to a cognitive, then to a socio-cognitive focus, in order to stress the significance of the social contexts in determining how visitors interact with exhibits. The physical context has a large impact on the quality of learning and therefore the engagement and learning which takes place. Informal learning centres, such as museums score highly on the novel and physical appeal. However, classrooms in schools can also be creatively organised to appeal to pupils with colourful eye-catching displays, accessible resources, and a safe, friendly atmosphere.

Research by Beard and Wilson (2002) and Bixler *et al.* (2002) suggests that outdoor learning offers opportunities for explorative play, freedom, creativity, enjoyment, incidental learning and social competency due to its experimental nature. Waite and Rea (2007) agreed that memory for learning outdoors endures and is associated with positive responses from children and teachers. Their study however did not look at how learning in the classroom compared to this, so cannot indicate that learning outside is preferential, but suggests it enhances the skills already introduced. Children not only learn in school but also through play, conversations and recreational activities (Kola-Olusanya, 2005; Jarman, 2005). However, opportunities for children to learn about the environment through play and recreational activities have unfortunately diminished due to 'stranger danger' and health and safety concerns (Malone and Trantor, 2003; Davis *et al.*, 2006).

However, play is now valued in schools as a vital part of child development (DfES, 2007; Wood and Attfield, 2005). Curiosity begins with exploration and play which promotes questioning and communication of ideas. Play is essential to learning as pupils take control and develop solutions to the problems that arise naturally through their explorations (Johnston, 2000). Solomon (1997) agrees that there are two fundamental rules which are necessary to foster children's curiosity: firstly the control must lie with the learner and secondly the teaching input must not restrict the learner's thought or decision-making processes.

The complexity of a play environment has been shown to influence the amount of play that takes place (Fjørtoft, 2001). The natural world represents a highly complex environment in which there is a large amount of stimulation, and therefore has been found to result in high levels of meaningful play. It has been shown that the presence of a natural environment near to a playground will result in increased creativity of play during break times (Lindholm, 1995).

Natural environments are ideal as a setting for play and have been shown to have positive effects on the physical development of young children. In one study of 5–7 year olds in Norway those children that had daily access to a natural forest setting in order to play were seen to display a greater improvement in motor fitness, balance and co-ordination, in comparison to children who had access to a standard playground setting (Fjørtoft, 2004).

It has also been found that use of experience of natural environments within school education can have particularly positive effects upon those children that may be from socially deprived backgrounds, living in sub-standard accommodation and with little or no exposure to the natural world through their home life (Wells and Evans, 2003). Research has also shown that exposure to natural settings can have very positive effects on children who suffer from Attention-deficit/hyperactivity disorder (ADHD), with individuals showing reduced attention deficit symptoms (Kuo and Faber Taylor, 2004).

The previous Government's Learning Outside the Classroom Manifesto (DfES, 2006) has strong aims to encourage a more widespread use of educational opportunities away from the classroom. The manifesto promotes that learning outside the classroom is not an end in itself but the authors see it as a vehicle to develop the capacity to learn. Through learning in this manner they believe that it will enable children to construct their own learning and be able to live successfully in the world that surrounds them. They state that there is strong evidence that good quality learning outside the classroom adds much value to classroom learning. That it can lead to a deeper understanding of the concepts that span traditional subject boundaries and which are frequently difficult to teach effectively using classroom methods alone (DfES, 2006, p6).

> *Learning outside of the classroom can build bridges between theory and reality, schools and communities, young people and their futures. Quality learning experiences in 'real' situations have the capacity to raise achievement across a range of subjects and to develop better personal and social skills.*
>
> (DfES, 2006)

Within the new National Curriculum (NC) for 2014 (DfE, 2013), there is no reference to informal learning. However, Magraw (2014) states that the forest school can supports the NC and other National Frameworks including creative thinking, key skills and personalised learning.

The TLRP (James and Pollard, 2006) project advocates ten evidence-informed principles to guide policy and practice. The aims of the principles are to *help teachers, school leaders and policymakers to decide how best to direct their efforts and resources for the benefit of pupils' learning and achievement* (James and Pollard, 2006, p8). Informal learning is recognised as one of these principles and is described in Principle 8:

> *8. **Effective pedagogy recognises the significance of informal learning**. Informal learning, such as learning out of school or away from the workplace, should be recognised as at least as significant as formal learning and should therefore be valued and appropriately utilised in formal processes.*
>
> (James and Pollard, 2006)

Furthermore, the Institute for Outdoor Education (2014) states there are many valuable reasons why outdoor learning matters. Firstly, environmental issues are steadily becoming more important in the political agenda and through first-hand experience of the natural world outdoor learning encourages the development of personal values and opinions. In addition, outdoor learning provides a totally different environment for learning, which may allow children who usually struggle in formal settings to become motivated and capable learners, and learners who already excel in formal settings may become more versatile learners. Swarbrick *et al.* (2004) suggested that high quality learning within an outdoor environment may result in increased academic ability, nurture creativity, stimulate and motivate children to learn, increase self-esteem, and may reduce behavioural and attendance issues.

Bentley (1998) believes that we need to change a traditional way of thinking. We see the school as a distinct formal organisation where learning is organized, defined and contained. Instead, we should concentrate on the individual and teach them to learn from the informal environment surrounding them. Rogers (1969) focused his ideas of education by placing the individual at the centre of learning and the main role of teachers is to be the facilitators of learning. He believed that teachers should create supportive learning environments where they could work with pupils to achieve mutually agreed goals. Rogers' research showed that pupils preferred classrooms where they collaborated, carried out their own investigations and taught each other.

However the present education system does not reflect these views and Claxton (2008) believes there is an over emphasis on assessment of knowledge, skill and understanding, neglecting qualities such as imagination, intuition and intrinsic curiosity – vital for innovation and creativity. He believes we need to cultivate young minds that are geared towards a modern world economy that demands creativity and innovation. Robinson (2002) and Malaguzzi (1987) have also spoken of how schools and educators are responsible for killing creativity. Robinson believes the education system is outmoded. It provides children an education, which may provide them with the ability to answer set questions about a body of knowledge in an exam, but not the skills to be a valuable asset in the workplace.

In more recent years there has been recognition that creative approaches to learning can motivate pupils and raise school standards (Ofsted, 2010). Inspectors found that in schools with good teaching, there was no conflict between the National Curriculum and creative approaches to learning. It is recognised that all children are capable of creativity from an early age onwards (Craft, 2005; Runco 2003) and indeed have a huge creative potential for creativity when encouraged in the right manner (Malaguzzi, 1987; Robinson, 2006; Runco, 2003; Sharp, 2004). A shift in pedadagy is advocated towards a more inclusive approach (Craft, 2005), where the environment is permissive and safe (Runco, 2007) and where learners are in control of their learning process (Woods, 2002).

Robinson (2002) argues that schools have provided an education system that merely divides the workplace into those who are academic and those that are not. The education system fails to discover the potential in many and they leave school as academic failures. Therefore, we need to consider how to change this. Wynn and Harris (2012) discuss the need for a curriculum teaching not only science, technology, engineering and maths (STEM) but also art (STEAM). They argue that by fusing art with science, it helps pupils develop new ways of perceiving the world, which in turn helps innovation. The area of science and technology requires people with minds that are creative to propel innovation and development forward. We should be considering adapting our education system to respond to these specific needs. Robinson and Aronica (2009, p248) state:

> *The curriculum should be personalized... learning happens in the minds and souls of individuals – not in the databases of multiple-choice tests. The current processes of education do not take account of individual learning styles and talents... in that way they offend the principles of distinctiveness.*
>
> (Robinson and Aronica, 2009)

Government policy, recent initiatives in education and research make clear why and how it is important that effective pedagogy recognises the significance of informal learning and briefly notes some ways in which schools can make changes in order to make the most of the advantages of informal learning practices, which can promote creativity. However, given the theoretical and research based evidence to support informal learning, it needs to be recognised that there are barriers a teacher might encounter in trying to implement informal learning. Many teachers feel uncomfortable taking children outside of the classroom, even in the school grounds. This is often due to lacking experience of teaching outside of a traditional classroom (Carrier, 2009). Also many teachers find the increased emphasis on testing children such as SATs testing in England at odds with implementing informal learning strategies. Informal learning often requires more time and resources. As the pressure increases to do well in the national tests, time and resources are often ear marked for test preparation and teaching to the test. Martina *et al.* (2009) when trying to use a problem-based and integrated environmental health programme into a school found difficulties, as teachers could not give sufficient time to it as they had to prepare children for tests.

Finally, if teachers are increasingly worried about health and safety issues related to informal learning and litigation if there are any accidents when taking children on out-of-site visits, then good preparation and planning can make informal learning outside the classroom more effective and safer (Lakin, 2006) and teachers need to know the importance of and how to follow the government's checklist of safe practice when taking children outdoors.

The relationship between informal learning/formal learning

Eshach (2007) believes that sharp distinctions between formal and informal learning is inappropriate as there are other factors than physical setting that governs learning. Cox-Peterson *et al.* (2003) identified that simply because learning takes place outside of the classroom does not in itself make that learning informal. They describe how some learning centres, particularly with older students, still use a tour format to show students around museums. This instructionist method of teaching, where a person simply dispenses their knowledge, is not dissimilar to what the students may frequently experience during their day-to-day classroom teaching. It is therefore not an informal experience, and may not carry the same benefits as a visit where students are free to explore their ideas. In addition, as Malcolm *et al.* (2003) also point out, learning cannot often be simply categorised into formal and informal modes. They propose that both are inextricably linked and there are significant elements of formal learning in informal situations, and vice versa.

Hofstein and Rosenfeld (1996) indicate that informal learning activities can be conducted in a formal classroom setting. They made the recommendation that future research should not focus on whether more teaching should take place outside the classroom, but on how this learning technique can be combined with learning inside the classroom to enhance children's education. Therefore, it is important not to make simple assumptions about the type of learning children can experience in a classroom environment or whilst visiting an informal learning centre.

Ellis (1990) considers a continuum in which there are no set definitions for formal and informal learning (Figure 6.2). On this are two extremes: at A children are left to learn through complete self-discovery and at B children learn through highly structured, compulsory education. Schools would be placed towards the formal end of the spectrum (point Y) and locations outside of schools, such as museums, farms, Interactive Science Centres towards the opposite end (Point X).

The Informal and Formal Learning Spectrum

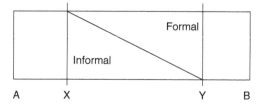

Figure 6.2 The informal and formal learning spectrum

Adapted from Ellis, J (1990) Informal Education: A Christian Perspective, [Online], Available: **www.infed.org**

REFLECTIVE TASK

Draw a real or imaginary line on the Ellis diagram to reflect where you think you are on the informal/formal continuum. Draw a second line, which is where you would ideally like to be on the Ellis diagram. Are there any obstacles in achieving this position? Think about and justify the position you have indicated.

The graph (Figure 6.3) is a visual representation of how formal and informal learning can be viewed (adapted from Sefton-Green, 2004, p7). A score of 1 represents formality of learning or environment. This is either where the learning is dictated by the teacher, with the learner having no choice, or where the environment is formal such as a classroom or lecture theatre. A score of -1 represents informality. This is either where the learner has complete control over their learning, or where the environment is informal, for example as on a school trip to a farm or the woods.

Activities such as a guided tour around a museum could be placed somewhere in the top left hand quadrant. The top right quadrant would be occupied by a quite regimented lesson in the classroom. The bottom right could be occupied by a less formal lesson in the classroom, such as one where the learners are free to design their own investigations. Learning in the bottom left quadrant could occur almost anywhere, for example out on the playground at break time.

The figure illustrates well that just because a child is in an informal learning environment it does not always necessarily mean they are experiencing informal learning and vice-versa. Ramey-Gassert *et al.* (1994) also suggest that different types of learning may be suited to different environments, that a novel, informal environment is better for active learning, and encouraging curiosity, but that some conceptual knowledge is better taught in the classroom. They suggest that both are necessary for a rounded education. In terms of the formal curriculum there is a large amount of literature suggesting that numerous subjects can be taught informally on school grounds, including reading,

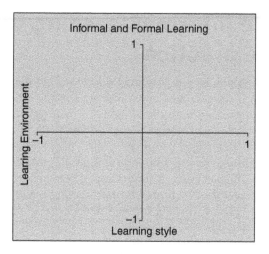

Figure 6.3 Graph viewing informal and formal learning

writing, mathematics, science, art, environmental studies and drama (Adams, 1990; Bell, 2001; Engel, 1991). Dillon *et al.* (2006) also found that outdoor learning opportunities, if effectively planned, taught and followed up, offered children methods of developing their knowledge and skills in a way, which enhanced their everyday learning experiences in the classroom.

PRACTICAL TASK PRACTICAL TASK PRACTICAL TASK PRACTICAL TASK PRACTICAL TASK

Consider exemplar lessons you have observed. Where would the lesson fit on the informal/formal learning grid (Figure 6.3)?

Now consider the whole and give teaching examples which would fit into each quadrant.

In reality formal and informal learning is complex, as expressed in this section, and often overlap as seen on the Ellis (1990) spectrum (Figure 6.2).

The work of McKenzie and Kernig (1975) looks at the use of informal education in the classroom. They define informal learning as:

> *activities which take place in a planned environment so arranged that each child is free to use time, space, materials and skilled adult help in order to advance in learning along the path indicated by his own interests and learning-style.*

> (McKenzie and Kernig, 1975, p11)

Indeed one of my main arguments is that informal learning is not defined by the environment and can and should be used in a classroom environment as well as outside the classroom. Also, current educational policies and frameworks, recognise informal learning as an essential component of children's learning, especially if it is blended with formal learning. I would also suggest that teachers could consider introducing more informal learning into their practice if they wish to develop creative, confident and motivated children.

Incorporate informal learning within your future practice

Finally, you need to consider the implications for informal learning in your own practice in schools to promote children's creativity. In analysing the literature you have probably now reflected and realized that the contexts for learning cannot be described as either formal or informal. Instead with reference to the 'hybrid approach' (Hofstein and Rosenfeld, 1996), to the 'free choice' approach (Falk, 2005; Falk and Dierking, 2000) and to the literature concerning lifelong learning (Eraut, 2000; Malcolm *et al.,* 2003) there are both formal and informal aspects in almost any learning situation, whether at school or in informal learning centres. The term informal learning environments has served as a unifying concept for various learning environments outside of the school for a long time. However, this term is not always helpful and it is important to recognise that learning in informal learning environments does not necessarily equate to informal learning. With regard to the formal/informal continuum (Ellis, 1990) there are both formal and informal aspects of learning regardless of characteristics of the learning environment. Formal and informal styles of learning may exist simultaneously to the educational benefit of the children. Similarly, within a school classroom formal learning may be delivered in the same lesson, for example by the teacher delivering the prescribed curriculum through a questions and answer format, followed by more informal learning represented by peer interaction.

The degree of formal/informal learning is very dependent on the level to which a learner has control over both the objectives and means of learning (Mocker and Spear, 1982). For example, self-directed learning would mean the learner having control of what they wanted to learn and the means of where and how they were going to learn. Often learners' choices evolve from their interaction with others in an activity in which they find themselves. This model has much in common with free-choice learning (Falk & Dierking, 2000). The idea of free choice emphasises the unique nature of out of school environments that allows the learner to identify several learning options, in a variety of spaces, and finally to choose a specific option, theme or space for learning. According to Falk (2005), the underlying motivation and interest of the learner is the reason for using free choice leaning. It is therefore important to stress the importance of how much autonomy and control a teacher gives to children to facilitate their own learning (Boekaerts and Minnaert,1999; Nias, 1988). This in turn will depend on the confidence of the teacher to operate such practices and the level of support from their school. If a teacher decides to operate more to the informal end of the spectrum, then the child is firmly being placed at the centre of the learning process (Rickinson, 2001) with their prior knowledge and experiences being taken into account in the educational process (Falk and Dierking, 2000). These characteristics of informal learning should be acknowledged and utilised, especially with the current emphasis in education on individual learning, creativity thinking and assessment.

It is my view that informal learning is significantly important and its recognition, understanding and application are vital for the creative development of children. Children spend a greater part of their lives learning outside the classroom environment from direct experiences, secondary sources, peers, family, and other adults. They learn things which interest them, which may or may not be relevant to the taught curriculum. So the key point is that teachers and educators need to recognise that children come to any learning situation with existing knowledge from a variety of experiences and contacts.

This is entirely consistent with the constructivist theories of education, but sometimes from my own experiences and observations I feel this is often forgotten or ignored by some teachers and educators.

Taking children on visits to new settings such as museums can be exciting, stimulating and motivating. This is because the physical environment is often specifically designed to encourage such responses. However, whilst the physical environment is often important to informal education it cannot define informal learning. Informal education can provide a multisensory experience and facilitate children to engage in a great deal of social dialogue and interaction with both peers and adults. Many children who might find it difficult in more formal school settings may well respond more positively and confidently to informal learning experiences. So, the characteristics of informal learning are as follows:

- Informal learning can take place on out of school visits to informal learning centres, visit to the woods, beach, park or urban environment. It can equally take place within the school grounds or classroom.
- Informal learning is consistent with a socio-constructivist model, which emphasises the importance of peer to peer and adult to peer discussions.
- Informal learning is multi-sensory by nature and often covers many different learning styles.
- Informal learning is characterised by being holistic in that it promotes not just knowledge and skills, but often learning which incorporates children's attitudes, confidence and self-esteem.
- Informal learning can encourage and foster creativity in children.

Teachers can utilise both informal and formal learning within their practice to maximise children's educational and creative development. This can best achieved over an academic year by using a combination of out of school visits, using school grounds or nearby outdoor areas and by incorporating informal learning in classroom practice. I have discovered that the school visits that are most effective are when teachers prepare their children well before a visit, adopt learner-orientated strategies during the visit, are willing and capable of mediating the experience with the children and subsequently follow-up the visit in a meaningful way back at school (Bowker, 2002). Price and Hein (1991) also stress the importance of preparation prior to a visit and Orion (1993) suggests that children need to be familiar with the learning aims, the environment and the kinds of activities they will participate in. Teachers can help children by drawing their attention to the special features at informal learning environments and by structuring and scaffolding their learning (Vygotsky, 1978). Otherwise, as Lucas (2000) points out there will be more off-task behaviour when the setting is unfamiliar.

Informal learning environments give children wonderful opportunities for experiential learning, which sometimes cannot be so easily achieved within a school. However, out of school visits may only be economically and logistically possible one or twice a year. Therefore, I think teachers need to and can be creative by thinking carefully about developing and using the school grounds for learning, including school gardening and Forest School education (Fjørtoft, 2001). School gardening and Forest School activities can for many children improve their self-esteem, confidence and motivation (Hoffman *et al.*, 2004; Bowker and Tearle, 2007). In turn these improvements can also have the benefit of indirectly affecting in a positive manner the children's cognitive and academic performance (Sheffield, 1992; Klemmer *et al.*, 2005; Bowker and Jasper, 2007).

Even within a classroom environment teachers can decide to use informal learning strategies successfully. The classroom layout in terms of its furniture, displays and resources can be altered to create a more informal learning environment. Teachers can adopt an informal teaching style where and when appropriate, which encourages autonomy of learning for their pupils. This can be achieved by creating an atmosphere, which encourages the children to ask questions and gives them the skills to work independently to find out the answers to their questions. Teachers using an informal learning style can also encourage good social learning, allowing children to work with peers in pairs and in groups. Informal learning can assist teachers to also develop good relationships with children, improving trust and respect, and vice-versa. Further, to maximise learning teachers need to consciously develop children's self-esteem, confidence, creativity and motivation. In this way children will be working for intrinsic values using characteristics of informal learning.

So, teachers could choose to introduce the opportunities for children to experience informal learning by:

- organising 'out of school' visits;
- using the local park, woods, beach, urban environment for learning;
- using the school grounds for learning, which may include school gardening and forest school teaching;
- providing opportunities for children to discuss and share their knowledge with peers;
- providing opportunities of developing children's learning through good mediation by knowledgeable adults;
- using the local community for teaching including using parental involvement;
- providing opportunities for practical experiences as well as theoretical discussions;
- providing interesting, stimulating and interactive learning environments including the classroom;
- giving time for play activities and exploration both inside and outside the classroom;
- promoting and encouraging independent learning;
- developing intrinsic values to learning;
- developing children's own sense of responsibility for their learning.

Of course many teachers already do many of these things, but perhaps do not realise that they are working in an informal manner. So it is more about teachers being more aware and conscious of informal learning and teaching, and the strategies they can adopt to blend it with more formal learning. I believe this can lead to them being very effective in delivering a creative education service to all the children in their care.

PRACTICAL TASK   PRACTICAL TASK   PRACTICAL TASK

How would you incorporate informal learning into your practice to promote children's creativity, motivation and intrinsic values to learning?

A SUMMARY OF **KEY POINTS**

In this chapter we have looked at both informal and formal learning. I have argued for effective pedagogy teachers need to be flexible in planning to use both types of learning in their practice. I have also discussed government policy, research and recent initiatives in education, which highlight the benefits of informal learning. I have further argued that informal learning can provide the environment to motivate and inspire children to think about learning in a more creative manner. The links between informal learning and creativity are strong and can raise children's confidence, cognition and enjoyment in their education.

MOVING *ON* > > > > > > MOVING *ON* > > > > > > MOVING *ON*

In your teaching, plan lessons or parts of lessons, which use informal as well as formal methods of teaching. Also, give children time, space and opportunities inside and outside the classroom for creative activities. It will not only enhance their learning of the National Curriculum and beyond, but will also make your own teaching more fulfilling and joyous. There is enough evidence to demonstrate that such methods work as long as you have the conviction and confidence to at least try them out.

REFERENCES REFERENCES **REFERENCES** REFERENCES REFERENCES REFERENCES

Adams, E (1990) *Learning through Landscapes: A report on the use, design, management and development of school grounds.* Winchester: Learning through Landscapes Trust.

Beard, C and Wilson, JP (2002) *The power of experiential learning: a handbook for trainers and educators.* London: Kogan Page.

Bell, AC (2001) The pedagogical potential of school grounds, in Grant, T and Littlejohn, G (eds) *Greening School Grounds: Creating Habitats for Learning.* Gariola Island, British Columbia: New Society. 9–11.

Bentley, T (1998) *Learning beyond the Classroom: Education for a changing world.* London: Routledge.

Bixler, R, Floyd, MF, Hammitt, WE (2002) Environmental socialization: quantitative tests of the childhood play hypothesis, *Environment and Behaviour*, 34(6), 795–818.

Boekaerts, M, and Minnaert, A (1999) Self-Regulation with Respect to Informal Learning, *International Journal of Educational Research*, 31(6), 533–544.

Bowker, R and Tearle, P (2007) Gardening as a learning environment: A study of children's perceptions and understanding of school gardens as part of an international project. *Learning Environments Research* 10(2), 83–100.

Bowker, R and Jasper, A (2007) Don't forget your leech socks! Children's learning at the Eden Project, *Research in Science & Technological Education,* 25(1), 135–150.

Bowker, R (2002) Evaluating teaching and learning strategies at the Eden Project, *Evaluation and Research in Education 16*(3), 123–135.

Braund, M and Reiss, M (2004) (eds) *Learning Science Outside the Classroom.* London: RoutledgeFalmer.

Carrier, SJ (2009) The effects of outdoor science lessons with elementary school students on pre-service teachers' self-efficacy, *Journal of Elementary Science Education*, 35, 28–40.

Claxton (2008) cited in NESSE seminar 10: Cultivating talent: educating for creativity and innovation. Available from: **www.nestweb.eu/content-resources-library/nesse-seminar-10-cultivating-talent-educating-creativity-and innovation** accessed 18/6/14.

Coffield, F (2000) *The necessity of informal learning.* The Policy Press, Hobbs Printers Ltd.

Colley, H, Hodkinson, P and Malcolm, J (2003) *Informality and Formality in Learning: A Report for the Learning and Skills Research Centre.* London: Learning and Skills Research Centre.

Cox-Peterson, AM, Marsh, DD, Kisiel, J and Melber, LM (2003) Investigation of guided school tours, student learning and science reform recommendation at a museum of natural history, *Journal of Research in Science Teaching*, 40 (2) 200–218.

Craft, A (2005) *Creativity in schools : tensions and dilemmas.* London: Routledge

Davis, B, Rea, T and Waite, S (2006) The special nature of the outdoors: Its contribution to the education of children aged 3–11, *Australian Journal of Outdoor Education*, 10(2), 3–12.

DfE (2012) Teachers' Standards available at **https://www.gov.uk/government/publications/teachers-standards** accessed 7/9/14.

Department for Education (2013) The National Curriculum in England: Key stages 1 and 2 framework document. Available from: **https://www.gov.uk/government/uploads/system/uploads/attachment_data/file/335133/PRIMARY_national_curriculum_220714.pdf** accessed 18/8/14.

Department for Education and Skills (2003) *Excellent and Enjoyment: A strategy for primary schools.* London: HMSO.

Department for Education and Skills (2006) *Manifesto for Learning Outside the Classroom*. London: HMSO.

Department for Education and Skills (2007) *The Early Years Foundation Stage*. London: HMSO.

Dewey, J (1916) *The democratic conception in education*. New York: The Free Press.

Dillon, J, Rickinson, M, Tearney, K, Morris, M, Young Choi, M, Sanders, D and Benefield, P (2006) The value of outdoor learning: evidence from research in the UK and elsewhere, *School Science Review*, 87 (320), 107–111.

Ellis, J (1990) Informal Education: A Christian Perspective, [Online], Available: **http://infed.org/archives/usinginformaleducation/ellis** accessed 18/8/14.

Engel, S (1991) The world is a white blanket: children write about nature, *Children's Environments Quarterly*, 8(2), 42–45.

Eraut, M (2000) Non-formal learning, implicit learning and tacit knowledge in professional work, in Coffield, F (ed.) (2000) *The Necessity of Informal Learning*, Bristol: The Policy Press.

Eshach, H (2007) Bridging in-school and out-of-school learning: Formal, non-formal, and informal education, *Journal of Science Education and Technology,* 16(2), 171–190.

Falk, JH and Dierking, LD (2000) *Visitor experiences and the making of meaning*. Walnut Creek: AltaMira Press.

Falk, JH (2005) Free-choice environmental learning: framing the discussion, *Environmental Education Research*, 11(3) 265–280.

Fjørtoft, I (2001) The natural environment as a playground for children: The impact of outdoor play activities in pre-primary school children, *Early Childhood Educational Journal,* 29(2), 111–117.

Fjørtoft, I (2004) Landscape as playscape: The effects of natural environments on children's play and motor development, *Children, Youth and Environments*, 14(2), 21–44.

Gerber, BL, Cavallo, AML and Marek, EA (2001) Relationships among informal learning environments, teaching procedures and scientific reasoning ability, *International Journal of Science Education*, 23 (5) 535–549.

Hoffman, AJ, Trepagnier, B, Cruz, A and Thompson, D (2004). Gardening activity as an effective measure in improving self-efficacy and self-esteem: Community college students learning effective living skills, *The Community College Enterprise*, 9, 231–239.

Hofstein, A and Rosenfeld, S (1996). Bridging the gap between formal and informal science learning. *Studies in Science Education 28*, 87–112.

Institute for Outdoor Education (2014) *Why Outdoor Education Matters*. Available at: **www.outdoor-learning.org/Default.aspx?tabid=210** accessed 18/8/14.

James, M and Pollard, A (2011) 'TLRP's ten principles for effective pedagogy: rationale, development, evidence, argument and impact', *Research Papers in Education,* 28(3): 275–328.

James, M and Pollard, A (eds) (2006) *Improving Teaching and Learning in Schools: a commentary by the Teaching and Learning Research Programme*, Swindon, ESRC.

Jarman, R (2005) Science learning through Scouting: an understudied context for informal science education, *International Journal of Science Education*, 27(4), 427–450.

Johnston, J. (2000) Making sense of the national criteria, in M De Boo (ed) *Laying the foundation in the early years*. Hertfordshire: The Association for Science Education, pp7–14

Klemmer, CD, Waliczek, TM and Zajicek, JM (2005) Growing Minds: The Effect of a School Gardening Program on the Science Achievement of Elementary Students, *HortTechnology,* 15(3), 448–452.

Kola-Olusanya *(2005)* Free-choice environmental education:Understanding where children learn outside of school, *Environmental Education Research,* 11(3), 297–307.

Kuo, FE and Faber Taylor, A (2004) A potential natural treatment for Attention-Deficit/Hyperactivity Disorder: Evidence from a national study, *American Journal of Public Health*, 94 (9), 1580–1586.

Lakin, L (2006) Science beyond the Classroom, *Journal of Biology Educator*, 40(2), 88–90.

Lindholm, G (1995) School yards- The significance of place properties to outdoor activities in schools, *Environment and Behaviour*, 23 (3), 259–293.

Lucas, KB (2000) One teacher's agenda for a class visit to an interactive science centre, *Science Education,* 84(4), 524–544.

Magraw, L (2014) Links between the Forest School ethos, the National Curriculum (NC) and other National Frameworks. Available from: **www.leics.gov.uk/links_to_the_curriculum_and_other_national_framework.pdf** accessed 18/8/14.

Malaguzzi, L (1987). The hundred languages of children. The hundred languages of children (I cento linguaggi dei bambini. Exhibition catalogue), 16–21.

Malcolm, J, Hodkinson, P and Colley, H (2003) Interrelationship between informal and formal learning, *Journal of Workplace Learning*, 15, 313–318.

Malone, K and Tranter, P (2003) Children's Environmental Learning and the Use, Design and Management of Schoolgrounds, *Children, Youth and Environments*, 13(2). Available from: **www.colorado.edu/journals/cye/13_2/Malone_Tranter/ChildrensEnvLearning.htm** accessed 28/6/14.

Martina, CA, Hursh, D and Markowitz, D (2009) Contradictions in educational policy: implementing integrated problem-based environmental health curriculum in a high stakes environment, *Environmental Education Research*, 15 (3), 279–297.

McKenzie, M and Kernig, W (1975), *The Challenge of Informal Education*. London: Darton, Longman and Todd Ltd.

Mocker, DW and Spear, GE (1982) *Lifelong learning: formal, non-formal, informal, and self-directed*. Columbus: Adult, Career, and Vocational Education.

Mooney, CG (2000) *Theories of Childhood: An Introduction to Dewey, Montessori, Erikson, Piaget and Vygotsky*. Michigan: Redleaf Press.

Nias, J (1988), *Informal primary education in action: Teachers' accounts* in Blyth, A (ed) Informal Primary Education Today: Essays and studies. Lewes: Falmer.

Ofsted (2010) Learning: creative approaches that raise standards. Available at **www.ofsted.gov.uk/publications/080266** accessed 10/5/14.

Orion, N (1993) A model for the development and implementation of field trips as an integral part of the science curriculum, *School Science and Mathematics*, 93(6), 325–331.

Price, S and Hein, GE (1991) More than a field trip: science programmes for elementary school groups at museums. *International Journal of Education,* 13 (5), 505–519.

Ramey-Gassert, L, Walberg III, HJ and Walberg, HJ (1994). Re-examining connections: museums as science learning environments, *Science Education*, 78 (4) 345–363.

Rickinson, M (2001) Learners and Learning in Environmental Education: a critical review of the evidence, *Environmental Education Research*, 7(3), 207–320.

Rivkin, M (1998) 'Happy play in grassy places': The importance of the outdoor environment in Dewey's Educational Ideal, *Early Childhood Educational Journal*, 25(3), 199–202.

Robinson, K (2001) *Out of our minds: learning to be creative*. Oxford: Capstone.

Robinson, K (2002) *Out of our minds*. UK: Palatino.

Robinson, K (2006) Do schools kill creativity?: TED.

Robinson, K and Aronica, L (2009) *The Element-how finding your passion changes everything.* London: Penguin Books.

Rogers, C (1969) *Freedom to Learn: A View of What Education Might Become (1st ed.).* Columbus, Ohio: Charles E. Merrill Publishing Company.

Runco, MA (2003). Education for Creative Potential. *Scandinavian Journal of Educational Research*, 47(3), 317–324.

Runco, MA (2007) *Creativity: theories and themes: research, development, and practice.* Amsterdam; London: Elsevier Academic Press.

Sefton-Green (2004) Literature Review in informal Learning with Technology Outside School: Report 7 Bristol: Futurelab.

Sharp, C (2004). Developing Young Children's Creativity: what can we learn from research? *Topic*, 32, 5–12.

Sheffield, BK (1992). *The affective and cognitive effects of an interdisciplinary garden-based curriculum on underachieving elementary students*. Doctoral Dissertation, University of South Carolina, Columbia, SC.

Solomon, J (1997) Is how we teach science more important than what we teach? *Primary Science Review*, 49, 3–5.

St John, M and Perry, D (1993) A framework for evaluation and research, science, infrastructure and relationships. in Bicknell, S and Farmelo, G (eds) *Museum Visitor Studies in the 90s*. London: Science Museum.

Swarbrick, N, Eastwood, G, and Tutton, K (2004) Self-esteem and successful interaction as part of the forest school project, *Support For Learning*, 19(3), 142–146.

The Campaign for Learning (2014) *Becoming a Better Learner.* Available at: **www.campaign-for-learning.org.uk/cfl/assets/documents/OtherDocuments/Becoming%20a%20better%20learner. pdf** accessed 9/4/14.

Tofield, S, Coll, RK, Vyle, B and Bolstad, R (2003) Zoos as a source of free choice learning, *Research in Science and Technological Education*, 21 (1) 67–99.

Uzzell, D (1993) Contrasting psychological perspectives on exhibition evaluation, in: Bichnell S and Farmelo, G (eds), *Museum Visitor Studies in the '90s* pp. 125–129, London, Science Museum.

Vygotsky, LS (1978) *Mind in Society: The Development of higher psychological processes*. Cambridge: Harvard University Press.

Waite, S and Rea, T (2007) Enjoying teaching and learning outside the classroom, in D. Hayes (ed) *Joyful Teaching and Learning in the Primary School*, 52–62. Exeter: Learning Matters.

Wellington, J (1990) Formal and informal learning in science: the role of the interactive science centres, *Physics Education,* 25 (1990), 247–252.

Wells, NM, and Evans, GW (2003) Nearby nature: A buffer of life stress among rural children, *Environment and Behaviour*, 32, 775–795.

Wood, E and Attfield, J (2005) *Play, learning and the early childhood curriculum* (2nd edition). London: Paul Chapman Publishing.

Woods, P (2002). Teaching and learning in the new millennium, in Sugrue, C and Day C (eds), *Developing Teachers and Teaching Practice* (pp73–91). London: RoutledgeFalmer.

Wynn, T and Harris, J (2012) Toward a STEM and Arts Curriculum: creating the teacher team, *Arts Education,* 9, 42–47.

PART 2
CREATIVITY IN THE CORE CURRICULUM

7
Creativity and literacy
Liz Chamberlain

Chapter objectives

By the end of this chapter you should have:

- **an understanding of the links between speaking and listening, reading and writing;**
- **considered the literacy environment in your own classroom;**
- **familiarised yourself with the place of English in the national curriculum (2014);**
- **gained an awareness of the importance of a creative approach to writing;**
- **reflected on your role in motivating children to write.**

This chapter addresses the following Teachers' Standards (DfE, 2012):

- **promote good progress and outcomes by children;**
- **demonstrate good subject and curriculum knowledge;**
- **plan and teach well-structured lessons.**

Introduction

This chapter outlines the ways in which schools adopt creative approaches to English lessons with specific reference to exciting ideas for writing tasks.

Getting the whole school writing

An alien spaceship crash-landed in the playground today!

Imagine a child going home and telling a parent that today lessons had been a bit different, and that on arrival they had been a little surprised to discover that an alien spaceship had crashed-landed in the school playground. What, I wonder would the reaction be? But, this is precisely the approach that many schools are taking to engage the whole school with writing. What teachers have realised is that children need something to write about; something they are interested in, something they have experienced and, more importantly, something that has a real audience and in essence gives children a sense of ownership over the writing (Graves, 1983). In the case of this school, children from Reception to Year 6 were involved in creating the world's biggest newspaper, which was then displayed in the school hall for parents and children to enjoy. To add to the authenticity of the experience, the English Subject Leader invited a journalist from the local newspaper to talk to the children about how to 'write' their articles. By the end of the school day, teachers and pupils alike were delighted with the outcome and they were all talking about writing.

This chapter will discuss creative approaches like this, with the aim of sharing some of the innovative approaches schools are adopting when planning English activities. It will also examine how, as a writing teacher (Bearne, 2002), rather than a teacher of writing, your role is vital.

REFLECTIVE TASK

Think of the best writing lesson you have seen. What was it that made it such a good lesson?

List the key factors that made this lesson so effective.

Consider:

- the role of the teacher;
- what the children were being asked to do;
- what factors (other than the Programmes of Study) the teacher drew on when planning the lesson;
- the aim of the writing; and
- the audience for the writing.

Creating a landscape of language

The average five year old, in the UK, spends five hours a day in the classroom, over the course of a year, which is a total of 950 hours (Smith and Call, 2003). Your classroom therefore needs to be a place that is interesting and inspiring – not just for the children but also for you. When you walk into your own classroom for the first time, take stock of how it feels. Is this a place where reading and writing are valued?

If we want children to enjoy learning, then reading and writing need to be everywhere. It should be obvious to every child what topic they are learning about through the wall and practical displays. You can scaffold children's learning with word walls that children can refer to when writing, by displaying 'tricky' words as a reminder when spelling. Or choose a poem, write it out, put it up and let children respond (Rosen, 2007). Let children be explorers in their classroom and see it as a place where there is always something new to discover. Have a book of the week, nominate a child to bring in a favourite book from home and display it in a prominent place. Let the child explain why the book is important to them and allow other children to respond. Before you know it, there will be a unique library of favourites. The national curriculum highlights that, *Reading also feeds pupils' imagination and opens up a treasure-house of wonder and joy for curious young minds*. (DfE, 2013, p4). Put reading for pleasure at the heart of your teaching by reading daily to your class (regardless of the year group), which will ensure that the children in your class have access to quality children's literature that you can share and enjoy together.

A report by the National Literacy Trust (Clark and Poulton, 2011) suggests that children who have books of their own enjoy reading more than those who do not. Therefore, ensure your book corner is well-stocked, so that children have access to a range of reading material; quality literature, poetry, non-fiction, magazines, annuals or comics. This might encourage them to go home and share reading with their parents or they might visit the local library, which will in turn further support them as readers (Goodwin, 2010). Ask the children to help plan the book-corner, let them decide on the theme and what to include: they might choose cushions, chairs, a listening station, boxes of books or a special entrance.

Not only does this kind of approach encourage children to read for pleasure, it also helps them as writers, as Vygotsky reminds us, *reading and writing are two halves of the same process* (as cited in Barrs, 2004, p267; Flynn and Stainthorp, 2006).

Find a table, have a range of stationery and writing implements available and call it a writing area. This is a common feature of Key Stage 1 classrooms, but increasingly Key Stage 2 teachers are realising the benefits of children being able to write with sparkly pens on different kinds of paper. Let children re-discover the pleasure of physically writing. Themed role-play areas create exciting opportunities for all kinds of English activities: in speaking and listening, the children can play in role, or they can use puppets and props to engage them in a range of literate problem-solving activities (Bayley and Palmer, 2004). For example:

A garden centre   Writing labels for plants, instructions for growing vegetables, listing opening times, designing seed packets

A café   Compiling menus, taking orders, creating recipes, replying to letters of complaint, writing a restaurant review

Even Key Stage 2 can enjoy role-play and, by using Helen Bromley's idea of *Storyboxes* (cited Bearne, 2002), they can enter an imagined world of Ancient Egypt, a pirate ship or even to learn more about the experience of an evacuee from World War II. By using artefacts included in the box, children can engage in high-level discussion and collaborative talk where they are genuinely responding to a shared experience (Mercer, 2000). Imagine the writing that would follow from exploring the following:

Evacuee's storybox   A ration book, a letter from a grieving mother, a watch, a train ticket, a medal, a torn family photograph

Alex Rider's storybox   A stopwatch, torch, a fading photograph of his parents, carabiner and rope, invisible ink, mobile phone, envelope with coded letter

Rather than you, as the teacher, deciding on the genre, allow children the opportunity to choose how they would like to respond, through poetry, a diary entry, a historically accurate report, or through an exciting narrative. Cremin *et al*. (2006) would argue that teachers should refrain from determining the genre and to allow children to 'seize the moment' to write and their research suggests that when children take ownership of the writing, the quality improves.

Consider what essential elements you are going to include in your classroom so that visitors will know that yours is a classroom rich in language, where books are celebrated and children's writing is valued. How will children know that you are a writing teacher?

The national curriculum for English

Within the Programmes of Study for English (DfE, 2013) there are three important areas that children across both key stages need to cover and these are: spoken language, reading (including both word reading and comprehension) and writing. The aims of the PoS, while broad and bold in their goal to promote high standards of language and literacy, contain within them the opportunity for teachers to respond imaginatively and to engage children with exciting approaches in the teaching of English.

Unlike previous government curriculum guidance (DfES, 2003), there is no mention of the word 'creative' within the English curriculum (2013), but there is specific reference to teachers' own creativity, in that the curriculum guidance provides the structure but it is the teacher who, *constructs exciting lessons* (DfE, 2013, p5). Therefore, it is important as new teachers that you take advantage of the flexibility offered and, this, coupled with your secure subject knowledge will ensure your lessons inspire and enthuse.

Reinvigorating writing: Who is it for?

In recent years, some teachers may have suggested that the aim of writing was to introduce children to a range of different genres, both fiction and non-fiction, with a sprinkling of poetry (Cremin *et al.*, 2006). As a Year 6 teacher, this would have been reduced to being able to identify key features of different genres and to be able to use them, confidently, within their own writing. While on one level this is successful, Ofsted (2009) found that in the lessons they observed, there was an over-emphasis on the technical competencies rather than children developing their skills *in* writing (p26). However, what effective teachers of literacy have always done is to ensure there is a purpose for any writing activity (Medwell, Wray, Poulson and Fox, 2002; Hall and Harding, 2003). The children in the alien spaceship scenario were motivated not only by the experience but also by the idea that they needed, somehow, to capture this moment and to share it with as many people as possible. This is the aim of writing. It is the way that we share our innermost thoughts with others and it is this very fact that makes writing so difficult, not only technically, but socially and emotionally.

As Margaret Meek reminds us,

> *To read is to think about meaning; to write is to make thinking visible as language. To do both is to become both the teller and the told in the dialogue of the imagination.*

(Meek, 1991, p48)

A Year 5 pupil, who has good initial ideas but has poor handwriting, may find it hard to write things down. Conversely, the Year 3 pupil who writes reams and reams about best friends and favourite pets and always brings the narrative element to every genre of writing needs a different type of support. Therefore, as a teacher, it is important to know whether it is the physical aspects of writing that need supporting, as in the case of the Year 5 pupil, or whether, as for the prolific Year 3 writer, it is being introduced to more sophisticated styles of authorship.

Frank Smith (1994) suggested that in order to understand the complexities and challenges of writing, it was helpful to separate it into two specific areas – transcriptional skills and compositional skills – and these terms are reflected in the national curriculum for writing. The transcriptional element, is concerned with handwriting, spelling, punctuation and possibly some aspects of grammar, but you may argue that word choices and sentence construction are more to do with the author's voice and belong in the compositional dimension. As practitioners, these are areas of writing that we are more confident in talking about; we can comment on the handwriting, correct the spelling and make mention of the effort involved (Black and Wiliam, 2003).

However, the missing part in that writing equation is the development of authorship or compositional skills, the aspects of the writing that contain the thoughts and ideas – the important bit containing all the ideas that you want to tell people about (Smith, 1994). This is harder to teach or mark, as it is not so easy to give children an imagination or to provide the words for them. However, what you can do is provide children with experiences that they want to write about, because in essence, if a child does not have anything to write about, then writing is going to remain hard. But, if you offer children exciting experiences both within and beyond the classroom, they are more likely to be motivated to write. This will be especially true when you plan for writing from the English Programmes of Study, as the rather complex process of writing is presented rather routinely as children needing to develop 'competency' in writing across the two dimensions of transcription and composition (DfE, 2013). Therefore, it is important to find ways of helping children in your classes to see writing as more than a set of skills: it should be something not only achievable and enjoyable but also relevant to their lives (Cremin, *et al.*, 2006).

REFLECTIVE TASK

Think of a child who is a good writer. What are you basing this judgement on? How would you describe them as a writer? Consider what transcriptional and compositional skills they brought to the process and how you would support them on the next stage of their writing journey.

Having generated a reason or purpose for writing, writing also needs an audience. Children need to know, not only what the writing is to be about and what it will include, but they also need to know who the writing is for (Graves, 1983). This goes beyond knowing what genre to write in and the appropriate language and layout features, but it is about being clear about the audience i.e. Who is going to read the writing? In the case of the alien spaceship, all the children knew they were creating an article for a newspaper that would be read, not only by other children, but also by their parents and the wider community. Therefore, knowing their audience and having a real reason to write influenced their style of writing. In the process, they learned and used the conventions of a newspaper report, and this was the purpose and audience that lay at the heart of the activity.

However, setting children authentic reasons for writing should be approached with caution, as teachers can sometimes get it wrong. For example, when planning for a persuasive unit of work, teachers often create scenarios that they hope will enthuse the children and these might include, writing to the headteacher to abolish school uniform or sending emails to the local council asking them to halt the redevelopment of the school playfield. These might be real-life situations but they are unlikely to be actually happening, so if the task simply pretends to be for a genuine audience then there is no emotional investment for children. Instead, ask the children to write about something that is important to them, something they feel strongly about – and compare the quality of the writing. Teachers who heed this advice go on to devise inspiring lessons such as: children writing and delivering speeches to the local council persuading them to do something about the real rubbish problem in their local area; sending emails to favourite authors asking probing questions about their books; or sending sequel script suggestions to film companies. By following through with both the writing task and by providing an authentic audience, these types of lessons provide children with the opportunity to be creative and imaginative.

Increasingly, as curriculum moves away from genre-specific teaching and learning, the purpose for writing is being put firmly at the forefront. So, while in the old Primary Framework (DCSF, 2006) units of work were listed under specific genres: narrative (adventure, myths and legends, descriptive etc.), non-narrative (persuasive, explanatory, instructional etc.) and poetry (a variety of forms), it is perhaps useful to think more broadly and incorporate a number of genres within a specific unit of work. For example, if as part of a Year 4 topic on the Victorian seaside, the English unit is 'To entertain' then children might write and tell their own music hall jokes, compose a murder mystery set in an old hotel or even create instructions about how to make puppets in a Punch and Judy show. This approach will enable you to plan for all three aspects of English, spoken language, reading and writing and make appropriate links that reflect their inter-relatedness. James Britton stressed *reading and writing float on a sea of talk* (1970). Over 40 years later, this principle is reflected in the current national curriculum: 'Spoken language underpins the development of reading and writing' (DfE, 2013, p3).

REFLECTIVE TASK

- Which of the genres for narrative, non-narrative and poetry are you confident about?
- If Year 6 are studying a sustainability project and the focus of English is, 'To persuade', which different genres could be included?
- If Year 2 are learning about Mary Seacole and the English focus is, 'To inform', which of the different genres might you expect to see children learning about?

Planning for writing

As previously highlighted, children who have a sense of ownership in their writing and who are writing about topics they have chosen are likely to be more motivated writers (Graves, 1983). For some teachers, there is an apparent conflict between the demands of the curriculum and the opportunity to be imaginative. However, effective teachers of literacy know that by adopting a more creative approach to writing, children are more likely to engage and are therefore more likely to succeed in their writing (Hall & Harding, 2003).

As you read the following learning outcomes for the different year groups, consider what you know about children's learning and the need for a real audience for writing. What kind of creative approaches could you take to the following units of work?

Year group, purpose and possible genres	National Curriculum

Year 1
Purpose: To entertain
Story writing, note-taking, instructions, invitations, descriptive writing
	In reading comprehension, pupils should be taught to:
	
	• develop pleasure in reading, motivation to read, vocabulary and understanding by:
	
	  o listening to and discussing a wide range of poems, stories and non-fiction at a level beyond that at which they can read independently
	  o becoming very familiar with key stories, fairy stories and traditional tales, retelling them and considering their particular characteristics
	  o learning to appreciate rhymes and poems, and to recite some by heart
	
	• understand both the books they can already read accurately and fluently and those they listen to by:
	
	  o making inferences on the basis of what is being said and done
	  o predicting what might happen on the basis of what has been read so far
	
	In writing,
	
	  o discuss what they have written with the teacher or other pupils
	  o read aloud their writing clearly enough to be heard by their peers and the teacher

Suggestions:
Create a role-play area of favourite fairy tales with a range of props, puppets and storybooks, and make a story throne with a crown for the storyteller. As a teacher tell stories and encourage children to learn them by heart, send stories home to practise. Use video cameras to capture stories, create freeze-frames, use role on the wall to find out more about the characters. Be creative with the character profile. Is it a 'Wanted' poster for the Big Bad Wolf, a letter of complaint about Goldilocks, a census for Old King Cole of all the characters in the land? Host a midsummer's ball and teach the children to dance. Write and send out invitations and interview the guests while they entertain the Prince.

| **Lower Key Stage 2 Year 3**
Purpose: To inform
Instruction writing, scripts, blogs, information writing | In reading comprehension, pupils should be taught to:
• develop positive attitudes to reading and understanding of what they read by:
  o listening to and discussing a wide range of fiction, poetry, plays, non-fiction and reference books or textbooks
  o reading books that are structured in different ways and reading for a range of purposes
• retrieve and record information from non-fiction
• participate in discussion about both books that are read to them and those they can read for themselves, taking turns and listening to what others say |

(Continued)

(Continued)

Year group, purpose and possible genres	National Curriculum

	In writing, pupils should be taught to:
	• plan their writing by:
	   o discussing writing similar to that which they are planning to write in order to understand and learn from its structure, vocabulary and grammar
	   o discussing and recording ideas
	• evaluate and edit by:
	   o assessing the effectiveness of their own and others' writing and suggesting improvements

Suggestions:
Create a kitchen role-play area, watch TV clips of cookery programmes, write instructions for making fruit salad for Sports Day and hand out pre-prepared instructions for parents to make at home. Upload onto the school website and encourage parents to leave comments and photographs sharing the success of their recipes. Create a podcast to capture the experience of all those attending Sports Day.

Ideas for meaningful writing activities

As the new curriculum finds its place within practice and, as a new teacher, you become more confident, it is important that you keep these creative responses at the heart of your English activities. So, how do schools manage to offer a creative approach while balancing the demands of the curriculum?

Two schools involved in *Everybody Writes*, a web-based project aimed at celebrating innovative approaches to writing, decided to take a fresh look at the writing opportunities within their own school and how they could bring a creative element to their planning.

CASE STUDY

Letter-writing for the whole school

Forest School wanted to review their letter-writing unit of work for Year 5, as they felt that it needed reinvigorating. The school decided to get the whole school writing with Year 2 sending love letters to parents on Valentine's Day, Nursery children writing letters of apology to Goldilocks, while Year 4 children designed stamps for letters they really posted, and sent messages in balloons.

However, Year 5 took things a little further:

WANTED

Young, skinny, wiry fellows.

Not over 18.

Must be expert riders.

Willing to risk death daily.

Orphans preferred.

Intrigued by the above advert, children were inspired by the exciting but short-lived Pony Express and enjoyed the thrill of finding out about the lone horse riders that raced across the United States in the time of Wild West. This is in itself inspired discussion. but the school went one step further and made contact with the Pony Express Museum in Missouri who put the school in touch with a local school. This then led to email contact and the children in Forest School were able to learn more about a far-off country and make a host of new friends. So, from a very modest approach to writing within school, the international link added a new and exciting element.

CASE STUDY

Townhill Primary School

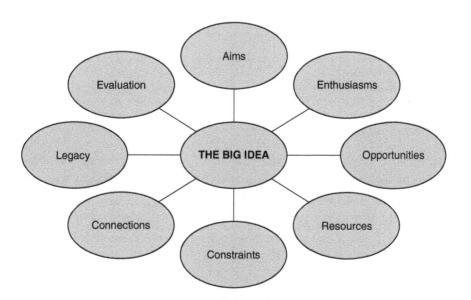

Figure 7.1 'The Big Idea' by Everybody Writes (2008)

Townhill Primary School were keen to raise the profile of writing within their school and the *aim* was to encourage pupils to see writing as something fun that they *chose* to engage with. The school ran a very successful gardening club and therefore identified nature and gardening as *enthusiasms* that could be drawn on. The school held an annual Arts Week in June and saw this as an *opportunity* to undertake a

(Continued)

(Continued)

cross-curricular project involving writing. Their *big idea* then was to hold an Everybody Writes Day during Arts Week, collapsing the curriculum for the day and involving all pupils in transforming the outdoor space into a poetry playground.

Pupils were involved in generating poems that hung from the trees in the playground, lined the borders of the gardens, stretched across footpaths, with favourite words carved onto stepping-stones. In transforming an under-used corner of the playground into a new outdoor theatre space, children now had a place where poetry could be performed, plays enacted, and speeches delivered. The playground was saturated with language and poetry with pupils keen to use the outdoor space during playtimes. The biggest *resource* they had was staff giving up their time and finding ways to involve the whole school community, the headteacher, teaching assistants, site manager and parents. As with any project there were funding *constraints* and, as this was a whole-school project, this was solved by the headteacher. In using established *connections*, the school involved a local artist and poet to bring an additional creative element to the project. The school now has a lasting *legacy* in the shape of a poetry playground with children who enjoy playing with language and see writing as relevant to them.

More inspirational ideas for using the school grounds:

- create a writing space;
- explore secret spaces;
- read stories under a story tree;
- find a space for a stage;
- plant a word garden;
- inspire with pebble poetry;
- go on a poetry journey.

A SUMMARY OF **KEY POINTS**

➤ **Ensure your classroom is a language-rich classroom, with role-play areas, a writing space (indoors and outdoors), a well-stocked book corner, a classroom rich with words to support writing, together with a sprinkling of poetry to enjoy.**

➤ **When planning, consider how to combine speaking and listening, reading and writing activities.**

➤ **Be aware that writing is hard and makes many demands on children and ensure you are flexible with time but be realistic about learning.**

➤ **Writing involves compositional and transcriptional elements.**

➤ **Seek out creative opportunities when planning writing for real audiences.**

MOVING *ON* > > > > > > MOVING *ON* > > > > > > MOVING *ON*

Having read this chapter, you should have a better understanding of the many demands placed on children when engaging with writing (Flynn and Stainthorp, 2006). You realise the importance of children needing to be inspired and have experiences to write about, but you are also aware of the tensions that can arise with the expectations of the national curriculum (2013). As teachers reflect on what they know about effective literacy teaching, a more flexible approach is being adopted but with an emphasis on high expectations about what children can achieve. By slowing down the writing process, time can be planned in for pre-writing activities, where ideas can be generated through talk, drama and discussion and will result in an experience that needs to be captured (Bearne, 2002). Pie Corbett talks about teachers inspiring children in such a way that they are on the edge of their seats *wondering what writing task will come their way* (2005, p6). Just as Bruner suggested that *knowing is a process not a product* (1966, p72), creativity should also be viewed as a process, not a one-off event (Grainger, Goouch amd Lambirth (2005, p16). This should be at the heart of your thinking when you start to plan for English activities within your own class. What will your legacy be?

REFERENCES REFERENCES **REFERENCES** REFERENCES REFERENCES REFERENCES

Barrs, M (2004) 'The Reader in the Writer' in *The RoutledgeFalmer Reader in Language and Literacy*. London: RoutledgeFalmer.

Bayley, R and Palmer, S (2004) *Foundations of literacy*. Stafford: Network Educational Press.

Bearne, E (2002) *Making progress in writing.* London: RoutledgeFalmer.

Black and Wiliam (2003) *Assessment for Learning: Putting it into Practice*. Glasgow: Open University Press.

Britton, J (1970) *Language and Learning*. Oxford: Heinemann.

Bromley, H (1998) in Bearne, E (1998) *Use of Language Across the Primary Curriculum*. Oxford: RoutledgeFalmer.

Bruner, JS (1966) *Toward a theory of instruction*. Cambridge, MA: Harvard University Press.

Clark, C and Poulton, L (2011) *Book ownership and its relation to reading enjoyment, attitudes, behaviour and attainment.* London: National Literacy Trust.

Corbett, P (2005) *How to teach fiction writing at Key Stage 2*. Oxon: David Fulton.

Cremin, T, Goouch, K, Blakemore, L, Goff, E and Macdonald, R (2006) 'Connecting drama and writing: seizing the moment to write' in *Research in Drama Education* 11, (3) pp. 273–291.

Department for Children, Schools and Families (2006) *Primary Framework for Mathematics and Literacy*. London: HMSO.

DfE (2012) Teachers' Standards available at **https://www.gov.uk/government/publications/teachers-standards** accessed 7/9/14.

Department for Education (2013) *English programmes of study: key stages 1 and 2. National curriculum in English*. London: DfE.

Department for Education and Skills (DfES) (2003) *Excellence and Enjoyment*. London: HMSO.

Flynn, N and Stainthorp, R (2006) *The Learning and Teaching of Reading and Writing.* Bognor Regis: John Wiley & Sons Ltd.

Goodwin, P (2010) *The Literate Classroom*. London: David Fulton Books.

Grainger, T, Goouch, K, Lambirth, A (2005) *Developing voice and verve in the classroom*. Oxon: Routledge.

Graves, DH (1983) *Writing: Teachers & children at work*. London: Heinemann Educational Books.

Hall, K and Harding, A (2003) 'A systematic review of effective literacy teaching in the 4 to 14 age range in mainstream schooling' in *Research Evidence in Education Library*. London: EPPI Centre, Social Science Research Unit, Institute of Education.

Medwell, J, Wray, D, Poulson, L and Fox, R (2002) *Teaching literacy effectively in the primary school*. London: Routledge.

Meek, M (1991) *On being literate*. The Bodley Head: London.

Mercer, N (2000) *Words and Minds: How we use language to think together*. London: Routledge.

Ofsted (2009) *English at the Crossroads.* London: Ofsted.

Rosen, M (2007) The poetry friendly classroom, online, available at **http://www.michaelrosen.co.uk/poetryfriendly.html,** accessed 10/8/14.

Smith, A and Call, N (2003) *The ALPS Approach.* Stafford: Network Educational Press.

Smith, F (1994) *Writing and the Writer*. New Jersey: Lawrence Erlbaum Associates.

Useful websites

www.booktrust.org.uk/programmes/primary/everybody-writes/ accessed 10/8/14

- with more details about the alien space-ship crash landing, letter writing to the Pony Express, Poetry Garden.

www.michaelrosen.co.uk/poetryfriendly.html accessed 10/8/14

- Michael Rosen's poetry-friendly classroom

www.ukla.org/news/new_ukla_curriculum_review_and_planning_tool_available_as_a_free_ download/ accessed 10/8/14

- Curriculum Review and Planning Tool

8
Creative mathematics
Mary Briggs

Chapter objectives

By the end of this chapter you will have:

- considered whether mathematics is a creative subject;
- considered whether creative mathematics is only for the most able;
- considered what it means to teach to encourage creativity in mathematics;
- considered what it means to teach mathematics creatively;
- considered the implications for practice.

This chapter addresses the following Teachers' Standards (DfE, 2012):

- establish a safe and stimulating environment for pupils, rooted in mutual respect;
- encourage pupils to take a responsible and conscientious attitude to their own work and study;
- have a secure knowledge of the relevant subject(s) and curriculum areas, foster and maintain pupils' interest in the subject, and address misunderstandings;
- have a secure understanding of how a range of factors can inhibit pupils' ability to learn, and how best to overcome these.

Introduction: the problem with mathematics

Creativity and mathematics or creative mathematics appears for many to be a contradiction in terms. Mathematics has a reputation for being either right or wrong: where can the creativity be in that? For many people there is no room for discussion as mathematics is seen as a way of proving other areas of study – 'the ultimate truth'. Yet mathematicians discuss the elegance in proofs and the creative patterns in algebra and fractals. The majority of people learning and teaching mathematics do not ever get to study at the level where creativity would appear to really get started.

Our views of mathematics are influenced by the fact that is it often seen as a utilitarian subject. Mathematics taught at school is a basic skill and needed for the real world. Yet how much mathematics do we use in our real lives? Most of us might say we use measures, aspects of number and estimating in our everyday activities. We might see problem-solving as part of mathematics and therefore an aspect we might use in our lives outside education. We may even see problem-solving as creative if there are a number of solutions to a given problem. One way of conceptualising creativity in mathematics is offered by Clark (2009) *as the mental processes involved in 'meaning making' in the mathematics classroom.*

Before looking at the issue of creativity within mathematics in detail, it would be worth considering your own perspective on this issue. Do you think mathematics is a creative subject? Is creativity situated in specific topics within mathematics or is it possible to see creativity throughout mathematics?

Curriculum issues

A key issue with mathematics is the curriculum that children are offered to explore the breadth of domain of mathematics. The new curriculum (DFE 2013) at the time of writing states as its aims fluency in the fundamentals of reasoning mathematically, with problem solving at the heart of this approach. Coupled with the emphasis in the guidance about making connections within and across mathematical ideas, the reader might consider this an excellent starting point for developing creativity in mathematics. The detailed expectations of the curriculum delivery, however, emphasise different facets of learning and teaching with a focus on more procedural aspects of the subject through practice, memorizing and attention to precision and fluency.

Look carefully at the curriculum you will be teaching from the aims to the detail of the expectations. What does this tell you about the conceptions of the subject and the relationship with creativity?

Look also at any scheme materials used in your school. What is the focus of attention in these materials? Are there tasks which emphasise the procedural aspects of the subject or the more creative aspects?

The case for creativity in mathematics

Mathematicians' view of their work is often framed in the use of specific mathematical vocabulary and, therefore, unless we speak mathematically fluently, can appear inaccessible. The following quote from King (1992) demonstrates something of that difficulty and a view of mathematics that may be very different to our own.

> The word 'produce' as used here seems slightly awkward and it would be more natural to replace it with the word 'create' or 'discover'. But I have used the word produce... to describe the work of mathematicians because it is a continuing controversy in mathematical circles as to whether new mathematics is created or discovered... The idea that mathematics, as a physical world seems to exists, independent of human thought and activity is a notion at least as old as the philosophy of Plato... a second view claims that mathematical structures are created and that they have no existence independent of the person that created them. This notion meshes well with the nature of modern pure mathematics.
>
> (King, 1992, p41)

Society's view of mathematics tends to focus on arithmetic and correct answers to calculations. Mathematics is seen as providing the evidence for other subjects, the proof that things are true if you can prove them mathematically.

The following, about the American poet Robert Frost, is a good parallel with mathematics in that it shows us how a subject or phenomenon is itself a way of looking and serves a wider purpose than the strictly utilitarian. You may know that Frost lived in the farming area of Vermont and was inspired to write poetry through the imagery of the farmers' daily lives.

> *...he understood, as do all true artists, that it is metaphor and symbol, and not plain reality, that is memorable and significant. Mathematicians, like poets, see value in metaphor and analogy. The lines they draw are made, not only of words, but of graceful symbols: summations and integrals, infinities turning on themselves like self-swallowing snakes, and fractals like snowflakes that, as you blink your eye, turn to lunar landscapes. Mathematicians write their poetry with mathematics.*
>
> (King, 1992, p11)

Mathematicians see their subject as having a poetic quality as well as the potential for ambiguity and interpretation.

The challenge to teach mathematics creatively

Mathematics by its nature is often seen as a visual subject with symbols written on a page. Tall et al. (2001) suggest that learners need to move towards the abstraction of mathematics to become flexible in their approaches, particularly to calculation, in order to become successful mathematicians. They focus on the child's attention during actions on objects when calculating. Often 5+3 can be seen as an array of objects that children imagine combining to find the total quantity. For some children seeing arithmetic in terms of mental images of objects persists and this prevents them from moving into the higher realms of mathematics. These children rely heavily on counting strategies, which increase the possibility for errors with increasing number size. The higher achievers seem to focus more on the symbolism itself. They utilise known facts and move away from counting strategies more quickly, seeing the relationship between numbers. These skills enable the children to engage more easily with the creative opportunities in mathematics. The ability to visualise in the abstract is a key skill in success in mathematics and not just in relation to number. It is a clear prerequisite skill for success in geometry. Creative activities in mathematics should give learners an opportunity to explore the possibilities, working in ways that motivate and engage their interest.

This means looking beyond the structure of the Primary National Strategy (DfES, 2006) for mathematics three-part lesson structure and differentiation through the use of three levels of tasks, often in the form of worksheets in the main activity phase of the lesson. It also required a shift in thinking about 'personalised learning' from being an entitlement to progressing two levels a year to address children's interests to allow exploration of subjects such as mathematics.

To address this, activities should be used to show how creativity could be enhanced through visual, verbal and kinaesthetic approaches. This links to areas discussed in relation to learning styles, which have gained predominance in recent years. Care is required as children who can flexibly move between learning styles are more successful learners. Children who struggle are often focused on their preferred learning styles alone.

Teaching to encourage creativity

Mann (2006) suggests that the way mathematics teaching is approached by teachers actually limits the creativity within the subject either in relation to learning or teaching. This key issue is supported by the work of Bolden *et al.* (2010) who focused on pre-service teachers. Within this group, conceptions of creativity in mathematics were predominantly associated with the use of resources and technology. As a result their conceptions focused on the idea of 'teaching creatively' rather than 'teaching for creativity'.

Reactions to children's responses are crucial in identifying what is actually happening when children complete a task. Are they demonstrating misconceptions in mathematics or bored so they decide to work creatively with the task given? The result may initially appear to be an incorrect answer. An example would be a child's response to 12 + 23 = giving an answer of 8. Without a discussion with the child, it is not possible to interpret exactly what is going on. It may hide a creative playing with numbers rather than a concern. It is important to listen carefully to children in order to accurately identify their understanding and the approaches they have taken with tasks.

Bolden *et al.* (2010) indicate that teachers may experience difficulties of *identifying ways of encouraging and assessing creativity in the classroom* and this is clearly linked to their conceptions of creativity in mathematics.

Current definitions of creativity

The DfEE (1999) report on creativity provides a definition, which is broken down into four characteristics. Creative thinking, or behaving creatively, can be seen as:

- imaginative;
- purposeful;
- original; and
- of value.

If we look at mathematics we can see that thinking mathematically can be purposeful and of value as we can solve problems with mathematical skills and knowledge. There is a considerable debate about whether problem-solving is actually a creative aspect of mathematics, and this will be discussed in more detail later. We value calculations and measuring where accuracy is important for safety or economy. The imaginative and original behaviours in mathematics appear at first to be more difficult to access. We might see children creating original methods of solving problems, repeating patterns or creating games.

Young children thinking creatively

Young children are fascinated by words and playing with rhyming, often making up new words. They do this with counting rhymes, counting words and their mathematical mark making (Carruthers and Worthington, 2006). These are areas that we might cite as creative activities within the subject of English or literacy. If you listen to children playing they will invent words for quantities as part of playing with language, language for a specific purpose. Mathematics can be seen as language that we learn to speak. We also learn that precise language can be used to describe situations, events or classify. Two-year-old Alex was overheard trying some of these things out as he was talking to his toys: *Tigger has a tail ... Alex has no tail*. This small boy was playing with his classification of objects including self, all part of beginning to think mathematically. For his parents, this might be a source of celebration, but like many small children they choose their own time to explore ideas and for these tired parents this was two o'clock in the morning!

For young children it may be simple connections between the mathematical skills they are learning and the situations they find themselves in. An example of this is a small girl Ellen of about three who was asked by her mother if there were enough drinks for her mother, her brother and herself. Ellen proceeded to count *1, 2...* and then instead of saying three, she said *me*, and then decided that there were enough drinks for everyone. Ellen was making her own original connections between her counting skills and the need to use one to one correspondence to find out if there were enough drinks for everyone. QCA (2004) describes how you can spot creativity and gives as examples making connections and seeing relationships in mathematics. Ellen is clearly demonstrating a very early start to making connections in order to solve a problem.

Mathematical creativity occurs anywhere young children make connections between what they see and their emerging knowledge of mathematics. I witnessed an example of this when three-year-old Ben was eating his tea of sausage and chips and suddenly he announced: *I've got a number. It's a number seven*. His chips were stuck together at one end to form the shape of a number seven. The adults sitting at the table chatting about other things when he made the connections for himself did not prompt him to look at his food. He showed by his observations that he was already thinking creatively about mathematics and well on his way to being a confident mathematician.

REFLECTIVE TASK
REFLECTIVE TASK

If you are working with young children, you may be able to think of examples similar to those already outlined that will allow you to think about mathematical activity differently from previous interpretation, as creative or evidence of creativity.

More able

Wilson and Briggs (2002) looked at more able children's approaches to solving mathematical problems for example:

a and b are whole numbers. What could they be? a / b = 4.125

One child, Zoe, took time to make sense of the problem from the outset, using her insight to plan a strategic response. She took control of the task, exploited connections and relationships, producing an elegant solution. After thinking for some time, she voiced that she saw the problem as: *See how many times you have to do the 4.125 to make a whole number*. Zoe recognised the relationship:

$$4 \cdot 125 \times b = a$$

This enabled her to develop the strategy of multiplying 4.125 to make a whole number. But rather than trying numbers randomly, she exploited what she knew about decimals in order to obtain:

$$4 \cdot 125 \times 2 = 8 \cdot 25$$
$$8.25 \times 2 = 16 \cdot 5$$
$$16 \cdot 5 \times 2 = 33$$

This is an example of a creative approach using the elegance of the mathematics as well as her previous knowledge.

Is creative mathematics only for the most able?

Since the 1980s there has been a developing focus of attention on children who are 'gifted and talented' and this has been linked to numerous additional programmes for these children. One key issue for teachers is how to identify and support these particular learners. Porter (2005) describes some of the difficulties of identification with young children. She suggests that teachers tend to under-identify both the gifted children who appear to engage with activities very slowly and those who are creative and do not conform. At the same time, it is possible to overestimate the abilities of children who engage with a task readily, cooperate easily and perhaps more tellingly conform to the expectations of adults.

Although Porter's work is focusing on gifted children, generally she raises specific issues in relation to mathematics and particularly in relation to children with learning difficulties. We do not associate 'giftedness' with any difficulties, yet Porter (2005) clearly sets out examples of children with a gift in one or more areas of the curriculum but appear to have difficulties in others. This has significant implications for a stance, which allows access to creative mathematics only to the most able. Children with the difficulties Porter describes may well be denied access to the opportunities to be creative in their strongest area. Porter describes the difficulties for teachers to be able to identify these children as more able, as their difficulties may mask their true abilities. To avoid this situation, access for all to be creative with mathematics would allow children to show their real abilities and offer teachers a different situation in which to accurately assess their potential.

Engaging all learners with the potential for enjoying, and therefore seeing the creativity possible within the subject, is a key challenge for teachers. Robinson and Koshy (2004) suggest that we look at school mathematics as partitioned into three elements: procedures, application and elegance. They see the way forward for increasing the creativity in mathematics by providing opportunities for children to learn all three elements in order to introduce them to the *more beautiful aspects of mathematics*. Mann (2006) again focused on the more able students and advocates taking risks in mathematics which may be seen as easier or slightly safer with the gifted learners.

Briggs (1998) interviewed mathematicians as part of an oral history project focusing on successful mathematicians and their early experiences of mathematics. In these interviews, one area explored was when their attention shifted specifically towards mathematics and they showed an early indication of where their interests might lie in the future. All those interviewed identified as their research focus areas of mathematics aimed at those under the age of ten, which is important information for those teaching young children.

This would seem to be backed up by the intentions behind the National Curriculum, which included recommendations for mathematics to be seen as a creative subject. DfES/QCA (1999) states that *Mathematics is a creative discipline. It can stimulate moments of pleasure and wonder when pupils solve a problem for the first time, discover a more elegant solution to that problem, or suddenly see hidden connections* (p14). In the current version of the curriculum there are echoes of these intentions in the purposes of study: *A high-quality mathematics education therefore provides a foundation for understanding the world, the ability to reason mathematically, an appreciation of the beauty and power of mathematics, and a sense of enjoyment and curiosity about the subject* (DfE, 2013). These are not recommendations for a few, but an entitlement for all children to be able to engage with mathematics as a creative subject, and this is where the role of the teacher in facilitating access to this approach to mathematics is paramount.

What does it mean to teach mathematics creatively?

The Primary National Strategy (DfES, 2006) for mathematics, often described as the 'numeracy hour', began its initial implementation in schools in September 1999. Martin Hughes (1999) describes the strategy as *undoubtedly the most prescriptive approach to primary mathematics ever developed in this country* (p4). Has this changed the way we think of teaching mathematics? Definitely. Does it mean that there we see less creativity in teaching mathematics? Possibly. Has it influenced the subsequent policy development of the mathematics curriculum? Definitely.

REFLECTIVE TASK

REFLECTIVE TASK

Can you think of someone who you consider teaches creatively? Does this include their teaching of mathematics? What are the key elements of their teaching that make it creative? Try to list these elements yourself. If appropriate share with your school-based tutor or mentor as part of the development of your teaching and the children's learning.

Comment

These are difficult questions and could suggest that you are looking for continuous evidence of flair and imagination. The issue with this interpretation is that a high level of imaginative teaching can be a clear aspiration but can be hard to sustain across all topics/subjects and may even set unrealistic expectations. This is not to say that this should not be the aim of teaching mathematics. However, we may consider that many people teaching mathematics in the early years and primary age range do not have positive feelings about the subject. These feelings about mathematics are likely to affect approaches to teaching the subject to children.

The National Numeracy Strategy (DfEE, 1999) made significant changes to approaches to teaching mathematics. The first area of change was the emphasis on numeracy, as opposed to mathematics, and a clear focus on numeracy skills for everyday life. The second was the structure of the lesson into three clear parts, and for some teachers a narrowing of the flexibility in approach and organisation of the lessons that was apparently there before. A conversation with a colleague from a school which had recently been inspected led to a discussion about creative teaching and in which subjects it occurred. (This was a school which had been very successful with its inspection, and many of the lessons had been graded highly.) His perception of the lessons that were graded at the highest levels was where the teachers were taking some risks with the lesson formats and the activities selected. Interestingly, the perception was that none of these lessons were within the 'core' curriculum. The power of the inspection in this case was perhaps limiting the creativity among this group of teachers, though the discussion extended beyond the inspection period and patterns had begun to emerge. The influence of a structure to the lessons, particularly in mathematics, was apparent for this school. It was felt that, somehow, the ability to structure the lessons flexibly had become emblematic of the school's development work on creativity, teaching and learning. The changes in the curriculum since the decline in the Primary Strategy have emphasised a 'back to basics' approach – and in mathematics this includes more focus on formal writing arithmetic using algorithms and learning and testing tables knowledge. These skills are important but an overemphasis on these areas increases the likelihood of children's anxieties around getting the right answers and viewing mathematics as a boring and uninteresting subject.

A problem-solving approach

One way of working on enhancing a creative and more open approach of teaching is to offer problems which can be used with children of a wide range of ability and therefore can be used within any class, not a specific class for the most able children. Problem solving is part of the current National Curriculum yet the steer that is given is towards word problems to practise the use of arithmetic skills and associated reading and comprehension skills. This does not develop the wider problem-solving skills that employers are looking for with potential strategic thinkers. Problem solving can be an approach to utilising mathematical skills in creative ways. Briggs (2000) argued this particularly in relation to the early years and in response to moving away from the use of worksheets within the main activity phase of numeracy lessons. The focus is much more on what makes good activities. The Practical Task box below is a suggested checklist for deciding what makes a really 'good' task.

PRACTICAL TASK   PRACTICAL TASK   PRACTICAL TASK   PRACTICAL TASK   PRACTICAL TASK

Is my activity:

- **accessible to all;**
- **possible to extend;**
- **possible to narrow;**
- **enjoyable?**

Does it offer/present:

- **a practical starting point;**
- **opportunities for mathematical discussion;**
- **a reason for children to record their ideas;**
- **opportunities for repetition without becoming meaningless both for teachers and children;**
- **clarity of underlying mathematics?**

Think about activities you use in your classroom. How do they compare to this list? Can you find an activity that fits all these criteria? How might you use an activity that fits all these criteria in a mathematics lesson? If appropriate share with your school-based tutor or mentor as part of the development of your teaching and the children's learning.

Vale *et al.* (2012) have conducted a more specific focus within problem solving research *on pattern problem solving tasks as a means of fostering creativity in mathematics*. Their work takes the problem solving tasks into early algebraic thinking. They suggest a definition for mathematical creativity based on Mann (2006) which includes:

- divergent and convergent thinking;
- three components/dimensions – fluency, flexibility and originality (novelty);
- problem solving and problem posing (including elaboration and generalisation).

(Vale *et al.*, 2012, pp17–18)

This builds on the work of Mann (2006), who suggests problem solving enables a more divergent view of learning and teaching in mathematics. He also used the term 'creative student' as a learner that has alternative views. As a direct result of the focus on procedures in mathematics we are perhaps less likely to acknowledge learners' views in the classroom.

Think about activities you use in your classroom, particularly if you are working with older learners. Do the activities give opportunities to explore these elements? Can you find activities that fit all these elements? What differences would you expect to see in the teaching and learning that takes place in a lesson given this focus?

Open tasks for children

The teacher can use open task materials in flexible ways that respond to the needs and previous experience of the learners. Organisations like NRICH provide resources which support the most able, but this is within the context of a broad interpretation and view of enrichment, not within a context of provision simply targeting the most able. Good enrichment education is good education for all. Good mathematics education should incorporate an approach that is an enriching and stimulating experience for all children and, some would argue, the teacher, too, in order to stimulate their development in teaching and continue their interest in learning. NRICH suggest that this approach should include content opportunities designed to:

- develop and use problem-solving strategies;
- encourage mathematical thinking;
- include historical cultural contexts;
- offer opportunities for mathematical extension.

Therefore, this enrichment is not simply learning facts and demonstrating skills. Mathematical skills and knowledge can be precursors to, and also outcomes of, an enrichment curriculum.

The aim of an enrichment curriculum is to support:

- a problem-solving approach;
- improving pupil attitudes;
- a growing appreciation of mathematics;
- the development of conceptual structures.

(Adapted from Ernest, 2000)

This sounds like a tall order for a teacher and does require the use of a creative approach to planning. It does not mean that teachers must reinvent the wheel but take simple ideas and adapt them for their pupils. Ideas can be adapted from a number of sources, such as old textbooks, puzzle books or notes from old courses. It may appear as though in order to teach mathematics creatively you need to alter your teaching radically, and yet the smallest things can change the teaching and learning for the children and make a lesson successful for the learners. Thinking creatively about mathematics teaching is about starting from what you know and adding to it.

Creative mathematics teaching in practice

An example of creative mathematics teaching in practice was observed in a student teacher's mathematics lesson with a Year 3 class who were working on multiplying by 10. This is an area where there are lots of opportunities for children to acquire misconceptions, the most obvious being that to multiply by 10 just add a zero. This works for whole numbers but does not make any difference to the number if over-generalised to decimals. The creativity in this lesson was in the modelling of what happens to numbers when multiplied by 10. The student had set up three large hoops on the floor for the whole class to see marked as hundreds, tens and ones. Children were asked to come out to the front and hold a digit card standing in the tens and ones hoops to make the number 14. Another child was asked to join them but stand initially a little way from the hoops holding a zero or nought. This child became 'naughty nought'.

The student with the children then modelled what happened when the zero was added to the original number pushing (gently) the digits along the hoops to increase their place value. This was completed after they had undertaken discussion about multiplying by 10 and what happened to the numbers with some children clearly spotting a generalisable pattern of adding a zero. The student felt it was important for the children to see and understand what was actually happening to the number. Digital pictures were taken by one of the class to form a display after the lesson to remind children of what had happened to the digits to form a new number after the intervention of 'naughty nought'. This was a creative, simple but effective model for all the children in the class regardless of ability. This approach begins to make links for the children between aspects of mathematics, which is a key finding from the study into effective teachers of numeracy (Askew *et al.*, 1997).

The need to engage children in their learning is a topic of discussion in many countries in relation to mathematics. In Germany, Meissner (2000) describes a project entitled 'We build a village' which concentrated on geometry to further concepts of both plane and three-dimensional geometry in primary schools. In this module for primary grades (age about eight-to-ten years) the children worked with about 35 different solids, made of styrofoam, wood, paper-nets or plastic. The activities for the children were diverse and consisted of: sorting and classifying, folding, drawing, cutting, constructing nets, using plasticine, and building solids and houses with these models. At the end of the module (of about seven lessons) the children built their own village with a grocery store, a church, a school, houses, as well as a creek, streets and parking areas. This kind of topic approach to teaching and learning is moving back into the primary curriculum with the introduction of the ideas from the Primary Strategy (DfES, 2003) and the subsequent continuing professional development materials. This is enabling teachers to look again at the ways they are constructing the learning to engage children with mathematics and to learn to become creative mathematicians.

Other approaches to being creative with mathematics teaching can be seen in the use of children's current interests to motivate and stimulate curiosity. Briggs *et al.* (2002) are an example of an approach drawing upon the interest created by the phenomenon of the Harry Potter books. All the activities described in the article are based around the theme of ideas from the wizarding books. The object of the creative approach is to enliven and enrich the mathematics lesson and to offer children a stimulus that they might then go on to develop by themselves. The activities also allow teachers to make connections for the children between aspects of mathematics (Askew *et al.*, 1997).

Sheffield (2009) suggests that a key area to develop mathematical creativity is the questioning that is used in learning and teaching. This includes the questions that the children might pose and answer, as well as the kinds of questions that the teacher might ask. Although this work focused on developing the more able, they are applicable to all learners. The suggested questions can be categorized as who, what, when, where, why and how.

Who?

- Who started this task in this way?
- Who did it differently?
- Who has a different approach?

What?

- What do you notice first?

When?

- When is it appropriate to use this approach?
- When is it not?

Where?

- Where can you find similar tasks?

Why?

- Why might you need more information?

How?

- How does this compare with other problems/tasks/approaches?

REFLECTIVE TASK

REFLECTIVE TASK

Think about the interests of the children you teach. Can you construct activities that will engage their interest with mathematics and help them to appreciate the creative opportunities within the subject? Find out about the approaches to teaching implemented as a result of National Curriculum and the testing of specific skills. What effect has this had on teaching mathematics creatively?

Think specifically about the questioning that either a teacher you are observing is using or that you use in the classroom. How can this encourage the development of creative mathematics?

A SUMMARY OF **KEY POINTS**

Cross (2004), now a retired HMI, wrote passionately about the important issues for her in mathematics teaching, which included: How do we engage children in their own learning? How do we engage them with mathematics and encourage them to want to know more? Her article also included a key quotation from the non-statutory guidance written to accompany the first version of the National Curriculum in 1989. It states that:

> *Mathematics is not only taught because it is useful. It should be a source of delight and wonder, offering pupils intellectual excitement and an appreciation of its essential creativity* (NCC, 1989).

Teaching mathematics in this way makes demands on us as teachers, especially if we have not had good experiences of mathematics teaching as learners. This requires us to:

> ➤ reappraise our preconceptions of mathematics as having no creative potential;

> ➤ look beyond the current structures for lesson planning in mathematics;

> ➤ ensure that we develop ways of teaching which encourage problem-solving and open tasks which make use of children's preferred learning styles;

> ➤ observe children closely so we can identify their interests and their creative use of mathematics not just in mathematics lessons;

> ➤ study closely the development of children of all abilities in our classes so that we do not fall into the trap of providing creative activities only for the most able or as extension activities for children who finish activities quickly.

MOVING *ON* > > > > > > MOVING *ON* > > > > > > MOVING *ON*

You will find it useful to discuss how teachers in your placement setting/school are developing their approaches to creative teaching and learning of mathematics. If your placement has a teacher with specific responsibility for mathematics and/or the creative curriculum across the school see if you can make a time to talk to this person in more detail about the school's policies and procedures and their role in co-ordinating that approach. Particularly you may want to discuss the following areas:

- planning for different types of mathematics lessons;
- mathematics across the curriculum;
- how records of observations of children are made not just in the early years and how this might be used as a starting point for personalised learning focusing on specific child interests.

You might also consider:

- What kind of resources could you collect to support a creative approach to teaching mathematics such as stories and games?
- How you can share creative teaching approaches with other students.
- Are there issues for your mathematical subject knowledge to identify, and support creativity in mathematics?

REFERENCES REFERENCES **REFERENCES** REFERENCES **REFERENCES** REFERENCES

Askew, M, Brown, M, Rhodes, V, Wiliam, D and Johnson, D (1997) *Effective teachers of numeracy: a report of a study carried out for the Teacher Training Agency*. London: King's College, University of London.

Bolden, DS, Harries, T, Newton, DP (2010) Pre-service primary teachers conceptions of creativity in mathematics. *Educational Studies in mathematics*. 73(2), 143–157.

Briggs, M (1998) The right baggage?, in Olivier, A and Newstead, K (eds) Proceedings of the 22nd Conference of the International Group for the Psychology of Mathematics Education, Stellenbosch, South Africa. Vol. 2, 152–9.

Briggs, M (2000) Feel free to be *flexible,* Special: *Children*, Hertfordshire: Questions pp1–8.

Briggs, M, Daniell, J, Farncombe, J, Lenton, N, and Stonehouse, A (2002) Wizarding Maths. *Mathematics Teaching*, 180, 23–7.

Carruthers, E and Worthington, M (2006)*Children's Mathematics: Making Marks, Making Meaning*. (2ndEdition) London: Paul Chapman Publishing.

Clark, J (2009). A nodes model for creativity in mathematics education. In: BERA Annual Conference, 2–5 September 2009, Manchester, UK.

Cross, K (2004) Engagement and Excitement in Mathematics. *Mathematics Teaching*, 189, 4–6.

DfE (2012) Teachers' Standards available at **https://www.gov.uk/government/publications/teachers-standards** accessed 7/9/14.

DfE (2013) *Mathematics programmes of study: key stages 1 and 2 National curriculum in England*. London: DfE.

Department for Education and Employment (DfEE) (1999) *All our futures: National Advisory Committee for Creativity and Culture in Education Report*. London: DfEE.

DfES (2003) *Excellence and enjoyment: a strategy for primary schools*. Nottingham: DfES.

DfES (2006) Primary National Strategy. London: DfEs/Crown Copyright.Ernest, P (2000) Teaching and learning mathematics, in Koshy, V, Ernest, P, and Casey, R. *Mathematics for Primary Teachers*. Abingdon: Routledge.

Ernest, P (2000) Teaching and Learning Mathematics, in Koshy, V, Ernest, P and Cassey, R *Mathematics for Primary Teachers*. Abingdon: Routledge.

Hughes, M (1999) The National Numeracy Strategy: are we getting it right? *The Psychology of Education Review*, 23:2, 3–7.

King, J (1992) *The art of mathematics*. New York and London: Plenum Press.

Mann, E.L (2006) Creativity: the essence of mathematics. *Journal for the Education of the Gifted*. 30(2), 236–60.

Meissner, H (2000) Creativity in Mathematics Education, in the Proceedings of the Mathematics Education Study Group (MESG), August 7–8, Tokyo, Japan.

National Curriculum Council (1989) *Mathematics: non-statutory guidance*. York: NCC/HMSO. Ofsted (2003) *Expecting the unexpected*. HMI **www.ofsted.gov.uk** accessed 11/8/2014.

QCA (2004) *Creativity: Find it! Promote it!* London: QCA Publications.

Porter, L (2005) *Gifted young children: A guide for teachers and parents* (2nd edition). Buckingham: Open University Press.

Robinson, D and Koshy, V (2004) Creative mathematics: allowing caged birds to fly, in Fisher, R, and Williams, M (eds) *Unlocking creativity: teaching across the curriculum*. London: David Fulton.

Sheffield, L (2009) Developing mathematical creativity – questions may be the answer' in Leikin, R., Berman, A., and Koichu, B. (eds.) Creativity in Mathematics and the Education of Gifted Students. Rotterdam: Sense Publications, 57–100.

Tall, D, Gray, E, Bin Ali, M, Crowley, L, De Marios, P, McGovern, M, Pitta, D, Pinto, M, Thomas, M and Yusof, Y (2001) Symbols and bifurcation between procedural and conceptual thinking. *Canadian Journal of Mathematics and Technology Education*, 1:1, 81–104.

Vale, I, Pimental, T, Cabrita, I, Barbosa, A, Fonesca, L (2012) Pattern problem solving tasks as a means of fostering creativity in mathematics. In Tso, TM (ed.) Proceedings of the 36th Conference of the International Group for the Psychology of Mathematics Education. Vol 4, 171–178. Taipei: Taiwan.

Wilson, K and Briggs, M (2002) Able and gifted: judging by appearances? *Mathematics Teaching*, 180, 34–6.

FURTHER READING FURTHER READING **FURTHER READING** FURTHER READING

Briggs, M and Davis, S (2008) *Mathematics in the early years and primary classroom (creative teaching)*. Abingdon: Routledge. (Second edition due in 2014.)

Briggs, M (2013) *Teaching and Learning Early Years Mathematics*: Subject and Pedagogic Knowledge. Northwich: Critical Publishing.

9
What is creativity in science education?
Jane Johnston

Chapter objectives

By the end of this chapter you should:

- understand the nature of creativity in science education;
- understand the importance of creativity in science teaching on learning and learners;
- understand and overcome the difficulties of being creative in teaching and learning.

This chapter will address the following Teachers' Standards (DfE, 2012):

- establish a safe and stimulating environment for pupils, rooted in mutual respect;
- encourage pupils to take a responsible and conscientious attitude to their own work and study;
- have a secure knowledge of the relevant subject(s) and curriculum areas, foster and maintain pupils' interest in the subject, and address misunderstandings.

Introduction

Science is not often thought of as creative, but rather as a body of certain and unchanging knowledge. This narrow view does not acknowledge the tentative nature of scientific theories and the creativity of scientific discoveries, which broaden our understanding of the universe, changing the way we think and the way we view the world. Children's pictures (see Figure 9.1), show scientists as white, male and white-coated, although the addition of 'thought bubbles', exclamation marks and the use of words such as 'Eureka!', indicate an element of invention, discovery and innovation, if not

Figure 9.1 A stereotypical picture of a scientist (Johnston, 2005, p110)

creativity. Children's oral responses to the question 'what is science?' do not appear to identify any creative elements (Crompton, 2013). The reason for this seeming anomaly is that creativity is not only difficult to define (see Naylor and Keogh, 2012) and used synonymously with words such as originality, but also has different meanings in science and technology than the arts.

REFLECTIVE TASK

What picture comes into your mind when you think of science?

How would you draw a picture of a scientist?

Do you think the stereotypical image of science and scientists is outdated?

It is necessary to extend our understanding of creativity in order to see how science can be creative and we should include creativity of thinking and problem-solving (de Bono, 1992), as well as discovery and innovation. In recent years our understanding of creativity in science has increased with deeper research being undertaken (e.g. CLS, 2012; CLS, 2013) and this has enabled us to build on previous definitions (Beetlestone, 1998). Creativity's importance in education has previously been recognised (DfES, 2003), although there are tensions in government calls to provide schools with *renewed freedom and authority will make a significant contribution to improving schools* (DfE, 2010) and advocated increased prescription in the same document and in the national curriculum (DfE, 2013). It is worrying that primary science in the national curriculum (DfE, 2013) is reduced to requirements to identify and recognise, rather than emphasising creative thinking. Creativity in science involves making links or connections and taking intellectual/cognitive risks (Johnston, 2013). The conceptual framework for the *Creative Little Scientists* project (CLS, 2012), builds on Beetlestone's (1998) six-part definition of creativity as involving learning, representation, productivity, originality, thinking creatively/problem-solving, universe/creation-nature. The project identified how teaching and learning using inquiry-based science education (IBSE) and approaches which foreground creativity (Creative Approaches, CA) can enhance learning through common synergies such as:

- play and exploration;
- motivation and affect;
- dialogue and collaboration;
- problem solving and agency;
- questioning and curiosity;
- reflection and reasoning.

Historically, science has been innovative, involving discovery and creative thinking and with creative scientists as risk takers. Leonardo da Vinci is considered to one of the greatest artists and scientists, producing significant works of art and scientific ideas, which have been used to support understanding (e.g. human anatomy) and technological advances (e.g. aircraft design). Newton, Archimedes and Curie demonstrated creativity of thought which led to improved understanding of our world (e.g. Newton extended understanding of gravitational force and light) and technological advances (e.g. Archimedes ideas led to the use of levers to help lift heavy objects and Curie's discoveries led to radiotherapy). Other scientists, such as Darwin and Galileo took great risks in communicating their ideas to a world, that was unwilling and unready to accept them, and faced public humiliation and incarceration.

Our science education has an important influence on our perception and understanding of science. Differences in understanding appear to result from societal and educational emphasis (Ofsted, 2003; Osborne and Dillon, 2008; DfE, 2013), views of the world and science education (Johnston *et al.*, 1998), although a contrasting view is offered in a review of curricula as part of the Primary Review (Hall and Øzerk, 2008). It may be that whereas different countries may have similar curricula, the emphases may be different. For example, sometimes primary science education has a biological and geographical emphasis (Finland, Bosnia), with chemistry, physics and mathematics being taught as secondary sciences, is mainly knowledge-based and curriculum-focused (England post-National Curriculum, Macedonia and Japan), or skills-based and child-centred (England pre-National Curriculum).

PRACTICAL TASK   PRACTICAL TASK   PRACTICAL TASK   PRACTICAL TASK   PRACTICAL TASK

Learning about scientists and their discoveries can help develop a better understanding about the nature of science and scientific discoveries. This is advocated in the revised national curriculum (DfE, 2013) although some of the 'scientists' identified are not always the most scientific or creative.

- Try learning about Leonardo da Vinci through reading extracts from his notebooks and explore gravitational force by making paper helicopters. Explore what happens when you use different types of paper/card or different sizes or add extra paperclips or fold the wings the opposite way.

- Read the story of Darwin's voyage on the Beagle and sort pictures of animals or collections of plants according to observable features. Look at teeth, skull shapes, leaf shape or seeds and think what this tells us about the animal/plant.

- Retell the story of Archimedes and then explore how different objects affect the water level of a tank of water. Does the weight or size make a difference?

See also Johnston (2013) for a fuller list of historical scientists and links to creative science education.

What is creativity in science education?

Creative science education is a complex inter-relationship between science and education – made difficult because of the different natures of science and education. Science is commonly viewed as a body of empirical, non-political knowledge. Education is felt to reflect changes in society and views, is inherently political and values all knowledge and understanding and is therefore less static in its development than science. Science education sits somewhat uncomfortably between science and education and is viewed differently depending on whether viewed, initially, from a science or education strength. Where science is the stronger partner, then progress in science education can be slowed by the empirical view of the nature of science. Science

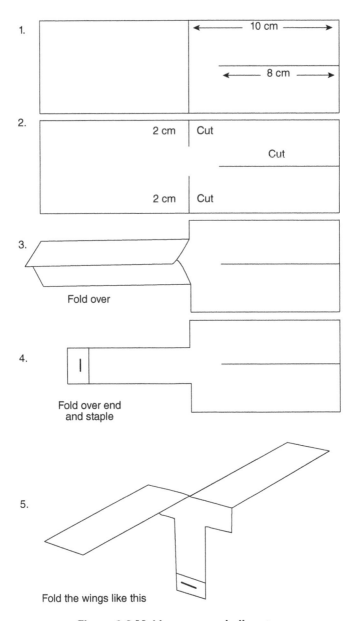

Figure 9.2 Making a paper helicopter

education in the national curriculum (DfE, 2013) focuses on factual learning the views of science, although creativity is increasingly more valued by society (Osborne and Dillon, 2008) and emphasized in government publication (DfES, 2003; QCA, 2003; DfE, 2010) and journals (see for example, Teaching, Thinking and Creativity, an on-line journal of articles on creative teaching). As the 2010 White Paper identified, *the guidance on the National Curriculum is weighing teachers down and squeezing out room for innovation, creativity, deep learning and intellectual exploration* (DfE, 2010, p40).

However, the solution that the National Curriculum *should set out only the essential knowledge and understanding that all children should acquire and leave teachers to decide how to teach this most effectively* (DfE, 2010, p40) is unhelpful to teachers who struggle to be creative after a long period where creativity was only encouraged in paper and not practice.

Making connections is considered to be an important aspect of creativity (Duffy, 1998) and creativity in science education involves making connections between aspects of learning across the curriculum (DfES, 2003; CLS, 2012; CLS, 2013). In this way science education will not focus solely on the acquisition of limited scientific knowledge, but involve the development of scientific understanding, skills and attitudes, integrating other subjects through real-life contexts so that knowledge and skills can be applied in real situations; that is, the development of scientific literacy.

Creative science education involves practitioners with subject and pedagogical knowledge who adapt their teaching to suit the learning objectives, children and context. Creative science education does not follow rigidly imposed methodologies or statutory requirements, which adversely affect pedagogical practice and reduced the practical component of much science teaching. Recent research (CLS, 2013) indicates the importance of both individual teacher and school understanding of the synergies between practical science and creativity. Creative science education is active and child-centred, involving individual problem-solving and exploration and not more passive learning approaches which published schemes, CD ROMs and schemes of work appear to advocate. Creative science practitioners make their own decisions about teaching styles and learning experiences, producing novel ideas for achieving objectives to the benefit of the children's learning. They are enthusiastic about science education and balance the needs of the whole curriculum with those of children's creative development (Boden, 2001). Excellent science practitioners have been identified (Fraser and Tobin, 1993) as those who manage their classrooms effectively, use teaching strategies which focus on the children's understanding, provide learning environments which suit the children's learning preferences, have a strong content knowledge and encourage children's involvement in classroom discussions and activities. More recently, excellent science teachers have been recognised by Chartered Science Teacher Status (see Association for Science Education and Science Council websites) as those whose teaching is informed by the personal scholarship and research.

REFLECTIVE TASK

Look at Figure 9.3 and decide what you think is good teaching and learning in science.

Pedagogical approaches in science can fall along two continua, constructivist/ positivist & traditionalist/ post-modernist (Longbottom, 1999) as seen in Figure 9.3.

Highly-structured, teacher-led approaches are ones in which the teacher imparts scientific knowledge, demonstrates concepts and instructs pupils in the use of equipment. These approaches fall within the

(Continued)

(Continued)

traditionalist/positivist sector and are the least creative type of approaches. More creative are teacher-led explorations, where the teacher sets up and structures explorations and investigations to enable pupils to construct their own scientific conceptions and develop skills. These fall into the traditionalist/constructivist sector. Even more creative science education involves exploration and discovery where teachers guide pupils and support the construction of understandings through scientific challenge and discourse. These type of approaches fall into the constructivist/post-modernist sector. Other creative approaches engage pupils in the discussion and argumentation of scientific understanding and abstract ideas and these fall into the positivist/post-modernist sector.

TRADITIONALIST
Emphasis on authority, dissemination, imparting knowledge and training skills

Highly structured teacher-led instruction/ demonstration

Teacher-led exploration

Structured teacher-led instruction/ demonstration

Structured teacher-led exploration

POSITIVIST

CONSTRUCTIVIST
Constructing understanding from experience

Pursuit of knowledge as a truth

Exploration

Debate/discussion/argumentation

Discovery

POST-MODERNIST
Emphasis on engaging with issues/ideas and challenging interpretations

Figure 9.3 How pedagogical approaches fit into the constructivist/positivist and traditionalist/post-modernist continua (Longbottom, 1999)

Student and teacher views of creativity in science education

In one piece of research (Johnston and Ahtee, 2006), I compared 98 student teachers' attitudes, towards teaching physics activities with their attitudes towards teaching their mother tongue (English), mathematics, and science using a previously validated semantic differential questionnaire with 20 bipolar adjective pairs (Ahtee and Rikkinen, 1995; Ahtee and Tella, 1995). The semantic differential (SD) is a method of observing and measuring the connotative meaning of concepts (Osgood *et al.*, 1967). The scoring adopted was +2, +1, 0, −1, −2 with high positive scores signifying a positive attitude. The bipolar adjectives were grouped in four broad categories with five pairs in each.

- *Level of Difficulty* (easy/difficult, self-evident/abstract, commonplace/mystical, simple/complicated, productive/trivial);
- *Level of Interest and Involvement* (interesting/boring, gripping/undesirable, active/passive, social/individual, practical/theoretical);
- *Perceived Nature* (free/compulsory, open/closed, creative/non-creative, cheerful/sad, broadening/constricting);
- *Perceived Value* (valuable/worthless, profound/superficial, wise/foolish, selfish/unselfish, sublime/ridiculous).

PRACTICAL TASK PRACTICAL TASK PRACTICAL TASK PRACTICAL TASK PRACTICAL TASK

Decide for yourself which of the bipolar adjectives (as above) you feel describes science

Compare your results with the students in Figure 9.4.

The results, as seen in Figure 9.4, show that science education is viewed as less creative than English teaching, but physics education is not viewed as creative and mathematics (sometimes referred to as the purest of sciences) is considered to be the least creative educational subject.

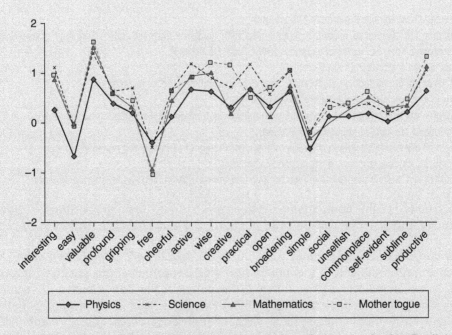

Figure 9.4 Student teachers' attitudes to the teaching of science, physics, English (mother tongue) and mathematics

I once asked experienced teachers (see Johnston, 2013) to explore their perception of science education by asking them to identify how it fitted into the constructivist/positivist and traditionalist/post-modernist continua described earlier and shown in Figure 9.3 (Longbottom, 1999). This indicated that teachers had a more creative perception of science education, with recognition of its multi-faceted nature and the importance of scientific learning relevant to everyday life. However, I was unsure whether these views were reflected in the science that is taught in school and so, in a further piece of research, student teachers' espoused philosophical views of primary science teaching were compared with their planning and practice.

The student group involved ten science specialist initial teacher training students at the beginning of their second year of undergraduate work. At the start of a module on the science curriculum, the students were asked to identify their pedagogical views on science education by identifying where they felt science education fitted into the two continua shown in Figure 9.4. Of the 10 students involved, five placed science teaching and learning at the centre of the continua. Four students felt that science teaching and learning was firmly in the constructivist/post-modernist sector and one student felt that it was very slightly in the positivist/traditionalist sector. There followed some teaching on good practice in science teaching and learning and individual planning of science teaching. Finally, student interaction with 30 Year 3 children, whilst engaged in 'discovery learning approach', was observed. Observations of their practice identified the approaches as falling into four out of five categories, from highly creative guided discovery to highly structured, teacher-led imposition of knowledge,

1. Guided discovery and exploration (0 students):
   Children are allowed to explore independently, with guidance from the teacher, by way of appropriate interaction, such as incidental questions (DES, 1967: DfES 2003).
2. Teacher-led exploration (4 students):
   Children are led through an exploration, with almost complete teacher involvement.
3. Structured teacher-led exploration (3 students):
   Children are led through an exploration, with teacher instructions and complete teacher involvement.
4. Structured teacher-led imposition (1 student):
   Children are directly taught knowledge through instruction, questioning and practical activity.
5. Highly structured, teacher-led imposition (2 students):
   Children are directly taught knowledge through instruction, questioning and teacher demonstration.

The results for the comparison between the student teachers' espoused views, planning and practice can be seen in Figure 9.5 and shows that there is very little correlation between their espoused views, planning and practice. The *Creative Little Scientists* project findings (CLS, 2013) endorse these findings and identify that teachers find it difficult to identify and provide opportunities for creativity in practice. This may indicate a tension between espoused beliefs on the nature of science education and the implicit message within the science national curriculum, both past and present, which emphasizes science as *knowledge consisting of relationships between self-evident variables that are related in regular law-like ways* (Monk and Dillon 2000, p80) – in other words, science as empiricism. This is not a new phenomenon, as research has found (e.g. Taber, 2002) that the wealth of knowledge on constructivist science teaching has not had a significant effect on the content of science education. However, this tension can only have a negative impact on creative teaching and learning, as new practitioners struggle to come to terms with the ideological rhetoric of creative science education and pragmatic classroom reality. There is indeed a need for coherence between policy and practice (van den Akker, 2010; CLS, 2013).

Student	Views	Planning	Practice
1	Central	Exploratory (C/PM)	Structured teacher-led exploration with a focus on knowledge (T/C)
2	Central	Structured teacher-led (T/P)	Highly structured, teacher-led with a focus on knowledge (T/P)
3	Traditionalist/Positivist (T/P)	Exploratory (C/PM)	Structured teacher-led exploration with a focus on knowledge (T/C)
4	Central	Structured teacher-led exploratory (T/C)	Teacher-led exploration with a focus on knowledge (T/C)
5	Constructivist/Post-modernist (C/PM)	Structured exploratory (T/C)	Teacher-led exploration with a focus on knowledge (T/C)
6	Central	Structured teacher-led (T/P)	Highly structured, teacher-led with a focus on knowledge (T/P)
7	Constructivist/Post-modernist (C/PM)	Exploratory group work with teacher cue cards (T/C)	Teacher-led exploration with a focus on knowledge (T/C)
8	Constructivist/Post-modernist (C/PM)	Structured teacher-led with some problem-solving (T/P)	Teacher-led exploration with a focus on knowledge (T/C)
9	Constructivist/Post-modernist (C/PM)	Structured teacher-led (T/P)	Structured teacher-led with a focus on knowledge (T/P)
10	Central	Teacher-led experiment (T/P)	Structured teacher-led exploration with a focus on knowledge (T/C)

Key	T/C = Traditionalist/Constructivist	C/PM = Constructivist/Post-modernist
	PM/P = Post-modernist/Positivist	T/P = Traditionalist/Positivist

Figure 9.5 The relationship between the student teachers' views on science education, planning and practice

REFLECTIVE TASK
BEFLECTIVE TASK

Compare your planning and practice to your ideas in Figure 9.3. Is there a gap between your beliefs about good teaching and learning in science and how you teach?

Problem-solving or inquiry-based science activities can help learners of all ages develop scientific understandings as well as understandings of the nature of science. These can be simple problem solving activities in the sand tray, such as *How can you make a stronger sand castle?* They can involve children making a strong bridge or a waterproof hat. They can involve solving collaborative problems, such as designing and making a one-minute timer, a series of energy transfers which take one minute from start to finish. For example, lighting a candle can burn through a thread and release a ramp, down which a ball bearing will roll. This may roll down a maze and then be attracted to a magnet pushing a needle into a balloon which bursts. This variation of a mousetrap game can be undertaken by learners of all ages, as they will apply and build upon their initial knowledge and produce a timer which demonstrates their understanding of different types of energy transfers (light, heat, mechanical, kinetic, magnetic and sound). In some recent research (Johnston, 2013), I identified that problem-solving activities were significantly better at generating predictions and hypotheses with scientific causal links than explorations and exploratory play and supported more developed thinking skills.

Why is creativity in science education important?

While there have been disputes among psychologists as to whether creativity is a characteristic of the highly intelligent (e.g. Munn, 1966), it is also considered to be a potential in all of us which needs encouragement and motivation to flourish (Medawar, 1969). Creative science education is recognised by the European Commission (2011) as needing to foster positive attitudes, enhance knowledge about the world, develop skills and understandings associated with inquiry and promote a questioning and investigative approach to learning. It will involve planning for and responding to creative pupil ideas and this has been found (QCA, 2003) to develop curiosity, motivation, self-esteem and academic achievement, as well as having a positive effect on adult life skills. Creative children are more likely to be creative adults, who can solve problems, take risks and be motivated to continue to learn, because *education is not the filling of a pail but the lighting of a fire* (incidentally, this quote of uncertain derivation is often incorrectly attributed to the poet WB Yeats).

REFLECTIVE TASK

Creative science educational experiences have three essential elements: they should be practical, memorable and interactive. The importance of practical exploratory approaches in scientific development is well established (see Harlen, 2012) and has been seen in many learning models in science, including the constructivist approach (Scott, 1987), which has become increasingly popular in science education. Practical science will develop important scientific skills and generic cognitive skills, such as problem-solving and thinking skills. Scientific thinking skills can be developed by:

- **challenging children's ideas, by getting them to test out their hypotheses;**
- **setting problems for them to solve;**
- **discussing their ideas and compare with the ideas of others;**
- **encouraging them to make causal links;**

> Through practical activities and discussion of ideas (Alexander, 2008) children develop thinking in science in the early years (Johnston 2011) and in older children (Erduran, 2012; Shayer and Adey, 2002). Through explorations, problem-solving and discussions, children begin to explain their ideas, think hypothetically (Erduran, 2012; CLS , 2012) and make causal links between phenomena and their hypothetical ideas. They can also identify their metacognitive processes, i.e. how they solved problems or the thinking behind their interpretations and hypotheses (Shayer and Adey, 2002; Fisher, 2003).
>
> Consider how thinking skills can be developed within the National Curriculum (DfE, 2013). How can you teach the statutory requirements to promote creativity in children?

I once asked Key Stage 1 children to explore a collection of toys in a toy box, after reading *Kipper's Toybox* (Inkpen, 1992). They handled the toys and were encouraged to play with them, exploring how they worked. The children were then encouraged to sort the toys according to their properties, putting them into sorting hoops. All the spinning toys were put into one hoop, all the magnetic toys in another, pushing toys in another and jumping toys in another. A magnetic gyroscope which spins on a metal frame with two metal rails, caused a few problems as this was both a spinner and magnetic. One child decided that we could place the gyroscope between the spinning and magnetic hoops, so that it touched both. Another child suggested that we could separate the two parts of the gyroscope and put the spinning part in the spinning hoop and the metal frame in the magnetic hoop (although it was not itself magnetic). A third child suggested an alternative solution, by overlapping the hoops so that there was another section for magnetic spinning toys. This was a good example of children developing and using their thinking skills to solve simple problems. Further research looking at the skill of observation in children from 4 to 11 years of age (Johnston, 2012) has identified the importance of providing time, space and support for children to enable them to think creatively and solve problems. *Cognitive acceleration*, whole class, group debates or discussions which involve an element of argument are proven to be successful in developing skills and understandings in science and across primary education as well as generic thinking skills (Shayer and Adey, 2002; Johnston, 2013; CLS, 2012).

Memorable science education supports the development of important motivating attitudes (Johnston, 2005; CLS, 2012), such as curiosity, which is essential in harnessing children's interest, encouraging them to take risks, make scientific discoveries and construct scientific understandings. Attitudes can usually be observed in some kind of behaviour and the importance of the resulting behaviours is thought to affect development in science (Johnston, 2013). Attitudes can be:

- generic, that is those needed throughout education (co-operation and perseverance);
- scientific, that is those that are important in science education (respect for evidence and tentativeness);
- affective or emotional (enthusiasm);
- cognitive (curiosity, respect for evidence, thoughtfulness, reflection, tentativeness, questioning);
- social or behavioural (co-operation, collaboration, tolerance, flexibility, independence, perseverance, leadership, responsibility, tenaciousness).

Creative science education can help to develop many of these attitudes, by motivating children to want to explore and discover, encouraging them to work co-operatively and support their cognitive development.

Children need to interact with their environment, their peers and supportive adults in creative science experiences. Creative science learning environments will encourage cognitive development; *encompassing milieus, in which the messages of learning and work are manifest and inviting* (Gardner, 1991, p204). Interacting with others will encourage them to consider the ideas of others and develop thinking skills (Shayer and Adey, 2002). Interaction with supportive adults can challenge ideas and interpretations, with the role of the adult being to facilitate learning rather than impart knowledge, recognizing that creative science education is an active rather than a passive experience in which an adult supports children in the development of skills and understandings, which can later be applied in other contexts and everyday life.

Why is it difficult to be a creative science teacher?

Creative science teaching and learning is thought to pose problems particularly regarding time, coverage, control, safety and achievement of learning objectives. In practice, creative science can effectively address all these issues and make learning fun for both practitioner and child.

The science curriculum contains an enormous amount of material and one pedagogical solution is to impart knowledge, as this takes less time than exploration, discovery or investigation. The difficulty of covering the curriculum, together with the understandable fear of a whole class practically exploring and investigating in science, sometimes leads to the type of teaching approaches advocated in literacy and numeracy. This means that some science lessons become whole-class demonstrations which impart knowledge to children en masse. For teachers who are lacking in confidence in science and inexperienced in teaching this approach to science education appears to be an effective way to manage the demands of the curriculum and maintain good levels of behaviour, controlling children's learning and ensuring safety. In fact, such an approach leads to poor-quality learning. Effective science learning occurs through teaching approaches which engage and interest children (CLS, 2012), approaches which are practical, developing skills alongside understandings and paying attention to detail rather than coverage and where practitioners facilitate individual or small group learning, bearing in mind individual learning abilities and styles (Gardner, 1983).

Science curricula often address ideas and knowledge in a *fragmented way* (Osborne and Dillon, 2008, p8) and so a recommendation from a report on science education in Europe is that there should be *more innovative curricula and ways of organising the teaching of science that address the issue of low student motivation* (Osborne and Dillon, 2008, p8). This is also endorsed by the more recent report from the European Commission (2011) and identifies the need to apply creative ideas more specifically to teaching and learning (see also DfE, 2010). The very large demands of the science curriculum can be effectively covered by practically focusing on small aspects of conceptual understanding rather than *fragmented* knowledge and when set in a motivating context which children can relate to. Practical work (explorations, investigations, problem-solving and guided discovery) will support the development of scientific skills through working scientifically (DfE, 2013) which cannot be achieved in a non-practical way. The focus on conceptual understanding will help children to apply their scientific knowledge in new contexts and support their development in other scientific concepts. Effective and creative science education does take time for children to explore investigate and discover new ideas. It does involve giving children time and encouragement to support their explorations, discoveries and also support their behaviour. Behaviour is improved by child-centred, creative scientific activities; in fact, we can have greater control over behaviour and learning by being less controlling. It is therefore worrying that there are indications from research (Murphy, *et al.*, 2005; SCORE, 2008) that teachers are undertaking less practical work. The demands of the 'knowledge-based' national curriculum, behavioural management issues and assessment demands are all contributory factors.

Whole-class directed scientific learning does not allow children to develop their own understanding, implying that all children need the same experiences and that the practitioner knows exactly what is best for each learner. In fact, children's development is more effective when they are motivated to learn, take ownership over their own learning and work with practitioners to develop knowledge, understanding, skills and attitudes.

Within the primary strategy, creative science education becomes a reality by:

- *making learning vivid and real, by developing understanding through enquiry, creativity, e-learning and group problem-solving;*
- *making learning an enjoyable and challenging experience, by stimulating learning through matching teaching to learning styles and preferences;*
- *enriching the learning experience, by developing learning skills across the curriculum.*

(DfES, 2003, p29)

For many practitioners the problem is how to incorporate the features of effective creative science education, but maintain the rigour and focus on key objectives for development and learning. Scientific concepts, knowledge and skills are static and unchanging, so that creative science activities are almost impossible to deliver. We need to remember that many aspects of science will be new for children and have the potential to inspire them. We can also be creative in our teaching, especially when we become confident ourselves in scientific understanding. Every teacher has the potential for creativity, in the same way that every child has. Too often our creativity in science education is adversely affected by our lack of scientific understanding and we are unable to use our creativity in our teaching.

REFLECTIVE TASK

Do creative children need creative teachers?

If we lack creativity in our teaching, we will structure and control all aspects of learning and restrict any creativity on the part of children. They will be unable to take alternative viewpoints, solve problems, challenge interpretations and their understandings are likely to be less sophisticated. If we allow children some freedom to explore their own ideas and value their alternative views of the world, then we support creativity and learning.

How can you be more creative in your science teaching?

How can we be more creative in our teaching?

Effective, creative science teaching and learning can be best achieved by providing motivating exploratory and investigatory experiences for children. One form of creative science involves structured exploratory discovery learning (Johnston, 2004). Discovery learning (DES, 1967) was popular in the 1960s and 1970s, although over time it was seen to involve children playing without purpose or learning objectives and did not take into account existing conceptual ideas of the world they had developed from birth. This definition has been updated for modern teaching and so an exploratory discovery approach is one where:

- *the child is central to the learning;*
- *children explore and discover things about the world around them, which stem from their own initial curiosity;*
- *children construct their own understandings through exploration and from the experience of discovery, as well as develop important skills and attitudes;*
- *teachers support and encourage children to ensure that their explorations and discoveries are meaningful to them;*
- *teachers utilize knowledge about the children as learners (e.g. Gardner 1983) and pedagogical theory and practice to provide an excellent learning environment.*

(Johnston, 2004, pp21–22).

An example of a creative discovery approach is a potions lesson (after Harry Potter, Rowling, 1997, see Johnston, 2005), which I have carried out with children from Year 2 to Year 6. This begins as a fairly formal lesson with me wearing an academic gown and in role as a Hogwart's supply teacher. During the lesson, the children predict and investigate what will happen if they mix small amounts of substances with water in clear plastic beakers. The substances include unidentified solids (salt, sugar, cornflour, talcum powder, bicarbonate of soda and plaster of Paris) and liquids (white vinegar, detergent, lemonade, cooking oil, lemon juice and colour change bubble bath). Through investigation the children will experience dissolving (salt and sugar), solutions (cornflour, bicarbonate of soda, lemon juice), density (talcum powder, oil and plaster of Paris) and colour change (bubble bath). Later, the lesson becomes more exploratory with children discovering what happens when they mix different substances together in different proportions (vinegar and bicarbonate of soda fizz, plaster of Paris and water produce heat) and they can even write instructions for their potion and identify what effects it will have through an advertisement or jingle. In this way children are developing scientific skills (observation, prediction and hypothesis) and understanding (the way materials change when mixed) through a creative, cross curricular activity that will motivate them.

Problem-solving is another example of creative science and can vary from the small challenges given to children while they explore or play to specific problems that involve the use of scientific skills and knowledge, sometimes in a technological context. While young children play in the sand, water or discover materials through a potion exploration, the practitioner can challenge them by asking questions,

- What will happen if you add water to the sand?
- How can you make a water spout?
- How can you make the potion change colour/fizz/...?

Design a ball sorter where balls of different sizes and made of different materials (polystyrene balls, marbles, ball bearings, golf balls, table tennis balls, tennis balls etc) have to be sorted by a machine made out of a large cardboard box and other junk materials.

Criteria for sorting can include size, density, mass, magnetic etc.

You can also do this activity with children. They are expected to work together in small groups to make accurate, original machines which sort the balls in a number of different ways. At the end of the activity, the machines can be tested and certificates given to groups for originality of design, accuracy of sorting, number of different ways of sorting and group collaboration skills. In this way children are developing skills in designing and making (DT) as well as planning and knowledge and understanding of forces and materials. You can make sure that each group receives a certificate and this can be an added motivational factor.

For younger children, play areas such as a garden centre or bakery (Johnston, 2013) can lead to scientific learning about plant growth or materials and properties in a cross-curricular way. In these play experiences, children can develop their own understandings at a rate and in a way that is appropriate. Some children will learn best when interacting with other children, while others will be much more solitary in their play but still make good developmental progress.

A SUMMARY OF **KEY POINTS**

➢ Creativity is not a description that is generally attributed to science.

➢ Historically, creativity is an essential factor in the scientific discoveries of many famous scientists, such as Darwin, Leonardo da Vinci and Archimedes.

➢ Science education sits in a difficult position between more creative education and less creative and less flexible science.

➢ Creative science educational experiences should be practical, memorable and interactive.

➢ Children need creative teachers to be creative learners.

➢ Creative science teaching involves challenging and changing approaches and adapting teaching to suit learners.

➢ The problems of including creative science activities in teaching are time, coverage, control, safety and achievement. However, the benefits in terms of future development outweigh the problems.

MOVING *ON* > > > > > >   MOVING *ON* > > > > > >   MOVING *ON*

- Try planning and teaching some creative science activities and evaluate their effect on children's learning and behaviour.
- Try working with more experienced and confident science teachers, within your school, to make the experience more rewarding for you professionally and personally and to help you to understand the scientific concepts underpinning the activities.

- Look for external support from the Association for Science Education, local and national science education conferences and publications and websites (see below for some useful websites).

REFERENCES REFERENCES **REFERENCES** REFERENCES REFERENCES REFERENCES

Ahtee, M and Rikkinen, H (1995) Luokanopettajaksi opiskelevien mielikuvia fysiikasta, kemiasta, biologiasta ja maantieteestä, Dimensio (Primary student teachers' images about physics, chemistry, biology and geography), 59, pp. 54–58.

Ahtee, M and Tella, S (1995) Future class teachers' images of their school-time teachers of physics, mathematics and foreign languages. In Tella, S. (ed.) *Juuret ja arvot: Etnisyys ja eettisyys – aineen opettaminen monikultturisessa oppimisympäristössä. (Roots and values: Ethnicity and ethics – Teaching a subject in a multi-cultural learning environment.)* Proceedings of a subject-didactic symposium in Helsinki. Department of Teacher Education. University of Helsinki. Research Report 150, 180–200.

Alexander, R (2008) *Towards Dialogic Teaching: Rethinking Classroom Talk (4th Edition).* York: Dialogos.

Beetlestone, F (1998) *Creative Children, Imaginative Teaching.* Buckingham: Open University Press.

Boden, MA (2001) Creativity and Knowledge in Craft, A, Jeffrey, B. and Leibling, M. (2001) *Creativity in Education.* London: Continuum.

CLS (2012) *Creative Little Scientists: Enabling Creativity through Science and Mathematics in Preschool and First Years of Primary Education. D2.2 Conceptual Framework.* Available at **www.creative-little-scientists.eu** accessed 11/8/14.

CLS (2013) *Creative Little Scientists: Enabling Creativity through Science and Mathematics in Preschool and First Years of Primary Education. D4.3 Country Reports*

Report 9 of 9: Country Report on in-depth field work in the UK. Available at **www.creative-little-scientists.eu** accessed 11/8/14.

Crompton, Z (2013) 'What is Science? Some Research from Primary Schools.' In Education in Science No. 253 September 2013 pp. 12–13.

de Bono (1992) *Serious Creativity.* London: Harper Collins.

DES (1967) *Children and their Primary school. A report of the Central Advisory Council for Education (England) Vol. 1: Report.* London: HMSO.

DfE (2010) *The Importance of Teaching. The Schools White Paper 2010.* London: HMSO.

DfE (2012) Teachers' Standards available at **https://www.gov.uk/government/publications/teachers-standards** accessed 7/9/14.

DfE (2013) *Science Programmes of Study: Key Stages 1 and 2. National Curriculum in England.* London: HMSO.

DfES (2003) *Excellence and Enjoyment. A strategy for primary schools.* London: DfES.

Duffy, B. (1998) *Supporting Creativity and Imagination in the Early Years* Buckingham: Open University Press.

Erduran, S (2012) 'The Role of Dialogue and Argumentation'. In Oversby, J (ed) (2012) *ASE Guide to Research in Science Education.* Hatfield: ASE pp. 106–116.

European Commission, (2011) *Science education in Europe: National policies practices and research*, Education, Audiovisual and Culture Executive Agency EACEAE9 Eurydice, Brussels: Education, Audiovisual and Culture Executive Agency.

Fisher, R (2003) *Teaching Thinking* London: Continuum.

Fraser, B and Tobin, K (1993) Exemplary science and mathematics teachers. In B. Fraser (ed), *Research Implications for Science and Mathematics Teachers, Volume 1.* Perth, WA: National Key Centre for School Science and Mathematics, Curtin University of Technology.

Gardner, H (1983) *Frames of Mind: The Theory of Multiple Intelligences.* London: Heinemann.

Gardner, H (1991) *The Unschooled Mind.* London: Fontana.

Hall, K and Øzerk, K (2008) *Primary Curriculum and Assessment: England and other countries. Primary Review Interim Report.* Cambridge: Primary Review, University of Cambridge.

Harlen, W (2012) 'Scientific Inquiry'. In Oversby, J (ed) (2012) *ASE Guide to Research in Science Education.* Hatfield: ASE pp98–105.

Inkpen, M (1992) *Kipper's Toybox.* London: Hodder.

Johnston, J (2004) The Value of Exploration and Discovery in *Primary Science Review* 85: 21–23 Nov/Dec 2004.

Johnston, J (2005) *Early Explorations in Science Second Edition.* Buckingham: Open University Press.

Johnston, J (2011) 'Children Talking; Teachers Supporting Science'. *Journal of Emergent Science.* No. 1 pp14–22 **www.ase.org.uk/journals/** accessed 11/8/14.

Johnston, J (2012). The Development and Support of Observational Skills in children Under 4 Years of Age. *Journal of Emergent Science.* No. 2 **www.ase.org.uk/journals/** accessed 11/8/14.

Johnston, J (2013) *Emergent Science. Teaching Birth to 8.* London: Routledge.

Johnston, J, Ahtee, M and Hayes, M (1998) 'Elementary Teachers' Perceptions of Science and Science Teaching: Comparisons between Finland and England'. Kartinen, S. (ed.) Matemaattisten aineiden opetus ja opiminem. Oulu: Oulun yliopistopaino: 13–30.

Johnston, J and Ahtee, M (2006) 'What are Primary Student Teachers' Attitudes, Subject Knowledge and Pedagogical Content Knowledge Needs in a Physics Topic?' Teaching and Teacher Education Vol. 22. No. 4: 1–10.

Longbottom, J (1999) Science Education for Democracy: Dilemmas, Decisions, Autonomy and Anarchy. Paper presented to the *European Science Education Research Association Second International Conference,* Kiel, Germany.

Medawar, PB (1969) *Induction and Intuition in Scientific Thought. Memoirs of the American Philosophical Society. Jayne Lectures 1968.* London: Methuen.

Monk, M and Dillon, J (2000) 'The Nature of Science Knowledge' in Monk, M and Osborne, J (eds) *Good Practice in Science Teaching: What research has to say.* Buckingham: Open University Press.

Munn, N (1966) *Psychology, 5th edn.* London: Harrap.

Murphy, P, Beggs, J and Russell, T. (2005) *Primary Horizons: Starting Out in Science* London: Wellcome Trust.

Naylor, S and Keogh, B (2012) 'Creativity in Science'. In Oversby, J (ed) (2012) *ASE Guide to Research in Science Education.* Hatfield: ASE pp83–90.

Ofsted (2003) The Education of Six Year Olds in England, Denmark and Finland London: HMI.

Osborne, J and Dillon, J (2008) *Science Education in Europe: Critical Reflections. A Report to the Nuffield Foundation.* London: Nuffield Foundation.

Osgood, CE, Suci, GJ and Tannenbaum, P. H. (1967) *The Measurement of Meaning* (Chicago, University of Illinois Press).

QCA (2003) *Creativity: Find it Promote it.* London: QCA/DFEE.

Rowling, JK (1997) *Harry Potter and the Philosopher's* Stone London: Bloomsbury.

SCORE (Science Community Representing Education), (2008) *Practical Work in Science: A Report and Proposal for a Strategic Framework.* London: Gatsby Technical Education Projects.

Scott, P (1987) *A Constructivist View of Teaching and Learning Science.* Leeds: Leeds University.

Shayer, M and Adey, P (2002) (eds.) *Learning Intelligence. Cognitive Acceleration Across the Curriculum from 5 to 15 Years,* Buckingham; Open University Press.

Taber, KS (2002) 'The constructivist view of learning: how can it inform assessment?' invited presentation to the *University of Cambridge Local Examinations Syndicate (UCLES) Research and Evaluation Division (RED).* 27th May 2002.

van den Akker, J (2010) Building bridges: how research improve curriculum policies and classroom practices. Beyond Lisbon 2010: perspectives from research and development for education policy in Europe. Available at: **curriculuminnovation.mixxt.org/networks/files/download.101462** accessed 11/8/14.

Useful Websites

Association for Science Education **www.ase.org.uk**

Science Council **www.sciencecouncil.org**

Teaching, Thinking and Creativity www.teachingtimeslibrary.co.uk

Creative Little Scientists **www.creative-little-scientists.eu**

- all websites *accessed 11/8/14.*

PART 3
CREATIVITY IN THE FOUNDATION CURRICULUM

10
Thinking about creativity: developing ideas and making things happen
Avril Loveless

Chapter objectives

This chapter will raise some questions and discussions to help you to think about:

- **how we might recognise creativity in ourselves, in other people, in our communities and in our wider societies;**
- **how these ideas about creativity can be expressed and developed through using digital tools;**
- **how we might approach our own teaching to reflect creativity for our pupils and for ourselves.**

This chapter addresses the following Teachers' Standards (DfE, 2012):

- **set high expectations which inspire, motivate and challenge pupils;**
- **promote good progress and outcomes by children;**
- **demonstrate good subject and curriculum knowledge;**
- **plan and teach well-structured lessons;**
- **adapt teaching to respond to the strengths and needs of all pupils.**

Introduction

How can teachers recognise and promote creativity in their pupils, without a personal understanding of the experience of being creative themselves? This chapter will address some of the conceptual frameworks that we can use to help us recognise and think about creativity, and illustrate some of these theoretical approaches by describing creative practices in a project using digital tools to develop ideas and make things happen.

What makes a person creative?

Poets, sculptors, engineers, photographers, software designers, geographers, jazz musicians, film directors, writers, theologians, political activists and teachers are not often presented together in the same list. This list represents some of the people in my immediate group of friends who I would consider to be 'creative' – but this leaves out many others who express their creativity without having a formal occupation or label. My grandmother Alice, for example, was a 'carder'. She worked in a cotton mill, raised her children in the first half of the twentieth century, and was renowned in the family for her imaginative solutions to practical problems – such as a Heath-Robinson con-traption for washing those awkward upstairs windows. Why should I be thinking about a jazz musician, a teacher and my grandmother in the first paragraph of a chapter in a book on 'Creativity'? What is it that these people have in common, yet enables them to express their individuality and difference? How do we recognise those qualities in their lives? Why do we think that we – as individuals, communities and societies – are richer for knowing such people and for being engaged by their creativity? What wider role do teachers play in both being creative themselves and encouraging creativity in others?

I believe that teaching is a creative activity that requires approaches to imagination, inspiration, preparation, engagement, improvisation and interactive relationship that the more commonly accepted 'creative' professions demand. Teachers in all stages of their professional lives, from initial teacher education to continuing professional development and postgraduate study, need to make time and space to think about creativity in their own lives, as well as in their teaching.

REFLECTIVE TASK

- Make a list – or diagram if you don't like lists – of people you know, who you would describe as 'creative'. Try to identify what it is that you recognise in them.

- Make another list, or diagram, of words and phrases that help you to describe the creative 'qualities' that you see and experience in these people.

Seeing creativity as an interaction

Creativity is possible in all areas of human activity and it draws from all areas of human intelligence.

(Robinson, 2001, p138)

There are some challenging questions to consider when thinking about creativity in education:

- Where do we find creativity? Is it 'in' individual people, or groups, or societies?
- Are there conditions under which creativity can thrive more easily than others, and how does creativity express itself in, or despite adversity?
- How might our understandings of creativity be shaped by wider social, cultural and economic interests?
- How might our education systems, from classrooms to national policy, provide opportunities for creative experiences which engage in the full cycle of creative interactions?

A useful way of looking at, and trying to describe and explain our understandings of crea-tivity, is to consider it as an interaction between characteristics of people and communities, creative processes, subject domains and wider social and cultural contexts. In the 1950s to 1970s, psychologists' interest in creativity focused on areas of personality, cognition and the stimulation of creativity in individuals, but awareness of the influence of social contexts and environments on the creativity of individuals and groups and organisations has developed in the last 20 or 30 years (Rhyammar and Brolin, 1999). *All Our Futures*, the report of the National Advisory Committee on Creative and Cultural Education, defined creativity as, *imaginative activity fashioned so as to produce outcomes that are both original and of value* (NACCCE, 1999, p29). This definition is helpful in that it expresses five characteristics of creativity which can be considered for individual people, as well as the local and wider communities and cultures in which they act:

- *Using imagination* – the process of imaging, supposing and generating ideas which are original, providing an alternative to the expected, the conventional, or the routine;
- *A fashioning process* – the active and deliberate focus of attention and skills in order to shape, refine and manage an idea;
- *Pursuing purpose* – the application of imagination to produce tangible outcomes from purposeful goals. Motivation and sustained engagement are important to the solving of the problem. A quality of experience in the creative activities of fashioning and pursuing purpose have been described as 'flow', where the person's capacity was being stretched despite elements of challenge, difficulty or risk (Csikszentmihalyi, 1996);
- *Being original* – the originality of an outcome which can be at different levels of achievement: individual originality in relation to a person's own previous work; relative originality in relation to a peer group; and historic originality in relation to works which are completely new and unique, such as those produced by Fermat, Hokusai and Thelonius Monk;
- *Judging value* – the evaluative mode of thought which is reciprocal to the generative mode of imaginative activity and provides critical, reflective review from individuals and peers.

Creativity and individuals

If we were asked to name our creative role models, it is likely that we would include many exceptional, perhaps famous, individuals who have expressed creative ideas, activities and outcomes which have enabled us to experience the world differently in some way. They are recognised as contributing ideas and work that is considered to be original and of value in our society. My personal list might include such people as Norman Foster, an architect; Jane Austen, a writer; Picasso, a painter; Isambard Kingdom Brunel, an engineer; Rosalind Franklin, a scientist; Bill Evans, a jazz musician; Emeric Pressburger, a screen writer; Akira Kurosawa, a film director; Anthony Gormley, a sculptor; Anthony DeMello, a priest; and Helen Levitt, a photographer. (Such a list might say quite a lot about how I see and hear the world, and how such people have influenced me). Craft describes the creativity that we ascribe to such exceptional people as 'Big C' creativity, yet she also highlights our concern with the creative potential of all individuals: 'little c creativity' and 'possibility thinking' in a creative approach to life for everybody (Craft, 2000, p3).

There are many examples of the attempts of different writers and thinkers to recognise and describe the personal qualities of creative individuals. Shallcross (1981) described them as: openness to experience; independence; self-confidence; willingness to take risk; sense of humour or playfulness; enjoyment of experimentation; sensitivity; lack of a feeling of being threatened; personal courage; unconventionality; flexibility; preference for complexity; goal orientation; internal control; originality; self-reliance; persistence (cited in Craft, 2000, p13). Another perspective on such personal qualities is described in Sternberg and Lubart's 'confluence model', in which six resources converge: intellectual abilities; knowledge; styles of thinking; personality; motivation and environment (Sternberg and Lubart, 1999) Robinson also offers a useful approach to thinking about individuals being actively creative within a medium, in which they have control, and are able to play, take risks, and exercise critical judgement (Robinson, 2001).

Csikszentmihalyi identifies a common characteristic of creative people as *'flow'* – the automatic, effortless, yet highly focused state of consciousness when engaged in activities, often painful, risky or difficult, which stretch a person's capacity whilst involving an element of novelty or discovery (Csikszentmihalyi, 1996). He elaborates the description of this characteristic in identifying nine elements which such activity provides:

- clear goals;
- immediate feedback;
- balance between challenges and skills;
- merging of action and awareness;
- elimination of distractions;
- lack of fear of failure;
- lack of self-consciousness;
- distortion of sense of time;
- autotelic activity (enjoyment for its own sake).

Individual states of intuition, rumination, reverie, even boredom, play a role in creativity and problem-solving and some studies indicate how creativity is enhanced in a state of reverie and imagery (Claxton, 2000). Such states are not just 'letting it flow' or 'leaving it to luck', but acknowledging a way of knowing which is not necessarily conscious and draws upon resources of knowledge, skill and experience in order to make new combinations, explorations and transformations (Boden, 1992).

It is interesting that these descriptions of creative characteristics, can also be recognised in discussions of what it takes to be a good learner. Alice, in her adventures in Wonderland, met the Mock Turtle and Gryphon who told her about their lessons in Reeling, Writhing and the different branches of Arithmetic – Ambition, Distraction, Uglification and Derision. Guy Claxton speaks of a different classification of the '3Rs', indeed, he names four: Resilience, Reflection, Resourcefulness and Relationship (Claxton, 1999). Good learners, and creative people, need to be able to encounter and cope with puzzles, problems, seeming failure and disappointment, in order to learn from these experiences and demonstrate perseverance and resilience. They also develop their abilities to think about patterns and connections, and reflect upon how new situations might relate to earlier experiences or need novel solutions. They know how to draw upon a wide range of resources to help them solve problems, from materials and memories to networks of other people. They also know how to be aware of, and engage in, relationship with other people and places.

REFLECTIVE TASK
REFLECTIVE TASK

- **Who would you describe as creative people who have enabled you to think differently about aspects of the world?**
- **How have they demonstrated imagination, fashioning, purpose, originality and value in their field?**
- **How have you been able to demonstrate various creative characteristics in your own life?**
- **How have you been able to demonstrate resilience, reflection, resourcefulness and relationship in your own life?**

Creativity and communities

Generative ideas emerge from joint thinking, from significant conversations, and from sustained, shared struggles to achieve new insights by partners in thought.

(John-Steiner, 2000, p3)

The creativity of individuals can flourish or be stifled within the communities in which they act. These communities can be in families, peer-groups, schools, workplaces, and wider society and culture, and are also expressed in the physical as well as cultural environments in which we develop. It is, therefore important to recognise the potential of interactions between people and their communities, and the opportunities for design of environments for nurturing creativity within those communities.

Western individualism – and romantic images of poverty-stricken artists struggling to create their work in isolated garrets – have contributed to our ideas of creativity being located within individuals. These people, however, rarely work in isolation. Their ideas and outcomes may be highly original and iconoclastic, but they are likely to have been generated through interaction with other people's ideas and reactions. It is no accident that many exceptionally creative people tell tales of their supportive families, or engaging network of friends, or group of like-minded people in studios or laboratories. Vera John-Steiner's work with creative people, explores the essential nature of their collaborations with others, in which they can challenge, discuss and try out their ideas (John-Steiner, 2000). She discusses the influences upon creative work of the intimate relationship between partners such as Simone de Beauvoir and Jean-Paul Sartre, or Pierre and Marie Curie – and highlights the patterns of collaboration between artists such as Picasso and Braque who encouraged and challenged each other, learned from each other, and were transformed by working together. As well as these 'Big C' creative collaborations, she notes a large number of groups who work together and acknowledge the shared nature of their thinking and knowing – from writing plays to scientific discoveries.

An interesting focus of her work is on the importance of mentorship and inter-generational creative collaborations, in which senior participants provide continuity, guidance and a 'new embodiment' of complex knowledge by working with younger people with energy and fresh approaches to questions in the field. Our traditions of 'apprenticeship' are rooted in this type of collaboration in which experts think and work with novices to mutual benefit, and provide interesting models for the relationships between teachers and pupils as 'expert' and 'novice' learners.

Of all the communities and places in our society, one might expect that schools would be creative and enriching learning communities. We are, however, sadly familiar with experiences of schools in which approaches to active learning and the development of creativity have been lacking in the general ethos, the physical environment, the organisation of the curriculum and the appropriation of the pressures for improvement measured by attainment in a narrow range. Bragg and Manchester's study of creativity and ethos in a primary school drew attention to the ways in which the concept of 'ethos' is a nebulous and contested term which can be used to denote conformity in behaviour and effective performance. They defined ethos as: embodying values and vision which are official and unofficial; often taken for granted and not easily articulated by insiders; emerging from everyday processes of relationships and interactions: and the material and social aspects of the environment; and continually negotiated (Bragg and Manchester, 2011).

One example of a school which addresses these issues and expresses its identity as a creative community is Coombes County Infant and Nursery School. Jeffrey and Woods (2003) offer an inspiring account of the Coombes' ethos, described through the themes of dynamism, appreciation, captivation and care which permeates the learning and teaching activities. The everyday knowledge of the wider community is drawn upon and celebrated in the activities of the school that are grounded in the cycles of the natural world, and local and global communities. The learning environment encompasses all the space, both inside and outside the school. It draws upon the imaginative development of the school grounds as extensions to the physical space of the classrooms, corridors, resource areas and meeting halls, attaching the curriculum to the cycles and connections of natural life on the doorstep and in the wider world. The spaces in the school are 'Aladdin's caves', representing the range of activity and experience through resources and displays which provoke responses, questions, enquiry, development of ideas and celebration of the pupils' achievements.

> *What matters is not just the substantive knowledge, but the maze-like structure of the knowledge and the interdependence of its many different parts and forms.*

> (Jeffrey and Woods, 2003, p94)

REFLECTIVE TASK

- Think about the different communities in which you have lived, worked and engaged with other people. What were the characteristics of those you felt encouraged your creativity, and what were the characteristics of those you felt inhibited your creativity?

- How would you envisage developing the physical and virtual spaces in your own classroom and school to promote a creative learning environment, ethos and community?

Creative processes

Anthony DeMello described an image of God's relationship with creation developed in Hindu India as God 'dancing' creation.

> *He is the dancer, creation is his dance. The dance is different from the dancer; yet it has no existence apart from him. You cannot take it home in a box if it pleases you. The moment the dancer stops, the dance ceases to be.*

> (De Mello, 1984, p14)

Creativity can be thought of as the 'dance', which does not exist separately from the people who are performing the dance. Creative processes are an expression of the individuals and groups engaging in them, not activities that are independent of them. They can be modelled, encouraged, and nurtured, rather than transmitted. Being able to take risks is the next level in which the person engages in the 'creativity cycle' of preparation, letting go, germination, assimilation, completion and preparation. Robinson emphasises the need to recognise that creativity involves *doing something* – in different subject areas, with different media and materials: *Whatever the task, creativity is not just an internal mental process: it involves action. In a sense, it is applied imagination.* (Robinson, 2001, p115). These processes express, shape and encourage creativity as an approach to life.

Trying to identify creative processes helps us to think about how we recognise when creativity 'is going on'. We can't lift off the top of people's heads to see if they are thinking more creative thoughts at one time rather than another; but we can see and discuss how they express creativity through their behaviours, activities, experiences and outcomes. The NACCCE definition of creativity encompasses processes of imagining, fashioning, pursuit of purpose, and evaluation of originality and value. We can also overlay these processes with behaviours of questioning and challenging, making connections and seeing relationships, envisaging what might be, playing with ideas, representing ideas and evaluating the effects of ideas.

Thus people and communities engage in these processes using a wide variety of tools and media to express and fashion their imaginative ideas. A musician, a mathematician, or a marine biologist would each approach their endeavours by asking 'what's going on here and would happen if....'; playing with ideas and materials; paying close attention to cause and effects; practising and refining techniques and skills; standing back and evaluating the outcomes; and learning from experiences in order to engage in the processes in new situations. Sculptors might work with stone; engineers with steel; photographers with film; multimedia designers with pixels – each is working and fashioning with chosen media to represent and express their imaginings. Digital technologies can be used as tools in creative activity in physical and virtual learning environments, and for developing ideas; making connections; creating and making; collaboration and communication and evaluation (Loveless, 2007a).

REFLECTIVE TASK

- Think of a variety of creative outcomes or artefacts – from a dance to a design for a new toothbrush or a digital representation – and imagine how the 'creators' engaged in a range of creative processes in order to realise their ideas.
- List the different media and tools that were used to create these outcomes.
- When do you have the opportunities to pose a problem and apply your imagination?

Creativity in subject domains

Where is the life we have lost in living?
Where is the wisdom we have lost in knowledge?
Where is the knowledge we have lost in information?

(T.S. Eliot 'The Rock', 1934)

Creativity is, of course, not confined to particular subject domains, such as art, drama, music and design and technology, but can be expressed in all areas of our knowledge and 'ways of knowing'. Our understandings of 'learning domains' as 'subjects' are related to our understandings about the nature of knowledge.

The structure of the National Curriculum and the training of teachers to offer a 'subject specialism' in their teaching, indicates how school curriculum and assessment systems are rooted in a view of subject knowledge. Pupils also learn from people with recognised subject expertise beyond school settings and many schools offer opportunities to engage with 'experts' or 'practitioners'. These 'experts', such as artists, musicians, scientists, engineers, writers, historians, sports men and women, can model their own high levels of practice which draws upon their deep conceptual understanding, knowledge and skills within authentic contexts in the subject area. This approach to learning from the expertise of others is reflected in theories of learning in *communities of practice* and by apprenticeship in *legitimate peripheral participation* (Lave and Wenger 1991).

It is argued that creative individuals within subject domains demonstrate knowledge and understanding of the concepts and traditions within the domain while knowing how to 'break the rules' in order to present original combinations of ideas. This can be illustrated in the ways a jazz musician, for example, can improvise to high levels when grounded in the history, philosophy, technique and practice of jazz (Nachmanovitch, 1990, Humphreys and Hyland, 2002, Loveless 2007b). The conceptual understanding of subject 'experts' enables them to make decisions about the appropriate use of tools and technologies to support and explore creative processes of imagination, fashioning, pursuing purpose, being original and judging value within the field. Looking closely at how 'experts' are creative in their different areas offers vivid illustrations of the relationship between subject knowledge and creative processes. In my own work in teacher education I have had the opportunity and privilege to work with scientists, artists, photographers, sculptors, film-makers and writers who work alongside pupils and teachers in schools. We have often witnessed how these practitioners – who are immersed in, and passionate about, their practice – can represent and draw out a deeper conceptual understanding from the pupils in their creative work (Loveless 1999a, 1999b; Loveless and Taylor 2000; Hawkey 2001).

The 'Body and Soul' project in Brighton focused on the narratives of creative practitioners in a variety of subject domains as they described the stories of their own 'learning lives' (Loveless, 2012). They were not necessarily accredited teachers, but were recognised in their own communities as playing important roles in other people's learning. Although from different fields and ways of working, they each demonstrated '3-D' characteristics in their creative and educational practices. They exhibited conceptual depth in their understanding of, and engagement in, their domain: from visual arts to science and political theatre; contextual scope in their awareness of the implications of their relationships with people, ways of knowing, politics and power; and pedagogic reach in the personal and conceptual connections they made with learners and the pedagogic strategies they employed. Hall, Thomson and Russell also noted some differences in pedagogic approaches between creative practitioners and classroom teachers, where creative practitioners focused on the learner's control and pace in order to perform, persevere and subject their outcomes to critical review for improvement (Hall *et al.*, 2007).

REFLECTIVE TASK

- Who are the creative practitioners in your own favourite subject areas?
- What have they contributed to our knowledge and practice in these domains?

Creativity in social and cultural contexts

Heavier-than-air flying machines are impossible.

(Lord Kelvin (1824–1907), ca. 1895,
British mathematician and physicist)

The wider contexts in which we promote and reward, or stifle and disregard creative people and practices, act as 'gateways' to recognition or marginalisation of creative activities in our societies. Teachers who are interested in developing creativity need to be able to 'read the world' in order to recognise, not only the subject and local contexts in which creativity can be expressed and acknowledged, but also the wider cultural, political and economic spheres in which creativity is encouraged.

Recent research in communities of practice also presents a view of learning as social, situated and characterised by interaction and communication between individuals (Wenger, 1998). Leach (2001) cites examples of creative individuals, such as Nobel Prize winners who benefit from association with other creative people within their communities which supported and celebrated the creative process. Feldman, Csikszentmihalyi and Gardner (1994) propose that creativity arises from the interaction between the 'intelligence' of *individuals*, the *domain* or areas of human endeavour, disciplines, crafts or pursuits, and the *field*, such as people, institutions, award mechanisms and 'knowledgeable others' through which judgements of individual performances in society are made.

Csikszentmihalyi develops his discussion of the *field* as a component of creativity, wherein other individuals act as 'gatekeepers' to a domain by recognising, preserving and remembering creative outcomes (Csikszentmihalyi, 1996). He presents a systems model in which creativity is in the interaction between a person's thoughts and actions, their knowledge and skills within a domain and a sociocultural context which can encourage, evaluate and reward. In such a systems model, the recognition and value of creativity is related as much to the wider context of *domains* and *fields* as much as to *individuals*. This has important implications for thinking about creativity and learning, where the context could be a school classroom, education system or a large corporation that can either nurture or dismiss the development of creative individuals, groups and communities. There can be a tension, however, between the current policy of promoting creativity in education that can be linked to political and economic imperatives, and the place of creative people and communities who can be challenging and disruptive to the status quo.

There are concerns that both the definition of creativity and the practical experience of creative processes become simplistic, unproblematic and unable to reflect the complexities and challenges of developing creativity in the wider spheres of curriculum and pedagogy for the twenty-first century. Hartley draws attention to the ways in which government and business are attending to creativity and emotional literacy in education, attaching them to *practice which remains decidedly performance-driven, standardised and monitored* (p16), and harnessing them for instrumental purposes in the knowledge and service-based economy (Hartley 2003; Troman *et al.*, 2007).

Creativity as recognised in individuals and communities, niches and domains can be appropriated to link up characteristics of personal well-being to requirements of economic innovation and international competitiveness. Loveless and Williamson draw attention to the ways in which creativity can be thought about, not only as psychological concepts, but also in economic and policy developments (Loveless and Williamson, 2013). Creativity is promoted in imperatives in reform in global economic and educational policy developments, from policy briefings of the World Bank (Yusuf, 2007), to 'NextGen', the 2011 review of the skills needed in the UK video games and visual effects industries (Livingstone and Hope, 2011). The European Year of Creativity and Innovation was declared in 2009, bringing together diverse groups interested in the implications of creativity for economic development and education systems (Cachia *et al*., 2010). The connection between the surface detail of consumerism and lifestyle and the deeper construction of workers as people being required to be continually innovative, competitive and entrepreneurial has been described as a corporatist model or *creativity with attitude* (Pope, 2005: 26–7). McGuigan understands these ways in which creativity has been appropriated as *cool capitalism* (McGuigan, 2009), and Osborne writes of *compulsory creativity*:

> *Creativity is a value which, though we may believe we choose it ourselves, may in fact make us complicit with what today might be seen as the most conservative of norms; compulsory individualism, compulsory innovation, compulsory performativity and productiveness, the compulsory validation of the putatively new.*

> (Osborne, 2003, p507)

Being creative is not easy or straightforward, indeed, not always desirable in every situation. In our work with creative practitioners, teachers, children and policy makers engaged in a variety of 'creative experiences' in projects, workshops and consultations in recent years, we have been aware of the dangers of creativity being perceived as just the elements of 'having good ideas' or 'making pretty things'; rather than the challenging, and often painful or frustrating, experience that characterizes the practices of creative people – the 'hard fun' and the 'flow' (Papert, 1993; Csikszentmihalyi, 1996). Teachers who wish to promote creativity in the lives of their pupils need to be able to model and share the range of creative experiences from their own lives – as individuals working in communities which are shaped by engagement in, and resistance to, the wider social, economic, cultural and political arenas in which education takes place. Craft, Claxton and Gardner have drawn our attention to the desirability of creativity being characterised and enriched by wisdom and trust within our wider community and society, providing a foundation for Good Work which is excellent, creative and ethical in our lives with others (Craft *et al*., 2008).

REFLECTIVE TASK

- How does a view of creativity as an interaction between people and communities, creative processes, subject domains and wider social and cultural contexts help you to understand your own creative experiences and possibilities?
- How would you like to describe yourself as a creative teacher?

Creativity in context: student teachers working with children

I feel that I have been able to engage with creative processes in ways that I haven't had the opportunity to do before. I feel that being able to work in small groups during session one and then in pairs during session two, allowed me to be creative with my peers. I have been able to use my imagination to develop my ideas and to be creative with other people's ideas. I feel that I have also seen that creativity is a process rather than simply one activity. I have seen that there is a process from developing an idea to working with that idea and then developing it further with the technology.

(Jan, student teacher)

If it is useful to think about creativity as an interaction between people and communities, processes, subjects and the wider social and cultural contexts, what might that look like in a real case study for teacher education? The following example focuses, not on the technologies used, but on the underlying creative processes that bring the activities to life. The Creativity and Professional Development Project at the University of Brighton focused on student teachers, and one of the aims of the project was to develop a conceptual framework for looking at creativity in the context of the use of digital tools in Primary classrooms. The students were given opportunities to experience working to a creative brief at their own level, as well as working with young children in school (Loveless *et al.*, 2006).

The framework for creativity and digital tools attempted to describe the interaction between three elements of creative practices with information and communications technologies:

- creative processes – for example, using imagination, fashioning, pursuing purpose and evaluating originality and value;
- the features of ICT – for example, provisionality, interactivity, capacity, range, speed, automatic functions, multimodality;
- and ICT capability as an expression of elements of higher order thinking – for example, finding things out, developing ideas and making things happen, exchanging and sharing information, and reviewing, modifying and evaluating work as it progresses, through a breadth of study.

The study focused on the experiences of a group of 16 student teachers, all ICT specialists in primary education, working collaboratively in using digital technologies to support creative digital video activities in primary schools. They worked with ten 'digital media labs' of portable ICT resources which included a laptop, digital video camera, digital camera, music keyboards and software for image and sound editing and manipulation. The student teachers were given two days to familiarise themselves with the resources by investigating what the hardware and software could do, working in groups of four. Firstly, they were shown the key features of the DV cameras and editing software, and then given two hours to make a mini-movie to a brief of getting someone through a door in only ten shots. The following week they were asked to work with digital still cameras and music composition software to create a slideshow that evoked memories of childhood toys.

After another two half days of visiting schools and planning, the groups spent two days working in small groups in two Primary schools – one class of five-year-old children and one class of ten-year-old children. Each group of children worked on making a digital movie from starting points emerging from the children's ideas – from stories shared in class, to music videos and original dramas. Half a day was spent in viewing and evaluating the outcomes from all the groups, and a final half day was used as an exhibition of the groups' work and critical reflections. Group feedback from this exhibition informed the students' individual presentation of their module assignment.

By engaging with the project, and analysing their experiences, the student teachers reflected upon their personal understandings of creativity, the contribution of ICT as a tool, and their own professional development. Their own definitions of creativity were wide-ranging, from 'creative' qualities in all individuals, to a focus on having ideas, or the making of tangible products. Many discussed the experience of being engaged in activities that they thought were creative, and emphasised not only the ideas and outcomes, but also on the feelings in that engagement. They described enjoyment, enquiry, excitement which lead to their greater involvement, and desire to follow things through. Many focused on the opportunities, and frustrations, of working in groups to develop creative ideas. They commented on the experience of offering their ideas to the group and learning how to adjust them, rethink and develop new ideas through discussion. One group highlighted the word 'compromise' in describing this experience, and acknowledged the difficulty of having to put aside, or compromise their personal ideas within the group activity. After the presentation of all the work, the students remarked upon their feelings of pride and achievement in what they had done. They later observed that their own experiences of generating ideas in groups, excitement and frustration in shooting and editing images, and enjoyment and pride in exhibiting the final movies were echoed in the children's experiences. They also recognised that their earlier experiences with playing and exploring with the equipment had enabled them to support the children's ideas in a more flexible manner. All recognised how they personally had engaged with a cycle of creativity activities and processes, from developing initial ideas, through fashioning and reworking, to presentation and evaluation.

In considering how they thought the digital tools have helped or hindered them in being creative in these activities, they highlighted the affordances of ICT to try out lots of ideas, revise and make choices. They described how they felt that they had used their imagination and collaborated to produce a mini video story. In order to do this they had to master the use of the technology, collaborate, pool ideas, discard ideas that did not work, edit their work and show it to their colleagues. The provisionality of the technology enabled them to try things, then discard or edit them easily. The immediacy of seeing their work in progress, without the constraints of limited film footage, allowed them to move on quickly to produce an acceptable product. There were, of course, feelings of frustration and impatience in learning to use new techniques with unfamiliar technology, but the groups developed strategies to share their knowledge with each other.

The focus on creativity and ICT afforded the opportunity to practise and advance their ICT capability in a context that was more challenging than many of their previous school placements. As well as learning to work with colleagues, they acknowledged the need for teaching strategies to support creative and collaborative group work for the children. Despite being experienced and successful student teachers nearing the end of their training, they recognised that they learned much by working with small groups of children.

An important aspect of the project was the challenge it raised for the students' working within the wider context of systems of primary schools and teacher education. They recognised the usual constraints of timetable, curriculum and assessment targets – for the children and for themselves. Designing opportunities for student teachers to experience, model and evaluate creativity in their practice is a challenge in the context of a schooling and teacher training system characterised by centralised pedagogy, monitoring and inspection, and aspirations focused on standards of achievement in a limited range of 'measures'. A conceptual framework for creativity and ICT must describe not only the interaction in the activities themselves, but also the interactions between the activities and the wider contexts of policy and practice as they affect people, and communities. By engaging in creative practices within the C&PD project, the student teachers experienced tensions and resolutions that helped them to 'read the world' in which they were acting in a more informed and interrogative manner.

REFLECTIVE TASK

- Look back at your own experiences of being creative in your life. What have you learned from those experiences? How will you take this into your own teaching?
- How would you like to express and develop your own creativity and creative habits of mind? What practical steps can you take to make that happen? How can you build a network of like-minded people to support and encourage each other?

A SUMMARY OF **KEY POINTS**

> A useful way of looking at creativity is to consider it as an interaction between characteristics of people and communities, creative processes, subject domains and wider social and cultural contexts.

> Creativity can be described as combining the following five characteristics: using the imagination; a fashioning process; pursuing purposes; seeking originality; and judging values.

> Creative people need to be able to encounter and cope with puzzles, problems, seeming failure and disappointment, in order to learn from these experiences and demonstrate perseverance and resilience. They also develop their abilities to think about patterns and connections, and reflect upon how new situations might relate to earlier experiences or need novel solutions.

> Creative people rarely work in isolation. Their ideas and outcomes are likely to have been generated through interaction with other people's ideas and reactions.

> A challenge for schools to think creatively in this regard is to draw upon the everyday knowledge of local and global communities; and to promote imaginative use of school environments as extensions to the physical space of classrooms.

> Being creative is not easy or straightforward, indeed, not always desirable in every situation. Tensions can arise when pursuing creativity: for example, between individual teachers, who challenge the status quo of pedagogical and curricular recommendations, and their schools.

> Teachers who wish to promote creativity in the lives of their pupils need to be able to model and share the range of creative experiences from their own lives.

MOVING *ON* > > > > > > MOVING *ON* > > > > > > MOVING *ON*

In order to develop your understanding and expression of teaching as a creative act, and yourself and your pupils as a creative people, you should think about how you might:

- realise creativity in your own life experiences;
- recognise and engage with other people in your community and networks who can inspire, support and sustain creativity;

- identify creative 'niches' and environments in which pupils' creativity can be fostered;
- draw upon creative connections within and between subjects;
- understand the potential and constraints of wider social and cultural contexts for creativity beyond the boundaries of classroom and school.

REFERENCES REFERENCES **REFERENCES** REFERENCES REFERENCES REFERENCES

Boden, M (1992) *The creative mind*. London: Abacus.

Bragg, S and Manchester, H (2011) *Creativity, school ethos and the creative partnerships programme*.

Cachia, R, Ferrari, A, Ala-Mutka, K and Punie, Y (2010) Creative learning and innovative teaching: final report on the study on creativity and innovation in education in EU member states. Seville, Institute for Prospective Technological Studies (IPTS). 24675 EN.

Claxton, G (1999) *Wise up*. London, Bloomsbury.

Claxton, G (2000) The anatomy of intuition. *The intuitive practitioner*. Atkinson, T and Claxton, G Buckingham, PA: Open University Press.

Craft, A (2000) *Creativity across the primary curriculum: framing and developing practice*. Abingdon: Routledge.

Craft, A, Claxton, G and Gardner, H (eds) (2008). *Creativity, wisdom, and trusteeship*. Thousand Oaks, CA: Corwin Press.

Csikszentmihalyi, M (1996) *Creativity: flow and the psychology of discovery and invention*. New York: HarperCollins.

De Mello, A (1984) *The song of the bird*. New York: Doubleday.

DfE (2012) Teachers' Standards available at **https://www.gov.uk/government/publications/teachers-standards** accessed 7/9/14.

Eliot, TS (1934) *The Rock*. London: Faber & Faber.

Feldman, DH, Csikszentmihalyi, M and Gardner, H (1994) *Changing the world: a framework for the study of creativity*. Westport, CT and London: Praeger.

Hall, C, Thomson, P and Russell, L (2007) Teaching like an artist: the pedagogic identities and practices of artists in schools. *British Journal of Sociology of Education* 28(5): 605–619.

Hartley, D (2003) The Instrumentalisation of the Expressive in Education. *British Journal of Educational Studies* 51(1): 6–19.

Hawkey, R (2001) Science beyond school: representation or re-presentation? in Loveless, A and Ellis, V (eds) *ICT, pedagogy and the curriculum: subject to change*. Abingdon: Routledge.

Humphreys, M and Hyland, T (2002) Theory, Practice and Performance in Teaching: professionalism, intuition and jazz. *Educational Studies* 28(1): 5–15.

Jeffrey, B and Woods, P (2003). *The creative school: a framework for success, quality and effectiveness*. Abingdon and New York: RoutledgeFalmer.

John-Steiner, V (2000) *Creative Collaboration* New York: Oxford University Press.

Kelvin, WT (Circa. 1985) cited in **http://scienceworld.wolfram.com/biography/Kelvin.html** accessed 8/10/14.

Lave, J and Wenger, E (1991) Situated learning. Legitimate peripheral participation. Cambridge: Cambridge University Press.

Leach, J (2001) A hundred possibilities: creativity, community and ICT in Jeffrey, CAB and Leibling, M (eds) *Creativity in education*. London: Continuum.

Livingstone, I and Hope, A (2011) *Next gen: Transforming the UK into the world's leading talent hub for the video games and visual effects industries*. London: NESTA.

Loveless, A (1999a) Art on the net evaluation: Report to South East Arts, Lighthouse and DCMS. Brighton: University of Brighton.

Loveless, A (1999b). A digital big breakfast: The Glebe School Project in Sefton-Green, J (ed) *Young people, creativity and new technology: the challenge of digital arts*. Abingdon: Routledge.

Loveless, A (2007a). *Creativity, technology and learning: a review of recent literature* (Update). Bristol:Futurelab.

Loveless, A (2007b). Preparing to teach with ICT: subject knowledge, Didaktik and improvisation. *The Curriculum Journal* 18(4).

Loveless, A (2012) Body and Soul: a study of narratives of learning lives of creative people who teach, in Goodson, IF, Loveless, AM and Stephens, D (eds) *Explorations in Narrative Research*. Rotterdam: Sense Publishers.

Loveless, A, Burton, J and Turvey, K (2006) Developing conceptual frameworks for creativity, ICT and teacher education. *Thinking Skills and Creativity* 1(1): 3–13.

Loveless, A and Taylor, T (2000). Creativity, Visual Literacy and ICT, in Leask, M and Meadows, J (eds) *Teaching and Learning with ICT in the Primary School* 65–80. Abingdon: Routledge.

Loveless, A and Williamson, B (2013) *Learning identities in a digital age: rethinking creativity, education and technology*. Abingdon and New York: Routledge.

McGuigan, J (2009) *Cool Capitalism*. London: Pluto Press.

NACCCE (1999) *All our futures: creativity, culture and education*. Sudbury: National Advisory Committee on Creative and Cultural Education: DfEE and DCMS.

Nachmanovitch, S (1990) *Free play: improvisation in life and art*. New York: Jeremy P Tarcher/Putnam a member of Penguin/Putnam Inc.

Osborne, T (2003) Against 'creativity': a philistine rant. *Economy and Society* 32 (4): 507–525.

Papert, S (1993) *The children's machine: rethinking school in the age of the computer*. New York, London, Toronto, Sydney, Tokyo and Singapore: Harvester Wheatsheaf.

Pope, R (2005) *Creativity: theory, history, practice*. Abingdon: Routledge.

Rhyammar, L and Brolin, C (1999) Creativity research: historical considerations and main lines of development. *Scandinavian Journal of Educational Research* 43(3): 259–273.

Robinson, K (2001) *Out of our minds: learning to be creative*. Chichester: Capstone Publishing Ltd.

Sternberg, RJ and Lubart, TI (1999) The concept of creativity: prospects and paradigms, in Sternberg, RJ (ed) *Handbook of Creativity*. Cambridge: Cambridge University Press.

Troman, G, Jeffrey, B and Raggl, A (2007) Creativity and perfomativity policies in primary school cultures. *Journal of Education Policy* 22(5): 549–572.

Wenger, E (1998) *Communities of practice: learning, meaning and identity*. Cambridge: Cambridge University Press.

Yusuf, S (2007). From creativity to innovation, World Bank policy research working paper 4262. Washington DC: World Bank.

11
Creativity and primary art and design education
Paul Key

Chapter objectives

By the end of this chapter you should have:

- **extended an awareness and understanding of creativity;**
- **extended an awareness and understanding of learning in art and design;**
- **developed an awareness and understanding of the relationship between creativity and art and design;**
- **developed an awareness and understanding of the role of the teacher in supporting the relationship between creativity and art and design.**

This chapter addresses the following Teachers' Standards (DfE, 2012):

- **set high expectations which inspire, motivate and challenge pupils;**
- **promote good progress and outcomes by pupils;**
- **demonstrate good subject and curriculum knowledge;**
- **plan and teach well-structured lessons.**

Introduction

The purpose of this chapter is to raise your awareness and understanding of the relationships between creativity and primary art and design education. This will be established by considering a range of perspectives on the nature of creativity, from policy, research and practice, and how these perspectives can be applied to art and design education. From this position the chapter will explore the role of the teacher in reflecting on and applying this understanding to classroom practice through more general principles of teaching, with a view towards establishing a purposeful and engaging creative art and design educational experience for primary phase children.

The relationship between creativity and art and design education

As Gentle (1985) identifies, primary school art and design education provides children with important opportunities to *develop a language of visual, tactile and spatial responses* (1985:96) to ideas, feelings and experiences. This language includes the marks and gestures which characterise drawings and paintings, the manipulation and joining of materials to construct and model three-dimensional work, the layering and extraction of surfaces to support printmaking, the employment of repetition or rotation to develop pattern, or the addition of threads and stitches to adorn and embellish textile pieces. A purposeful education in art and design can support, enrich and refine this language. This can be attained through well-considered and purposeful curriculum opportunities and timely teaching interventions, which support not only the outcomes of art and design, but the processes which support their production. In addition to the central aspect of making in art and design education, children also learn about artists, designers and craft makers, and the contributions these creative practitioners make to our lives and to our cultures.

It is also recognised that art and design, like other areas of arts education, has a close association with creativity. This is evident in school settings where teachers and pupils will refer to art and design lessons as opportunities to 'be creative'. Children are encouraged 'to be creative' with ideas, to imagine new ways of combining materials, invent ways of applying paint, create characters and stories combining drawing and animation, or develop imaginative responses to observations of texture and pattern, combining print and stitch. However, the various chapters of this publication, and readings from elsewhere, will have highlighted that this association is far from exclusive to art and design, and one that is not always guaranteed. For example, art and design lessons may sometimes miss opportunities for children to explore or develop ideas in creative ways, or limit opportunities to experiment and be imaginative with materials and techniques. Elsewhere in the curriculum, children can also be fully engaged in processes of creative thinking, for example in science education or physical education, as they work out or invent solutions to challenging problems, test out ideas or make connections across learning experiences.

Where the association or relationship between art and design education and creativity is well understood and successfully applied to practice, the educational benefits can be identified. One such example is in the recognition that art and design educational experiences can foster and develop creative learning dispositions or 'habits' (Spencer, Lucas and Claxton, 2012): children learn to be creative. For example, where a project encourages children to explore overlooked visual qualities in the classroom, documented and recorded through photographs and explored through mixed-media images in sketchbooks, children have opportunities to develop and enhance transferable creative habits. In turn, the habits of creativity can be applied to the images, materials and ideas of the project. Children learn to make and think about art and design in creative ways; children produce creative outcomes.

To explore these relationships further, the following section of this chapter will consider more carefully the nature of creativity and creative processes and how they can be applied to processes of learning in art and design education, this will be followed by a closer examination of the implications for classroom practice.

REFLECTIVE TASK

Reflect on your experiences of education and identify and consider areas of the curriculum which both support and are supported by creativity.

Perspectives on the nature of creativity

The revised national curriculum for England (DfE, 2013a) establishes a clear connection between creativity and art and design, suggesting in the Art and Design Purpose of Study that *Art, craft and design embody some of the highest forms of human creativity* (2013a, p182). This idea can be exemplified in aspects of human creativity which have imagined and constructed buildings, designed bridges, produced paintings, drawings, sculptures and photographs, directed films and crafted illustrations of unique originality and with a clear sense of creativity and imagination. Such examples demonstrate qualities of creativity which reflect the integration of the imagination, the pursuit of purpose, a sense of originality and the role of reflective value judgement. These areas, imagination, purpose, originality and value judgement were identified by the National Advisory Committee on Creativity and Cultural Education (NACCCE, 1999) and reported in the important document *All Our Futures: creativity, culture and education*.

While these areas provide an initial indication of the characteristics of creativity, which have been reworked and developed elsewhere (for example *Creativity Find It Promote It* developed by Qualification and Curriculum Authority, or QCA, 2004), other key ideas from the report are worth consideration. Perhaps most significantly, the report identifies a shift from more elite versions of creativity to democratic and inclusive terms. Where the *highest forms of creativity* identified in the national curriculum (DfE, 2013a) may well be evident in both our everyday and the more exceptional aspects of our lives, in educational contexts, creativity for individuals can be considered in more relative and relational terms. For example, a child exploring and inventing characters, retelling familiar experiences, or recording friends or relatives with drawing materials, can be described as engaging in creative activity, with a sense of purpose originality, imagination, and of personally-judged value. This notion of a democratic approach to creativity, co-existing with the more remarkable achievements of a smaller minority of people, is a powerful conception of creativity which can be employed across the curriculum.

To establish and maintain this compelling argument – that all children have the capacity for activity that can be described as creative – it becomes relevant to explore more carefully what is understood by the term creativity, with a view to applying this awareness to the suggested reciprocal relationship with art and design education.

Sharp's (2004) review of research and policy material on creativity in education identified *often hotly contested* (2004, p5) and much-debated views of definitions of creativity. Within single publications and across documentation, for example, the National Curriculum (DfEE, 1999) and the Early Years Foundation Stage (DCSF, 2000), Sharp identifies 'creative thinking' 'creative development' and 'being creative' as terms expressed without a common or shared understanding. However, she identifies a relatively shared view that creativity when considered as a process, involves a range of inter-related components. The components she identifies as being most common, and which closely reflect the work of the NACCCE (1999) are:

- imagination;
- originality (the ability to come up with ideas and products that are new and unusual);
- productivity (the ability to generate a variety of different ideas through divergent thinking);
- problem solving (application of knowledge and imagination to a given situation);
- the ability to produce an outcome of value and worth.

(Sharp, 2004)

A further observation made by the NACCCE, highlights creativity as involving both productive (generative) and evaluative processes. They suggest *helping young children to understand and manage this interaction between generative and evaluative thinking is a pivotal task of creative education* (NACCCE, 1999). Although the summary list from Sharp (2004) appears on first reading to be mostly centred on generative or productive aspects of creative activity, the importance of formative reflection and evaluation are at least implicit within these phases of activity.

Sharp's exploration of a democratic and broad understanding of creativity acknowledges all children as *having creative potential and to be capable of creative expression* (2004, p6). In this context, value is placed on not only the creative outcomes of children's work but importantly on their engagement in creative processes, as suggested earlier. This tendency to emphasise creative characteristics or attributes is one which places children centrally within the creative learning process. As a result, opportunities begin to emerge which enable teachers to recognise, value and develop these aspects of learning, as both generic learning dispositions (Spencer *et al.*, 2012) and their application to particular subjects or cross-curricular contexts.

REFLECTIVE TASK

Reflect on the key ideas established so far in this section of the chapter:

1. **identify examples of what the national curriculum (DfE, 2013a) describes as** *high forms* **of creativity, and consider them in relation to an elite view of creativity;**
2. **identify your own creative achievements and consider them in relation to a democratic view of creativity;**
3. **consider the challenges of trying to define creativity.**

In their development of the work of the NACCCE, the Qualifications and Curriculum Authority (QCA, 2004), identified a range of dispositions of creative activity, shown below in bold, and in turn began to suggest the personal attributes or behaviours which enable such activity:

Questioning and challenging: asking questions such as 'why does it happen this way?, 'what if we tried it that way?', responding to tasks or problems in an unusual way, showing independent thinking.

Making connections and seeing relationships: using analogies, making unusual connections, applying knowledge and experience in a new context.

Envisaging what might be: seeing new possibilities, looking at things in different ways, asking 'what if?' or 'what else?'

Exploring ideas, keeping options open: exploring, experimenting, trying fresh approaches, anticipating and overcoming difficulties.

Reflecting critically on ideas, actions and outcomes: reviewing progress, inviting feedback and acting on it, putting forward constructive comments, ideas, and ways of doing things.

Creativity Find It Promote It (QCA, 2004)

More recently the Centre for Real World Learning (Spencer *et al.*, 2012), based at the University of Winchester, was commissioned by Creativity Culture and Education to research the 'viability of creating an assessment framework for tracking the development of young people's creativity in schools' (2012, p1). Their research conceptualised creativity in similar terms to those discussed here, as inclusive and democratic, cross-curricular, and when defined in generic terms, as having identifiable learning dispositions, with an ultimate application to personal and social growth. To recognise, value and develop such dispositions the research identified a manageable set of person centred creative processes, described as 'habits', which are extended through a further set of 'sub-habits'. Although the research focused on the viability and practical application of this framework, as a formative assessment tool, there also appears to be potential in using its structure to support planning practices, activity design and teaching interventions

The research identified the following habits and sub-habits:

Inquisitive Clearly creative individuals are good at uncovering and pursuing interesting and worthwhile questions in their creative domain

Wondering and questioning

Exploring and investigating

Challenging assumptions

Persistent The role of determination in creativity has been repeatedly emphasised

Sticking with difficulty

Daring to be different

Tolerating uncertainty

Imaginative At the heart of a wide range of analyses of the creative personality is the ability to come up with imaginative solutions and possibilities

Playing with possibilities

Making connections

Using intuition

Collaborative Many current approaches to creativity, such as that of John-Steiner (2006), stress the social and collaborative nature of the creative process

Sharing the product

Giving and receiving feedback

Cooperating appropriately

Disciplined As a counter-balance to the dreamy, imaginative side of creativity, most authors also stress the need for knowledge and craft in shaping the creative product

Developing techniques

Reflecting critically

Crafting and improving

Figure 11.1 Habits and sub-habits of creative learning developed by the Centre for Real World Learning (Spencer *et al.*, 2012)

Conceiving creativity as a process of production and evaluation, and as a set of learning dispositions (while acknowledging variations across attempts to define a definitive set) can be very helpful in developing an inclusive and purposeful approach to art and design education. Where Addison (2010) extends this idea, in his theoretical exploration, he identifies an argument that establishes creativity *not so much as a possession, but more of a potential* (2010, p43) which, he continues, can be supported by the *fertile conditions* of pedagogic and social relationships. In these environments children are given opportunities to explore and investigate ideas in art and design, to pursue experiments beyond pre-determined outcomes, to see what happens when two materials are combined or a drawing is enlarged or a sequence of images is projected on to a school building. These artistic adventures are dependent on the environmental and relational conditions of the classroom, and will be explored in more detail as the chapter moves to the role of the teacher in supporting an education in art and design.

Although the creative process, when represented as a set of habits, appears to be a continuous one, there are many reminders that it ebbs and flows; having moments of clarity and purpose and moments of frustration and setback. The NACCCE (1999) for example identify *notable periods of engagement*: of focus withdrawal and breakthrough, which can influence timescales of creativity as sometimes being long and drawn out, or spontaneous and sudden. Awareness of these cycles of activity could have an impact on practice. For example, short sketchbook activities could take place each morning for five to ten minutes, stimulated by a word or image, projects could then be developed from sketchbooks, collaboratively across year groups and during an art week. This could encourage children to explore and develop ideas, sustain their work and stick with difficulty. Artists could be utilised to work alongside children to share skills or techniques, and exemplify the combination of working from intuition and tradition, and the challenges presented during creative processes.

These aspects of consideration have clear implications for planning and for managing the learning environment, and place a responsibility with teachers and children to learn and develop characteristics or attributes which enable them to work with the unforeseen and the unpredictable. Indeed these attributes can be applied to teachers and their capacity to work in the *fertile conditions* of creative activity.

While it may not be immediately obvious where all children or teachers exhibit creative characteristics, the art and design classroom or art and design lessons can provide clear opportunities for their development. Although some children may grow out of their playful willingness to make unlikely connections between images, materials and ideas, observations of young children tend to provide strong indications that the creative processes and outcomes of art and design matter to children. This is evident in children's experiments with materials, in their drawings and paintings, models and diagrams. Although these images and objects may appear to adults, or indeed the curriculum, as sometimes superficial or insignificant, when understood, their educational value can form the basis of a purposeful art and design education.

REFLECTIVE TASK

Consider your experiences of teaching or of observing teachers – were there examples of teachers adopting dispositions of creativity in their practice?

Developing an awareness and understanding of art and design education

Studies of art and design education reveal a range of inter-connected ideas, including those from learning theory and perceptions of learners, traditions of psychology, social theory, cultural theory and ideas of schooling, to the nature and role of vision, ideas about making meaning, humanist perspectives on education, and the role of the imagination. Inevitably as a field of study there are ideas which co-exist comfortably, and others which appear to polarise opinion. A similarly diverse and sometimes conflicting view of creativity appears to add to the complexity. However, these levels of uncertainty should not be used to deflect attention to other matters, instead they can be used as a reminder that whatever version of art and design education is presented, there will be others to be discovered and reconstructed through experience, challenge, compromise or success, in both theory and in practice.

While acknowledging this range of possibilities, there is a strong case to be made in identifying 'making' as a common and central aspect of art and design education. The value of making is identified as being both personally significant, in that it encourages children to have opportunities to make meaningful representations of ideas, feelings and experiences, through the images and objects they produce. Images and objects which help children tell stories, recall a visit to the park or an experience from television, communicate an idea about texture or colour, or invent the protagonist of a newly-told story. This level of purposeful making provides opportunities for children to behave like artists in having an opportunity *to have something to say* (Eisner 2002, p51).

As a result, children's personal and social development is enhanced through active engagement in making processes; reaffirming children as *contributors* to an otherwise *already made world* (Gormley in Hickman 2005, p7). Through the making process children take initially inanimate objects and use them to mediate, communicate and express ideas, feelings and experiences. Educational settings can encourage the conditions which support an *outlook* (Bentley 2005) to making, which enables the maker to be empowered through the very act of creative making, and to transfer this experience to broader community contexts. Creativity in the sense of an *outlook* becomes a *crucial means by which the individual can engage with his or her wider community* (Bentley 2005, p10).

Art and design education has a responsibility to support opportunities not just for making, but to recognise this central aspect alongside a number of other processes, knowledge areas and skills, and within the relationship to 'creativity'. This commitment to identifying learning in initially broad terms will help to support the development of learning experiences and teaching interventions. A summary of the proposals of the National Curriculum Council (NCC) (1990), Prentice (1999) and the National Curriculum (DfEE 1999) reveals a number of common areas of learning which are summarised in Figure 11.2.

Exploring and investigating: Prentice (1999) suggests *art (and design) makes available to children a richness of opportunity to investigate ideas and feelings in relation*

A summary of areas of learning in art and design		Starting points and areas of activity
Processes	Exploring and investigating Making Reviewing and reflecting Responding	Environments and habitats Ourselves and others Stories and events Objects and still-life
Knowledge	Artists, craftspeople and designers Traditions and techniques Materials Visual, spatial and tactile qualities	Drawing Painting Printmaking Textile
Skills	Perception Production Discussion	Sculpture Modelling Construction Photography and digital media Line Shape Texture Colour Pattern Form Space Composition

Figure 11.2 Summary of areas of activity and areas of learning in art and design

to an external world seen and an internal world imagined (1999, p152). Investigation and exploration play a key role in examining these worlds, through related processes of observation, documentation, recording and presenting. Children are asked to think and act through these processes to enrich their visual, spatial and tactile responses. From observation, from memory and from imagination (DfEE, 1999), children can be encouraged to take photographs, produce drawings, make maps, draw diagrams, list words, record sounds. Sketchbooks become invaluable as places to record and store these investigations and to demonstrate an increasingly intelligent approach to art and design activity, with opportunities to apply skills of observation, perception and production. The starting points for these explorations and investigations include environments and habitats, ourselves and others, stories and events, objects and still-life.

Making: Although some artists employ others to produce and execute work, or work on collaborative productions, making remains a central to artistic practices in and beyond educational contexts. Prentice (1999) reminds us *when children's creative work in art is rooted in personal experience and informed and enriched by a critical under-standing of works of art, making becomes more meaningful for the maker* (1999, p153). Importantly, the NCC (1990) remind us that making art is not simply a process of translating an idea into an image or object; ideas are *reassessed, reworked, refined and reshaped* (NCC 1990, p11). By engaging in practical making activities children acquire, practice and apply and skills of observation and production, experimenting with materials and crafting responses. Children will make work related to the traditions of drawing, painting, printmaking, textiles, sculpture, modelling, construction and photographic and digital media.

Evaluating and reflecting: Prentice (1999) suggests *of fundamental importance is the ability of children to recognise that alternative ways of seeing, of handling media and responding to works of art are possible*. The interaction between productive and reflective engagement can be facilitated for individuals or small groups or a whole class of pupils. The process is supported through the application of skills of perception and discussion, and the development of an art and design rich vocabulary. Commentary will include references to line, shape, colour, texture, colour, pattern, form, space and composition.

Responding: Engagement with the work of artists, craftspeople and designers, forms a significant part of a balanced art and design education. This enables pupils to develop and apply knowledge of artistic traditions to their own practice, while increasing awareness and understanding of the role of creative practitioners in reflecting and contributing to cultures across different times and places. In turn, children enhance their discursive and critical skills, which are reinforced with an increasingly rich art and design vocabulary.

Where the National Curriculum (DfEE, 1999) details a positive approach to primary art and design education which recognises and presents a commitment to areas of learning (similar to those above), and presents them within a development framework, the most recent national curriculum (DfE, 2013a) presents what could be thought of as a series of 'statements'. However, similarities to the areas of learning above can also be recognised, and are highlighted in **bold** in the extract below from the document's Purpose of Study and overall Aims for art and design:

Art and design

Purpose of study

Art, craft and design embody some of the highest forms of human creativity. A high-quality art and design education should engage, inspire and challenge pupils, equipping them with the **knowledge** and **skills** to **experiment**, invent and **create** their own works of art, craft and design. As pupils progress, they should be able to **think critically** and develop a more rigorous **understanding** of art and design. They should also **know** how art and design both reflect and shape our history, and contribute to the culture, creativity and wealth of our nation.

Aims

The national curriculum for art and design aims to ensure that all pupils:

- **produce** creative work, **exploring** their ideas and **recording** their experiences;
- become proficient in drawing, painting, sculpture and other art, craft and design techniques;
- **evaluate** and **analyse** creative works using the language of art, craft and design;
- **know** about great artists, craft makers and designers, and **understand** the historical and cultural development of their art forms.

Figure 11.3 Extract from the national curriculum (DfE, 2013, p182)

Beyond these areas of leaning in art and design, this chapter has proposed and emphasised that areas of learning can be supported by, and in turn support, creative learning dispositions. This relationship is reinforced by the National Society for Education in Art and Design (NSEAD). The society suggests Learning through Art and Design for the 21st Century serves broader and more creative aims of education (Figure 11.4).

Art and design activities should allow children to develop their own thinking and questioning skills. This will enable children to gain knowledge and understanding of the world around them and its people, and prepare them for the future by:

- Valuing diversity and individuality.
- Allowing time for reflection
- Promoting innovation, risk taking and problem solving.
- Promoting playfulness and curiosity.
- Ability to collaborate with other people and take the views of other people into account.
- Tolerance for ambiguity.
- Making links between unusual concepts and circumstances.
- Developing the imagination.
- Encourages experimental approaches.

Figure 11.4 Extract from NSEAD

REFLECTIVE TASK

Reflect on art and design lessons you may have taught or experienced as pupil. Can you identify starting points for learning, areas of activity, and areas of learning? Did the teacher make these areas of learning explicit?

Applying an understanding of creativity to areas of learning in art and design education

Where Addison (2010) recognises creativity as a potential to be supported through the *fertile conditions of pedagogical and social relationships* (Addison, 2010, p43), Carroll (1998) appears to suggest a similar approach. She identifies and suggests, *Rather than ask, how do we teach art, I ask, how do we cultivate artistic behaviour in our learners?* (1998, p76). Artistic behaviour in this sense is identified as enabling personal and communal meaning through the images and objects of art and design. Images and objects which extend an understanding and exploration of their material properties, and which encourage personal understanding of how these properties can communicate to other people; ideas of space, texture, colour, light, relationships, loneliness, celebration or joy. These are expressions are brought together through ways of thinking, feeling and acting which enable learners to observe, search for detail, solve problems, invent problems, think visually and spatially. As such Carroll concludes *art can be regarded as thought and feeling made visible.* (1998, p79)

This consideration of artistic behaviour builds on the recognition suggested earlier of the importance of images and objects to children, but also gives a sense of how thinking, feeling and acting through art and design is reliant on a relationship with the dispositions of creativity. To succeed in the potential artistic behaviours described by Carroll, or in the processes of learning suggested by Prentice, a creative approach to learning is required. However, as we have also discovered with art and design education, ideas about creativity can divide opinion. These levels of uncertainty should not be used to deflect attention to other matters, instead they can be used as a reminder that whatever version of creativity is presented, there will be others to be discovered and reconstructed through experience, challenge, compromise or success, in both theory and in practice.

Applying creative learning habits and sub-habits to primary art and design education

Figure 11.5 captures and presents the processes, knowledge and skills associated with art and design, alongside the relational creative learning habits and sub-habits (Spencer *et al.*, 2012). By presenting material in this way the intention is to reveal the potential in the Starting Points and Activity Areas in supporting this relationship.

Self-portraits traced directly to small mirrors can encourage children to *challenge assumptions* of how faces 'should be drawn'. The tracings can be copied and repeated to extend opportunities to *dare to be different* with materials, or enlarged to two-metre-high drawings, *playing with possibilities*. Artists and photographers working with portraits and self-portraits can be compared and contrasted, to *make connections* and *challenge*

A summary of areas of learning in art and design		Starting points and areas of activity	Application of creative learning habits and sub-habits
Processes	Exploring and investigating Making Reviewing and reflecting Responding	Environments and habitats Ourselves and others Stories and events Objects and still-life Drawing Painting Printmaking Textile Sculpture Modelling Construction Photographic and Digital imagery Line Shape Texture Colour Pattern Form Space	*Inquisitive* Wondering and questioning Exploring and investigating Challenging assumptions
Knowledge	Artists, craftspeople and designers Traditions and techniques Materials Visual, spatial and tactile qualities		*Persistent* Sticking with difficulty Daring to be different Tolerating uncertainty Using intuition *Imaginative* Playing with possibilities Making connections Using intuition *Collaborative* Sharing the product Giving and receiving feedback Cooperating appropriately *Disciplined* Developing techniques Reflecting critically Crafting and improving
Skills	Perception Production Discussion		

Figure 11.5 Application of creative learning habits and sub-habits to areas of activity and learning in art and design

assumptions. The *persistent* approach of artists can be adopted to develop images and objects, encouraging pupils to *craft and improve* their work, and to *stick with periods of difficulty*.

PRACTICAL TASK   PRACTICAL TASK   PRACTICAL TASK   PRACTICAL TASK   PRACTICAL TASK

Refer to Figure 11.5. Take one activity area, for example drawing, and work through the application of creative learning habits and sub-habits to that area of activity. Try to imagine activities in the classroom which would be the result of this application of creative habits to art and design.

'Cultivating' the relationship between creativity and art and design

Recognising and understanding the relationship between creativity and art and design is a positive step towards enhancing and developing practice. From this position there is scope to apply some general principles of teaching and learning to cultivating stimulating learning experiences for children.

One set of principles is presented in the guidance for teachers of art and design, across a range of age phases and educational sectors, developed by the Tertiary Art Education Group of Victoria (TAEV), Australia. The document 'Quality Art Teaching: what high quality art teachers know and do' (TAEV 2014 is particularly helpful in that it provides complimentary 'subject specific' guidance to the current generic guidance found in

---

Professional Knowledge

Knowledge of students (pupils): high-quality art teachers have a thorough knowledge of the pupils they teach. They understand the social and cultural contexts of their pupils and know how to cater for individual artistic preferences.

Knowledge of pupils as learners: high-quality art teachers see pupils as individuals... they encourage pupils to think divergently, take risks and think outside of the square.

Professional Practice

Art room learning environments: high-quality art teachers provide a trusting and supporting environment in which students can experiment, try new approaches and enjoy being 'different'.

Planning for artistic learning: high-quality art teachers plan organised art experiences that also allow for flexibility. They understand that art making is sometimes spontaneous yet at other times quite calculated and controlled.

Art teaching in action: high-quality art teachers motivate students to want to make art. They establish contexts and non-threatening situations in which creativity can occur. They facilitate problem solving experiences which encourage pupils to seek artistic solutions, take risks, experiment and refine ideas.

Figure 11.6 Extract from Quality Art Teaching: what high quality art teachers know and do (TAEV)

Teachers Standards (DfE, 2012). It identifies three broad areas: Professional Knowledge, Professional Qualities, Professional Practice. These broad areas are then more finely tuned, illustrating subsets of knowledge, attributes and practice. For this discussion, it is useful to identify areas of the subsets, as clear informants of successful practice in the application of creativity to art and design. They are a reminder of the need to understand the children with whom teachers work, to understand the nature of learning, and to understand and to put into practice an appropriate learning environment, planning, teaching and assessment arrangements. The examples extracted below are those which appear to support directly creativity and art and design.

Where teachers are able to enact such a principled pedagogy, there could be real purpose and value in the creative and artistic adventures of children. Such pedagogy may reflect what the UNESCO (2006) Road Map for Art Education describes as an *arts-rich pedagogy*,

A summary of areas of learning in art and design		Starting points and areas of activity	Application of habits and sub habits through *productive toolbox strategies*	Creative learning habits and sub-habits
Processes	Exploring and investigating Making Reviewing and reflecting Responding	Environments and habitats Ourselves and others Stories and events Objects and still-life	*Combine* *Juxtapose* *Diffuse* *Map* *Embellish* *Rotate* *Mirror* *Canon* *Edit* *Filter* *Extract* *Select* *Sort* *Sequence* *Categorise*	*Inquisitive* Wondering and questioning Exploring and investigating Challenging assumptions *Persistent* Sticking with difficulty Daring to be different Tolerating uncertainty Using intuition *Imaginative* Playing with possibilities Making connections
Knowledge	Artists, craftspeople and designers Traditions and techniques Materials Visual, spatial and tactile qualities	Drawing Painting Printmaking Textile Sculpture Modelling Construction Digital imagery		
Skills	Perception Production Discussion	Line Shape Texture Colour Pattern Form Space	*Order* *Mask* *Layer* *Zoom* *Magnify* *Repeat* *Loop* *Accumulate* *Mark* *Recur* *Uncover* *Excavate* *Accent* *Dissect* *Scale*	Using intuition *Collaborative* Sharing the product Giving and receiving feedback Cooperating appropriately *Disciplined* Developing techniques Reflecting critically Crafting and improving

Figure 11.7 Application of habits and sub-habits to activity areas and areas of learning in art and design through 'productive toolbox' strategies

in that adopted teaching approaches are shaped by and reflect artistic behaviours. As Eisner (2003) would suggest, in this context teaching can be considered as *artistry*.

To bridge principled pedagogy to classroom practice, teachers often employ strategic devices to support particular types of learning. For example, story maps are used to sequence and structure narrative events, talking frames can be used to support children's responses to art work in gallery settings (Charman, Rose, and Wilson 2006; Taylor, 1986), and *real life problems* can be presented to stimulate design-based solutions.

One strategy for creativity and art and design teaching would be to employ what we have described elsewhere (Key and Stillman, 2009) as a Productive Toolbox. The Productive Toolbox was developed and adapted from Waters (1994), as part of the Higher Education, the Arts and Schools (HEARTS) project. In his review of arts practice, surveyed from a range of Higher Education institutions and courses, Waters (1994) presents a *toolbox of productive metaphors* to identify common or shared artistic practices and describes them as *compositional strategies for working across media* (Waters, 1994, p75). The metaphors are offered as an evolving and emerging lexicon. The productive terms which form the lexicon, listed below, and named collectively as the Productive Toolbox, illustrate the actions taken by artists when working with ideas, feelings and experiences. They are another set of habits, often explored or investigated intuitively by artists, to develop imaginative and inventive responses. In a similar way to which story tellers absorb the structures of a *story map*, and apply it at times intuitively to their story telling, artists do something similar. Where the Productive Toolbox is educationally useful is in its application to exploration and investigation, making, reviewing and responding to work. Children can be introduced to the productive terms, shown examples of how artists apply them to materials, images, objects, observations or ideas. As a result, a drawing could be combined with a photograph, a print embellished with stitch, or an image magnified and projected through digital microscope and projector.

REFLECTIVE TASK

Reflect on the key ideas within this section of the chapter:

1. **Identify the related areas which teachers need to consider when supporting learners and learning.**

2. **Consider and reflect on your own practice in relation to the suggestions of the TAEV document 'Quality Art Teaching: what quality art teachers know and do'.**

3. **Consider the usefulness of 'strategies' when teaching. Think about the possibilities and challenges of adopting the Productive Toolbox as a strategy for teaching primary art and design education.**

Making this strategy work in the classroom would in turn be determined by consideration of the learning environment, of an understanding of the pupils involved, of their learning needs and of their social and environmental context. A 'word' a day could be approached in sketchbooks, or a Key Stage could be introduced to a number of 'words' as part of an arts week, or a year group could identify 'words' in their analysis of artists work and employ them in their own investigations. In these ways the 'words' become a key tool for teaching. They act as prompts for investigation or exploration, prompts for purposeful and creative learning in art and design. For example:

- produce a *sequence* of images of your drawings, photocopied and coloured with different *combinations*;
- *layer* materials to produce qualities of texture and surface;
- *cover* parts of drawings with paper and *mask* areas as you apply coloured materials;
- *magnify* an area of a painting with the aid of an overhead projector;
- change the scale of your work, *reduce* and *enlarge* on the photocopier;
- use a data projector to project *juxtaposed* words and images onto the outside of the building;
- *map* routes made around the classroom in one day;
- do the same for a week;
- draw the movement of a football player during a game on television, don't look at the drawing as you *mark* their movement;
- *embellish* and *decorate* work using the colour schemes of particular artists;
- *select* a series of images and present them in a *sequence* to show your lunch time experience;
- *document* the lunch time experience as a fold out book;
- *sort* your favourite toys by size, colour, texture, fabric, colour;
- photograph each *category*;
- cover your page in graphite, rub out sections with an erasure to *excavate* an image;
- *accumulate* flotsam and jetsam and *sequence* as a colour wheel;
- *map* the horizon on paper taped to the classroom window;
- take *photographs* looking down and up at points around the school;
- *combine* the photographs as though they were *mirror* images;
- *zoom* in on locations around the school .

A SUMMARY OF **KEY POINTS**

The chapter has introduced and made connections between a number of ideas. To summarise these ideas and to make them work in practice, it is suggested you keep thinking about:

➢ **an inclusive approach to creativity;**

➢ **creativity thought of as learning dispositions or habits;**

➢ **ways of describing learning in art and design;**

➢ **the relationship between creative learning habits and art and design;**

➢ **ways to cultivate this relationship through the application of teaching approaches and strategies.**

MOVING *ON* > > > > > > MOVING *ON* > > > > > > MOVING *ON*

Examples of good practice in primary art and design education reveal what is possible when pupils and teachers embrace the relationship between creativity and art and design and understand their contributions to children's education. Examples from OFSTED subject reports (Drawing Together 2009 and Making a Mark 2012), the Big Draw events, projects involving artists across the country including the work of Art4All in Kirklees, and the pioneering work of Room 13 all demonstrate what is possible. But perhaps what they demonstrate most of all is that the possibilities are achieved when teachers and schools are prepared to give something a go. They show in their own practice a commitment to, and courage towards, the very habits of creativity which they are trying to cultivate in children.

REFERENCES REFERENCES **REFERENCES** REFERENCES REFERENCES REFERENCES

Addison, N (2010) *Developing Creative Potential: learning through embodied practices* in Addison, N, Burgess, L, Steers, J, Trowell, J (eds) (2010) Understanding Art Education: engaging reflexively with practice. London: Routledge.

Bentley, T (2005) *So Giotto Drew On Rock: Children's Right to Art and Everyday Democracy,* available at: **www.demos.co.uk/publications/sogiottodrewonrocks** accessed 12/8/14.

Carroll, K (1998) *Cultivating Artistic Behaviours* in Simpson, J, Delaney, J, Carroll, K, Hamilton, C, Kay, S, Kerlavage, M and Olson, J (eds) (1998) Creating Meaning Through Art: teacher as choice maker. New Jersey: Merrill Prentice Hall.

Charman,H, Rose,C and Wilson,G (eds) (2006) *The art gallery handbook : a resource for teachers.* London: Tate.

DCSF (2000) Early Years Foundation Stage Statutory Framework. Nottingham: DCSF Publications.

DfE (2013) National Curriculum in England: Key Stages 1 and 2 Framework Document available at **https://www.gov.uk/government/publications/national-curriculum-in-england-primary-curriculum** accessed 12/8/14.

DfE (2012) Teachers' Standards available at **https://www.gov.uk/government/publications/teachers-standards** accessed 7/9/14.

DfEE (1999) *The National Curriculum*. London: HMSO.

Eisner, EW (2002) *The Arts and the Creation of Mind*. London: Yale University Press.

Eisner, EW (2003) *Artistry in Education* in the *Scandinavian Journal of Educational Research, Vol. 47, No. 3, pp 373–384.*

Gentle, K (1985) *Children and Art Teaching*. Beckenham: Croom Helm.

Hickman, R (2005) *Why we Make Art and Why it is Taught*. Bristol: Intellect Books.

John-Steiner, V (2006) *Creative Collaboration*. Cambridge: Cambridge University Press.

Key, P and Stillman, J (2009) *Teaching Primary Art and Design*. Exeter: Learning Matters.

NACCCE (1999) *All Our Futures: Creativity, Culture and Education.* Report from the National Advisory Committee on Creative and Cultural Education, to the Secretaries of State for Education and Employment, and Culture, Media and Sport, DfEE.

National Curriculum Council (NCC) Arts in Schools Project Team (1990) *The Arts 5–16 Practice and Innovation* Essex: Oliver and Boyd.

NSEAD **www.nsead.org** accessed 12/8/14.

OFSTED (2009) *Drawing Together: art, craft and design in schools 2005–08*. London: OFSTED.

OFSTED (2012) *Making a Mark: art, craft and design in schools 2008–12*. London: OFSTED.

Prentice, R (1999) 'Art: Visual Thinking' in Riley, J. & Prentice, R.(Eds.) *The Curriculum for 7–11 year olds.* London: Paul Chapman.

Qualification and Curriculum Authority (QCA) (2004) *Creativity Find It Promote It*. Suffolk: QCA Publications.

Sharp, C (2004) *Developing young children's creativity: what can we learn from research?* in Topic Autumn 2004, Issue 32.

Spencer, E, Lucas, B and Claxton, G (2012) *Progression in Creativity: Developing new forms of assessment*, Newcastle: CCE.

Taylor, R (1986) *Educating for Art*. Harlow: Longman.

Tertiary Art Education Group of Victoria (TAEV) *Art Teaching: what high quality art teachers know and do*, available at **www.arteducation.org.au/index.php/members-centre/art-education-advocacy-and-policy-development** accessed 12/8/14.

UNESCO (2006) *Road Map for Arts Education*, available at **www.unesco.org/new/en/culture/themes/creativity/arts-education/official-texts/road-map/** accessed 12/8/14.

Waters, S (1994) *Living Without Boundaries*. Bath: Bath College of Higher Education Press.

Other useful websites

Arts4All collaborative creativity in Kirklees **http://kirkleesarts4all.blogspot.co.uk** accessed 7/9/14.

Room 13 **http://room13international.org** accessed 7/9/14.

12
What has creativity got to do with citizenship education?
Richard Woolley and Hilary Claire

Chapter objectives

This chapter will raise some questions about citizenship education (CE) to help you to think about:

- the importance, for the future of our society, of creating people with vision;
- values in citizenship education;
- qualities and characteristics of people who can think creatively about citizenship issues;
- the creative teacher of citizenship;
- the creative curriculum in citizenship.

This chapter will not concentrate on explaining citizenship education, but on exploring the conditions and possibilities in the curriculum for creative responses to citizenship education. If you are unsure about its contents and remit look at Part 1 of *Teaching Citizenship in Primary Schools* (Claire, 2004).

This chapter addresses the following Teachers' Standards (DfE, 2012):

- demonstrate good subject and curriculum knowledge;
- adapt teaching to respond to the strengths and needs of all pupils.

Introduction

In England, the new curriculum for primary schools (DfE, 2013a) includes a non-statutory programme for citizenship (DfE, 2013b). The subject is not statutory until Key Stage 3 (from age 11 years) and until that point schools are to design their own curriculum content in addition to that outlined in the National Curriculum documents. Every school is required to provide a curriculum that is broad and balanced (DfE, 2013a, p5) and that promotes the *spiritual, moral, cultural, mental and physical development of pupils at the school and of society* (DfE 2013a, p5) – and that prepares pupils for the opportunities and experiences that they will face in later life. This places responsibility on individual schools and teams of teachers to develop an ethos and learning plan that has citizenship issues at their heart and requires teachers to be creative in their approaches to learning in order to integrate a consideration of values, social justice, moral responsibility and mutual respect into learning.

Ofsted, the school inspect body in England (2010, pp5, 6), found that:

> Teachers were seen to promote creative learning most purposefully and effectively when encouraging pupils to question and challenge, make connections and see relationships, speculate, keep options open while pursuing a line of enquiry, and reflect critically on ideas, actions and results.

Promoting such skills and attributes with children is very much in line with the approach to citizenship education that is outlined in this chapter, where children are enabled, in safe and secure environments, to broaden their thinking, explore new ideas, and consider potential solutions to problems and challenges in their locality and the world.

The global context of citizenship education

In the last 20 years there have been arresting examples of citizens confronting their history and creatively developing new systems of governance to promote social justice – Northern Ireland, nations which were part of the former USSR, and South Africa. Historically, there have been examples of people dissatisfied with existing systems who determined to develop democracy and citizenship in new ways – Ancient Athens, England at the time of the Civil War, the Glorious Revolution and throughout the nineteenth century, America and France at the end of the eighteenth century, and the Russian Revolution. Now, international conflict, climate change and other environmental hazards challenge the future of our children. In addition, there are issues about how the rich world can take on it responsibility to the poor in Africa and elsewhere.

In all these circumstances – historical and contemporary – people have to think with vision (not just pragmatically) about the nature of society and people's relationship to government and each other, locally and globally. The Robinson Report (NACCCE, 1999) was unequivocal, claiming that Britain's economic prosperity and social cohesion depended on unlocking the potential of every young person and enabling them to face an uncertain and demanding future (NACCCE, 1999). We have every reason to believe that as the twenty-first century rolls on, creative as well as pragmatic and principled thinking about social, economic and political problems and solutions will be essential. When children are asked about their future, they tell us clearly that they fear war, racism, crime and environmental meltdown (Hicks and Holden, 1995; Holden 2005).

REFLECTIVE TASK

Consider your own conception of citizenship education.

- To what extent is it founded in political processes, voting in elections and maintaining the rule of law?
- To what extent is it rooted in values, for example solving problems in the local community, addressing issues of fairness and injustice, or developing a sense of self-worth, self-identity and respect for others?
- How do your responses relate to the prescribed curriculum for your setting?

Creativity, citizenship and children's education

The statement at the beginning of the National Curriculum document for England (DfE, 2013a) acknowledges that children's education should encourage wider visions of a future society, not just fit them for the status quo. It states that the curriculum should *introduce pupils to the best that has been thought and said; and [help] engender an appreciation of human creativity and achievement* (DfE 2013a, p6). Sometimes encapsulated in the terms 'minimalist' and 'maximalist', there is a continuum in citizenship education: at one pole, a conservative desire to maintain the status quo, at the other, a conviction that citizenship education is about moving us along the road towards social justice (see Claire, 2001, pp1–2). The former concentrates on knowing about public systems and obedience to the law; the latter envisions and is prepared to work for wider ideals.

But even the conservatives, who would like to keep things as they are, are forced to deal with changing, often unexpected, circumstances. The old ideas do not always work; old dogs must learn new tricks; creative solutions become essential. So, creativity becomes fundamental to citizenship, whether at the radical or the conservative end of the continuum, or at points in between. Participative, active citizens of all political persuasions will need the ability to construe problems and consider creative solutions. Conformist/conventional thinking and attitudes will not lead to solutions in a changing world.

Creativity, democracy and values

Citizenship Education (CE) is imbued with values – as has been recognised from its inception in the curriculum. Government bodies have tried with little success to establish a set of common values that everyone should live by and ended up with lists that offend nobody and still leave us with controversies. Because CE is about the ways we organise society and live alongside one another, it is imperative that principles of human rights and social justice are the yardstick for systems and proposed changes. Still, the detail will always be contentious. When we ask children to consider creative solutions to social issues we must make sure that they constantly measure them against values which we debate in terms of principles and consequences. When we ask them to judge other people's creative proposals they must also refer to values.

This is because creativity can be the handmaid of evil as well as benign change. People are capable of creative problem-setting and creative solutions, but creativity does not automatically ensure justice. No doubt, gas chambers were perceived by Nazis as 'creative'. In South Africa in the early 1950s, the Nationalist Government came up with the 'creative' solution of apartheid, to solve what they had defined as the 'problem' of diverse groups living alongside one another. For the next forty years appalling injustice was perpetrated to carry out the so-called creative solution. Contrast a very different creative solution to economic and political problems: the New Deal in 1930s America. Following Keynesian economic theory which turned classical economics on its head, Roosevelt tackled poverty by providing work through government programmes. Indeed, Cropley (2001) argues that for a development or innovation to be creative it has also to be effective and ethical (for a more detailed discussion of creativity and its definitions see Compton, 2013).

Democracy requires citizens who can:

- analyse and synthesise idea and information from a variety of sources;
- evaluate the ways problems are defined and the possible consequences of proposed solutions; and
- resist brainwashing by powerful – even hegemonic – arguments.

They will need to be independent and capable of principled, creative lateral thought and imagination. They need the education and value systems to reject arguments such as those perpetrated by Nazis, white supremacists or fundamentalists, and realise that the problem itself has been wrongly defined. There are arguments that people who allow themselves to be led by the nose by their leaders have experienced an education which encouraged conformity and obedience, and punished any questioning of authority figures (Adorno, 1950). We are not advocating anarchy in the classroom: order is fundamental to successful teaching. However, we believe that being open-minded to alternative perspectives grows with the experience of creative debate and opportunities to come up with your own creative solutions to issues.

REFLECTIVE TASK

We are suggesting that citizenship is linked to creativity though the following requirements for a free democratic society:

- **creative thinking about problems and solutions in society;**
- **independent minds governed by principled moral thinking and capable of resisting pressure to conform;**
- **the presence of an opposition which critiques the status quo and offers alternative programmes and goals.**

Any critique which cannot offer alternatives will be negative, limited and backward-looking:

- **Envisioning alternatives, whether radical or conservative, required thinking outside the box, perceiving possibilities and being psychologically prepared to take risks and face challenges.**

What is citizenship education about anyway?

The thoughts illustrated in Figure 12.1, developed by a group of practising teachers and teacher educators, may help you with an overview of its concepts.

The diagram shows that citizenship education comprises a number of concepts, skills and personal characteristics.

PRACTICAL TASK PRACTICAL TASK PRACTICAL TASK PRACTICAL TASK PRACTICAL TASK

Taking the ideas from Figure 12.1 try to group them according to common themes, concepts, skills and personal characteristics.

- **Is there a better way to present this information visually? As a web or a list?**
- **How many of the ideas connect to the others or cross over with them?**
- **How many of these areas fit comfortably with other curriculum areas, so that you can integrate citizenship education in imaginative and creative ways with other learning and teaching?**

Figure 12.1 Citizenship education

Self-esteem and identity development: links with creativity and citizenship

In the National Curriculum guidelines for primary schools, Personal, Social and Health Education (PSHE) and Citizenship Education are closely related. Though PSHE may appear to be about personal qualities, they are essential to CE because pupils will grow into and hopefully influence the *social world*. High self-esteem and identity development are central to citizenship: to respect others' identity, understand their situation and grant them 'worth', even if they are very different from you, you must first respect yourself and your own worth, and feel confident about your own identity. George Mead (1934) explained how judgements and responses from *significant others contribute* to identity development and self-esteem. Peers and teachers in school as well as parents/carers and community members are critically significant for young children.

More recently, Jeffrey (2004a, 2004b) explained, using his own research, that we develop our identity and our capabilities in a social world: the very experience of creative learning in a creative context, contributes to positive self-esteem and social identity – all the more when a young learners' group experience is enjoyable, active, social and emotionally engaging. Indeed, the Robinson Report (NACCCE, 1999) emphasised two justifications for creative approaches in education: first, to address the kind of future we want for the human race; and second, to employ creative teaching and learning can promote children's self-esteem. It follows that we need to consider the environment and ethos that children will experience and how these can help them develop a strong sense of their own worth and identity, alongside an appreciation of others.

Citizenship, creativity and taking risks

Much theoretical writing about creativity emphasises the centrality of taking risks in one's thinking and planning. If your 'big new idea' goes against conventional thinking, you may not dare voice it for fear of an incredulous reception or jeering. Risk-taking is not just a physical thing like bungee jumping, though you may get an adrenalin rush as you prepare to argue a minority position. It is psychologically and emotionally charged: you are exposed and on your own. Even if you have a metaphorical map, it will be incomplete, warn of precipices or have blank bits. Think about the women who campaigned to be allowed to enter higher education – or any other campaign which went against the status quo. They had to be courageous, not just have persuasive arguments. We need to remember of course that something well-tried and familiar for adults may not be so for young children. This applies to the risk-taking they may feel if we ask them to work in unfamiliar ways, or to think for themselves – without the water wings of the worksheets or the familiar textbooks. For some children, something as ordinary as working in a group where you have to take a role or expose your views to others will be highly risky. So along with high self-esteem, children who are asked to think creatively and unconventionally about the social world need courage – and they need the conditions which nurture their courage and do not undermine it.

Given how important their social world is to children, preparing the ground for taking risks in the ways they think about problems and solutions is essential. Do remember that taking risks with thinking is a greater challenge for some children than for others; this applies to children in Year 6 as well as those in the Foundation Stage. So you will want to consider a psychologically supportive environment which encourages children to think outside the box without fear of ridicule. Perhaps it means working with trusted friends and having the solidarity of a group to back your ideas. Perhaps it means working through role play or games, or with puppets, or some other distancing technique, which allows them to play safely with new ideas.

PRACTICAL TASK PRACTICAL TASK **PRACTICAL TASK** PRACTICAL TASK **PRACTICAL TASK**

Rules, playing and creativity

Margaret Boden (2001) emphasises that the psychological ability to work without clear rules or to change the rules is an oft-ignored aspect of creativity. It follows that the classroom ethos we establish must encourage and not punish children for critiquing the rules and, where appropriate, changing them. Beyond that, the capacity to play with ideas – even play with rules – encourages creative thinking. So you might encourage your pupils to envisage a 'what if' world – where animals are in charge; where children are really adults' equals, where there are no adults, where the cars all vanish overnight. Some 'playing with ideas' will be seriously related to real events – suppose you were part of the unpredicted devastation wreaked by a tsunami, a cyclone or a drought which turned you from a wealthy farmer to a refugee. The

(Continued)

(Continued)

'imaginings' that such work invites are part of encouraging the kind of empathy as well as creativity children will need later, as concerned and proactive global citizens.

Consider one of the 'what if' examples above:

- **How easy is it to imagine alternative ways of thinking or living?**
- **What implications or consequences can you identify for the example you have chosen?**
- **How might considering alternative viewpoints help children to consider diverse views and ways of seeing the world? Might this help them to become more empathetic citizens?**

Children who have a strong sense of identity, self-worth and self-confidence can make choices for themselves, discuss and advocate what they would like to see happen – and why; listen carefully to alternative points of view, and be prepared to change their minds. Teachers can help to lay the foundations for concepts, skills and knowledge which will develop as the child matures towards adulthood. This means in practice that, from the nursery and throughout primary school, we consider confidence and identity building as children learn both to listen and to 'hear' others' positions and express their own ideas with confidence and without undue criticism. Thinking unconventionally and creatively can mean playing with ideas, imagining, letting go of rules and taking risks. Reducing the social and psychological risks will facilitate creating thinking.

The school curriculum, creativity and citizenship

Creative Citizenship Education is about looking at our social world with critical eyes, identifying what we would like to improve, and then developing realistic, appropriate ideas and plans.

'Mirrors and windows... roots and wings'

Someone has said that we need mirrors to reflect our world, and windows opening out to wider horizons and possibilities; roots so that we know who we are and feel strongly connected, and wings so that we can fly, fantasise, hope and dream. These seem perfect metaphors for creative CE. You must start with the mirrors and roots, so that you are not misinformed, alienated, apathetic and disengaged. To change things you need to understand what you are dealing with in terms of economic, historical, social and political realities. But without the windows and the wings there can be no visions of the future. The notion of *teaching for tomorrow* (Hicks and Holden, 1995) is best exemplified through the work of development education associations, the global citizenship movement and World Studies Trust (see Hicks, 2003). Their active pedagogy is admirably suited to work in citizenship. Much of their focus has been on global connections, particularly using geography as the vehicle. A range of useful resources are available from Oxfam **(www. oxfam.org.uk/education)** and Teachers in Development Education **(www.tidec.org)**. However, the principles of *teaching for tomorrow* apply across the curriculum and connect at all points with CE.

Teachers and the curriculum

So far, we have considered the personal qualities which may be important for creative thinking generally and in CE specifically. Within the child's experience in school, starting with the youngest, there are some other necessary conditions for nurturing qualities and attitudes of creative citizenship. This requires:

Creative, democratic and empowering teachers who:

- are committed to developing creative citizens for the future;
- create a classroom climate in which children experience democracy first-hand;
- see possibilities of developing children's ability to engage with the present and the future;
- know how to develop an ethos of collaboration and trust – both essential because of the risks and dynamics of thinking creatively;
- know how to set up up opportunities for creative thinking about their society – whether 'blue skies' thinking or pragmatic.

A creative curriculum which:

- enriches children's knowledge about society through biographies, stories and situations which challenge and stimulate their understandings of possible actions and ways of life in the world;
- develops qualities and capabilities of empathy, creative problem-setting and problem-solving;
- develops and encourages higher-order thinking skills.

The creative teacher

Having your own vision about creative teaching

We have said that CE can be either at the minimalist or the maximalist end of a continuum. Creativity in your classroom will depend on your philosophy of education and interpretation of your own role. People with a highly instrumental and minimalist view of CE are unlikely to want to encourage creativity or open-ended situations in which children pose problems about society and try to tackle them. But we do need to consider that we are preparing young children for the rapidly changing twenty-first century.

Being able to take risks as a teacher

Many experienced teachers know that it is possible to crush children's creativity into ready-made moulds where they parrot the expected answers and do what they have to do to get good marks or teacher approval or stay out of trouble. Moving children on from this conformist, uncreative approach to their own learning may have to start with the teacher her/himself being prepared to take some risks. In *Teaching Citizenship in Primary Schools* there is an account of a teacher called Paula who, faced with discipline problems in her Year 6 class, responded empathetically and creatively to the children – and simultaneously found solutions to their and her difficulties (see Claire, 2004, pp87–9). An important message from Paula's story was that she had to take a number of risks herself. She had to break free from a repressive school system which did not give children space to bring their concerns to teachers' attention; she had to take a risk that listening to children's perspective on some difficult issues might open *Pandora's box*, as she put it herself. Basically, she had to be prepared to trust herself and the children sufficiently to set something new moving without knowing quite where it would go. This is a really important message to those of you who hope to encourage children's creative response to citizenship issues. It is not just yourself you will have to trust, your own good sense, judgement, ability to create and manage a much more open classroom – but you will have to trust the children, too.

Managing a collaborative and trusting classroom

To get 'there' from 'here' will be quite easy if the school ethos already ensures that children work collaboratively, take responsibility seriously and know how to manage themselves in situations where they have considerable autonomy. For others, the very opposite may be the case. You will need to set yourself and the children small achievable goals towards greater collaboration, responsibility and autonomy on the journey towards a more distant goal of encouraging creative responses to citizenship issues. You will need to make your *responsibility objectives* as clear as you would the day's plans for literacy. You will need to use all the strategies you know for positive behaviour management, clear boundary setting, discussion about how they are doing and the progress you hope for (e.g. listening to each other, working with people who are not part of their clique, actively participating, etc.). You will go for group reward systems, intrinsic motivation and collaboration, not individual competition and extrinsic rewards. You will avoid damaging criticism. Your 'further goal' will be about working together towards solutions to societal problems – because they think it is worthwhile, not because they will get a gold star.

Your goal of building greater trust between children should not be confined to Circle Time. Use games and PE. Think about puppets, role play, pair and small-group work on stories, design, art and maths as possible opportunities for children to learn to talk more openly, listen and work together in trusting respectful ways.

Creative teaching: perceiving opportunities

Your vision of your role as a teacher and how you encourage learning and your intention to build greater trust and autonomy may mean some quite creative curriculum innovations. You will need to look for opportunities and plan to implement them.

Boden (2001) explores the relationship between knowledge and creativity and points out that creative thinking develops from what we already know, not in a vacuum. We transform what we already know by changing some of the rules; we think more creatively through engaging with other people's ideas – maybe through reading or through collaborative planning or conversation. CE is privileged, because you can use any other subject you choose to further its aims – and combine them in any ways you think will work. So you might get children to consider how they would like to improve an area of wasteland near their school (which would certainly be a citizenship topic) and your work could include some design and technology, science, art, letter writing, making a PowerPoint presentation and role play. You might use a painting in a museum to reflect on emblematic, cultural representations of power, celebration or religious difference (for example, Andre´ Fougeron's *American Civilisation* which is in Tate Modern – in the centre a man worships a car, surrounded by images of war and poverty – or the *Delhi Durbar* painting in the Bristol Museum of Empire and Commonwealth History (see Harnett *et al.*, (2005)). This will be the starting point for children to think about their own values, the people with power in their own society and how it is expressed.

Or you might start with the traditional Indian art of puppet-making to help children think about deforestation (Growney, 2005). Growney taught a primary class about puppet-makers substituting papier mâché for wood through a cross-curricular project in global citizenship, involving picture books like *The People Who Hugged Trees*, making puppets, perspective, talking about the different people involved in forestry, and work on sustainable development.

REFLECTIVE TASK

Reflect on some work that you have recently done with children. Could you have introduced a citizenship theme, for example about rights and responsibilities, identity, understanding other people's perspectives, what might we do when we feel excluded or bullied? Perhaps you asked the children to write poems, or explore themes in a text – could this have gone in other directions? One Year 4 teacher helped her children to develop role-play alternative non-violent endings to *Romeo and Juliet* – which is about peaceful conflict resolution in CE.

The creative curriculum: beyond instrumentalism

Inspiring children and enriching their knowledge base

You can support children's creative thinking about their own and others' identity, human rights, possible futures, their potential power and their relationships through introducing them to a range of analytic tools and concepts that move them beyond their current experiences and understandings. This is Vygotsky's *zone of proximal development* (1978) in practice – building into the unknown with scaffolding. It is fundamental to a wider vision of education, beyond instrumentalism. For citizenship, it may mean helping children to think about their world in terms of concepts such as the following:

- *The individual's relationship to society* e.g. how far aspects of a competitive, individualistic, materialistic society create difficulties between individuals, communities and internationally, and how far such characteristics promote dynamic and progress. You could use a story like *The Selfish Giant* (Bowler and Wilde, 2012) to help children to grasp these difficult ideas, going beyond the story itself, to talk about contemporary, realistic issues, and where we need to share and work collaboratively in society.
- *Gender relationships* e.g. how far conventional ideas about roles, rights and responsibilities get skewed into oppressive power plays and how far they serve stability. (Anthony Browne's *Piggybook* (1996) could stimulate such thinking).
- *Self-expression and instrumentalism* e.g. what is the point of artistic endeavours whether personal or communal – should the government spend money on free art galleries and sculptures in public places?
- *Should the wealthy 'north' take responsibility for the poverty and instability in some part of the 'south'* (less developed countries)? Are we our 'brothers' keeper'? A story from the Christian Bible could be the starting point.
- *Is war always justified?* Perhaps start with songs about soldiers like The Dixie Chicks' *Travellin' Soldier,* which was banned at the time of the 2004 Iraq War, Bruce Springsteen's *Youngstown,* or John Lennon's *Imagine.*

You are unlikely to use the abstract words but stories, poetry, music and art are important ways to open children's minds to critiquing their own society and possibilities for progress. Remember that everyone needs ideas to bounce off – even the most creative people stand on the shoulders of the giants who came before them. It is also about progression in learning – you offer images, stories and ideas which young children may not comprehend in depth, but which will form the basis for their conceptualisation of possibilities in the future. You can also explore the affective domain – considering how emotions and empathy help us to understand and respond to a range of issues.

Here are some more ideas:

- *Using a poem* – some examples:

White Comedy

I waz whitemailed
By a white witch,
Wid white magic
An' white lies,
Branded by a white sheep
I slaved as a whitesmith
Near a white spot
Where I suffered whitewater fever.
Whitelisted as a whiteleg
I waz in de white book
As a master of white art,
It waz like white death.

Benjamin Zephaniah, from 'Propa Propaganda'

Peace
Some say that Peace is calm and relaxing
And some say it takes your problems away.
Some say it makes your heart glow
And some say it is utter madness.

Does it look like a jigsaw muddled up?
Or does it look like an angel?
Does it stick with you all the way?
Or does it wave goodbye?

Katherine, age 11, cited in Adams, Hyde and
Woolley (2008: 74)

- *Using a story*

Engaging stories that highlight issues include: Anthony Browne's *Willy and Hugh* (all about bullying, friendship, the power of gangs) or *Piggybook* (a mum refuses to do the housework and her children and husband find out just what 'women's work' entails); Mary Hoffman: *Amazing Grace* (possible futures, breaking the stereotypes);

- *Using role play*

Develop a scenario between a group who would like to stop parents taking their children to school in individual cars, and those who support it (individual rights *versus* environmental pollution and traffic);

- Diamond-ranking

Provide a range of roles and job titles, including an artist, musician, doctor, teacher and childminder (see Claire, 2004, pp11–12; Clough and Holden, 2002, pp55–7). Consider the merits of each role and rank them according to various criteria, including perceived importance. The discussion may be more valuable than the final ranking;

- *Philosophy for children*

Use text (which could be from a newspaper), a cartoon, a photo or painting act as stimuli for children's own questions (see Claire 2004, Chapter 3 and Woolley 2010, Chapter 2 for more on Philosophy for Children).

Children cannot be expected to think creatively about an environment with beautiful innovative buildings or inspiring landscapes if they have never seen any – even in pictures. So perhaps bring in pictures of Gaudi's architecture in Barcelona, or Corbusier's estates on the outskirts of Paris, which in their time were supposed to offer a brave new world to working people (but have not ultimately fulfilled this vision).

More ideas for stimulating creative thinking about citizenship concepts

Historical and current examples

For opportunities to learn including starting with people and groups who wanted to change things, and considering their values and motivation:

- Martin Luther King, Mohandas (Mahatma) Gandhi, Nelson Mandela, Maya Angelou, Eglantine Jebb (who founded the Save the Children Fund) – all concerned with social justice and human rights.
- People concerned with the environment and uses and abuses of science and technology, e.g. Rachel
- Carson, a progenitor of the environmental movement; Arundhati Roy who campaigns in India; Greenpeace; WWF.
- People concerned with the effects of war and conflict, e.g. Save the Children Fund, UNICEF, Amnesty International.
- Anne Frank Educational Trust, Holocaust Education Trust, Red Cross, Medecins sans Frontieres.

Starting with fiction

Much children's fiction is about 'quest' and challenge, difficult choices, fighting the dragons and the giants or confronting evil, and personal qualities – courage, vision. From Philip Pullman, Anne Fine or Lemony Snicket to feminist and traditional fairy tales, myths and legends, there are opportunities to get children thinking about their values, concerns and their own willingness to become engaged. The important thing for teachers is to consider how pupils can engage with dominant discourses and critiques, moving from the metaphorical and fictional to today's real world. What are 'our dragons'? What qualities do we need to slay them? What choices should we carefully think through?

Linking with art and music

Certain artists represent reality or challenge the status quo, so that we see the world differently. Some theorists believe that without exposure to critical art we are 'dumbed down' into passivity and political apathy (Adorno, 1991). To harness this material for creative CE means being prepared to include the political and social content of art and music, not just concentrate on form. Think about Picasso's *Guernica*, Dubuffet's drawings of wartime Paris or poster art from round the world. These resources are intended to do more than extend children's cultural base. After the discussion, children should themselves try and use art, photography or posters to interpret contemporary issues.

Drama techniques

Role play, simulations and other drama techniques might well be your most powerful vehicles for creative work in CE: they can liberate creativity, allowing children to play with new ideas and new personae in safe contexts, to imagine and consider 'what if?'

Preparing for local study in the primary history curriculum, some students worked with newspaper cuttings about various historical campaigns, which included keeping a hospital open, stopping nuclear waste going through the borough, a *Rock Against Racism* concert in the late 1970s, the dustmen's strike and a march of unemployed workers in the 1920s. They quickly appreciated the opportunity to use cross-curricular approaches to explore historical issues about rights, responsibilities and advocacy and take this into contemporary concerns. So, their plans included using the photos and articles to set up freeze-frames, with children taking different positions which were then animated, the class writing letters to the press, holding a debate, making a simulated TV programme and learning some of the songs from the old campaigns. They would follow through by identifying a contemporary concern and planning a campaign themselves, learning about the range of possible ways to make your voice heard: making banners, designing leaflets and holding meetings.

A SUMMARY OF **KEY POINTS**

In this short chapter it has only been possible to skim the surface of a huge subject, but we hope that creative teachers will use these ideas as a springboard, and in turn empower their pupils to think and plan creatively for their own future. Toss a pebble into a pool – watch the ripples spread. The surprises and the rewards are great when you become a creative teacher, so that CE for your pupils is creative, liberating and empowering.

➢ **Creativity is fundamental to citizenship. Participative, active citizens of all political persuasions will need the ability to construe problems and consider creative solutions. They will need to be independent, and capable of principled, lateral thought and imagination; they will also need to be able to realise when 'problems' have been wrongly defined. Creativity does not automatically ensure justice.**

➢ **Central to citizenship education are high self-esteem and development of identity. To respect others' identity, understand their situation and grant them 'worth', you must first respect yourself and your own worth, and feel confident about your own identity.**

> ➤ Remember that taking risks with children and working with them to explore and change perceptions are greater challenges for some children than for others: this applies to pupils in Year 6 as much as those in the Foundation Stage.

> ➤ Try to conceptualise citizenship education as a journey towards a more distant goal of encouraging creative responses to wider societal issues. Set yourself and the children small achievable goals towards greater collaboration, responsibility and autonomy on this journey. Make your 'responsibility objectives' as clear as you would the day's plans for literacy.

> ➤ Citizenship education is privileged, because you can use any other subject you choose to further its aims – and combine them in any ways you think will work. Your goal of building greater trust between children should not be confined to circle time.

MOVING *ON* > > > > > > MOVING *ON* > > > > > > MOVING *ON*

- You may feel that some of the issues that children will raise will be controversial, and feel understandably nervous about this. Choose an issue that is particularly prominent in the news media at the present time. Create a mind map of questions which you anticipate children might ask. What is your own response to each question? Which questions might you find it difficult to address and what strategies could you use to avoid being defensive and to help children to work towards their own solutions/attitudes? An exploration of a range of issues including war and peace, climate change, democracy and sustainable development can be found in *The Challenge of Teaching Controversial Issues* (Claire and Holden (eds), 2007), and further issues including anti-racist education, diverse ways of being family, bereavement and consumerism can be found in *Tackling Controversial Issues in the Primary School* (Woolley, 2010).
- Using Oxfam's *Education for Global Citizenship: a guide for schools* (available to download at **www.oxfam. org.uk/education/gc/**), consider the range of citizenship-related skills that can be integrated into your teaching. Develop your lesson-planning format to include an area to include citizenship skills which will run alongside other curriculum areas. Explore the effectiveness of including such cross-curricular links as part of your daily or weekly evaluations.
- Choose one of the strategies outlined in this chapter (e.g. using poetry, freeze frame, photographs or artists' work) and develop an activity to undertake with a group of children to explore ideas about possible futures. How might the people be feeling in the situation that is portrayed? How does the situation or issue make the children feel? How would the children wish to change the situation presented? What possible alternatives can they think of?

REFERENCES REFERENCES **REFERENCES** REFERENCES REFERENCES REFERENCES

Adams, K, Hyde, B and Woolley, R (2008) *The spiritual dimension of childhood*. London: Jessica Kingsley Publishers.

Adorno, TW (1950) *The authoritarian personality*. New York: Harper & Bros.

Adorno, TW (1991) *The culture industry: selected essays on mass culture*. Abingdon: Routledge.

Boden, MA (2001) Creativity and knowledge, in Craft, A. Jeffrey, B and Leibling, M (eds) *Creativity in education*. London: Continuum.

Bowler, Bill and Wilde, O (2012) *The Selfish Giant*. Oxford: Oxford University Press.

Browne, A (1996) *Piggybook*. London: Walker Books.

Browne, A (1998) *Willy and Hugh*. London: Red Fox.

Claire, H (2001) *Not aliens: primary school children and the PSHE/citizenship curriculum*. Stoke-on-Trent: Trentham Books.

Claire, H (ed.) (2004) *Teaching citizenship in primary schools*. Exeter: Learning Matters.

Claire, H and Holden, C (2007) *The challenge of teaching controversial issues*. Stoke-on-Trent: Trentham Books.

Clough, N and Holden C (2002) *Education for Citizenship: ideas into action.* London: RoutledgeFalmer.

Compton, A (2013) Creativity in K Taylor and R Woolley (eds) *Values and Vision in Primary Education.* Maidenhead: Open University Press.

Cropley, A (2001) *Creativity in education and learning,* London: Kogan Page.

DfE (2012) Teachers' Standards available at **https://www.gov.uk/government/publications/teachers-standards** accessed 7/9/14.

Department for Education (DfE) (2013a) *The National Curriculum in England: key stages 1 and 2 framework document*. London: Department for Education. See website: **https://www.gov.uk/government/uploads/system/uploads/attachment_data/file/254357/PRIMARY_national_curriculum_11–9–13_2.pdf** accessed 12/8/14.

Department for Education (DfE) (2013b) *National Curriculum non-statutory guidance for Citizenship*. Sine loco: Department for Education. See website: www.education.gov.uk/schools/teachingandlearning/curriculum/primary/b00198824/citizenship accessed 12/8/14.

Growney, C (2005) *Primary design and technology and citizenship*. See website: **www.citized.info/pdf/commarticles/Cathy_Growneys.html** accessed 12/8/14.

Harnett, P with Pettigrew, A and Newman, E (2005) My 'self' and the wider world: Interpreting the British Empire and Commonwealth Museum.

See website: **www.citized.info/pdf/commarticles/Penelope_Harnett.pdf** accessed 7/9/14.

Hicks, D (2003) Thirty years of global education: a reminder of key principles and precedents. *Educational Review*, 55:3, 265–75.

Hicks, D and Holden, C (1995) *Visions of the future: why we need to teach for tomorrow*. Stoke-on-Trent: Trentham Books.

Hoffman, M (2007) *Amazing Grace*. London: Frances Lincoln.

Holden, C (2005) The citizenship challenge: educating children about the real world and real issues, in Ross, A (ed.) *Teaching citizenship*. London: CiCe, University of North London.

Jeffrey, B (2004a) *End of award report: creative learning and student perspectives* (CLASP) *project,* submitted to ESRC, November.

Jeffrey, B (2004b) Meaningful creative learning: learners' perspectives. Paper given at the ECER conference, Crete.

Matthews, A (2003) *Romeo and Juliet (Shakespeare Stories).* London: Orchard Books.

Mead, G (1934) *Mind, self, and society*, Morris, CW (ed.). Chicago, IL: University of Chicago.

National Advisory Committee on Creative and Cultural Education (NACCCE) (1999) *All our futures: creativity, culture and education* (The Robinson Report). London: DfEE.

Ofsted (2010) *Learning: Creative approaches that raise standards*. London: Ofsted.

Oxfam website at: **www.oxfam.org.uk/education** accessed 12/8/14.

Rose, Deborah Lee (2001) *The People Who Hugged the Trees: an environmental folktale*. Sine loco: Roberts Rinehart.

Teachers in Development Education website at: **www.tidec.org** accessed 12/8/14.

Vygotsky, LS (1978) in M. Cole, V. John-Steiner, S. Scribner and E. Souberman (eds) *Mind in Society*. Cambridge, MA: Harvard University Press.

Woolley, R (2010) *Tackling Controversial Issues in the Primary School: facing life's challenges with your learners.* London: Routledge.

Zephaniah, B (1996) *Propa Propaganda*. Newcastle-upon-Tyne: Bloodaxe.

13
Creativity in primary design and technology
Dan Davies and Alan Howe

Chapter objectives

The objectives of this chapter are to:

- argue for the importance of design and technology to children's creative development;
- suggest creative starting points for design and technology activity;
- introduce the notion of social creativity.

This chapter addresses the following Teachers' Standards (DfE, 2012):

- establish a safe and stimulating environment for pupils, rooted in mutual respect;
- demonstrate knowledge and understanding of how pupils learn and how this impacts on teaching;
- have a secure knowledge of the relevant subject(s) and curriculum areas, foster and maintain pupils' interest in the subject, and address misunderstandings;
- impart knowledge and develop understanding through effective use of lesson time;
- demonstrate an awareness of the physical, social and intellectual development of children, and know how to adapt teaching to support pupils' education at different stages of development.

Introduction

Design and technology (D&T) can claim to be at the heart of any curriculum that seeks to develop children's creativity, and was originally conceived as such. In the original proposals for the subject in the National Curriculum, the Design and Technology Working Group (1988) suggested that it involves:*The development of design and technology capability to operate effectively and **creatively** in the made world* (para 1.2; our bold).

PRACTICAL TASK PRACTICAL TASK PRACTICAL TASK PRACTICAL TASK PRACTICAL TASK

In the current national curriculum in England (DfE, 2012), a 'Purpose of study' statement for each subject is included prior to the programmes of study. How many of these statements refer to creativity?

You will have discovered that five of the introductory 'Purpose of study' statements for subjects in the national curriculum claim to contribute to children's creativity, yet design and technology – alongside art & design and music – mentions it twice! What makes D&T such a creative subject?

Well, firstly, if we take the oft-quoted definition from the highly influential report *All Our Futures* (NACCCE, 1999): *Imaginative activity fashioned so as to **produce outcomes** that are both original and of value* (our bold), we can see that the emphasis upon production is central to D&T activities. D&T is a hands-on activity in which children make real, tangible objects. It is, however, also 'minds-on', involving a balance between doing and thinking, action and reflection. The act of designing inevitably involves imagining something that does not yet exist. At its best, D&T offers children open-ended tasks which do not have a prescribed 'right answer' and involve an element of choice (of shape, colour, materials, function, etc.) so that their outcomes will all be original. Evaluation is also central to the 'minds-on' dimension of D&T; children need to learn to appraise others' designs as well as their own.

Secondly, Koestler's (1964) definition of creativity as *the ability to make connections between previously unconnected ideas* seems to describe well the sorts of ways in which designers think (e.g. linking clockwork and radio, or cyclones and vacuum cleaners). D&T can provide children with opportunities to bring together ideas from different areas of the curriculum (e.g. knowledge about materials, electricity or nutrition from science, understanding of 3D shapes and measurement from mathematics, people's different needs and lifestyles from geography). D&T draws particularly on children's *visual literacy* – their ability to 'read' colour and form, patterns and symbols, and to reassemble these elements into aesthetically pleasing outcomes. It shares this with art and design, and can perhaps claim to represent a third major form of representation, alongside words and numbers.

Thirdly, accounts of creative processes also seem to echo those that designers or children might undertake in the course of a D&T project. For example, Dust (1999) suggests that at least four phases of creativity are commonly identified, to which we have added imaginary examples from the development of the Dyson vacuum cleaner:

1. **Preparation** – investigating the problem and gathering data (e.g. trying out many vacuum cleaners to measure their loss of suction as the bag fills up).
2. **Incubation** – usually an unconscious/subconscious phase (e.g. going away and thinking about something else, perhaps observing tornadoes or water flowing down plugholes).
3. **Illumination/revelation** – the insight, the moment of creation (e.g. if we could make two 'mini-tornadoes', one inside the other, it would suck air into a vacuum cleaner powerfully).
4. **Verification/reframing** – the 'testing', usually through communicating the outcome to peers or 'gatekeepers' in the 'field' or domain (e.g. making hundreds of models and prototypes, taking them around trade fairs, showing them to manufacturers).

If we consider these against the processes identified in the National Curriculum Programme of Study (PoS) for D&T (DfE, 2013a) (Figure 13.1) we can see striking correspondences. You will notice that the steps in the process do not occur in the same order, but we need to remember that in both cases they *do not generally occur in a tidy linear path: they often overlap and the process can be entered and left at any stage* (NGfL Scotland, 2003). There is also no equivalent of *incubation* in D&T as prescribed by the National Curriculum, although there seems to be a recognition by teachers that children should be given more time to think and discuss ideas during the school day.

Dust's (1999) synthesis of creative processes	D&T National Curriculum Programme of Study
Preparation	4. Knowledge and understanding of materials and components
	3. Evaluating processes and products
Incubation	
Illumination/revelation	1. Developing, planning and communicating ideas
Verification/reframing	2. Working with tools, equipment, materials and components to make quality products
	3. Evaluating processes and products

Figure 13.1 Correspondence between models of creative and D&T processes

The fourth reason why D&T and creativity go together is concerned with thinking skills. One of the *creative thinking skills* identified in the National Curriculum is *problem-solving*. Problem-solving is a thinking skill that has received much attention over the years, and the strategies to solve practical problems have long been promoted in D&T (see, for example, Roden, 1999). The extent to which it is generic or transferable is debatable (if you can solve mathematical problems, it does not necessarily mean you can solve design problems), but its importance in D&T is profound. Design problems tend to be 'wicked'; they are not clearly defined like mathematical problems and involve many factors such as materials, technology and human lifestyles. This sometimes makes them not look like problems at all: *design and make sandwiches for a picnic* sounds more like an opportunity for trying out new combinations of fillings. Playing around with ideas, another characteristic of creative D&T, is a problem-solving activity, although within a low-stress, relatively unstructured framework. We do not necessarily need to set children artificial 'problems' (for example, *build a tower to support a marble*) but we do need to support them in developing strategies that will help them think through problems in the midst of designing and making. For a food technologist, designing a sandwich that will stick together, taste pleasant and not make the bread too soggy presents a whole range of challenging problems – it's no picnic!

Creativity and values in D&T

Before we look in detail at classroom practice we need to consider why we want children to be creative in D&T and how we will know whether they have been. This involves applying value judgements: what is your response to a child who has creatively combined materials to make an innovative weapon? If we analyse further the national curriculum 'Purpose of study' statement, it becomes clear that design and technology is a *future-oriented* subject in that children are being asked to imagine how things might be different and better. David Orr claims that:

> Students in the [future] will need to know how to create a civilisation that runs on sunlight, conserves energy, preserves biodiversity, protects soils and forests, develops sustainable local economies and restores the damage inflicted on the earth. In order to achieve such ecological education we need to transform our schools and universities.

(Orr, 1993, p16)

Orr is applying his values – which are associated with education for sustainable development – to identify problems that, in his opinion, require creative solutions.

We do not often ask children to think very far into the future, but what could we design to improve people's lives in ten or 20 years' time? Perhaps in order to engage children's creativity we need to be setting more 'blue-sky' design projects, inviting children to project themselves forward in time.

REFLECTIVE TASK

Hicks and Holden (1995) reported on a survey of children's visions of the future. They found that while half the children at age seven thought about their own personal futures often, less than a quarter reflected on the future for their local area. Encouragingly, 41 per cent claimed to think about the future of the world often, with a further third considering it *sometimes*. While the majority considered that their own futures would improve, they were less optimistic about other people and the planet as a whole. 11 year olds in particular were worried about increasing pollution, poverty and wars:

> *Their choice for preferred futures indicates that many would like a future based on greater environmental awareness, and their action as individuals reinforces this as an area of concern.*

> (Hicks and Holden, 1995, p78)

In your experience, are children encouraged to think about *a better future* during D&T lessons?

The findings of Hicks and Holden will not surprise any teacher who has discussed global issues with his or her class. The problem lies (as with all of us) in the differences between what children say and what they do. At a mundane level, their apparently wasteful use of resources in a design and technology project (cutting a circle out of the middle of a piece of card for example) may frustrate us. Often it is that they have not made the connections between the big ideas of environmentalism (e.g. deforestation) and their individual choices (how much paper to use).

So a further dimension of decision-making for children can be to introduce eco-choice points in a project in which they are given the relevant environmental information to make sustainable decisions. Batheaston Primary School used its international links to obtain recycling data from different European Countries, then compared the rates of decomposition of different materials by burying them. They used the information to design class gardens, which grow food for the school canteen to reduce food miles. Children were also involved in the design of animal boxes and a weather station in the school grounds, together with a Mediterranean garden, withy dome, bark trail, sand pit, fossil wall and range of limestone rocks from a local mine (**www.batheastonprimary. co.uk**). Children worked with sculptor Edwina Bridgeman on a number of installations, as part of the 5x5x5 = creativity project (**www.5x5x5creativity.org.uk**).

PRACTICAL TASK

How could common classroom designing and making activities such as fairground rides, coats or fruit salads be adapted to engage children with values consistent with sustainable development?

Starting points for creativity in D&T

Through looking at what experienced teachers do in the classroom (Howe *et al.*, 2001), we have identified three ways that teachers provide motivational and inspirational starting points for D&T activities that support the development of children's creativity. These are:

- building on children's interests;
- identifying real opportunities;
- using relevant contexts.

For example, in a reception class making wheeled vehicles, we observed how the class teacher used the children's interests to identify a context for learning:

> *[The children] had lots of experience of working with a variety of construction kits on a small scale. There was a class 'craze' for making ever more elaborate wheeled vehicles. Katherine, the class teacher, wanted to capitalise and build on this enthusiasm. This led to her making formative assessments about what the children were able to do, their language development, their knowledge and understanding of the world and their interests. She had also identified a need to give the children opportunities to work on a larger scale and to develop the skills of cutting and joining wood... To begin the project, Katherine discussed with the class their recently made wheeled models, and introduced a new word – 'axle'. She showed them how an axle could be used to link pairs of wheels and allow them to turn. Some children were able to make freehand labelled drawings of vehicles whilst others used the models as designs for the next stage . . . The children discovered how PVA glue and elastic bands might be used to join pieces of wood through this activity. At times they became engrossed in this to such an extent [Figure 13.2] that they lost a sense of time and place – they were 'in the flow...'*
>
> (Howe *et al.*, 2001, pp22–3)

Figure 13.2 Developing wheeled vehicles from children's initial interest

Csikszentmilhalyi (1997, 2002) coined the phrase *in the flow* to describe the most productive and fulfilling phases of the creative process, a state he characterises by intense concentration, absorption, pleasure and lack of awareness of time passing. By providing children with real opportunities, their sense of engagement with the task can carry them into this state. For example, at Bromley Heath Infants School in South Gloucestershire, D&T co-ordinator Sarah Stillie chose to take advantage of the new housing development being built locally to provide children with the opportunity of observing structures at various stages of completion, and consider ways in which the development would impact upon the local community. She was also anxious to provide children with a sense of the social setting within which homes are bought and sold, so set up an estate agency in the classroom role-play area, complete with ICT-generated advertisements, index files, property descriptions and key tags. When children came to undertake the design-and-make assignment (DMA) she wanted them to be able to consider the particular needs of individuals, so set up a 'fantasy' scenario in which children would design for story characters. They were to group the resulting models in a housing development ('Fairytale land') which considered issues of access, space and traffic.

A classroom role-play area is also an example of a relevant context. In other examples we have seen, contexts were provided through the use of story or by referring to needs within the school – to help someone to put on an assembly or to redesign a library. Relevant contexts are particularly important in helping young children to design for others, because without significant scaffolding many find it very difficult to think beyond their own needs and wants. For example, the children in the autumn of Year 1 at St Philip's Primary School, Bath, carried out a D&T task to make a sandwich that they would like to eat. The starting point was, therefore, a discussion about their own preferences. Their teacher had judged that it would be too demanding for them to think of the needs of others while, at the same time, meeting the requirements to plan before making and remembering safe and hygienic practices. Later in the year, when the children were more secure with the notion of designing and making, she 'scaffolded' their transition from egocentricity to awareness of the perspectives of others during work on playgrounds. The class went to look at a playground as the starting point for thinking about the equipment different age groups would like and where a playground should be sited so as not to offend residents.

REFLECTIVE TASK

Are the teachers above teaching for creativity, teaching creatively, or both?

Helping children to generate creative ideas

Having *good ideas* is fundamental to creativity; it is an obvious point to make, yet do we actually teach children in a way that develops their ability to think creatively? A study of 5,000 pupils undertaken by Nicholl *et al*. (2008) found that many sometimes struggled to develop original ideas, a situation they described as *design fixation*. By 'original' we refer here not only to inventing new products but also to considering new ways of looking at things and doing things. It is also important to note that we are using the *ideas* in the plural here. We want children to be able to come up with a number of possibilities, then evaluate their potential before proceeding. This is related to a measure of creativity – *ideational fluency* – in common usage in the USA. We want to avoid situations where children say *I can't think of anything!* or on the other hand proceed with the first idea that occurred to them. This is not to say that every time children do D&T they should come up with three ideas and choose the 'best' one. That would be too formulaic, however, we do believe children should have the opportunity to think before proceeding.

The D&T curriculum provides a framework for allowing children time to think by suggesting they should investigate and evaluate *a range of existing products* (DfE, 2013b, p193). Although the processes of D&T can occur in any order and begin at any point (see Table 13.1 above) we believe there is a strong case for beginning with *evaluation*. D&T and evaluation have a *special relationship*, and it is difficult to think of a great innovation in design that has come about without a keen awareness of what has been done before. We need not worry that by exposing children to existing products they will simply *copy* them – some degree of transformation is inevitable in the process of making an idea their own. The key to making an evaluation activity a spur to generative thought is the teacher's choice of a range of different design solutions around a common theme, and the *scaffolding* of children's ability to *interrogate* these objects.

For example, we can use questioning which focuses children's attention on key aspects of the objects being evaluated. This needs to begin with questions that encourage closer observation and initial investigation, such as:

- What shapes can you see?
- What materials have been used?
- How many pieces have been used in construction?
- What does it feel/taste/smell like?

Next, we can ask children to consider the human factors behind the design of the product being evaluated, and to think about future developments as this may provide a springboard for their own ideas:

- Who do you think this product was designed for? How can you tell?
- Describe how they would use it – can you imagine any difficulties they might have?
- Could you improve upon the product, and if so, how?
- How would you redesign it for a different user (perhaps for a child, an elderly person, an astronaut, a fictional character)?

So, through evaluation of the made world, children's ideas can be sparked and their creativity enhanced. Handled in the wrong way, however, looking at what already exists can be an inhibitor to creative thought. Such a situation could arise if the children see only one or two alternatives, if they think the teacher values one solution above others, or if one product seems perfectly suited to the design brief they have been set.

A set of techniques developed by Robert Eberle (1997) and known by the acronym SCAMPER can be usefully applied to D&T contexts to enable children to see existing artefacts or products in a new way and so aid *ideational fluency*:

Substitute: What if we substituted one material with another in this bag or vehicle?
Combine: What if we combine the ideas from these two pupils or groups?

Adapt: What if we adapt this idea to be more environmentally friendly?

Modify: What if we magnify this shape to make something much bigger? (e.g. a cup becomes a house). What if we 'magnify' this aerial photo to make a fabric design?

Put to other uses: What if we use this bag as a hat or that hat as a bag?

Eliminate: What if we remove as much material as possible from this design?

Reverse: What if we turn this inside-out or upside-down? (Eberle, R, 1997)

Another common way of supporting idea generation is brainstorming or blue-sky thinking. Essentially this is an uninterrupted process during which a teacher might invite immediate responses to a given scenario, e.g. *a wolf-proof house* for the three little pigs. Children throw any words or ideas that occur to them into the *pot* for recording on a large sheet of paper or interactive whiteboard. The ground rules are to avoid evaluating the ideas immediately, and certainly not to laugh at them! Such a flow of ideas in response to a problem or scenario can be enhanced if the thinkers work in small groups initially to allow a chance for discussion. The discussion may start from a very open-ended question – *what winds you up?* – or completing the statement – *we really must do something about...* Another technique is for ideas to be written or drawn on paper aeroplanes – this literally allows ideas to be *tossed around* for others to pick up and add to. The playfulness of the situation can encourage playfulness in thinking. Once the initial *storm* has passed, we can then sort through the contributions and evaluate them against criteria decided by the group, e.g. practicality, aesthetics, or expense.

Alternatively, we can use a strategy called *linking-thinking*. Linking ideas, as we have seen, is a fundamental part of creativity. There are a number of techniques that can help this linking-thinking in the classroom. Relating a product in an analogous way can throw up new possibilities, for example:

> *Packages are like...*
> *...nuts (strong, keep the contents safe, hard to open)*
> *...homes (keep contents dry, secure, insulated, reflect the owner's character).*

Develop the analogy for the item to be packaged:

> *If my new sweet was growing on a tree, it would look like this . . . be displayed like this... be dispersed like this... be consumed by... and so on.*

Some children might find the visual a more powerful stimulation than words. Visual triggers might come from:

- random shapes/scribbles/doodles;
- images from photos or clippings;
- digital photos that have been manipulated;
- shapes in nature – fruits, river deltas, frost patterns.

In generating ideas, children might be asked to act out an aspect of the life of the intended user or even the intended product. Some adult designers have actually done this – dressing like a pregnant woman or visually impaired person. Examples for role-play could include:

- looking after a baby;
- coping in a classroom without bending;
- if I were a package I would be...
- a day in the life of a shoe.

Social creativity in D&T

As teachers, should we concentrate on enabling individuals to be creative or should we concentrate on developing a creative classroom ethos? Siraj-Blatchford (1996) discusses how, in the classroom, children can move from being involved in *collective design* – working as a group with support from the teacher – to, in later years, a *design collective* in which children draw on earlier experiences and learned skills to design and make with autonomy alongside their peers. He suggests that if children are part of successful design collectives during the primary years, then they are more likely to progress to challenging tasks with confidence.

One of the key findings from research into children's creativity is the central importance of peers, supportive adults and role models in inspiring and stimulating children. Our own research in this field – the Young Designers on Location project (Davies *et al.*, 2004) – suggests that the most important kinds of encounters for stimulating children's creativity are those involving practising designers, technologists, artists, architects and engineers – we will call them *design-related professionals*. Children respond instinctively to the apprenticeship model of education offered by the designer in the classroom, rather than to the more rigid, curriculum-led attempts to *teach children to design*. By sharing their own work practices with examples, it seemed that the designers working on the project helped to create a climate of confidence and trust, while maintaining *high ambient levels of creative activity* through acting as *co-workers*, modelling behaviours and demonstrating practice. The professionals also demonstrated *explicit expressions of confidence in the creative abilities of those within the environment* (Harrington, 1990) through a discussion of children's own creativity – demonstrating both a democratic view of creativity and a metacognitive dimension to their teaching. By the end of the project, when relationships had had time to establish, the interactions between children and designers were very productive. They were genuinely able to *bounce ideas* off each other and challenge formulaic thinking.

The project above describes a situation where the distinction between the roles of adult and child had begun to dissolve. This poses the class teacher a real challenge – can this radical shift of roles be allowed to happen in a 'normal' classroom? The role of the *more knowledgeable other* is like that suggested by Bruner (1996) in *scaffolding* children's learning, as evidenced in the way Steve Heal worked with his Year 5/6 class in helping them to prioritise design criteria (Davies and Heal, 2006). Another way forward is to consider different uses of curriculum time. Many schools have made a step in this direction through *D&T weeks*, where different ways of working can be developed and where different relationships can take hold. This different use of time, when combined with some input from those who work in the design world – perhaps in the form of an afternoon visit or short residency – can provide an ideal context for a *creative ecosystem* to be developed.

Creative making in D&T

We have discussed creative and generative thinking as a part of designing, yet there is more thinking to be done when making. At any point, the introduction of one of the strategies we have described above might refresh or refocus minds. D&T is an iterative process moving backwards and forwards between activities *inside* and *outside the head*

(Kimbell *et al.*, 1991) so it is appropriate for children to employ procedures in different orders – for example by starting with making. In order to develop their creative ideas, children may find it helpful and motivating to get their hands on materials as soon as possible. This can involve play, by which we mean handling objects and exploring them in a relatively unstructured way. In a primary classroom children might be encouraged to handle objects such as the materials they will later be using (as in the wheeled vehicles example above). This will allow children to develop their knowledge of the properties of materials and will allow them to imagine how the materials might be put to use. Ideal materials that allow shapes and forms to be developed in a temporary way include:

- clay – to explore a form for a storage container, candle holder or vehicle body;
- pipe-cleaners or art straws – to allow exploration of stable shapes for a photo frame, furniture or play-ground equipment;
- paper – to allow exploration of card mechanisms, patterns for garments, patterns for bags or shoes;
- construction kits – to allow exploration of mechanisms for vehicles or toys, hinges for storage boxes, stable shapes, strong shapes.

The power of computing in developing children's ideas before and during making is considerable. For example, using a site such as www.dtonline.org to explore packaging design, simple computer-aided design software such as TABS+ which allows children to make 3D models and prints out 2D nets, or 'My World' which allows young children to make a number of decisions, for example in relation to designing a house, can all help to develop creative solutions.

REFLECTIVE TASK

Should teachers give children freedom to design and make, or should they teach them skills beforehand?

This question of balance between intervention and non-intervention has been at the heart of debates about teaching for creativity. In D&T there are certain skills that children can learn – to do with thinking and making. The tension between a skills-based approach to developing creativity (what Gardner (1999) identifies as deriving from an Eastern, Confucian tradition with an emphasis on *mastery*) and one that is more *constructive*, with an emphasis on process, was highlighted in our own work with 11 year olds and *design-related professionals* (Davies *et al.*, 2004). Those with more skills input produced outcomes of higher quality, though children who had been encouraged to reflect on their own creativity and *follow their own path* were less conventional. This reflects research by DATA/Nuffield (2003), who advocate an approach combining skills input with *surprise* activities to stimulate unusual solutions. The National Grid for Learning in Scotland (2003) urged teachers to go beyond the *creative ecosystem* to a more directive role in children's capability:

> *Although a creative climate and an encouraging adult are essential they are not enough to develop creativity. The teacher's role, beyond encouragement, involves intervening, actively teaching creative techniques and strategies.*

> (NGfL, 2003)

Although young children may exhibit *preconventional* creativity (Rosenblatt and Winner, 1988) before exposure to specific D&T knowledge and skills, our own view is that *postconventional* creativity (i.e. that which transcends convention) is associated with explicit teaching of knowledge and skills. Through making with a range of materials, children will develop knowledge of their properties, together with skills of cutting, fixing, joining and manipulating that will enable them to realise their creativity with fewer frustrations. There is no substitute for this first-hand experience.

Sometimes children can get *stuck* and give up, or return again and again to making the same limited range of things. To move children on and help them transcend their existing set of ideas for solving the problem, we can intervene in a number of ways:

- by introducing a new set of materials;
- by asking the child to share their project and ideas with the rest of the class;
- by showing a new technique for cutting, joining or combining.

One way in which we can support children in their development of problem-solving is to make the strategies they are using more explicit through questioning. This will promote *self-knowledge*, or *metacognition*, widely regarded as essential if you want to get better at something. For example, during an activity to design and make homes for story characters (see above) class teacher Sarah Stillie gathered the children on the carpet for a joint problem-solving session. Each pair had to present their progress and discuss their problems – plus the ways in which they had tried to overcome them – with the wider group, who made suggestions about the way forward.

PRACTICAL TASK   PRACTICAL TASK   PRACTICAL TASK   PRACTICAL TASK   PRACTICAL TASK

Another way of looking at creative teaching of D&T is to consider what a D&T teacher should not do (Fasciato and Rogers, 2005). Can you imagine what the most uncreative D&T teaching would be like?

A SUMMARY OF **KEY POINTS**

In this chapter, we have suggested that in order to develop children's creativity through D&T teachers should:

➢ develop a supportive 'ecosystem';

➢ be playful with ideas, spaces, time and resources;

➢ make connections, when planning, between learning and children's lives;

➢ teach skills and knowledge, but in a way that helps children to solve their own problems;

➢ develop cross-curricular links with other learning areas.

MOVING *ON* > > > > > > MOVING *ON* > > > > > > MOVING *ON*

After teaching some design and technology, a teacher will want to know if the lesson is a success. There are at least two ways of asking this: *Did I put on a good performance and ensure the lesson ran smoothly and to plan?* or (and this is the key question in the context of this chapter) *Did I teach in a way that enabled children to demonstrate their creativity?* In order to answer the question next time you are evaluating a lesson, the following factors could be considered.

In the lesson, was there:

- a non-threatening atmosphere in which children were secure enough to take risks and make mistakes – or were they always looking to me for reassurance and the 'right answer'?
- opportunity for play and experimentation – did I allow the children to try things for themselves in an open-ended way?
- opportunity for generative thought – where lots of ideas were expressed and greeted openly?
- an activity presented in an exciting context – did the children find the context motivating and worthwhile?
- a chance for children to choose resources and methods?
- opportunity for critical reflection in a supportive environment – did the class appraise their own and each other's work constructively?

If you can answer yes to at least one of these questions, then you are on the way to teaching design and technology both creatively and for creativity.

REFERENCES REFERENCES **REFERENCES** REFERENCES **REFERENCES** REFERENCES

Bruner, JS (1996) *The culture of education*. Cambridge, MA: Harvard University Press.

Csikszentmihalyi, M (1997) *Creativity, flow and the psychology of discovery and invention*. London: Rider.

Csikszentmihalyi, M (2002) *Flow*. London: Rider.

Davies, D and Heal, S (2006) 'Ground Control to Moonbase': communications technology in primary D&T, in Norman, E, Spendlove, D and Owen-Jackson, G (eds) *Designing the Future: The D&T Association International Research Conference 2006*. Wellesbourne: DATA. 33–40.

Davies, D, Howe, A and Haywood, S (2004) Building a creative ecosystem – the Young Designers on Location Project. *International Journal of Art and Design Education*, 23:3, 278–89.

DfE (2012) Teachers' Standards available at **https://www.gov.uk/government/publications/teachers-standards** accessed 7/9/14.

Department for Education (DfE) (2013a) *Design and technology programmes of study: key stages 1 and 2*. London: DfE. **https://www.gov.uk/government/uploads/system/uploads/attachment_data/file/239041/PRIMARY_national_curriculum_-_Design_and_technology.pdf** accessed 13/8/14.

Department for Education (DfE) (2013b) *The national curriculum in England: Framework document*. London: DfE.

Design and Technology Association (DATA)/Nuffield Foundation (2003) *Creativity in crisis?* Wellesbourne: DATA.

Dust, K (1999) *Motive, Means and Opportunity: Creativity Research Review*. London: NESTA.

Eberle, R (1997) *SCAMPER: Creative Games and Activities for Imagination Development*. Austin, TX: Prufrock Press.

Fasciato, M, and Rogers, M (2005) Creativity in practice. What not to do. In E. Norman, D. Spendlove and P. Grover (eds) *Inspire and Educate*.

DATA International Research Conference 2005 Proceedings. Wellesbourne: Design and Technology Association.

Gardner, H (1999) *The Disciplined Mind*. New York: Prentice Hall.

Harrington, DM (1990) The ecology of human creativity: a psychological perspective, in Runco, MA and Albert, RS (eds) *Theories of creativity*. London: Sage.

Hicks, D and Holden, C (1995) *Visions of the future:why we need to teach for tomorrow*. Stoke-on-Trent: Trentham Books.

Howe, A, Davies, D and Ritchie, R (2001) *Primary design and technology for the future: creativity, culture and citizenship in the curriculum*. London: David Fulton.

Kimbell, R, Stables, K, Wheeler, T, Wozniak, A and Kelly, AV (1991) *The assessment of performance in design and technology*. London: Evaluation and Monitoring Unit (EMU), School Examinations and Assessment Council (SEAC).

Koestler, A (1964) *The act of creation.* London: Macmillan.

National Advisory Committee on Creative and Cultural Education (NACCCE) (1999) *All our futures: creativity, culture and education (The Robinson Report).* London: DfEE.

National Curriculum Design and Technology Working Group (1988) *Interim Report.* London: Department of Education and Science/Welsh Office.

National Grid for Learning in Scotland (NGfL Scotland) (2003) *Creativity in education online.* See website: **www.educationscotland.gov.uk/learningteachingandassessment/approaches/creativity/** accessed 12/8/14.

Nicholl, B, McLellan, R and Kotob, W (2008) *Understanding creativity for creative understanding.* Cambridge: University of Cambridge Faculty of Education.

Orr, D (1993) Schools for the 21st century. *Resurgence*, 160 (September/October).

Roden, C (1999) How children's problem-solving strategies develop at Key Stage 1. *Journal of Design and Technology Education*, 4:1, 21–7.

Rosenblatt, E and Winner, E (1988) The art of children's drawing. *Journal of Aesthetic Education*, 22: 3–15.

Siraj-Blatchford, J (1996) *Learning Technology, Science and Social Justice*. Nottingham: Education Now Publishing.

Other websites

www.batheastonprimary.co.uk

www.dtonline.org

www.5x5x5creativity.org.uk

– all accessed 12/8/14

14
Creative primary geography
Simon Catling

Chapter objectives

By the end of this chapter you should:

- appreciate that geography can be imaginative and creative;
- recognise that harnessing children's geographies is vital in enabling creative geographical learning;
- be aware of the characteristics and principles underpinning creative geography teaching and learning, including curriculum making;
- identify and consider how to use a variety of approaches to creative teaching and learning in primary geography.

This chapter addresses the following Teachers' Standards (DfE, 2012):

- demonstrate good subject knowledge and maintain children's interest in the subject;
- show awareness of children's prior knowledge and capabilities and build on these;
- promote children's subject learning and intellectual curiosity;
- provide engaging subject lessons and curriculum through effective planning;
- provide motivating and challenging aspirations for all pupils through stimulating teaching.

Introduction

Geography is an active subject, at the heart of which lies creativity. Throughout its history geography has taken creative and imaginative turns in its explorations, investigations and explanations of our world (Törnqvist, 2011). It is a discipline and subject which constantly fosters and requires new thinking to help us all understand the Earth, its physical and human characteristics and functions, places and how we use and (re)make them, and what we can do to right the damage we create and improve our places and the planet. We can think of creativity in a number of ways. Usually we associate it with imagination and being imaginative, creating new ways of looking at or making something, whether an idea or object. It is, therefore, about understanding the world about us as much as it may involve something fictional or imagined. In this context, creativity implies resourcefulness in producing ideas as well as objects and can be linked to the creation and use of images, for instance imagining what a place might look like or what it may be like to visit. It links to processes as well as to products, including signs and symbols that represent ways of understanding, such as words, pictures and maps. It can also be thought of as a frame of mind, an attitude to undertaking tasks. In many senses, creativity is a way of responding to challenges, but creativity in itself is equally challenging.

Creativity is a key element of constructivist learning, how we make or create our own knowledge of the world, initiating, adapting, assimilating, and recreating learning from new contexts to revise, even reject and renew, current understandings or schema. This can be influenced by the way we perceive events, our environment and the people involved. Creativity is not a single entity; rather it has a number of overlapping meanings. It is not straightforward, therefore, to pin down simply in terms of originality or of having purpose and value; at times creativity appears intuitive or serendipitous, as when the solution to a problem might *spring to mind* rather than appear to be based in explicit and analytic thought. In this sense creativity is active and generative (NACCCE, 1999; Scoffham, 2013a, 2013c). It is about new insights, new perspectives, new alternatives and new possibilities, whether personally or for the wider world. Creativity is fundamental to learning as much as it is vital to the way disciplines or subjects evolve. Creativity is as much an aspect of geography as any other subject.

Creativity for geographers involves several different things. There are images to be created, whether they are maps, photographs, film, field sketches or models to show the world. There is the capacity to understand how the world works, the processes that create our natural and human environments and lives and the imaging and imagining that helps our understanding of these processes. Where we need to find, revise and provide our familiar resources, such as food, water and energy, housing or waste removal services, there are problems to solve, and we need to imagine how these will look and what impact they will have; indeed we will have to consider whether or not we make these developments and changes. Geography requires the use of imagination, the capacity to innovate, to be problem-solvers, and creativity (Craft, 2005). Barnes (2010) notes that creativity is not often associated with geography, even in the minds of novice teachers (Davies, *et al.*, 2004, Compton, 2013), yet it is clearly essential in geographical learning (GA, 2012; Lambert and Owens, 2013).

The revision of the national curriculum offers opportunities for creative approaches in teaching and learning, particularly through what the government refers to as inspirational teaching, with primary teachers given greater freedom to create and make their own curriculum (DfE, 2010). The revised programmes of study for Geography in key stages 1 and 2 (DfE, 2013b) provide a set of content statements but do not, helpfully, direct how they might be taught. The potential for geography teaching and learning is to be creative and proactive, and to make links that provide integrated learning, for instance through using topicality to find out about what is happening internationally in the world, initiated by news items, linking these with enquiry skills, including using websites, globes, atlases and Google maps, and in making short presentations about what has been found out. This keeps children aware of the events, places and environmental matters in the wider world (DfE, 2013b), but it can apply equally to being informed about the local area, wider region and nationally. It is also true for the Foundation Stage, particularly in relation to children's play-based interactions with places and their evolving experiences in the local area (Conway *et al.*, 2008).

This chapter examines aspects of and approaches to creativity in primary geography. It considers teaching creatively as well as engaging children in learning that is creative (Craft, 2005, 2011). It has been argued that creative teaching is fundamentally aligned to effective teaching, that effective teaching involves dimensions of creativity, whether in opening children's eyes to new perspectives and helping them create new understandings or by involving them in developing approaches to undertake their studies and fostering insight through their self-developed activities (Ofsted, 2010). The latter can be appreciated as teaching *for* creativity, in that it is concerned with the empowerment of the learner, where the child is a co-participant alongside the teacher in constructing their approaches to learning. The argument is that this provides the basis for creative learning, exhibited through five *behaviours*: asking questions, making connections, imagining what might be, exploring options, and reflecting critically (Craft, Cremin and Burnard, 2008). To these we might add: being empathetic – understanding others' perspectives and feelings. These are all elements of an enquiry approach in geography (Martin, 2004; Catling and Willy, 2009; Dinkele, 2010; Roberts, 2013) that supports strongly teaching for creativity and creative learning.

REFLECTIVE TASK

Before you read further, consider how geography can be a creative subject. List three ways to teach creatively and three ways in which children's creativity might be developed in geography.

Children's creative geographies

Studies of children's geographies have enabled us to recognise that children's place and environmental experience is a *given* in their lives (Freeman and Tranter, 2011) and can be drawn upon in various ways when we plan our geography teaching. Indeed, children's perspectives are a key creative aspect of curriculum making in primary geography (Catling, 2013), enabling us to identify and work with the ways in which children engage with, think and feel about the world. These 'worlds' represent children's geographical imaginations, their constructions of experience in the world, and how they make sense and use of it as they grow through childhood (Catling, 2006a, 2006b, 2011).

Children's *action world* is the environment of their daily experiences, of going to school and coming home, of playing outside and indoors, of shopping with their parents, and of visiting their friends and relatives. It is their engagement with their environment, and it enables their creative development of environmental knowledge and spatial understanding. It is the source for their mental maps of familiar places and the basis for extending their fields of activity into new areas. Children associate people with places and this human interaction helps to create their sense of place. In their *peopled world* others influence their experiences of places, guide and encourage their environmental experience, impact on their routines and activities and provide them with information and perspectives about the world around them. This occurs both at first hand and also through *experiencing* the media: television, computer games, film and mobile technologies.

Children's perceptions and images of their own places and of the wider world are influenced by their experience and their understandings. Their feelings, in turn, impact on how they assimilate and appreciate new encounters with places and the wider world whether through visits or the media. Their *perceived world* interacts with their action and people worlds to influence how they make use of the affordances their locality and of other places provide, and what sense they construct of other places and peoples. Children's *valued world* encompasses their place and environmental likes and dislikes, their attachment to or detachment from places, of where they prefer to be or are determined to avoid, of who they want to be with in particular places, of sites that are special to them – their feelings for and senses of place.

It is evident that their experience of places and the environment enables children to construct their *information world*, their tacit and shared knowledge of the local and wider world. Their inquisitiveness involves them in interacting with a wide variety of environmental information, which they inter-relate to create understandings about places, enabling them to use places not always as adults imagine. Yet other aspects of their knowledge remain particular, partial and unconnected, an assemblage of facts and/or misconceptions. Their environmental experiences enable children to develop their *competence world*, the range of skills they employ to make use of places. These involve refining their inquisitiveness such that their investigative skills are more directly useful, constructing their wayfinding and navigational skills, and connecting these with map making and use. Children's own experiences in their home and local area, with their family, friends and strangers, through play equipment and story and information books, and through television and computer programmes and increasingly by mobile communication technology provide their *source world*. It is a world that is often presented to children in mediated and selective encounters. It is also a world in which children are increasingly creating their own sources, through blogs and in virtual environments such as Facebook.

A vital way in which children make sense of the world they inhabit is through their *imagined worlds*. Play enables children to explore the activities and actions of people, to mimic and play out what they have observed occurring in, for instance, the supermarket or a journey, alongside the use of toys or other objects as props to construct environments at their own scale or in miniature, creating a beach scene or building and role playing characters in an imagined street or on a farm. Children's imagination is fired by stories set in places and about lives and events occurring there, both familiar and novel. There are connections here with children's *future worlds*. In noticing what places are like, the various ways in which people live in them and what they do or happens to them, provokes in children a sense of what might be. This is influenced by their own experiences with family, friends and society. From a young age, children become concerned about injustice, for people and the environment – often intertwined – and a desire to see change effected for a fairer world. They have a sense of a *preferable world*. This connects with children's *commitment world*. Children's sense of injustice and welfare leads to more than identifying what might be alternatives and preferences for the future. It leads to a desire to act, and as such to the frustration of inactivity, not simply of their own impotence but the inactivity of others locally and on the larger stage. The development of ethical awareness means for many children the move to commitment to make improvements, to take action to create a fairer and better world, focused usually on the lives of others.

REFLECTIVE TASK
REFLECTIVE TASK

Consider your own experience of places and your awareness of the *distant* world through secondary sources, and those of children and young people with whom you have worked in or out of school. For each of the ten worlds of children's geographies outlined above provide a personal example and one you might know of or can infer from another person's experience.

Applying research: challenging children's learning

Creativity in primary geography involves harnessing and integrating both the creative subject of geography and the creative nature of children's geographies. The literature on creative teaching and learning can be applied to teaching geography with younger children (Bruce, 2004; Craft, 2005, 2011; Cremin and Barnes, 2010; Conway, 2008; Compton, 2013). Emerging strongly from this literature is the notion of challenge in pedagogy, that creative teaching is focused on challenging children in their learning, both intellectually and through self-expression, which best work together. Challenge is used here not as a singular notion but severally. Before exploring this a little further, it is relevant to note some of the characteristics exhibited in pedagogical strategies when teachers construct creative learning contexts (Rawling and Westaway, 2003; Barnes, 2010; Craft, 2005; Cremin and Barnes, 2010; Johnstone and Halocha, 2007; GA, 2012; Scoffham, 2013a). These include:

- being clear about the nature and focus of the topic that is to be studied but setting it up in an open way to which the children contribute;
- providing stimulating and motivating introductions and tasks to generate interest and engagement in learning;
- setting clear structures for lessons and tasks, for instance in the use of available sources and/or materials, time limits and types of outcome;
- ensuring there is enough time to develop ideas within a time limit for undertaking the task;
- providing a safe, secure and supportive learning environment, where children can *go beyond what is expected*, not necessarily in a linear fashion;
- providing a context for the children such that they recognise the relevance and pertinence of the tasks;
- being committed to developing understanding through the tasks set which are designed to make demands on children;
- encouraging the use of discussion and sharing and the use of vocabulary and expression to explore and develop tasks and outcomes;
- ensuring that children encounter alternative approaches to tackling tasks through the example set by the teacher;
- being flexible and open to making use of the unexpected, whether this comes from the children or an outside source;
- engaging children in the use of evaluative criteria such that they can identify and explain the quality of what they have achieved and consider their next moves.

Implicit in these pedagogical characteristics is the idea of *challenge*, not least for the teacher intending to adopt them. They are also key aspects of curriculum making in primary geography (Catling, 2013), which depend for their full effectiveness on a teacher's subject knowledge and their confidence in employing a range of teaching strategies (Ofsted, 2010, 2011). So in what senses is challenge being used here? There are various ways in which the notion of challenge can be applied.

- The obvious characteristic of challenge is that of making demands on children in terms of higher order thinking skills, which involve problem-solving approaches, careful scrutiny and evaluation and well-argued and presented outcomes, for instance in examining a local problem about car parking or access for disabled pedestrians and identifying ways in which these might be overcome.
- This includes the curiosity to explore and follow lines of enquiry where they lead. It also means taking a questioning and critical stance in that the interest is not to accept the conventional, indeed any, response without taking a hard look at it. This focus might be used when examining and comparing tourist information about particular destinations, questioning what is shown and why as well as considering what might be missing from the brochures and website information and why.

- This might well require risk taking, where it is not clear where enquiries might lead and may not have straightforward resolutions, if any. It involves engaging with uncertainty and the unknown and a willingness to come up with novel, even messy, solutions as necessary (Pickering, 2013). For example, children might investigate a site in their village, suburb or town for a new housing development to help meet housing needs locally, particularly if it is a live and controversial issue. This will involve considering different perspectives, the needs and issues involved, possible solutions which may be uncomfortable for some or all, and making the arguments for different decisions.
- Linked closely to this is the requirement for openmindedness, in which children do not close off options to explore or viewpoints to examine but where they are concerned to identify as many possibilities as possible, evaluating limitations before rejecting them, and returning to them later if circumstances warrant it. Considering the need to provide clean water supplies and sanitation for a particular community may involve just such an approach for while a solution may seem obvious it may not be as straightforward as first appears, perhaps having unhelpful consequences.
- Another element of challenge involves a willingness to be unconventional, not to take the more likely option, even to follow up what will become controversial because it evokes strong and mixed responses and will need to be well-considered and argued. A geography topic might explore the impacts and developing potential for the use of tablet computers and mobile phones in shaping how we keep aware of what is happening in the world and maintain contact with people. It should explore how this is reshaping of our geographical awareness as well as some of the concerns about the use of such technologies in our classrooms which can bring the world 'in' and take us 'out'.
- Related to these last two is another element, that of speculation, which is the capacity to think laterally. This is about keeping one's options open and playing around with different ideas to come up with alternatives, characterised at times as *thinking outside the box*. It links with possibilities thinking (Craft, Cremin and Burnard, 2008). This might involve children looking at ways they might develop the facilities in and uses of their playgrounds, making proposals which they display and which could be followed through, moving from the possible to the actual.
- A further characteristic of challenge is the capacity to identify, make connections and see relationships, as well as to notice *gaps*. Here we are involved in linking ideas and ways to generate solutions to the problems that are the subject of an enquiry. Children might examine the links which they have across the world, what these relationships are and what pattern they show on a world map. They can consider the empty spaces or non-existent links they notice and consider why this is. Perhaps they identify places to find out about, which enables them to use known and perhaps new sources of information in their enquiries.

PRACTICAL TASK PRACTICAL TASK PRACTICAL TASK PRACTICAL TASK PRACTICAL TASK

Select two of the challenges noted above and outline another example of a geographical topic for investigation.

Use your reading in other subjects about research in creativity in teaching and learning to identify one or more ways in which you could monitor and evaluate how your use of creativity can benefit children's geographical learning.

Creative approaches to teaching and learning geography

There are many ways to provide for creative learning in geography teaching. Scoffham (2013b) provides a variety of examples of creative approaches to teaching geography and to enabling creative learning by children, for instance through play, the use of stories, investigations in the immediate environment, cooking to create landscape and geological patterns, using art and music, finding out about locations and connections with mathematics, history and sustainability. At the heart of creative teaching lies enthusiasm, curiosity and the desire to learn. Keys to creative learning include children's greater engagement and control, co-operative working, asking questions, rethinking their learning and actively and practically developing their investigations (Scoffham, 2013a, 2013c). The following case studies illustrate a variety of approaches that employed creative approaches in children's investigations.

CASE STUDY

EXPLORING THE ENVIRONMENT IN FOREST SCHOOL

The Reception and Year 1 children regularly visited a piece of local scrub and sparse small woodland a short walk from their suburban school. One of the reasons for this was to engage these young children with a natural environment, which too few of them had the opportunity to do, since many lived in flats, played in concrete playgrounds and journeyed to shopping centres or similar urban sites by car or bus. They looked forward to their visits and much enjoyed them. The focus was on children's own interaction with this natural site, in which they could explore and create their own activities individually or in pairs and small groups, as they wished. It was carefully overseen by experienced and trained staff and included a time to gather for a drink and to eat round a fire. The weekly sessions across the year lasted about two hours.

As a creative approach to developing geographical encounters and learning, it provided these young children with the time, excitement and surprise of interacting with at first a new and later a more familiar but still unexpected environment. There was much going on, such as developing confidence, observational skills, experimentation, and new experiences, as the affordances offered by this place were noticed more fully by the children. Geography is founded on exploration and piecing together what we learn of places, creating our mental maps of an area and its features and possibilities, learning its reality and potential. Even in later sessions, children encountered areas they had not explored as their roaming through the site grew wider. Their initial experience introduced them to sites to which they returned weekly, knowing what they would find, though at times surprised by changes in seasons or because someone else had been there in the meantime. Engagement with their peers brought about new experiences and helped them to explore further in what to them was *a big place*. This was supported by the adults who occasionally set up trails of items to find to take the children into less used parts of the site.

The children would talk with each other and the adults about where they went, what they found and what they did. They created their own places as dens and imagined and acted out events and layouts drawn from television, stories and journeys. A site or area could be in a home or a street or a mall. The Forest School site offered opportunities for creativity in making shelters or bridges, for imagining places, for sitting and contemplating, for chatting with friends, and for learning through their senses of sight, touch, smell and hearing. Tools and other resources enabled them to investigate, delve and be fascinated. It offered learning about nature, about themselves, of new skills and relationships and pleasure and enjoyment. Forest School offers these opportunities for creative, self-directed learning, and much more (Williams-Siegfredsen, 2012; Knight, 2013a, 2013b; Watts, 2013). It provides developing familiarity, knowledge and engagement with a place at a scale large enough to need to explore and small enough to be safe. It provides geographical experiences which complement, even enhance, those of everyday life in urban settings.

CASE STUDY

A CREATIVE APPROACH TO STUDYING OUR LOCALITY

A Year 4 class began a study of their local area with group and then class discussions about what they knew about their locality, what they thought about it and how they felt about it. It became clear that they had a wide range of knowledge of their area between them, how variously they related to the area and that they had views about the state of the area. Drawing out their ideas and questions their teacher encouraged the children to work in four teams, each of which focused on a different way of looking at the locality, and each of which was to produce its own report. The four mini-topics were: *What is good about our place?*, *A clean neighbourhood?*, *What you can do here*, and *What we like here*. A variety of investigations developed. Opportunities for fieldwork were organised and many of the children were able to draw on their local knowledge and to follow up lines of enquiry outside school. Investigations involved interviews with family, friends and other local people; photographs of places liked or thought *scruffy*; mapping local shops and other useful services; sketches of particular features and views. The children were encouraged to be creative in preparing their reports. The teams drew on leaflets, posters and such like that they had come across for inspiration.

One produced a brochure to attract people to their area and emphasised what a good place to live in it is. Another provided a *clean up our neighbourhood* poster with photographs of unkempt sites and advice on what to do. The third team made a presentation about their and other children's favourite places using maps and photographs to show the sites. The fourth team produced a map leaflet to show what services were available and where they were.

The outcome was insightful, in that it provided four differing but overlapping perspectives on the geographies of their area. The children's favourite sites did not mesh with the views of a range of adults and teenagers on what was good about the locality, though there was some overlap with other people's ideas of what was scruffy about the area, such as the waste ground. Being creative in geography should involve looking at places and environmental matters from more than one angle and sharing and reflecting on these, as this class did. Creativity helps us to see the world differently and more roundedly.

CASE STUDY

FOSTERING CREATIVE THINKING USING *BELONGING*

Belonging (Baker, 2004) is a picture story without text. It presents the view from an upstairs window across the back garden to two local streets, similarly to her earlier book *Window* (Baker, 1994) which viewed the development of countryside at the urban fringe. Over a period of years, as a child grows from babyhood to being a first time parent, *Belonging* shows how the streets change. Initially there is decline in the quality of the area, then a gradual improvement and greening of the neighbourhood. The focus of the book, Baker (2004, p29) argues, is on the sense of belonging to the land. The story is about how communities contribute to and enhance or neglect at their peril their environment and how their nurturing creates the character of places and a sense of home.

Used with a mixed-age class of Years 1 and 2, the children were taken through the book by their teacher but not in one sitting. The story was introduced after the children had spent several minutes looking

(Continued)

(Continued)

out of their classroom window. They were given no particular brief but when they sat down they were asked what they had seen. The responses were uniformly about features. Using the big book version of the story, their teacher showed the children the first picture and asked them what they saw. Features and people were identified, but two children said that it looked rather tatty and another noticed the dog urinating! This led to two discussions. One was about how the area looked and what the children felt about it. The other focused on the couple in their back garden and their baby: what did the children think would happen to this family? Responses ranged from moving out to staying poor, with some ideas about the place *getting better* and that they would make a *nice garden*. Over the rest of the week several pages at a time were shown and discussed, the children encouraged to notice what had changed, to say what they felt about the changes, what they thought might happen next and what they would like to do to improve the area. The second half of the book provides opportunities to discuss creative ways to make an area more pleasant and attractive and about how it might be used by local people, including children like themselves.

The book generated three responses from the children. One was that among different groups of children there was increased sharing of their lives at home, what they did, what they liked to do and where to go, and so forth. A second was that, spontaneously, the children started talking about the views they saw from one or more of their windows at home, commenting on the view and the features, the state of the neighbourhood, how it looked different at night and how far and what they could see. The third was to suggest ideas about how the school playgrounds and field could be 'greened'. They moved from the story and home views to the view from their classroom window and to the somewhat barren nature of the play areas they used daily in school. This sparked further discussions, resulting in the children creating their own ideas and pictures about what sort of play areas in school they would like. They were aided here by the willingness of their teacher to go with where the children were taking their learning from the story, not in the direction she had planned but one which extended the sense of belonging to a place in the book and around home to the idea of school as a place of belonging. A creative approach to the use of the book led to opening up creative opportunities for the children, which did in the end lead to some additional resources for playtime use though not to some of the physical changes the children suggested. Creativity has an impact and can change minds, and the use of stories in geography can support this strongly (Tanner and Whittle, 2013).

CASE STUDY

GEOGRAPHY THROUGH ARTEFACTS

A Year 3 class were presented with a various artefacts from another culture and community in another part of the world. They included cooking utensils, cleaning equipment, storage jars, children's toys and musical instruments. They were set out as a display in the classroom. This set of commercially purchased items – all were originals, not copies – were provided for the class as a stimulus to involve the children in the study of a locality in a less economically developed region. The teacher drew on an approach he had used in history, not telling the children what the objects were or where they had come from but inviting them to select two or three objects in turn and working in twos and threes to say what they could about them, who might use them, for what and when. They were required to give a reason for their comments. They were also asked to see if they could say where in the world they came from. A large globe and atlases were available. The teacher recognised that their experience was limited and that this might prove a fruitless line of guesswork. The children responded well and the study of the locality went ahead. During the enquiry the teacher introduced photographs, newspaper extracts, postcards, clothing, food samples and other resources. The children pursued various lines of enquiry both self- and teacher-initiated. The creative start and use of a wide variety of resources, introduced in timely ways, engaged the children and maintained motivation. They came away more aware and empathetic to others elsewhere.

There was one point in this study when the children were asked what else would help them know more about the place they were studying. More resources from that part of the world was one of the responses. This sparked a creative, *left-field* moment for the teacher. He decided that he would adjust the geography and other parts of the curriculum to run a short topic on what their own local artefacts might be. He put it to the children that since they had received a collection of artefacts from another locality it would be helpful to people there if they could make their own set of artefacts for others to use to find out about their place. This approach used the '3 Ds' – develop, debate, decide – with the children: to develop their own ideas about what to include; to debate what might be included and why; and to decide what to include in their artefact set.

Suspending much of the intended curriculum for one week, the teacher focused the children on developing their ideas about which artefacts might tell other people about their lives in their place. Children worked in groups of four to come up with their lists and reasons why. The result was that many children brought into school one or more artefacts, including clothing, local postcards and newspapers, food packets, sweet and drink labels, photographs they or family members had taken (all labelled), as well as items similar to those they had initially been introduced to in the distant locality study, and much else. It proved not only highly stimulating but gave credibility to the risk in suspending the curriculum (an unusual practice here) and opened eyes to what the children felt was important to say about themselves and their neighbourhood. It also enabled them to consider what other items they would have liked access to for their distant locality study.

CASE STUDY

INVESTIGATING FOOD AND DRINK

Where do our food and water come from? How do they reach us? How do we use them? What is effect does all this have on us and others? These were some of the questions a Year 6 class investigated about key resources we take for granted and which are vitally important for us. This was a wide-ranging topic which touched on many aspects of geography, from developing knowledge about places on local, national and world maps, to appreciating the interdependence of places through food production, transportation and commerce, to investigating the relationship between rain and water supplies, the role of sewage farms and the links with health, among others. It was initiated by a discussion about what the children knew about what they ate and drank for lunch, whether in their packed lunched or school dinners. While they could describe what food they liked and did not, they had little sense of its sources. The starting point for investigations was recognition of ignorance about more than supermarket and market place sources – or the tap and the off-licence or pub! Their teacher gave them information about the sizeable number of children who do not know the sources of various meats and milk and cheese nationally. The children were personally challenged to address what they did not know, to work out how they would

(Continued)

(Continued)

investigate and how they might provide interesting information to help other children in the school know more about their food and drinks.

This was more than a geography topic, since there were clear links with science, health, design and technology, and ICT. This provided opportunities for experiments in blind tasting and cooking, a visit by a nutritionist, discussion with the school's cook, a fieldtrip to a farm and a visit to a local food store. Groups of children pursued topics selected from the range of possibilities which an early discussion identified as interesting and worthwhile to investigate. The challenge was to become as well informed as possible. Their teacher decided that he would add other challenges as the children worked on their topics. One concerned the ways in which foods such as bananas and chocolate arrived from their sources in our shops, with the children introduced to Oxfam resources on the journeys of these items. Another was to develop further the question arising from these about the fair distribution of costs, through using resources about fair trade. Some of this was challenging, for instance when the children debated the viewpoints, which different children had to argue, about the amount someone should be paid for their labour, who should take what share, and what they would be prepared to pay depending on interpretations of fairness for whom. The displays the children mounted for the rest of the school and parents evidenced their high level of engagement with this topic and their responses, such as the filmed fair trade debate, how packaging for chocolate might be more informative and look better, the sequence map of the distribution chain for tomatoes, and one group's view of the nutritional value of a good school meal!

These five examples illustrate how innovative and imaginative approaches to teaching geography can generate creative thinking and learning in children. Creativity and creative understanding are possibilities in all subjects; they can draw on approaches from each other.

PRACTICAL TASK   PRACTICAL TASK   PRACTICAL TASK   PRACTICAL TASK   PRACTICAL TASK

Read the classroom case studies outlined above and identify the ways in which creativity has been used in the teaching involved and what learning by the children appears to have taken place.

Being creative with geography in the national curriculum

The geography national curriculum requirements for key stages 1 and 2 (DfE, 2013b) are structured around:

- *locational knowledge*: knowing where places are and what they are like;
- *place knowledge*: of local areas and regions, including the UK, Europe and North and South America;
- *human and physical geography*: such as environmental vocabulary, settlements and land use, resources, trade, rivers, mountains including volcanoes, earthquakes, weather, climate and vegetation zones, and the water cycle; and
- *geographical skills and fieldwork*: reading globes and atlas maps, reading and making large scale maps, using photographs, taking and recording measurements, and undertaking fieldwork.

The first point to make is that the creative approach is to integrate all of these four aspects in all geographical studies. For instance, in looking at the local area use maps and photographs alongside fieldwork to explore the human and physical features of the area, such as using everyday vocabulary to name them with younger children and more geographical terms with older children. In doing this you will be noticing where features are and building children's mental maps of the locality. This may well be developed in considering the type of settlement and what characteristics it has, such as port facilities or being local service centre because of its commerce and market. You may well be able to look at shops and other businesses and consider where their food and water come from, as well as use this to identify connections with the wider region, country and world. You can also observe and record local weather and use this to consider the relevance of the water cycle and the disposal of waste water.

Secondly, using and applying the examples given throughout this chapter, you can investigate a local area, country or region in North or South America, and examine in those continents examples of volcanoes and other mountains, earthquakes and their effects, major rivers, the ranges of climates and vegetation, using not only reference books and the web but also seeking information from atlas maps and through Google maps, engaging and applying developing map reading skills. You might make links with a local school in Canada or the USA to share information and understanding about each other's places as settlements, the wider region and your countries. Alternatively, this link might be with a school in a country in South America if you have Spanish or Portuguese as your foreign language in key stage 2. You can certainly discuss how digital technologies aid your communication and enable you to find out about other parts of the world and its human and physical geography.

A third, vital creative approach to the geography requirements recognises that the listed content provides only a partial sense of geography, which must be addressed in every school's geography curriculum. The geography programmes make no reference to the enquiry approach to teaching and learning, which schools have used over the past 20 years, nor does it refer to the importance of sustainability in our places and environments and to our futures, both key aspect of earlier geography requirements (DfEE/QCA, 1999). These can be readily addressed and support stimulating and engaging ways of teaching and learning geography. Several examples above have illustrated the use of enquiries, built around questions about where places are, what they are like, what happens in them, how they change over time, what people feel about this, and what might develop in the future. Investigating food and water, as much as our use of other natural resources and energy, must consider how sustainable these are and the care we need to take in their provision and their use, given ever-increasing demands, national and global variations in access to resources and the effects, for instance, of such outcomes as poverty on people's lives.

There are many ways in which you can provide a creative geography curriculum, use creative teaching approaches and enable creative learning. Figure 14.1 identifies a wide variety of creative approaches to teaching geography. These can generate and motivate children in their geographical learning across the key stages. Even when you have been given a pre-structured geography topic to teach, you can draw on one or many of the ideas in Figure 14.1 to initiate and develop creative engagement in your teaching and your children's geographical learning.

At the heart of creativity in geography teaching lies taking responsibility for the children's learning and for developing and devising your teaching for and with them. This approach is known as *curriculum making*. There are two sets of characteristics which underpin

• give (and follow) route instructions with a map and/or compass • use vocabulary to describe features, layouts and areas without naming them (others work it out) • make and using maps to show particular aspects of places • take, annotate and display photographs of features, sites and places • draw field sketches • draw and write a picture postcard • make models of real or imagined places • use role play to debate an environmental change • create a picture sequence with drawings or photographs to show a route or development • make a wall frieze or collage to depict the 'look' of a street • plan and follow a trail around your neighbourhood to show particular aspects of it • use thought-tracking during a freeze frame in a role play to express views on an issue • investigate to write a formal report about a geographical topic or concern • write and illustrate a newspaper article about a topical local or global event • undertake surveys and interviews about, e.g., disability access, local v. chain shops • create a website about your school's neighbourhood, a place investigated or an environmental matter or concern	• write (shape) poetry and stories about or set in landscapes, urban sites, at the coast, alongside rivers or in mountains, or during a flood or earthquake • make equipment to gather data, e.g. about weather elements • organise a Planning Enquiry on a real or imagined development • make posters to encourage, e.g. using litter bins • arrange a debate about a topic environmental issue, e.g. food or water shortage • question visitors about their perception of the locality • plan, organise and undertake fieldwork in the local area or further afield • use hot seating to consider someone's viewpoint on an issue, e.g. a planner, shopkeeper, developer • use conscience alley at the end of a role play to involve the class in thinking about the views of the character walking between two rows • use drama and improvisation to act out scenes in, e.g. a meeting and debate about a global issue like climate change • undertake a simulation exercise to explore, e.g. a traffic/parking problem • make a presentation (perhaps using visual media) about, e.g. a place, an environmental issue • plan how changes might be made to an area, real or imagined, that people would like to see • make a video/audio tape recording about a local feature or issue	• create a display of artefacts about the local area or another place • make playmat maps for younger children to use, and trial them • arrange a meal using ingredients from around the world or from a particular part of the world • link with another UK or non-UK school and exchange information about your respective places • prepare a travel itinerary to visit another locality, how to get there, what you would take, what you might do • create a digital resource pack for your locality for use in a partner school and send it to them • create an activity sheet to be used to investigate a specific place or environmental topic • play with environmental toys, creating a model of your own, another or an imaginary place • evaluate the quality of places by developing criteria using rating scales • allocate pairs of children roles, e.g. as people in another locality, who then • hold an improvised conversation about their community

Figure 14.1 Examples of creative teaching activities to use to generate creative geographical learning

curriculum making (Catling, 2013). One set concerns your *attitudes*, while the other is about your *organisational and decision-making skills* as a curriculum maker. Attitudinally, you need to be confident that you are the person responsible for the curriculum for the children, that you are, thus, confident in yourself as a teacher, that, too, you are confident in the children, and that you see yourself as an active learner always developing your understanding of geography. Organisationally and as a decision-maker, you must be clear about the purposes of any topic you teach, but you need to limit your planning so that you can draw on the children's knowledge, potential and engagement to enhance and extend it. You provide an active and experiential approach for the children's learning and are open to discussion and debate, as well as being willing to modify with the children your (and their) intentions where more fruitful lines of enquiry open up. This requires that you are always looking to extend and apply your repertoire of teaching skills.

You can develop your creativity as a curriculum maker of your geography teaching and the children's learning by taking account of the examples of excellent practice advocated by Ofsted (2011). These examples of good practice are essentially creative not only in their topics and lessons but across the school where good, creative practice is implicit. An example to apply when investigating earthquakes and volcanoes is that used in by one Year 6 class to understand glaciers. Effective links with a local university postgraduate student encouraged innovative teaching approaches enabled the children to become engrossed and to develop experiments and explore the nature of glaciers, mountain and polar regions, and climate change (Ofsted, 2013b). In a second school, the use of outdoor learning and Forest School approaches involved Reception children developing their confidence through risk taking in a safe environment while building their knowledge of the outdoors locally and their sense of place (Ofsted, 2013a). A third example describes an enriched whole school geography curriculum that provides stimulating introductions to topics, such as an unexpected parcel arriving for a class, and a focus through topics which motivate children and build challenges and demands as they move through the school, the content of which is well integrated within the subject and with other subjects appropriately and imaginatively (Ofsted, 2013c). This third approach is strongly supported by the Geographical Association's Primary Geography Quality Mark criteria (Owens, 2013; GA, 2013).

Features of good practice in creative geography teaching and learning

As with all effective teaching there are a number of features of creative teaching that have underpinned the strategies and learning in the examples given above. They are important in developing geographical learning and enable teachers to provide the contexts for creative learning. They provide the environment for the *principles* inherent in the meanings of challenge in creative teaching and learning. These features include the following.

- *Clarity of focus*: being clear about what the children can learn from the topic and helping them to identify what they are learning as it develops.
- *Emphasise questioning and enquiries*: involve children in devising questions about the topic they are researching, e.g. What is it like? What is life like there? How might people there want it to develop? – and in selecting and structuring their geographical questions and their investigations, using and doing enquiry.
- *Engaging teaching approaches*: using children's perspectives, 'problematising' the topic, questioning the 'accepted', becoming aware of alternative possibilities, creating personal responses and meanings, making judgements and decisions and justifying them.

- *Focusing on children doing the thinking*: on interpreting, looking critically, making deductions or inferences, giving reasons, recognising limitations; justifying perspectives and conclusions; identifying what has been learnt. Always be prepared to challenge the children's views and arguments to enable them to hone them.
- *Evaluating learning*: involving children in appreciating what they have learnt and in identifying some of the gaps and limitations to their awareness, so as to help them realise and recognise their geographical learning.
- *Connecting with personal futures*: engaging children in thinking about ways in which their geographical studies and their understanding about their own geographies and learning might impact on their personal lives and the lives of others around them, how they might go about things differently in their use of and/or attitude to the environment, places and other peoples (Hicks, 2002).

A SUMMARY OF **KEY POINTS**

➢ **Geography is a creative subject.**

➢ **Children's geographies are both created through their experience and are creative in the ways in which they are aware of, appreciate and understand the world.**

➢ **The characteristics of creative pedagogies link well with the focus on challenge in creativity that is characteristic of creative geographical teaching and learning.**

➢ **Innovation, imagination and creativity are intertwined in approaches to good geography teaching and learning.**

➢ **Curriculum making in geography is a creative approach to teaching on which to draw. It returns responsibility to the teacher and involves the children fully.**

➢ **Effective geography learning and teaching will require creative approaches and engender creative learning within geography.**

MOVING *ON* > > > > > > MOVING *ON* > > > > > > MOVING *ON*

When you have your (next) opportunity to teach a geography topic or an interdisciplinary topic which includes geography, identify the approaches you can use to provide both creative teaching approaches and for creative learning for the children. Remember that it is you who can facilitate these opportunities for creative geographical teaching and learning by accepting the challenges and taking the risks in planning creative teaching. Try one activity, then another and a third...

REFERENCES REFERENCES **REFERENCES** REFERENCES REFERENCES REFERENCES

Baker, J (1994) *Window*. London: Walker Books.

Baker, J (2004) *Belonging*. London: Walker Books.

Barnes, J (2010) Geography, creativity and place, in Scoffham, S (ed) *Handbook of primary geography*. Sheffield: Geographical Association, 24–33.

Bruce, T (2004) *Cultivating creativity in babies, toddlers and young children*. London: Hodder Education.

Catling, S (2006a) What do 5-year-olds know of the world? – Geographical understanding and play in young children's early learning. Geography, 91:1, 55–74.

Catling, S (2006b) Younger children's geographical worlds and primary geography, in Schmeinck, D (ed) *Research on learning and teaching in primary geography*. Karslruhe: Padagogische Hochschule Karlsruhe, 9–35.

Catling, S (2011) Children's geographies in the primary school, in Butt, G (ed) *Geography, Education and the Future*. London: Continuum, 15–29

Catling, S (2013) Teachers' perspectives on curriculum making in Primary Geography in England, The Curriculum Journal, 24, 3, 427–454.

Catling, S and Willy, T (2009) *Teaching Primary Geography*. Exeter: Learning Matters.

Compton, A (2013) Creativity, in Taylor, K and Woolley, R (eds) *Values and Vision in Primary Education*. Maidenhead: Open University Press, 33–49.

Conway, D, Pointon, P and Greenwood, J (2008) 'If the world is round, how come the piece I'm standing on is flat?' Early years geography, in Whitebread, D and Coltman, P (eds) *Teaching and Learning in the Early Years*. London: Routledge, 377–398.

Craft A (2005) *Creativity in schools: Tensions and dilemmas*. Abingdon: Routledge.

Craft, A (2011) *Creativity and Education Futures: learning in a digital age*. Stoke on Trent: Trentham Books.

Craft, A, Cremin, T and Burnard, P (eds) (2008) *Creative learning 3–11 and how we document it*. Stoke-on-Trent: Trentham Books.

Cremin, T and Barnes, J (2010) Creativity in the curriculum, in Arthur, J, Grainger, T and Wray, D (eds) *Learning to teach in the primary school*. Abingdon: Routledge, 357–373.

Davies, D, Howe, A, Fasciato, M and Rogers, M (2004) How do trainee primary teachers understand creativity? Paper presented at the British Educational Research Association Annual Conference, University of Manchester, September 16–18. **www.leeds.ac.uk/educol/documents/00003727.htm** accessed 13/8/14.

DfE (Department for Education) (2010) The Importance of Teaching: The Schools White Paper 2010. London: TSO.

DfE (2012) Teachers' Standards available at **https://www.gov.uk/government/publications/teachers-standards** accessed 7/9/14.

DfE (2013a) Teachers' Standards (Early Years).

DfE (2013b) The National Curriculum in England: Framework document. **www.gov.uk/dfe/national-curriculum** accessed 13/8/14.

DfEE/QCA (Department for Education and Employment/Qualifications and Curriculum Authority) (1999) The National Curriculum Handbook for Primary Teachers in England. London: DfEE/QCA.

Dinkele, G (2010) Enquiries and investigations, in Scoffham, S (ed) Primary Geography Handbook. Sheffield: Geographical Association, 94–104.

Freeman, C and Tranter, P (2011) *Children and Their Urban Environment: Changing Worlds*. London: Earthscan.

GA (Geographical Association) (2012) Geography and Creativity. **www.geography.org.uk/cpdevents/curriculum/geographycreativity** accessed 26/8/14.

GA (2013) The Primary Geography Quality Mark. **www.geography.org.uk/cpdevents/primaryquality mark** accessed 26/8/14.

Hicks, D (2002) *Lessons for the future*. Abingdon: Routledge.

Johnstone, J and Halocha, J (2007) Planning for creative teaching, in Johnstone, J, Halocha, J and Chater, M *Developing teaching skills in the primary school*. Maidenhead: Open University Press.

Knight, S (2013a) *Forest School and Outdoor Learning in the Early Years*. London: Sage.

Knight, S (ed) (2013b) *International Perspectives on Forest School: Natural Spaces to Play and Learn*. London: Sage.

Lambert, D and Owens, P (2013) Geography, in Jones, R and Wise, D (eds) *Creativity in the Primary Curriculum*. London: David Fulton, 98–115.

Martin, F (2004) Creativity through geography, in Fisher, R and Williams, M (eds) *Unlocking creativity*. London: David Fulton, 117–32.

NACCCE (National Advisory Committee on Creative and Cultural Education) (1999) All our futures: creativity, culture and education. London: DfEE.

Ofsted (Office for Standards in Education) (2010) Learning: creative approaches that raise standards. **www.ofsted.gov.uk/resources/learning-creative-approaches-raise-standards** accessed 26/8/14.

Ofsted (2011) Geography: Making a world of difference. **www.ofsted.gov.uk/resources/geography-learning-make-world-of-difference** accessed 26/8/14.

Ofsted (2013a) Improving teaching and learning using the outdoor environment: Lavington Park Federation. **www.ofsted.gov.uk/resources/good-practice-resource-improving-teaching-and-learning-outdoor-environment-lavington-park-fede** accessed 26/8/14.

Ofsted (2013b) An enquiry-based approach to learning: St Anne's CofE Primary School. **www.ofsted.gov.uk/resources/good-practice-resource-enquiry-based-approach-learning-st-anne%E2%80%99s-cofe-primary-school** accessed 26/8/14.

Ofsted (2013c) A creative curriculum to support outstanding teaching and learning in geography: Corsham Primary School. **www.ofsted.gov.uk/resources/good-practice-resource-creative-curriculum-support-outstanding-teaching-and-learning-geography-corsh** accessed 26/8/14.

Owens, P (2013) More than just core knowledge? A framework for effective and high-quality primary geography, Education 3–13, 41, 4, 382–397.

Pickering, S (2013) Keeping geography messy, in Scoffham, S (ed) *Teaching geography creatively*. London: Routledge, 169–179.

Rawling, E and Westaway, J (2003) Exploring creativity. Primary Geographer, 50, 7–9.

Roberts, M (2013) *Geography through enquiry*. Sheffield: Geographical Association.

Scoffham, S (2013a) Geography and creativity: making connections, in Scoffham, S (ed) *Teaching geography creatively*. Abingdon: Routledge, 1–13.

Scoffham, S (ed) (2013b) *Teaching geography creatively*. Abingdon: Routledge.

Scoffham, S (2013c) Geography and creativity: Creating joyful and imaginative learners, Education 3–13, 41, 4, 368–382.

Tanner, J and Whittle, J (2013) *The everyday guide to primary geography: Story*. Sheffield: Geographical Association.

Törnqvist, G (2011) *The geography of creativity*. Cheltenham: Edward Elgar.

Watts, A (2013) *Outdoor learning through the seasons*. London: David Fulton.

Williams-Siegfredsen, J (2012) *Understanding the Danish Forest School approach*. London: David Fulton.

15
Creativity in primary history
Hilary Cooper

Chapter objectives

By the end of the chapter you will have considered:

- what is historical enquiry?;
- how generic criteria for creativity are interdependent with the processes of historical enquiry;
- how psychologists' definitions of creativity link to historical enquiry;
- how constructivist learning theories are related to creativity and historical enquiry;
- why a creative approach to learning history is essential;
- how developing creativity through history reflects recent documentation.

This chapter addresses the following Teachers' Standards (DfE, 2012):

- establish a safe and stimulating environment for pupils, rooted in mutual respect;
- demonstrate knowledge and understanding of how pupils learn and how this impacts on teaching;
- have a secure knowledge of the relevant subject(s) and curriculum areas, foster and maintain pupils' interest in the subject, and address misunderstandings;
- impart knowledge and develop understanding through effective use of lesson time;
- demonstrate an awareness of the physical, social and intellectual development of children, and know how to adapt teaching to support pupils' education at different stages of development;
- know and understand how to assess the relevant subject and curriculum areas.

Introduction

This chapter will help you to understand why creative thinking must be at the centre of teaching and learning in history. A series of examples will illustrate how these points apply to practice.

What is historical enquiry?

Historical enquiry, whether for an academic historian or at a simpler level for a primary school child, involves the same process. We find out about the past from a variety of sources, through traces of the past which remain, such as photographs, paintings, objects, buildings, statistics, maps, advertisements, newspaper accounts, diaries. We need to ask questions about the source. How was it made? Who made it? Why? What did it mean to the people who made and used it (Collingwood, 1939). Often there is no right or wrong answer. We need to say, 'probably', 'I think', 'perhaps', to give reasons and to listen to the reasons of others; we may possibly change our mind. Craft (2000) identifies 'possibility thinking' as creative. And we have to recognise that some things we may never know. This involves the creative thinking as identified by the psychologists who described it as producing a rich variety of ideas and tolerating what cannot be known.

In order to try to understand people and events in the past we also need to try to see things from their perspectives and to use historical imagination, imagination rooted in evidence, as described by Cox (1986); Jones (1968); Gardner (1993); Goleman (1996). Young children have a limited knowledge base but if, from the beginning, they learn how to make multiple suggestions about how people may have thought and felt they will, as they grow older, be able to make increasingly valid suggestions based on what is known, what is likely and what cannot be disproved (Cooper, 2007, p194).

Finally children, like historians, need to combine what they know and can 'guess' from the sources to construct an account of a past time, or event, or for the reasons for changes over time. To do this they need 'multi-dimensional creativity'. For these do not need to be written accounts; they could be 'museum displays', role play, models, picture stories, video or audio presentations or PowerPoint presentations (DfEE, 1999; Edwards and Springate, 1995). These interpretations may be different but be equally valid, just as historians' interpretations are, depending on particular interests, gender, ethnicity and perspectives and what is known at the time.

History also involves multi-dimensional creativity because history is an umbrella subject. It involves all aspects of societies from the past: music, art or literature which can all be integrated into a history topic. This involves not just interpreting them as sources but also engaging with the creativity within the subjects themselves.

Creativity and historical enquiry are interdependent

When I wrote this chapter for the second edition of *Creativity in Primary Education* there had been little exploration of what creativity means in the context of teaching and learning history. So a group of colleagues and I decided to analyse in detail what this might mean. *Teaching History Creatively* presents case studies illustrating our findings (Cooper, 2013). The case studies are based on the premise that all teachers and pupils can learn to be creative in teaching and learning history. Being creative does not necessarily involve dance, drama, music, art or being a great original thinker like Einstein or Tolstoy. Creativity and related creative ideas may simply be new to a person's way of thinking. Indeed by relating generic characteristics of history to the processes of historical enquiry we concluded that good teaching and learning in history must, by definition, be creative. First we identified what are generally agreed to be the characteristics of generic creativity.

What is 'creativity'?

- *Being curious* (Gardner, 1999).
- *Identifying problems and asking questions* to investigate them (Craft, 2004).
- *Considering different possibilities*. Being open-minded and *being able to consider a variety of possible responses or perspectives* in answer to a question (Craft, 2002).

- *Imagination* – seeing more than is immediately apparent or interpreting something in a way that is unusual (Elliott, 1971; Passmore, 1980; Kenny, 1989).
- *Risk-taking*, living with uncertainty, confidence and a 'can-do' approach.
- *Acting both individually* (Leach, 2001) *and collaboratively* (Craft, 2005).
- *Creating a product.* Creativity may involve generating new ideas or creative behaviour – although it is not always considered necessary to result in a product (Scruton, 1974).
- *Connectivity* – the making of connections between disparate and apparently unconnected elements.
- Creativity involves *content knowledge and procedural knowledge*. It is not 'free-floating' but requires knowledge, both of the enquiry processes of a subject (knowing how) (Ryle, 1979) and subject knowledge (knowing that); depth of understanding and knowledge depends on age and ability (Dewey, 1933; Montessori, 1949; Kant, 1989).

Creative teaching and learning of history

We linked these generic criteria to the processes of historical enquiry, which are embedded in investigating the past.

- *Being curious, defining areas of enquiry* – these may be related to individuals, groups or events; local, national, global, economic, political or social; focus on gender, ethnicity, music or art. (Popper, 1945; Hexter, 1961; Elton, 1970).
- *Identifying problems* – (e.g. Ferguson, 2011;Schama 2001, 2002, 2003) and asking questions to investigate then (e.g. Collingwood 1939); for example why did the fortunes of a street change or what changes did the railway cause in this town?
- *Considering different possibilities* – for example why might someone have behaved as they did; why was this source created and by whom?(Elton, 1967).
- *Imagination* – what might it have been like to live here or how might this have affected people's lives/ summoning up sights, sounds and smells different from our own (Collingwood, 1939, p7; Elton, 1970, p5).
- *Risk-taking* – suggesting various possibilities and listening to the suggestions of others, when evidence is incomplete or not understood (Cooper 2012, ch1–2).
- *Acting individually or collaboratively* – collaborative work is generally seen as generating creativity; for one reason it allows children to work together without competition, stress and anxiety. However Ng's (2003) research shows that there *needs to be a bala*nce between *direct teaching, individual* and *collaborative work*.
- *Creating a product* – selecting and combining evidence to create an account or interpretation of the past: a role play, display, a model or piece of writing (Cooper, 2012 ch. 3; Cooper, 2014).
- *Making connections* – understanding how we find out about the past and applying this to what we already know (e.g. Bruner, 1966).
- *Content knowledge and procedural knowledge* – it has thus been shown that every aspect of historical enquiry is creative. Creativity in each of these aspects also depends on the interaction between enquiry and content knowledge; for example knowledge to know whether creative interpretations are valid based on what is known, knowledge of what is reasonable and likely and some understanding of the different attitudes beliefs and values people in the past may have held and why.

We also took into account the role of classroom organization and ethos in teaching history, or any subject, creatively. Craft (2005) make a distinction between 'teaching creatively' (using imaginative approaches and 'making learning interesting and affective) and 'teaching for creativity (which develops creativity in the learner). This involves passing control to the learner, valuing learners' innovative contributions, ownership and control and being a co-participant in the learning although Craft later saw these as interdependent. Woods and Jeffrey (1996) research found that relevance, ownership and control led to innovation.

Lucas (2001) says that learners need to be *challenged*, have *goals* set and set their own. *Negative stress* should be *eliminated* and *feedback* should *enhance self-knowledge, self-esteem* and *motivation*.

- Many writers emphasise *the importance of teachers sharing in the process of enquiry*, being active partici-pants in experiences and modelling curiosity.
- Teachers also need to be *good listeners*; explaining something confirms what has been learned and can lead to ideas.
- *Learners need time to reflect* and to *extend* their learning outside school.

The case studies in *Teaching History Creatively* demonstrate these principles in practice.

Psychologists, creativity and historical enquiry

When, in the 1960s, psychologists attempted to define and even test creativity in an attempt to make the curriculum broader, more flexible and 'child-centred' they found it very difficult (Guilford, 1959; Torrance, 1965; Wallach and Kogan, 1965). They concluded that creativity is concerned with 'divergent thinking', with producing a variety of ideas (for example imagining uses for objects), tolerating what is not known and generating imaginative interpretations of situations which may be difficult to understand. Haddon and Lytton (1968) found that children develop this kind of thinking if they are in an environment where they are encouraged to think creatively, although many teachers did not recognise creative thinking because they preferred conformity. Psychologists also investigated children's ability to see things from another person's perspective. Donaldson (1978) and Cox (1986) concluded that children had been underestimated in their ability to do this, if an activity was interesting, through role play, conversation and looking at pictures.

Jones (1968) thought it essential that thinking should be related to emotions and imagination and suggested ways in which children can be encouraged to understand both themselves and the behaviour and feelings and ideas of other societies. More recently the concepts of multi-intelligences and emotional intelligence have become familiar. Research of the 1970s and 1980s recognises that both logic and imagination are involved in creativity, and research in the 1980s and 1990s recognised the importance of social interaction in fostering creativity (Craft, Jeffrey and Leibling, 2001).

Recent neuroscience research shows that learning depends on the development of multisensory networks of neurons distributed across the entire brain (Goswami and Bryant, 2008). For example a concept in history, say Elizabethan or The Industrial Revolution, may depend on neurons being simultaneously active in visual, spatial, memory, deductive and kinaesthetic regions of both hemispheres.

The National Advisory Council on Creative and Cultural Education (NACCCE, 1999) sums up previous research, defining creativity as:

- multi-dimensional – involving all fields of activity (Boden, 1990; Gardner, 1993);
- playing with ideas and making unusual connections;
- involving imagination and feelings as well as thinking (Goleman, 1996).

Creativity has been seen to include 'possibility thinking' (Craft, 2000) and the ability to transfer knowledge gained in one context to another in order to solve a problem (Seltzer and Bentley, 1999, p10). Others (e.g. Edwards and Springate, 1995) have suggested that creativity is fostered through expressing ideas in a wide variety of symbolic media and encouraging integration of subject areas through meaningful topics.

Constructivist learning theories, creativity and historical enquiry

The key constructivist theorists are Piaget, Vygotsky and Bruner. Much subsequent research has developed their work. Constructivist learning theories are based on the idea that we all construct, or create, our own understandings of the world through gradually building up our own mental maps, based on our personal experiences, and through discussion with others.

This is a continuing, active process. Piaget's work on reasoning (1928) applies to interpreting sources and his work on language (1926) explores how children gradually become able to make robust arguments to support their reasoning, using 'because'. Vygotsky (1986) emphasised the importance of working with others and of discussion, trial and error in order to clarify, modify and extend our understanding and learn new concepts. Craft *et al*. (2001) also saw creativity as linked to social interaction. Bruner (1966) emphasised the importance of presenting material in different ways, material children can explore physically (artefacts, tools, buildings, sites), visually (pictures, photographs, paintings, illustrations and diagrams), as well as through language. He argued that if material is presented in an appropriate way, children of any age can ask and answer questions at the heart of a subject. Bruner argues (1963) that if children learn the methods of enquiry at the heart of a discipline they can transfer this reasoning to new contexts and so avoid mental overload. Seltzer and Bentley (1999) saw this as part of the creative process.

History then can only be learned through engaging in historical enquiry. The work of psychologists and learning theorists has shown how this process involves creative thinking: making probabilistic inferences and causal arguments, discussing these with others, understanding different viewpoints and using imagination to understand how people in the past may have thought, felt and behaved. Learning history also involves creativity because it is multi-dimensional; it subsumes other dimensions of society, including art, literature and music. Constructing interpretations or accounts of an enquiry also involve multi-dimensional creativity involving different curriculum areas. Constructivist learning theory illustrates how children construct and create their own historical understanding.

Why a creative approach to history is important

Learning to ask and answer questions, to develop and defend arguments, to listen to others, to recognise that there may not be a right answer is part of social and emotional as well as cognitive development. Constructing our own histories includes family histories, local histories, histories of different places and recognising that there is no single history and that stories of the past can change. This values individuals and diversity and develops identities. Understanding how different valid interpretations are constructed is essential in a democratic society as is evident from previously Communist and Fascist countries who are trying to reconstruct their multifaceted histories, and in countries where views of the past are contested, such as South Africa and Northern Ireland.

Examples of developing creativity through history

History, play and creativity

In play children are motivated, they make choices, explore, are flexible and actively engaged. Imaginative play frees a child from the immediate environment. In play children behave beyond their age and daily behaviour (Vygotsky, 1978). Through 'Let's pretend play' about oral history, myths, legends, folk tales as well as about 'true' stories from the past children construct their own accounts. This, in an embryonic way, is how all accounts of the past are constructed; imagining, from what is known, why people felt, thought and acted as they did. They use experimental dialogue about supposed places and people in 'alternative worlds'.

Meadows and Cashdan (1988, p39), Vygotsky (1978) and Bruner (1987) say that social interaction with adults enhances the quality of learning through play. Adults can help children to sequence, repeat and retell stories, discuss what happens next and why, using the language of time through questioning and extended shared thinking. Who lived in the castle? What did they wear? What did they eat? Children learn probabilistic thinking; (what if?), to hypothesise, that there is not always a right answer and that others have different ideas. Winnicot (in Bruce, 1987, p71) suggested that adults are able to relate to powerful events, hero figures, music and paintings if they have related to them through play. Bruce (1987) claims that play forms a fundamental part of fostering a child's creativity. Garvey (1977) emphasised the importance of play which reconstructs stories about the past for social and emotional growth because it explores emotions, relationships and situations beyond their direct experience.

Children need to be involved in negotiating and organising the play (Bennett *et al.*, 1997). They need to learn to develop a story they know, sequence ideas, adopt roles and take turns. They may do this through sensitive adult intervention to extend language, model, mediate, question or to give some direction for a while. Teacher-directed activities are integrated with play through a topic approach, and through 'plan, do, review sessions', which encourage children to initiate and follow up ideas. Several aspects of the 3–5 curriculum and the Key Stage 1 curriculum can be assessed through and observing play and such conversations.

Creativity (DfEE, 1999)	Historical enquiry	Psychology	Constructivist learning Theory
Multi-dimensional thinking Expressing ideas in variety of media	Creating interpretations through role play, technologies, displays, paintings, etc.	Divergent thinking, Producing a variety of ideas Multi-intelligences Logic and imagination	Bruner – Presenting material in different ways (kinaesthetic, iconic, symbolic) Bruner – transferring knowledge and
Rational and emotional thinking	Imagination rooted in evidence	Generating imaginative solutions Understanding	thinking processes to new contexts
Playing with ideas and making connections	Causal thinking	behaviour and feelings of others Emotional intelligence	
Possibility thinking	Making inferences about sources;	Social interaction in problem-solving	Piaget – reasoning, causal argument,
Transfer knowledge and thinking to new contexts to solve a problem	tolerating what cannot be known	Seeing things from perspective of others through role play, looking at pictures, conversation.	Vygotsky – importance of social interaction in concept development; Zone of proximal development
Integrating subjects	Cross-curricular links within history	Tolerating what cannot be known	
Social Interaction		A subject is learned through multi-sensory networks	

Figure 15.1 Synopsis: creativity, history, psychology and learning theories

PRACTICAL TASK PRACTICAL TASK PRACTICAL TASK PRACTICAL TASK PRACTICAL TASK

Select a story set in a past time. Plan teacher-directed activities related to the story, and how you would initiate a related role-play area. List ways in which you might intervene in play in order to extend and assess thinking.

Case Study

A visit to a castle: Year 6 and Year 7

This case aimed to promote continuity between Key Stages 2 and 3 and to involve pupils in the role of historians, in each stage of a pupil-initiated historical enquiry (Cooper and West, 2009). In session one both classes worked in their own schools. They learned, through teacher questioning and information

(Continued)

(Continued)

based on a PowerPoint presentation showing the plan and photographs, the stages in which the castle was built and by whom, why it was built and why it was built where it was. Pupils then worked in groups to list questions they would like to investigate on a site visit. Their questions were then conflated into five enquiries:

- **How was the castle defended; where were the weakest points?**
- **Which part of the castle was built by Vieuxpont, Robert Clifford, Hugh Clifford? Why do you think so?**
- **What evidence is there of life in the castle in the days of Robert Clifford?**
- **How can we create a guide to the castle young children (or blind children) might enjoy.**
- **You are creating a TV series, romantic novel or ghost story based on locations in the castle. Record the locations which will be part of the story.**

On the site visit pupils worked in groups of three Year 6 and three Year 7 pupils. They selected the evidence they needed for their investigation and recorded it using notes, drawings, digital and video cameras.

In session three they combined and interpreted their data to create accounts (interpretations) of their findings. The final session took place in the secondary school.

Interpretations included role play against images of castle locations, models, television scripts, a video, an animation, a display board for young children, a toy (to encourage problem-solving and fantasy play) to be sold in the shop, an information board for younger children and a tactile tour for partially-sighted visitors.

REFLECTIVE TASK

Using Figure 15.1 identify the ways in which the case study uses creative approaches to find out about the castle.

Stimulating cross-curricular approaches to teaching history

I am conjuring up an image of a school in which I worked. It is an open plan school. The Key Stage 2 unit consists of a large space shared by four classes with a small 'quiet room' for each class and a drama studio leading off it. The history topic this term is Ancient Greece. In one corner of the unit is a kitchen area with dresser, table, chairs, sink, cooker. A group of children are preparing an Ancient Greek lunch of chick pea soup, bread, goats' cheese and olives, salted anchovies and pomegranates. The smell is delicious. In another corner a Greek Temple reaches from floor to ceiling, its pillars made from corrugated card and the steps from staging blocks. Here requests appropriate for Ancient Greek Gods can be offered to Zeus and the Gods whose stories are depicted around the walls. In a third corner a group of children are making replica Greek vases and dishes in the pottery area based on photographs. In the drama studio, another group are preparing their Assembly drama, based on stories from the Odyssey; Odysseus is negotiating the Straits of Messina while pupils' poems describing the drama are read to the accompaniment of various stringed instruments and pan pipes made in a design and technology lesson. Around the walls are huge paintings of Greek vases and inferences about the stories the pictures tell. They were made by projecting slides of Greek vases onto paper then painting the images. The curtains at one of the windows are screen printed with a design of laurel wreaths and temples.

PRACTICAL TASK PRACTICAL TASK PRACTICAL TASK PRACTICAL TASK PRACTICAL TASK

Plan activities related to another history study unit and linked to study units for design and technology, art and design, music and English which will help children to take ownership of their environment.

Art and historical imagination

Visual images, paintings, sculpture, photographs, cartoons from past times are important historical sources. Arnheim (1970, p31) said that, 'Every visual pattern, be it a painting, a building, an ornament, a chair . . . every work of art is a statement about something which makes a declaration about the nature of human existence.' Arnheim explains how paintings and sculptures that portray figures, objects, actions in a more or less realistic style nevertheless make no sense as reports of what life was like in the past until the viewer can read what each symbolises. This requires thought, language, discussion.

Dewey (1934) said that through an expressive object the artist and the active observer encounter each other, their material and mental environments and their culture at large; it demonstrates the connections between art and everyday experience. 'To emphasise what is aesthetic,' he said 'is to emphasise ways in which an aesthetic experience is a manifestation, a record, a celebration of a civilization . . . and an ultimate judgement on the quality of that civilization.'

Arnheim (1970) similarly linked visual perception and thought. He said that by collecting images of kinds of qualities, kinds of objects and kinds of events the mind grasps what they have in common and so organises experience into concepts. For example we may collect and group images of power, defeat, celebrations, noble deeds, poverty, wealth across the centuries, which become categorised as abstract concepts.

Dewey (1932) said that 'The imagination is the medium of appreciation in every field.'

Collingwood (1939, 1942, 1946) was concerned with the definition of historical imagination.

He reasoned that we can only speculate about the feelings of people in the past by speculating about the sources they leave behind. The more we know about a period the more likely are the suppositions we make.

Gombrich (1982) discusses ways in which strong feelings can be conveyed in images. For example 'The Kneeling Captive', (Bibliothe`que Nationale, Paris) demonstrates, through posture, the stark contrast in the statues of Imperial Rome between authority and submission.

Innumerable images of thirteenth-century saints, donors and worthies in churches, with their folded hands, evoke piety, although there is here a complex relationship between ritual and expression. Greek vases illustrate familiar narratives but nineteenth century paintings of domestic scenes tell stories about feelings – jealousy, fear, loss. Images in stained glass windows change metaphor into symbolic images. Egan (1992) emphasised the importance of forming and articulating vivid images in our teaching.

Gardner (1990, p31) having introduced his theory of multiple intelligences, concluded that the most promising way to integrate the various forms is through 'situated learning':

> *When students encounter various forms of knowing operating together in a natural situation, when they see accomplished adults move back and forwards between these forms, when they are themselves engaged in a rich and engaging project which calls on various modes of representation, when they have the opportunity to interact and communicate with individuals who evidence complementary forms of learning, these are the situations that facilitate a proper alignment amongst various forms of knowledge.*

PRACTICAL TASK   PRACTICAL TASK   PRACTICAL TASK   PRACTICAL TASK   PRACTICAL TASK

Using online sources (e.g. **www.nationalgallery.org.uk**; **www.npg.org.uk**) and in response to a specified unit of study, select the following.

- **A painting which makes a statement about aspects of human existence at the time.**
- **A work of art you think is a celebration of the civilization which produced it.**
- **A work of art which expresses people's feelings at the time.**
- **The narrative described on a Greek vase.**
- **A symbolic image.**

What questions might you ask children so that they can make suggestions about what each image can tell us about the time in which it was made? Cooper (2002, p101–24) suggests practical ways of using visual sources with young children.

Personal and social education through history

History is concerned with causes and effects of and motives for human behaviour. Historical enquiry attempts to understand the values and attitudes of people in the past. This involves rational interpretations, empathy and tolerance; all have creative potential. Slater (1995), Husbands (1996) and Claire (2005) provide excellent examples of how teachers may help children to engage with moral issues of the past. Pupils explore questions through hot-seating, drama, poetry and oral history. Would you help an escaping negro slave? Would you hide the Frank family? What would it feel like to be on the *Kindestransport*? They consider how governments terrorise and scapegoat a community.

Folk Tales are oral history which handed down the hopes, fears and values of daily life through a community. Two recent studies (Cooper and Ditchburn, 2009; Cooper, 2010) investigated whether Key Stage 2 pupils could retell traditional Turkish and Russian folk tales in contemporary contexts. Central to the Turkish tale was the importance of hospitality and also the importance of respecting the house rules of a host. The Russian tales were concerned with greed, with respect for others and with being careful about what you wish for. Children's interpretations were extremely insightful in a rich variety of familiar, contemporary contexts, suggesting that there are universal values underpinning individual differences.

In another study (Ager, 2009) children identify and evaluate, through a variety of activities, the reasons for Tudor voyages of exploration and settlement: science, trade, religious toleration, population growth, plunder, political rivalry. This small rural school booked an interactive video session with experts in the National Maritime Museum to discuss some of these issues (**www.rmg.co.uk**). Another focus was on the Roanoake Settlement in Virginia who were looking for a land of religious tolerance, the original support of the Amerindians, their ethnic differences, the pressure on food supplies and eventual conflict encompassed numerous moral predicaments.

REFLECTIVE TASK

Research the Roanoke Settlement (**www.dur.ac.uk/4schools/Roanoke/default.htm**). What value-laden issues arise? How might you explore them with a Key Stage 2 class?

A SUMMARY OF **KEY POINTS**

➢ Historical enquiry involves making inferences and deductions about historical sources and using concepts of time, cause and effect and motivation, in order to construct accounts of the past which may differ, depending on the interests of the historian, but be equally valid.

➢ This process is creative because it involves suggesting a variety of possibilities, it involves reasoning, emotion and imagination, in attempting to understand the feelings, thoughts and motives of people in the past.

➢ Learning history involves developing a sense of your own identity and of similarities and differences with others. It involves developing and defending arguments, listening to the views of others and recognising that there may be no single 'right answer'. This is part of social and emotional as well as cognitive growth.

➢ This reflects research into the generic concept of creativity and its application to psychology, and constructivist theories of learning.

➢ Finding out about the past and constructing interpretations of the past is cross-curricular; this reflects research in neuroscience.

MOVING *ON* > > > > > > MOVING *ON* > > > > > > MOVING *ON*

A checklist to ensure that your history teaching in future is creative

- Does it involve making deductions and inferences about a range of sources in order to construct interpretations of past times and changes over time in a variety of ways?

- Do sources include literature, music, statistics, art, maps and diagrams?
- Are interpretations constructed in different ways (using technologies, design and technology, art and design, literacy, mathematics, role play)?

REFERENCES REFERENCES **REFERENCES** REFERENCES REFERENCES REFERENCES

Ager, J (2009) Tudor exploration, in Cross-curricular approaches in the primary school, Rowley, C and Cooper, H (eds) London: Sage.

Arnheim, R (1970) Visual thinking. London: Faber and Faber.

Bennett, N, Wood, L, and Rogers, S (1997) Teaching through play: teachers' thinking and classroom practice. Buckingham: Open University Press.

Boden, M (1990, second edition, 2004) The creative mind: myths and mechanisms. Abingdon: Routledge.

Bruce, T (1987) Early childhood education. London: Hodder and Stoughton.

Bruner, JS (1963) The process of education. New York: Vintage Books.

Bruner, JS (1966) Towards a theory of instruction. Harvard, MA: Belknap Press.

Bruner, JS (1987) Making sense: the child's construction of the world. London: Methuen.

Claire, H (2005) History, citizenship and the primary curriculum, paper presented at the History in British Education Conference, Institute of Historical Research, London 14–15 February, accessed at **www.history.ac.uk/education/conference/claire.html** last accessed 9/12/08.

Collingwood, RG (1939) An autobiography. Oxford: Oxford University Press.

Collingwood, RG (1942) The new leviathan. Oxford: Oxford University Press.

Collingwood, RG (1946) The idea of history. Oxford: Clarendon Press.

Cooper, H (2002) *History in the Early Years* 2/e London: Routledge.

Cooper, H (2007) *History 3–11*. Abingdon: David Fulton.

Cooper, H (2010) Contemporary English Interpretations of Traditional Russian Folk Tales pp. 25–30, *The International Journal of Historical Learning Teaching and Research* Vol. 9.no.2.

Cooper, H. (2012) *History 5–11*, London: Routledge.

Cooper, H (2013) Teaching History Creatively. London: Routledge.

Cooper, H (2014) (ed.) *Writing History 7–11: historical writing in different genres*, London: Routledge.

Cooper, H and Ditchburn, E (2009) Folk Tales: universal Values Individual Differences, pp. 58–71, *The International Journal of Historical Learning Teaching and Research* Vol. 8 no.1

Cooper, H and Rowley C (2006) Geography 3–11: a guide for teachers. London: David Fulton.

Cooper, H and West, E (2009) Year 5/6 and Year 7 Historians visit Brougham Castle, in Cooper, H (ed) *Constructing History 11–19*, London: Sage.

Cox, MV (1986) The development of cognition and language. Brighton: Harvester Press.

Craft, A (2000) Creativity across the primary curriculum. Abingdon: Routledge.

Craft, A (2002) *Creativity and Early Years Education*, London: Continuum.

Craft, A (2004) Creative Thinking in the Early Years of Education, in Fryer, M (ed.) *Creativity and Cultural Diversity*. Leeds Creativity Centre Educational Trust.

Craft, A (2005) *Creativity in Schools: tensions and dilemmas*. Abingdon: Falmer.

Craft, A, Jeffrey, B and Leibling, M (2001) Creativity in education. London: Continuum.

DfE (2012) Teachers' Standards available at **https://www.gov.uk/government/publications/teachers-standards** accessed 7/9/14.

Department for Education and Employment (DfEE) (1999) National Advisory Committee for Creative and Cultural Education (NACCCE) *All Our Futures; creativity, culture and education,* London: DfEE.

Dewey, J (1932) *How we Think*, republished 2007. New York: PO Box 416, Old Chelsea Station.

Dewey, J (1933) *How we Think*, London: Harrap.

Dewey, J (1934) *Art as Experience*, republished 2009. New York: Berkley Publishing Group.

Donaldson, M (1978) *Children's minds*. London: Fontana.

Edwards, CP and Springate, KW (1995) The Lion Comes Out of the Stone: Helping Young Children Achieve Their Creative Potential. *Dimensions of Early Childhood* 23(4, Fall): 24–29.

Egan (1992) Imagination in teaching and learning. Abingdon: Routledge.

Elliott, RK (1971) Versions of Creativity, *Journal of Philosophy of Education* 5 (2): 139–52.

Elton, GR (1967) *The Practice of History*, London: Sydney University Press, Methuen.

Elton, GR (1970) What sort of history should we teach, in Ballard, M (ed) *New Movements in the Study and Teaching of History*. London: Temple Smith.

Ferguson, N (2011) *Civilisation: the West and the Rest*. New York: Penguin Press.

Gardner, H (1990) Art education and human development. Santa Monica, CA: The Getty Centre for Educational Arts.

Gardner, H. (1993) *Frames of Mind: the theory of multiple intelligences,* New York: Basic Books, 1993, London: Fontana Press.

Gardner, H (1993) Multiple intelligences: the theory in practice. New York: Harper Collins.

Gardner, H (1999) *Intelligence Reframed: multiple intelligences for the 21st century,* New York: Basic Books.

Garvey, C (1977) Play (The Developing Child Series), Bruner, JS, Cole, M and Lloyd, B (series eds). London: Collins/Fontana.

Goleman, D (1996) Emotional intelligence. London: Bloomsbury Publishing.

Gombrich, EH (1982) The image and the eye: further studies in the psychology of pictorial representation. Oxford: Phaidon.

Goswami, U and Bryant, P (2008) Children's cognitive development and learning, primary review research findings 2/1a. The Primary Review. Cambridge University Faculty of Education.

Guilford, JP (1959) Traits of creativity, in Anderson, HH (ed.) Creativity and its cultivation. New York: Harper, pp142–61.

Haddon, FA and Lytton, H (1968) Teaching approach and the development of divergent thinking abilities in primary schools. British Journal of Educational Psychology, 38, 171–80.

Hexter, JH (1961) *Reappraisals in History*, London: Longmans.

Husbands, C (1996) What is history teaching? Language, ideas and meaning in learning about the past. Buckingham: Open University Press.

Jones, RM (1968) Fantasy and feeling in education. London: London University Press.

Kant, J (1989) On Educations (trans. Churchton, A). Oxford: Oxford University Press.

Kenny, A (1989) *The Metaphysics of Mind*, Oxford: Oxford University Press.

Knight, P (1989) A study of children's understanding of people in the past. Education Review, 41:3.

Leach, J (2001) A hundred possibilities: creativity, community and ICT, in A. Craft, B. Jeffrey and M. Leibling (eds.) *Creativity in Education*: 175–93, London: Continuum.

Marshall, HE (1905) (second edition, 2005) Our island story. Cranbrook: Galore Park Publishing Limited.

Lucas, B (2001) Creative Teaching, teaching creatively and creative learning, in Craft, A and Jeffrey, B (eds) *Creativity in Education.* London: Continuum.

Meadows, S and Cashdan, A (1988) The child as thinker: the development and acquisition of cognition in childhood. Abingdon: Routledge.

Montessori, M (2007) *The Absorbent Mind*, Radford, VA:Wilder Publications (Originally published (1949) by Dell: New York).

National Advisory Committee on Creative and Cultural Education (NACCCE) (1999) *All Our Futures: creativity, culture and education*. London: Department for Education and Employment.

Ng, AK (2003) A cultural model of creative and conforming behavior, *Creativity Research Journal* 15(2) : 223–33.

Passmore, J (1980) *The Philosophy of Teaching*, London: Duckworth.

Piaget, J (1926) The language and thought of the child. Abingdon: Routledge.

Piaget, J (1928) The judgement and reasoning of the child. Abingdon: Routledge.

Popper, K (1945) *The Open Society and its Enemies* (5/e 1966, reprinted 1973), vol.:270. London: Routledge and Kegan Paul.

Ryle, G (1979) *On Thinking,* Oxford: Blackwell

Schama, S (2000) *A History of Britain, Vol. 1 At the Edge of the World,* London: Ebury Publishing.

Schama, S (2001) *A History of Britain Vol. 2 British Wars 1603–1776,* London: Ebury Publishing.

Schama, S (2002) *A History of Britain, Vol. 3 The Fate of Empire 1776–2000,* London: Ebury Publishing.

Scruton, R (1974) *Art and Imagination: a study in the philosophy of mind,* London: Methuen.

Seltzer, K and Bentley, T (1999) The creative age: knowledge and skills for the new economy. London: Demos.

Slater, J (1995) Teaching history in the new Europe. London: Cassell.

Torrance, EP (1965) Rewarding creative behaviour. Prentice Hall.

Vygotsky, LS (1978) *Mind in Society: Development of Higher Social Processes*, pp92–119. London: Harvard University Press.

Vygotsky, LS (1986) in Kozulin (ed) *Thought and* Language *(revised edition)* Massachusetts Institute of Technology.

Wallach, MA and Kogan, N (1965) Modes of thinking in young children. New York: Holt, Rinehart and Winston.

Woods, P and Jeffrey, B (1996) *Teachable Moments: the art of teaching in primary schools.* Buckingham: Open University Press.

Other websites

National Maritime Museum **www.rmg.ac.uk**

National Portrait Gallery **www.npg.org.uk**

The National Gallery **www.nationalgallery.org.uk**

The Settlement at Roanoke **www.dur.ac.uk/4schools/Roanoke/default.htm**

- all accessed 13/8/2014

16
Creativity in the music curriculum
Sarah Hennessy

Chapter objectives

By the end of this chapter you should have:

- developed confidence in your own and your children's ability to use your musical imagination;
- explored how to structure activities;
- understood the need to see yourself and your children as musicians.

This chapter addresses the following Teachers' Standards (DfES, 2012)

- demonstrate knowledge and understanding of how pupils learn and how this impacts on teaching;
- have a secure knowledge of the relevant subject(s) and curriculum areas, foster and maintain pupils' interest in the subject, and address misunderstandings;
- promote a love of learning and children's intellectual curiosity;
- contribute to the design and provision of an engaging curriculum.

Introduction

In this chapter I offer a rationale for music in the primary curriculum as a source and resource for creativity. It is well understood that many primary teachers, in training and with experience, are anxious about their abilities to teach music. This has much to do with the perception that teaching music requires advanced skills in singing, playing an instrument and reading notation. Using and strengthening the natural abilities to make music that we all have is much more important and while I do not believe that one can learn to teach music through merely reading about it, I do believe that teachers should give some time to reflecting on what informs their practice and what can support better practice. That being said, nothing can replace learning through practical musical engagement with colleagues and children. This is where confidence and understanding for teaching are nourished.

Confident teachers are much more likely to use their imagination, take risks and be responsive to their pupils. Confidence develops through sustained engagement with both musical thinking and activity. In this way we come to understand and appreciate the nature of music-making and learning in music. David Elliott (1995) refers to this view of learning as praxial, that is, not only learning through doing, but also music-making, which is located in a social and cultural context. Music is a human activity, something we do intentionally, thoughtfully and in response to our experiences.

Creativity in music learning

Not everything we learn in music demands creativity. There are skills we may want to master (such as playing a rhythm on a drum accurately and fluently), or knowledge we want to acquire (such as the origins of a particular piece of music). These need practice and study; but the motivation to learn these things should derive from the desire to try something new, develop a new idea, find a particular sound – in the pursuit of making music. And, even when mastering a skill, the activities or context for the practice can be given more meaning by the teacher's imaginative approach and their ability to enable children to find their own solutions.

Creativity in music learning is not an afterthought, something we think about if there's time or as an occasional break from 'work'. Creativity is an essential component of effective learning when the purpose of learning is to enable learners to act and think independently, to grow and change and ultimately to make an original and valuable contribution. Music in schools has not always reflected this view wholeheartedly for a number of reasons:

1. The National Curriculum in England was conceived in such a way as to promote a compartmentalised view of the primary curriculum with a focus on individual subjects, which appeared to discourage integration across subjects around themes or topics. This meant that timetables often became increasingly rigid, making it difficult to consider innovative or flexible approaches to learning.
2. An emphasis on Literacy and Numeracy (with their attendant Strategies) has reduced teachers' energies and motivation towards the rest of the curriculum.
3. There may be a tension in teachers' minds between the notion of work (individual, product oriented, knowledge acquisition, useful, systematic) and the pleasurable, 'non- academic' image of music (and the arts in general). Music may be seen as a luxury that, when the pressure is on, becomes expendable.
4. Creativity in music is inevitably noisy. Noisiness may be viewed as a negative condition in school: a quiet environment suggests studiousness, discipline, calmness, whereas noise means lack of control. Teachers may find it difficult to reconcile this in the context of music-making – and especially when encouraging exploration and experimentation with sound – a necessary element of creative music-making.
5. Musical creativity may be believed to be found only in advanced musicians.

There have also been, in the last few years, two major government-funded initiatives directly focused on improving music education at Key Stage 2:

- KS2 whole class instrumental and vocal tuition (often called Wider Opportunities) – in the first years of the initiative funding provided all schools with tuition for one year group for one year. In recent years the funding has been much reduced and Music Education Hubs (many based on the Music Service providers) continue to have responsibility for providing the expert tutors. Music tutors who are expected to work alongside classteachers to introduce the learning of instruments to one chosen year group. The idea is to stimulate interest which will continue beyond the 'free' year and encourage more children to take up specialist instrumental or vocal learning. The approach to teaching whole classes encompasses the National Curriculum programme of study for music so that listening, composing and improvising are also developed.
- Sing Up was a project aimed at improving singing in primary schools (see www.singup.org). Funding has now ceased but the website of resources is still available through a subscription. In this project, specialist singing leaders were employed to provided professional development for class teachers and work directly with children.

The renewed focus on developing performance skills through singing and learning an instrument may have inadvertently shifted the focus away from creative music-making.

Instrumental tuition (whether in large groups or one to one, can also involve playing by ear, improvising and composing; and In good practice, music teaching always aspires to an integration of listening, composing and performing. It is creativity which motivates and gives meaning to music learning of all kinds

Some readers might be surprised at the idea that music learning is not always concerned with creativity – surely the arts are synonymous with creativity? They certainly encompass creative thinking, inventiveness, innovation, novelty, risk-taking, problem-solving, speculation and meaning-making. But of course they also involve skill training, acquisition of knowledge about the art form, and analytical and critical thinking. Perhaps music in formal education, more than other art forms, has been rather imprisoned by these latter concerns to the neglect of the creative aspects. Composing may be seen as the preserve of a chosen few with exceptional talent, and the opportunities for creative music-making, more broadly defined, often struggle to be acknowledged in the other musical activities of performing and listening.

REFLECTIVE TASK

Consider your own experience, as a child, of learning music in and out of school. Are your memories positive or negative?

When I ask this of my students their memories are often coloured by a mixture of strong emotions:

- **the 'buzz' of being part of a performance event, of joining in and achieving something; or**
- **the fear of failure, the misery of rejection, or the drudgery and guilt surrounding practice.**

The 'buzz' is what we should all have the opportunity to experience; negative experiences are almost always the result of a teacher's judgement or teaching habits.

Do you recall making up your own music, or working creatively in a music class?

What is creative music-making?

A note to the reader

When I refer to 'musicians' I mean anyone who makes music, however simple or tentative.

When I refer to the music-making behaviours of young children these are often very close to the behaviours of novice musicians of any age. Experience through listening and making (and interactions with others) will all contribute to development – whether you are a five-year-old or a 25-year-old.

Musical creativity can be viewed as both a product and a process in which the musician/ music-maker expresses and communicates their ideas and feelings through:

- interpreting, adapting or arranging the music of others in a new way;
- joining in with a new part

- improvising;
- composing;
- making imaginative/unexpected connections with other media such as language, movement or visual images;
- combining with, or finding musical responses to poetry, dance, or art works.

We need to consider the differences between child and adult musicians – if we carry in our heads a perception of the latter then children's achievements will often seem inadequate and insubstantial. We need to learn to listen to what children's music is (Glover, 2000), not what is missing (not quite in tune, not in time, lacking in structure). It is easy to be critical when musical ability is based on a strict and unforgiving mastery of technical skills: if you cannot sing in tune – mime; if you can't keep time – stay quiet.

Frameworks for activities should allow children even at the very earliest stages of their development to use their musical imaginations and be creative. The originality, risk-taking and novelty will be relative to their experience and ability rather than relative to all possible music. As a teacher you may well hear these kinds of musical ideas many, many times in your classroom but what you are listening for is something that is new for that child or group at that moment (consider the idea of 'small c creativity' as discussed by Craft (2001)).

All music-making has the potential to be creative. Creative activities, in which children make their own choices or decisions, add something to or adapt a given idea, all involve creative musical thinking:

- contributing to or giving their own interpretation of a song;
- making an arrangement of a given piece of music (adding accompaniment and deciding how the piece is to be performed);
- inventing a short melodic pattern and developing it into a sequence or a complete piece;
- composing a backing track for a rap;
- improvising a rhythm in the gaps between another given rhythm;
- choosing sounds to represent the sound of waves on a beach, and deciding how to begin and end the 'sound picture'.

Teaching for creativity

There needs to be a distinction between creative teaching in music and teaching for creative music-making. The former can exist without the latter, but the latter is unlikely to result without the former.

Creative teaching involves finding imaginative, unusual, surprising, adventurous approaches to putting across concepts and knowledge, or to making skill building enjoyable and motivating. Children may learn more effectively and engage more fully with the lesson as a result, but there may be no creative opportunities for them in the experience. Learning to read notation using colours, puppets or funny faces is still about learning to read notation. Singing a song about the Vikings may be fun but may not be musically imaginative or challenging. However, asking the children to compose their own song (music as well as words) or composing music in response to a Norse myth could. Teaching for creativity requires a kind of 'letting go' on the part of the teacher, and providing a safe space in which the children can find challenge and new insights about music and about themselves.

There is not the space here to discuss in detail the role of music in supporting and enriching creative activities in the rest of the curriculum. Suffice it to say that bringing music and music-making into humanities, other arts, core subjects and physical education not only feeds the imagination and understanding, but also puts music in its proper context of being an integral part of the cultural and social world in which children learn. This is not to suggest that music should be artificially inserted into non-music topics. But where there are obvious links the opportunities should be exploited, not least to increase children's involvement with music!

The focus of the rest of this chapter will be on creative processes and activities within music learning.

Teaching songs

The song repertoire used in primary schools should encompass a wide range of styles and traditions. Popular music (as opposed to classical/high art music) in all traditions is created to be infinitely flexible and adaptable, learned aurally through joining in and in a social setting. Each time a song is sung it will change according to the abilities and feelings of the singers and the context in which it is sung.

When teaching a song, consider the opportunities for children to create their own interpretation. The material that exists (the words, the melody and the accompaniment when there is one) is only part of the music. Making decisions about how to sing the song (expressive elements: speed, dynamics, liveliness, calmness, etc.), how to arrange the song (solos, everyone together, how to begin, how many repeats and how to vary each repeat, etc.) and what to add in the way of accompaniment are all musical choices to be made and experimented with. In this way children learn about the many ways musical material can be changed to give different meaning or feeling. Of course instrumental music can also be explored in these ways.

PRACTICAL TASK PRACTICAL TASK PRACTICAL TASK PRACTICAL TASK PRACTICAL TASK

Suggested sequence of activities for teaching a song

- **Sing it through to give a sense of the whole. Ask children to listen out for anything they notice: repetitions, interesting words, surprises.**

- **Is the song a gentle, calming song or does it make you want to move (is it a work song or a going to sleep song, a story song or a love song, a funny/comic song or a protest song, a song for a single singer or a group)? Thinking about the meaning and context for the song will help in deciding how to sing it (i.e. how to interpret it in performance).**

- **Learn the chorus first. Children can invent their own pattern of movement (dance sequence, makaton, or just expressive gestures) to accompany it. From these the class choose movement patterns that they like (appropriate and manageable) and everyone practises – what happens if not everyone can manage it? Can the children solve the problem? Possible solutions include:**

(Continued)

(Continued)

- – simplify;
- – break into sections for different groups to perform in sequence;
- – practise;
- – differentiate so that some perform a more complex version of the pattern.
- The possibilities for different ways of singing encourage 'possibility thinking' (what if we sing it faster, change the dynamics, vary the number of voices singing together?).
- There are choices to be made to achieve a satisfying 'fit' of style and content.
- Not every idea will feel right.
- As children become more confident they might divide into groups to perform their own versions of the same song to each other.
- There may be a performance recorded on CD (song books often include this), or Youtube – how does that performance compare?

Skill building

Introductory skill-based activities are now a very familiar part of the music lesson. They give group focus, and introduce and establish the skills needed for listening and music-making. They are often devised as circle games: inventing and passing sounds; following the leader in making body sounds; echoing and sequencing clapped or sung patterns; keeping the pulse collectively and feeling silent beats; accompanying simple songs with actions and so on. In some ways these 'games' are disguised 'drills' – for children to practise in an enjoyable way. What will enable such games to become creative activities for the children is to invite them to make the 'game' their own – to invent variations, add new elements, play independently of the teacher as leader. Such activities should have a strong connection to the main activity of the lesson, so that, for instance, the rhythm patterns used in an echo game are used as the basis for improvising, or accompanying a song, or are listened out for in a listening piece.

Listening

On the face of it, listening may appear to be unrelated to a focus on creative music-making; but listening is crucial in developing skills, knowledge and understanding in the music – making process as well as listening as audience. Our musical imagination is engaged through repeated listenings; and thinking and talking about how music makes us feel, and about what's going on in the music. Listening and responding to music through movement and dance, painting, drawing or writing gives meaning and makes connections between different forms of expression and imagery. A multi-sensory approach feeds the imagination and expands possibilities for our own ideas. Listening to soundtracks of films and videos etc. can give a strong impetus to attentive listening and lead into creative work (www.literacyshed.com offers some excellent material). Attentive listening while creating music will develop the ability to change and refine ideas, to get closer to what we imagine. Listening to a piece of music can provide the starting point for children's creative work, or a moment during the process to listen how another composer has responded to the same idea. Giving time to listening to the music made in class (through live or recorded performances) affirms the value of children's work and encourages critical reflection.

Improvising

Improvising and composing are considered distinct activities but in the musical behaviours of young children and the inexperienced they overlap and merge. Improvising can be seen as a form of musical play (Hennessy, 1998b) spontaneous, of the moment, not fully worked out before it is sounded, a kind of musical doodling. It may not be intended to be communicated to anyone else: 'the musical stream that results may be highly-structured or more exploratory' (Glover, 2000). It is, however, inevitably based on what the performer can do at that moment – and so arises out of prior learning or experience. Often the design and layout of an instrument will dictate the gestures or patterns which result. It is not something that appears out of thin air even though it may appear to do so. Improvising at a more developed stage involves knowledge, skills and practice in order to create within a given musical frame or style – this is what jazz musicians do, for example. If musicians are encouraged to play with ideas, and play by ear (without notation), to not worry about every note sounding perfect and to play and sing along with others, they are more likely to develop the confidence to improvise. Songs and musical frameworks for instrumental work which include little gaps or sections within them for improvising are a 'safe' place for children to develop their improvising abilities in this direction. The Orff approach (see Buchanan *et al.*, 1996; Goodkin, 1997) promotes this way of working – starting from simple accessible ideas and providing supportive musical frameworks within which everyone can participate at their own level.

Composing

Composing involves a putting together of ideas – something planned and worked out. A composition is developed in stages with alterations, edits and revisions. In the hands of younger children the revision process may be barely touched upon – the inexperienced are more likely to accept the first idea which appears and stick to it. This will be compounded by lack of time in lessons and the teacher's degree of understanding of how to mediate the process of revision. Encouraging development and revisions requires careful handling – to gauge when enough is enough or when the musicians are keen (or willing) to stay with it. Knowledge of individual children, and their capacity for focus and critical thinking will inform the teacher's decision to encourage a group to work further with a piece or agree that, for now, it is ready to be performed, recorded and more or less 'fixed'.

Group compositions are more likely to have a discernible shape and structure where one can hear (and see) how the piece has been put together. The teacher may have asked for a particular structural feature to be used (repetitions, ostinato, ABA, canon, verse/chorus) but even when this is not done, children, especially when working with others, will invariably come up with a structure which organises who plays what when. Also children, especially when working in groups, may often impose a linear 'narrative' form on their work in the absence of a given structure. Musical structures involve repetition (exact or with variations), question and answer, contrast and silence. Finding ways of encouraging children to work with these elements will lead to more developed and musical outcomes and greater musical understanding. Jo Glover provides an in-depth explanation and discussion of the different ways in which children compose. She encourages us to understand children's music as a musical world quite distinct from adult music, and also argues for self-initiated composing (2000).

A note on notations

Many view musicianship as synonymous with being able to read and write conventional notation (i.e. dots on the stave), despite the fact that the vast majority of music-makers in the world do not use notations of any kind. Especially for young children in primary school, notation should always follow practical and aural engagement, not precede it. Notations of all kinds can and should, on occasion, be used to support and illuminate aspects of music learning. Paintings, sculptures, graphic art and invented symbols can all combine with music to offer starting points or structures for composing, responses to music or ways of analysing music. Inviting children to create their own notations will develop their understanding of the possibilities and limitations inherent in representing music in this way.

The creative process

As you can see there are different ways in which we can work creatively in music and which do not necessarily result in a completely new 'composition'. It is helpful to think of creativity in music as a process through which many different outcomes may emerge. In this process we can identify a number of phases or stages which are sequential and cumulative, but also cyclical, that is earlier stages may be revisited through the process. These stages are in many ways common to all creative processes whether in music or other disciplines. The particular aspect of the process in music which we need to acknowledge is time. As with dance and drama, experiencing music takes place in and through time. This temporal quality dictates much of the way we engage with music both in teaching and learning, and the process of creating in music should be framed by this understanding.

I have borrowed a model developed by Wallas (1926) and adapted it to provide a frame for how to recognise and plan for children's engagement with the creative process. Wallas identifies four phases which he names:

- preparation;
- incubation;
- illumination;
- verification.

Preparation

In the classroom this initial stage almost always commences with a 'commission' – a task instigated by the teacher as part of a unit of work. However, it could also arise from children's ideas and motives.

The preparation stage will encompass:

- the stimulus (e.g. pattern of movement, poem, a visit to a wood, a visual image, a sound or an existing piece of music) through which the structural or expressive framework is agreed – or given;

- initial focusing activity (listening game, exercise, song, conversation) exploring the elements which link the stimulus to musical ideas;
- establishing the mode of working (whole-class, groups, pairs) and providing some ground rules (scope of the piece and time available for working on it).

If the composition is to be based on small-group work, the teacher may also use this phase in a quite directed way in order to take the class through a model of the suggested way of working – the kinds of decisions they will need to make, and a chance to try out and listen to how the basic ideas can be worked on.

In the teacher's planning there needs to be careful thought given to how much freedom or constraint is permitted (Burnard and Younker, 2002). Too much freedom can be as difficult as too little and the balance between them varies according to the experience and dispositions of the children.

There is a tendency to believe that creativity must be entirely free, open and unfettered – the teacher's role is to *light the blue touch paper* and stand back. The teacher, in this view, just provides the initial stimulus, the resources, the space and the time – she has no function once the children are working other than to ensure that they stay on task and arrive at a product in the time available.

Fortunately this idea has been largely discredited and it is recognised that children learn more effectively when their experience is mediated by 'knowledgeable others' (Hennessy, 1998b). This clearly supports the notion of creativity as a social phenomenon.

REFLECTIVE TASK

If you were asked to compose a piece of music – anything you liked and for any purpose you chose – how would you feel? How would you approach the task?

You would have to make every decision from scratch and in effect decide on your own constraints (rules): how long, what structure, mood, melodic content, etc. If you have composed before you may feel undaunted by this and enjoy the freedom. If you have never composed or done very little, you might find this quite paralysing – even if you play an instrument or sing quite confidently.

Would this be easier alone or with others?

On the other hand composing a piece in which you can only use three notes on a recorder might feel much less threatening and more achievable. At the same time, for an experienced composer, limitations can be challenging and exciting.

It is evident that in creative activity we need both freedom and constraints – freedom to experiment, invent, find our own ideas; and constraints to support, challenge and give focus.

Incubation: exploring and experimenting

This is the phase which creates the most difficulties in the classroom context. It is likely to be noisy and therefore difficult to provide good conditions and difficult to gauge how long different groups or individuals need. Incubation might mean quite solitary thinking or a period of exploring, experimenting and the musical equivalent of doodling (noo-dling) with others. The teacher's role in this phase requires skills of facilitation and guid-ance rather than direct instruction. Children need to explore, experiment and improvise with the materials and ideas provided. Because of noise there has to be more manage-ment than perhaps seems appropriate – and more than one might need for other crea-tive activities such as poetry, drama, or visual art, for instance. Turn-taking, listening to each other, short periods of free play, whole-class involvement with opportunities for individual suggestions to be tried and tested, all need planning (many publications offer ideas on how to achieve this).

If you are able to use time flexibly you might consider planning for small groups to explore and experiment at different times through the week – if there is an adjacent space available. If this phase is stretched over several days in this way children may want to record their ideas for recall (i.e. audio recording or finding a way to notate).

If using electronic keyboards or computer software children can use headphones – and save or record their ideas.

Illumination: choosing and organising

This is the phase in which decisions are made about what to work with and what to dis-card. Once choices are made, the process of organising and refining takes place. As mentioned earlier young children may arrive at this stage very quickly – choosing the first idea they come up with. As they develop their understanding and skills they will become more discerning and more confident to discard or revise ideas. The teacher's role is to encourage and nurture this awareness through listening, sensitive questioning, suggestions for development, even challenging their decisions – in fact, scaffolding their learning (Hennessy, 1998).

Verification: rehearsing, performing and evaluating

Once the piece is composed (organised, assembled, fully fashioned) there comes the phase of 'fixing'. Rehearsal may still involve changes but essentially this is the stage prior to performing. In the classroom this is likely to be an event in which the composi-tion is performed 'live' to others (the rest of the class, another class, at an assembly) or recorded and played back.

Traditionally, the final product is viewed as the end of the process and the achievement should be celebrated. The accumulated experience will resonate in various ways and there should be time, after the event, for the children to evaluate their work and what they feel they learned. Articulating their reflections through writing, drawing or talking should help in developing a sense of ownership and independence.

We can see and hear what children can do in their acoustic compositions – no one is likely to compose something they cannot play themselves as most composing arises out of personal trial and error, so there is likely to be a close link between performing ability, musical understanding and the kinds of compositions children produce.

It is often suggested that there is no 'right' and 'wrong' in creative music-making – how-ever, there is fitness and unfitness, appropriateness and inappropriateness. These are in many ways subjective terms but they are inevitably informed by common cultural expe-riences and ideas about balance, the relationships between certain patterns and gestures in sound and what they signify in terms of feelings, movements, natural phenomena, etc. For instance, there are very recognisable and common musical representations of different intensities of rain. Young children will tend to find simple and literal responses to events or moods in a story – often fairly predictable. As they become more experienced and exposed to more and more possibilities they will challenge themselves and be challenged to move away from cliche´s and experiment with more novel ideas.

The contexts for musical creativity

Children are steeped in music from the moment they are born (and before) (Young, 2003) – in contemporary Britain it is impossible to avoid regular, daily contact and immersion in music. By the time children enter school they are likely to have acquired a well-developed repertoire of music through TV, radio, background music in shops and, hopefully, songs and bits of music encountered in play and social settings. In this way children learn to recognise how music is structured, to respond to rhythms, to predict the shape of a tune, to separate the familiar from the unfamiliar. They learn to move and dance to music and to recognise its mood. They adopt and adapt music within their play activity: babbling, cooing, chanting, singing, using objects as instruments and dancing. They are already musically experienced. This is part of enculturation – as we learn language, ways of behaving and ways of interacting in the family and social groups, we also absorb musical behaviours.

When children enter school we need to recognise and build on this knowledge and experience. Children will already be immersed in the music of their home culture and its relationship to what is offered in school can affirm or deny their own emerging musical self. A valuable and authentic way for teachers to learn about their children's musical lives is not only to invite them to create and share their own music in the classroom, but also to listen in on how children use music in their play.

Creative music-making will:

- reinforce and help to develop their musical ideas;
- increase and strengthen their abilities in controlling sound (technique);
- encourage social interactions through and around music;
- give meaning to their music learning.

School is only one of many places where music learning for children happens and one might argue that 'school' music is a genre all its own – made up of an exclusive repertoire never heard outside of school (unless to invoke 'school'). What primary schools can provide is a structured, safe and sociable setting for music-making. They can foster musical interactions so that children can then take their music-making into other settings: at home, with friends, at after-school clubs and community-based activities.

Creative activity carries a certain momentum which can depend on many factors:

- the relevance and imaginative potential of the initial stimulus and purpose of the task;
- an appropriate balance between constraint and freedom within the task;
- children having some real control over musical decisions – feeling that the music is theirs;
- the quality of the resources and environment in which the children are working;
- the successful match between the demand of the task and the abilities of the children; and
- responsive and encouraging teachers.

Atmospheric winds

The purpose of the lesson is to explore the contrast between long and short sounds; to develop skills in controlling long and short sounds, vocally and on wind instruments, and to create a composition which exploits the sound qualities children have explored.

Preparation

- Play an introductory 'game' to establish group focus for listening and vocal control, and to think about and invent long sounds and short sounds.

- Pass a vocal sound round the circle on the end of your finger – a steady horizontal movement, but wiggly or stabbing action will change the sound. First everyone reproduces the same then each invents their own. Different physical movement triggers a 'matching' vocal response and vice versa.

- Listen to a piece of music made up entirely of sustained sound and move to it (e.g. an excerpt from Atmosphere by Ligeti).

- In the circle listen to the music again and ask the group what they hear, how it makes them feel or what they imagine.

- Ask them to make long continuous sounds with their mouths or voices (humming, blowing, quiet singing on a single note, whistling) – contrast with very short sounds. Ask individual children to find gestures for conducting the class performing these two contrasting sounds.

Incubation

- Introduce lots of cardboard and plastic tubes of different lengths and diameters and ask children to find different ways of sounding them (blowing across the opening, blowing into the tube, tapping it on the ground). If there are children who play blown instruments (recorder, penny whistle, flute, trumpet, etc.) they can include these (as part of the overall texture or perhaps a specific contrasting section). This could lead to an exploration of pitched notes and how they sound in different combinations (do some tubes produce the same note? Do some notes sound comfortable together? Why? Can you alter the sound of your tube and control the way you play it – quietly, gradually getting louder?... and so on).

- Conduct (and let the children conduct) everyone playing short sounds and long sounds – altogether, in small groups, solos, combinations of short and long, only long high sounds, only short low sounds and so on.

Illumination

- Create a whole-class piece based on these sounds and patterns – considering repetitions and contrast. Don't forget silence! (Children decide on the content and structure, and fix this by showing the sequence visually – how?: graphics, streamers/ ribbons and unifix blocks, † do different colours show different 'colours' of sound?)

NB Blowing is quite tiring and might make children dizzy so you could add a contrasting section based on percussive sounds made with their soundmakers – maybe free improvisation (represented in the score by a scribble!).

Verification

- Once the piece is constructed and the score is fixed, the piece should be rehearsed to ensure everyone knows what they are doing and gets a feel for the overall sound and structure. Invite individual children to sit out and listen – to give feedback on balance, quality, etc. Record or perform to others. It could be combined with dance or become the atmospheric music for a drama.

Creating a musical environment

- For individual explorations and musical play for young children, a sound corner works well: devise an area of the classroom where instruments are available, perhaps at certain times of the day or week, e.g. a few chime bars, a xylophone with a variety of beaters, two or three different sized drums (see Hennessy, 1998, for detailed guidelines), or headphones plugged into a keyboard and an audio recorder for children to record their stories and songs.
- Build up the best possible range and quality of instruments for the classroom. This will take time, but resist buying cheap as the sound will be disappointing.
- Use poems and stories which have sound content or which evoke movement or atmospheres which can stimulate music-making.
- Exploit the musicality of speech and enjoy the sounds and rhythms of words.
- Look for opportunities to include music in other areas of the curriculum – not only as support for learning in that area but also to further musical aims.
- Include music for listening wherever possible – to feed the imagination, and enrich sensory experience.
- Invite parents or colleagues who play instruments to play to the children.
- Involve secondary school pupils in performing and helping with music-making.
- Exploit opportunities for involving community and professional musicians in special projects or ongoing support.

A SUMMARY OF **KEY POINTS**

> Teaching for creativity involves taking risks and being confident in your ability to use the imagination of your pupils, allowing the power and responsibility to shift between you and the children. It requires everyone to engage in the process, however limited their contribution might be: this includes the teacher.

> The music teacher's role is often one of managing the activity, asking questions, capturing interesting ideas and ensuring that all the children are able to participate at an appropriate level. It may also be necessary to arbitrate among different ideas (or where little is forthcoming, offer some) and suggest some structure.

> It is impossible to produce simple formulae for success as so much depends on the particular children you are working with, your knowledge of them and your own musical interests and enthusiasms. Creative activities you plan may not work, or work beautifully sometimes and not at other times.

> Teachers need to see themselves as artists alongside their pupils so that they can enter the musical world of children and thus come to understand how to nurture and support their explorations and discoveries.

MOVING *ON* > > > > > > MOVING *ON* > > > > > > MOVING *ON*

Supporting children's musical creativity requires you to be open-eared and open-minded about all kinds of music. It also requires a certain attitude of mind towards processes and possibilities. To teach creatively for creativity in music:

- try to see music as activity rather than fixed material that children must learn to master;
- look for musical possibilities in words, gestures, and everyday sounds; and find imaginative connections and stimuli in stories, poems, pictures and patterns;

- look for opportunities to collaborate with colleagues in developing imaginative connections between different curriculum areas;
- if you have musical interests pursue them for your own pleasure and learning but also look for opportunities to challenge yourself with new ways to make music.

REFERENCES REFERENCES **REFERENCES** REFERENCES REFERENCES REFERENCES

Buchanan, K, Chadwick, S and Dacey, L (1996) *Music connections: practical music for all primary class teachers, Key Stages 1 and 2*. London: Cramer Music.

Burnard, P. and Younker, B-A (2002) *Mapping pathways: fostering creativity in composition*. Music Education Research, 4:2, 245–62.

Craft, A (2001) Little c creativity, in Craft, A, Jeffrey, B, and Liebling, B (eds) *Creativity in education*. 45–61. London: Continuum.

DfE (2012) Teachers' Standards available at **https://www.gov.uk/government/publications/teachers-standards** accessed 7/9/14.

Department for Education and Skills (DfES) (2004b) *Excellence and enjoyment: a strategy for primary schools*. London: DfES.

Elliott, DJ (1995) *Music matters*. New York: Oxford University Press.

Glover, J (2000) *Children composing 4–14*. Abingdon: RoutledgeFalmer.

Goodkin, D (1997) *A rhyme in time: rhythm, speech activities and improvisation for the classroom*. Miami, FL: Warner Bros Publications.

Hennessy, S (1998a) *Coordinating music across the primary school*. Abingdon: Falmer Press.

Hennessy, S (1998b) Teaching composing in the primary curriculum, in Littledyke, M and Huxford, L (eds) *Teaching the primary curriculum for constructive learning*. London: David Fulton.

Wallas, B (1926) *The art of thought*. New York: Harcourt Brace & World.

Young, S (2003) *Music with the under-fours*. Abingdon: RoutledgeFalmer.

FURTHER READING FURTHER READING **FURTHER READING** FURTHER READING

Burnard,P and Murphy, R. (2013) Teaching Music Creatively, London: Routledge

Teaching materials (a selection)

Buchanan,K and Chadwick,S (1996) *Music Connections*, London: Cramer.

MacGregor, H (1995/6) *Listening to music, elements 5+*. London: A & C Black.

MacGregor, H (1995/6) *Listening to music, elements 7+*. London: A & C Black.

MacGregor, H (1995/6) *Listening to music, history*. London: A & C Black.

MacGregor, H and Gargrave, B (2002) *Let's go zudie-o*. London: A & C Black.

MacGregor, H and Gargrave, B (2004) *Let's go shoolie-shoo*. London: A & C Black.

Music Express (2003) London: A & C Black.

Orff-Schulwerk American Edition (1977–82) *Music for children, vols 1 and 2*. Schott.

Song books

Birkenshaw-Fleming L (1990) *Come on, everybody, let's sing*. New York: Holt, Rinehart & Winston.

Clark, V (2002) *High, low, dolly, pepper*. London: A & C Black.

East, H (1989) *Singing sack*. London: A & C Black.

Gadsby, D and Harrop, B (1982) *Flying a round*. London: A & C Black.

Sanderson, A (1995) *Banana splits*. London: A & C Black.

Stannard, K (2004) *Junior voiceworks series*. Oxford: Oxford University Press.

Thompson, D and Winfield, S (1991) *Junkanoo*. Harlow: Longman.

Thompson, D and Winfield, S (1991) *Whoopsy diddledy dandy dee*. Harlow: Longman.

Websites

www.bbc.co.uk – ideas for teachers, information and links to other sites

www.gridclub.com – teaching materials

www.literacyshed.com – a wide selection of short videos to stimulate creative writing and music, drama or art work with primary age children

www.mtrs.co.uk – ideas

www.orff.org.uk – Orff Society holds courses for teachers in creative approaches to music teaching and learning.

www.singup.org – providing award-winning resources

www.youthmusic.org.uk – major source of funding and resources for out-of-school music-making

-all websites accessed 7/9/14

17
Children, creativity and physical education
Sue Chedzoy

Chapter objectives

By the end of this chapter you should have:

- understood the processes involved in teaching physical education;
- developed your own philosophy about the value of physical education and fostering creativity;
- recognised what high-quality physical education looks like.

This chapter addresses the following Teachers' Standards (DfE, 2012):

- establish a safe and stimulating environment for pupils, rooted in mutual respect;
- demonstrate knowledge and understanding of how pupils learn and how this impacts on teaching;
- have a secure knowledge of the relevant subject(s) and curriculum areas, foster and maintain pupils' interest in the subject, and address misunderstandings;
- impart knowledge and develop understanding through effective use of lesson time;
- demonstrate an awareness of the physical, social and intellectual development of children, and know how to adapt teaching to support pupils' education at different stages of development;
- manage classes effectively, using approaches which are appropriate to pupils' needs in order to involve and motivate them.

Introduction

The purpose of this chapter is to try to help you to think through your own view of physical education (PE) and to recognise the potential of the subject for enabling children to be creative through movement, either alone or with others. Practical suggestions are made and the creative approach is underpinned with creative theory (Fryer, 1996; Steinberg *et al.*, 1997; Beetlestone, 1998; DfEE, 1999; Craft, 2000; Aires *et al.*, 2004) and good practice in the subject (Schools Council and Assessment Authority (SCAA), 1997; Bailey and Macfadyen, 2000; Hopper *et al.*, 2000; DfES/DCMS, 2004).*

The problem with physical education

For those of you who remember your lessons in PE as unpleasant experiences on the hockey or rugby fields, being freezing cold and wearing unflattering kit, not being able to vault a horse in the gymnasium while being observed by the rest of the class or struggling around a 1500-metre track, creativity and physical education may not seem to be naturally well-matched. It has to be said that many people have been put off the subject by a few teachers who adopted very didactic teaching styles, favoured the naturally gifted and focused on the activity rather than the child. Some of these teachers were generally insensitive to the individual needs of their pupils and failed to inspire in them a love and appreciation of physical activity. However, you might consider that remembering the negative aspects of your own experiences might help you to empathise with those children who potentially struggle with the subject and this could be a chance to put those things right for the children that you teach.

REFLECTIVE TASK

If you were to write down your views about PE, what would you say?

Some possible answers might include:

- It's about keeping fit and fitness is important for a healthy lifestyle.
- Healthy lifestyles combat illnesses such as heart disease and diabetes.
- It's a range of competitive, creative and challenge-type activities.
- It's only popular with sporty people.
- Everybody can be good at PE.
- It's different from other lessons.
- It's about keeping the Olympic legacy alive.

Depending on your own experiences you might emphasise some aspects more than others. When you have completed this exercise turn to Figure 17.1 to see how others have described PE.

Creativity in PE throughout the twentieth century

In the early days of the development of the subject, there were hardly any opportunities for pupils to be creative. At the beginning of the twentieth century there was concern that the nation's youth were unfit for joining the armed forces and the government introduced programmes of physical training into elementary schools, based on military drill. In these programmes there was little room for creativity (Board of Education, 1933).

In the 1940s the Ministry of Education took over responsibility for physical education from the Ministry of Health and the subject became more child-centred. Certainly the guidance for primary school teachers in the 1950s (Ministry of Education 1953a and 1953b) recognised the need to relate to children's creative potential within the physical education programme in primary schools. The Plowden Report had an impact on the curriculum which followed and in the early 1970s the government issued a document relating to the physical education curriculum in primary schools named 'Movement' (Department of Education and Science, 1972). This document gave very little specific guidance to teachers on how to foster creativity but it was expected that modern

Children, creativity and physical education

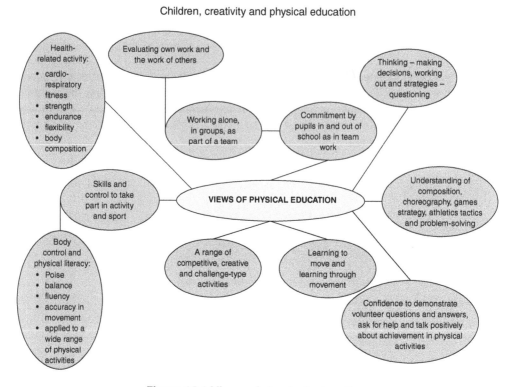

Figure 17.1 Views of physical education

educational dance and gymnastics were taught which encouraged a lot of exploration by children with very little structure.

In the National Curriculum for Physical Education (DES/WO, 1991) the teaching profession was guided towards involving children in the processes of planning, performing and evaluating their ideas and performances. It was intended that the process would underpin what children learn and do in physical education, changing the emphasis from a *product (activity) based curriculum to a process (learning) based curriculum* (Murdock, 2005). This made more explicit the way in which we should encourage children to be more involved in, for example, composing dances, creating original sequences in gymnastics and water-based activities, working out tactics and strategies in games and athletics activities and creating adventures outdoors. The very nature of the subject is about doing and so performance has always been at the heart of PE, but the concept of pupils planning and evaluating their work and the work of others had never been made so explicit in past guidance for teachers. This process relates well to the model of learning in other art forms in the primary curriculum such as music, art and drama, which involve the processes of composing, making and appreciating – and is very relevant today.

As Smith (2008) pointed out, Every Child Matters (ECM) provided an opportunity for teachers to be creative, to reflect on their philosophy for physical education, the curriculum, pedagogy and the whole child's physical education experience in school. See Smith (2008) and Council for Subject Associations (2008) for ideas on the contribution that physical education can make to the ECM agenda to have a significant impact on children's well-being. For a more detailed overview of developments in the United Kingdom, see Chedzoy (2012).

What does high-quality PE look like today?

When pupils are experiencing high-quality physical education, they appear to enjoy the subject, seldom miss physical education lessons, always bring their kit and encourage others to take part. They know and understand what they are trying to achieve and how to go about doing it. They know how to think for different activities, for example, composition in gymnastics activities, choreography in dance, games strategy, athletics tactics and problem-solving.

REFLECTIVE TASK
REFLECTIVE TASK

What does this mean in practice?

I personally feel that *thinking* has a major role in PE and the impact on learning is often underestimated. I would like you to consider the following:

- **How can you help children to *think* for different activities?**
- **What skills do you need to teach them to help them to be able to choreograph a simple dance or gymnastics sequence?**
- **What skills do they need to devise a games strategy?**
- **What skills do they need to be able to adopt a tactical approach to games or athletics?**
- **What skills do they need to solve problems in outdoor and adventurous activities and other areas of PE?**
- **How can you encourage them to think 'outside the box' in swimming?**

Children who receive high-quality PE know how to evaluate their own and others' work in a variety of activities. They recognise the contribution that physical education can make to a balanced, healthy, active lifestyle, and how success in aspects of the subject might affect their feelings about themselves.

Children who are experiencing high-quality PE have confidence in their ability. They are not afraid to show others what they can do: they volunteer questions and answers, ask for help and talk positively about their achievements, whatever their level of attainment. They explore and experiment with new activities without worrying about failing. Those who are more confident in an aspect of the subject are happy to help others.

However, the latest National Curriculum for the Physical Education programmes of study in England for Key Stages 1 and 2 (Department for Education, 2013) stresses that *a high-quality physical education curriculum inspires all pupils to succeed and excel in competitive sport and other physically-demanding activities.* As well as this, *it should provide opportunities for pupils to become physically confident in a way which supports their health and fitness.*

This guidance puts sport at the heart of the curriculum and states that *opportunities to compete in sport and other activities build character and help to embed values such as fairness and respect.*

It could be said that this is a retrograde step in the development of the subject, unless other aspects of the subject are carefully considered. Character building on the sports field was a feature of games and sports in public schools back in the 1800s. Surely we are not expected to subject our children to the notion of adopting 'a stiff upper lip' in losing and experiencing physical pain in the sports arena? We still need to consider how we can adopt creative teaching styles and approaches to the teaching of physical education, sports and dance, despite there being no direct reference to this in this National Curriculum guidance (DfE, 2013).

Mosston and Ashworth (2010) have written widely on teaching styles in physical education and reminded us that these fields are rich in opportunities to discover, design and invent. They identified the Divergent Discovery Teaching Style as a possible teaching style for a creative approach. They prompt us to remember that when children are given the opportunity of interpreting open-ended tasks, there is always another possible movement or another combination of movements that they might include. In creating games, there is always an additional piece of equipment that they may use, another way of passing the ball, or another strategy that might use to outwit their opponents. Most children are naturally inventive, that's what they do in their play activities – and teachers need to find ways to capitalise on their imaginative skills within the Physical Education curriculum.

REFLECTIVE TASK

In order to be creative in PE, children need to be and feel safe: both safe in the physical environment and safe to take risks.

- How can you help children to feel safe and secure in their physical space?
- What kind of ethos do you need to develop with your class to enable children to feel confident to explore and experiment in PE?
- How can you help children in your class to value and receive others' efforts and performances in PE with sensitivity?

Through high-quality PE, children are able to demonstrate improved skills and control, poise and balance. They are able to apply and adapt a wide range of skills and techniques effectively and have developed stamina, suppleness and strength to keep them going. Children experience a range of competitive, creative and challenging activities, both individually and as part of a group in high-quality PE programmes. They think about what they are doing and make appropriate decisions for themselves. They work independently and ask questions so that they can organise themselves and make progress. They devise ideas and strategies to help them to improve their performance. Children experiencing a high-quality PE programme show a desire to improve and achieve in relation to their own abilities; they are prepared to take time to practise and refine their performance and welcome the advice of others (DfES/ DCMS) (2004).

The Physical Education in the National Curriculum which has been taught in schools since 1999 (DfEE/QCA, 1999) required children to be taught dance, game activities and gymnastics activities every year throughout Key Stages 1 and 2, as well as athletics activities, outdoor adventurous activities and swimming at Key Stage 2. The four strands of the Physical Education National Curriculum included:

- acquiring and developing skills;
- selecting and applying skills and compositional ideas;
- evaluating and improving performance;
- knowledge and understanding of fitness and health.

The Attainment Target for Physical Education contained eight level descriptions with an additional description for exceptional performance and was central to planning in physical education. Gower (2005) reminded us these could be broken down into four aspects: a gradual increase in the complexity of the sequence of movement; an improvement in the demonstrated performance qualities; greater independence in the learning context; and a gradual challenge to the level of cognitive skills required throughout the level descriptions.

The most recent guidance is less prescriptive and the aims include ensuring that all pupils:

- develop competence to excel in a broad range of physical activities;
- are physically active for sustained periods of time;
- engage in competitive sports and activities;
- lead healthy, active lives.

Teachers need to recognise that previous guidance can be helpful when planning the new curriculum. There is more flexibility now; much of the earlier guidance can be helpful for schools to establish their own philosophy of the teaching of this subject and to formulate success criteria that suits the ethos of the school. Opportunities need to be created to give children as many chances as possible for independent learning and establishing success criteria which takes in to account innovative approaches to teaching Physical Education.

PRACTICAL TASK   PRACTICAL TASK   PRACTICAL TASK   PRACTICAL TASK   PRACTICAL TASK

Look at the National Curriculum for Physical Education

This has implications for the way you help children in their learning in all aspects of PE. You need to give them plenty of opportunities to be creative, to have opportunities to plan for themselves and to help them to develop a language with which to describe their own and others' work so that they are able to evaluate progress against given criteria.

REFLECTIVE TASK

- **What kind of environment do you think you need to foster in your classroom to enable children to be creative in PE?**
- **How can you help children to feel free to explore and experiment in the different aspects of PE?**
- **What knowledge, skills and understanding do children need as tools for creativity in this subject?**
- **How can you encourage other children in your class to value the originality of opinion, response to a task or different interpretation to a given task?**

All aspects of the National Curriculum for Physical Education lend themselves to developing and celebrating children's creativity. You as a teacher have the key to opening this up. First of all, you need to value the subject and feel reasonably confident in your own subject knowledge. You do not need to feel that you are an expert in all areas of activity, but you do need to feel secure in setting up a safe physical environment (see AfPE, 2012) and have a basic understanding about how children learn in and through physical education. Pickup (2012) has provided us with a very informative overview about the importance of Physical Education. You also need to help children to develop a movement vocabulary so that they are able to use these skills to form their individual movement patterns, whatever the area of activity.

PRACTICAL TASK   PRACTICAL TASK   PRACTICAL TASK   PRACTICAL TASK

Select one of the areas in the National Curriculum for Physical Education. Design a work card to give to a group of children to help them to devise an original dance, game, gymnastics, athletic, swimming or outdoor and adventurous activity.

- **What space will be available to them?**
- **What equipment will be available to them?**
- **How long will the activity need to last?**
- **What guidance will be required with regard to safety?**
- **Are there any cross-curricular links you would like the children to include?**
- **How can the activity be linked in some way to previous work to enable the children to use previously acquired skills?**

Creativity in athletic activities

Athletic activities in the primary school involve running, jumping and throwing activities. At this stage of children's development, it is important that they have success in these activities so that they feel good about themselves and recognise that, with practice, they are all capable of improving their performance. It is important that children are given time and plenty of opportunity to explore and experiment with different actions related to athletics, and that there is a fine balance between cooperative and competitive activity within the programme.

During the warm-ups for athletic activities, children can experiment with different ways of running and can work alone, in pairs or small groups to make up and create their own running activities (Bray, 1992). Examples might include: asking the children to devise a warm-up in a grid which involves running in different directions (forwards, backwards, to the left, to the right and diagonally); creating a maze to run through; around or over using hoops, bean bags, skipping ropes or low hurdles. Ask children to work in small groups and go on a journey in a single file: the first person in the line chooses the way of running, i.e. small steps, cross steps, large strides, or a variety of ways; and the rest of the group follow. The leader decides on the route and, on a signal, the person at the back jogs to the front and creates the running pattern and pathway.

Creating jumping patterns can also be fun either alone, in pairs or in groups. You may have taught the basic skills of jumping for distance or jumping for height. You could invite the children to create a pictorial series of movements using different take-off and landing techniques producing different patterns on the ground and in the air.

An example of larger-scale planning in athletics activities is where children in Year 2 in a first school were set the problem-solving exercise of planning the sports day for the whole school. The children selected the activities, gave them names, created their own record sheets, wrote and sent the invitations, planned and prepared the refreshments, and had a wonderful time learning across the curriculum (Chedzoy, 2000).

Other approaches have been outlined by Griggs (2012) and readers might find the frameworks which are described in his writing useful in developing imaginative athletic activities in their school.

Creativity in dance activities

Dance as a performing art seems to be the most obvious area of activity in the Physical Education National Curriculum to contribute to children's creativity. I am sure that if you have studied dance in your initial training, you are aware of the potential for developing children's creativity through the activity. Dance provides opportunities for artistic and aesthetic education, and experiences in which children can develop emotionally and learn to express moods and ideas symbolically. Dance can also help children to develop rhythmic and musical sensitivity and a knowledge and understanding of the art form. Dance education can also contribute to children's understanding of traditional dance forms from different times and places.

In dance you will encourage children to compose dances by exploring and improvising, making decisions and solving problems. Give them opportunities to share their ideas with others through practical demonstration or discussion. This will help them to shape and refine movement phrases to form dances. Through performance, children will develop physical skill and a repertoire of actions to travel, turn, jump and perform gestures to perform a set dance, express an idea, tell a story or communicate a mood. You need to give children time and opportunity to view dances, to appreciate their meaning, actions and qualitative and spatial features (Chedzoy, 1996).

There is such a wide range of stimuli for developing dance. These include other curriculum areas such as music, history, geography and art. Starting points for developing dance could be poems, stories, photographs, paintings, posters with different colours, text shapes and contrasts. Television adverts or film clips containing professional dance works may also be used to inspire children to create their own dances.

Even when teaching folk dancing, you can encourage children to adopt a creative approach. For example, teach the children some basic moves and figures such as do-si-do, arches, right-hand, left-hand star, promenade, and ask them to compose their own circle or line dance in small groups, using some of these figures involving meeting and parting.

Creativity in games activities

A high-quality games programme in the primary school will enable children to become confident and competent in a variety of invasion games, net/wall games and striking and fielding games.

Some people feel that all games teaching needs to be governed by the rules and regulations of the major game, or even their mini-versions such as high-five netball, uni-hoc, five-a-side football, pop lacrosse, tag rugby or short tennis. If you watch children playing games in the park or on the playground you will often see that they make up their own structures and rules – jumpers for goals and boundaries and carefully negotiated rules to help the game flow. Rules that are negotiated and agreed by the group are more likely to be adhered to by children – which for you as a teacher make things easier with regard to organisation. All governing bodies of sport advocate small-sided games for children of primary school age and if you are able to rely on children in your class playing games to their own rules, you do not have to referee or umpire to help keep order in the group.

You might also consider adopting a creative approach to helping children understand the principles involved in the tactics and strategies of games. For example, ask children to work in pairs to make up a game involving aiming at a target.

All ball games require the accurate sending of a ball/shuttlecock into space or to a goal or target. Focusing on this skill in an innovative way can be fun and also helps the children to understand the basic principles of play. Ask the children to select their own target from a range of equipment. The targets could be markings on the ground, wall or fences, such as circles, faces, animal shapes or rocket shapes, or children could draw their own targets with playground chalk. Posts, trees, skittles and hoops also make suitable targets. Ask the children to choose their own equipment to send to the target. This could be a small or large ball, a bean bag, a rubber quoit, or a uni-hoc stick and ball. Ask the children to decide on their own area of play and agree on any rules before play begins. Will there be a method of scoring? If so, how will the score be recorded?

At the end of the session, ask the children to show and share their ideas with others. Ask the children to evaluate their games. Ask questions such as: Is it easier to hit a target when you are close or far away? Is it easier to hit a big target or a small target? Is it easier to hit a target with a small ball or a big ball? Ask the children to give their game a name and ask them to write it up using the computer so it can be played by others at a later date (Chedzoy, 2000).

A refreshing approach to physical education is suggested by Lavin (2012) in his chapter 'There is always another way!' He gives us lots of suggestions for new approaches to teaching physical education including approaches to creative learning in a games context.

Creativity in gymnastics activities

Gymnastics activities is an area of the curriculum which can be a worry to both newly-qualified and experienced teachers, with all the inherent concerns about safety and progression. Once you have more experience, you might be comforted by the fact that children are in fact your best resource in this area of the curriculum. Their responses to your challenges will be rich and varied and if you can 'capture the moment' with good observational skills and ask children to show others in the class their movements, you will enable children to increase their 'movement vocabulary' so that they have more ideas with which to create longer and more complex sequences. The advice from Griggs (2007) is very helpful here: he suggests that to employ a creative approach to teaching gymnastics successfully, teachers need to use precise language in setting challenges and tasks. For example, instead of asking the children to *show me three ways to roll*, the guidance might be *to create three different movements which involves you turning your body connected by a balancing activity in between*. This might well result in more original and innovative outcomes for each individual child.

The most popular form of gymnastics taught in primary schools is educational or informal gymnastics (Reynolds, 2000). This approach is also sometimes described as curriculum gymnastics (Williams, 1997). In this form of gymnastics, the pupil works at his/her own level within a framework set by the teacher. This is rather different from formal gymnastics, in which the child has to perform stylised vaults and other prescribed gymnastic agilities. There are many good curriculum guides to help you to plan a progressive programme of curriculum gymnastics activities (Underwood, 1991; Benn and Benn, 1992; Williams, 1997; Devon LEA, 2002, Price, 2003). Very good advice has more recently been offered by Price (2012) and I would encourage teachers to read his chapter on gymnastics in the primary years and how to encourage your children to move with enhanced confidence, competence and imagination.

Creativity is at the heart of curriculum gymnastics. You are asking children to find different ways of travelling, jumping, balancing, turning, swinging, hanging, climbing and transferring weight from one area of the body to another. If you create a climate of mutual trust and encourage children to sensitively evaluate their own and others' work, they will enjoy creating their own original pieces of work. It is an area of the curriculum which should be accessible to all, regardless of physical shape or athletic ability. In assessing children's ability in this area of activity, as in other areas of the physical education curriculum, credit should be given for the child's ability to compose sequences and appreciate the aesthetic qualities of performance, as well as for the performance itself.

Creativity in outdoor and adventurous activities

The primary focus of teaching Outdoor and Adventurous Activities is to teach problem-solving skills, to focus on process, to learn to co-operate and to learn from group mistakes while participating. In a significant majority of Outdoor and Adventurous Activities, the skills, knowledge and understanding are almost immaterial to the primary focus, and do not significantly feature even as a secondary focus.

(Martin, 2000)

Outdoor and adventurous activities are defined as problem-solving activities which can be planned in and around the school environment, using existing facilities and taught to the whole class by their class teacher. This is opposed to outdoor pursuits and outdoor education which tend to need specialist facilities and specialist tuition.

No two solutions to problems set for children will be identical as children will need to cooperate with others, make decisions and work together to test themselves in a variety of situations, and the outcomes will always vary accordingly. Different forms of orienteering such as cross-country, score orienteering and line orienteering contain elements of navigation, decision-making and physical activity. (McNeill *et al.*, 1987; McNeill *et al.*, 1992; Chedzoy, 2000). Trails such as obstacle trails and string trails can present children with the challenge of making connections and seeing relationships. You can be imaginative in stimulating children's interest in their surroundings by taking photographs of features in the school and school grounds such as flowers, trees, shrubs, walls, murals and pond life and then backing these onto a firm fabric, giving each a number and setting up a trail for the children to follow. Another way of organising a trail is to create a texture trail, then give the children a base map, a wax crayon and a large sheet of paper with clues for the texture children should look for at given locations. Children then chase off to find them and make a rubbing of the texture, for example bark, brickwork, leaf or netting. You could encourage children to create their own texture trails.

For a more comprehensive overview of a rationale for outdoor and adventurous activities as an integral part of children's learning, and how schools can achieve this, see Wainwright (2012) and Wait (2011).

Creativity in swimming

Try not to always think of swimming in the primary school as only teaching children in straight lines to learn and refine the prescribed swimming strokes. Of course, you will wish children to develop water confidence and efficiency in moving through the water and to be able to fulfil the requirements of the National Curriculum for Physical Education (which, by the end of Key Stage 2, requires them be able to swim at least 25 metres and have a good knowledge and understanding of safe practice in and around water). However, children can have a great deal of fun and develop confidence in the water if you can think of interesting ways to help them to be creative in these lessons. In fact it is worth remembering that most activities which can be planned, performed and evaluated on land can also be enjoyed in the water. This can make things easier for you as a teacher, as you can help your children to transfer some of the ideas developed in the hall or on the field to be further explored in the water!

For children who are not confident in the water these activities will need to take place in shallow water, in which children are able to move with their flotation aids.

Use music – this might be over a sound system in a public pool or a suitably insulated deck if used pool-side, or use percussion to stimulate the movement. Ask the children to travel with big steps, little steps, high knees, forwards, backwards and sideways. Their way of travelling is planned by them and they can choose the arm actions to go with their stepping pattern. Ask the children to think about different still shapes and perform them – wide, narrow, twisted, curled. Ask the children to think of characters – how would they move in the water? Find different ways of turning, spinning and rolling around in the water.

For stronger swimmers, ask them to create different swimming patterns, joining front and back swimming strokes with a turn, spin or roll. Ask the children to make gestures in small groups to create Mexican waves (i.e. one performs a simple action which is repeated by the rest of the group one after the other). Make patterns with the water, sprinkling, swishing, splashing (not at each other!) and whirling using different body parts, i.e. fingers, toes, elbows or knees. Suggest that the children make up their own patterns, for example, picking up water in their hands and letting it fall through their fingers making patterns at different levels. Ask partners to share and join patterns together. You can ask the children to work in small groups together making circle patterns just as you might do in a folk dance so that the children compose their own patterns, for example, holding hands, travelling four steps to the right, followed by four steps to the left, walking together into the middle and lifting hands high to repeat. The task you might set them could be to *make up a pattern together* which involves everybody working in unison (all doing the same thing at the same time) which involves travelling (stepping, marching, swimming) meeting and parting.

A SUMMARY OF **KEY POINTS**

The development of physical education as a subject.

➢ **Understand the processes involved in teaching physical education today so that you can enable children to plan, perform and evaluate across the range of activities in the physical education curriculum.**

Your views about physical education.

➢ **Have a clearly-defined philosophy about the value of Physical Education and recognise the potential for fostering creativity across the whole of the physical education curriculum at Key Stages 1 and 2 (see J. Lavin (ed), 2008) and Lavin (2012).**

Recognise what high-quality physical education looks like.

➢ **Be able to facilitate creativity by helping children to think for and through different activities.**

➢ **Help children to develop skills of evaluation and a language with which they can evaluate their own and others' work.**

Create a safe environment in which children feel free and confident to take risks, explore and experiment and to create innovative and original episodes in and through movement.

➢ **This requires you to pay particular attention to the physical space and facilities.**

➢ **It also requires you to foster a climate of mutual respect where all children feel free to share and demonstrate their work without fear of failure or ridicule.**

MOVING *ON* > > > > > > MOVING *ON* > > > > > > MOVING *ON*

Never forget, your children are your best resource, always give them time and opportunity to develop and share their ideas with others. Take care to value each and every contribution in the creative process and encourage your children to do the same. Plan well, look ahead, seek advice and remember, a rich and stimulating physical education programme will lay the foundations for active healthy lifestyles. Every child deserves the chance to achieve their full potential (Lavin, 2008) and you can make a difference.

REFERENCES REFERENCES **REFERENCES** REFERENCES REFERENCES REFERENCES

Aires, J, Wright, J, Williams, L and Adkins, R (2004) The performing arts, in Jones, R and Wyse, D (eds) *Creativity in the primary curriculum.* London: David Fulton.

Association for Physical Education (AfPE)(2012) *Safe Practice in Physical Education and School Sport.* London: AfPE.

Bailey, R and Macfadyen, T (eds) (2000) *Teaching physical education 5–11.* London: Continuum.

Beetlestone, F (1998) *Creative children, imaginative teaching.* Buckingham: Open University Press.

Benn, T and Benn, B (1992) *Primary gymnastics – a multi-activities approach.* Cambridge: Cambridge University Press.

Board of Education (1933) *Syllabus of physical training for schools.* London: HMSO.

Bray, S (1992) *Fitness fun.* Crediton: Southgate Publishers.

Chedzoy, S (1996) *Physical education for teachers and coordinators at Key Stages 1 and 2.* London: David Fulton.

Chedzoy, S (2000) *Physical education in the school grounds.* Crediton: Southgate Publishers.

Chedzoy, S (2012) The development of the physical education curriculum in primary schools in the United Kingdom, in Griggs, G (ed) *An Introduction to Primary Physical Education.* London: Routledge. pp57–65.

Council for Subject Associations (CfSA) (2008) *Primary subjects: making every child matter.* Physical Education and Dance. CfSA.

Craft, A (2000) *Creativity across the primary curriculum: framing and developing practice.* Abingdon: RoutledgeFalmer.

Department for Education (DfE, 2012) Teachers' Standards available at **https://www.gov.uk/government/publications/teachers-standards** accessed 7/9/14

Department for Education (DfE) (2013) Physical Education programmes of study: key stages 1 and 2. National Curriculum in England. London: DfE

Department for Education and Employment (DfEE) (1999) *All our futures: creativity, culture and education. The National Advisory Committee's Report on Creative and Cultural Education.* London: HMSO.

Department for Education and Employment/Qualifications and Curriculum Authority (DfEE/QCA) (1999) Physical education: the National Curriculum for England. London: HMSO.

Department of Education and Science (DES) (1972) *Movement – physical education in the primary years.* London: HMSO.

Department of Education and Science/Welsh Office (DES/WO) (1991) *Physical education for ages 5 to 16: proposals of the Secretary of State for Education and Science and the Secretary of State for Wales.* London: HMSO.

Department for Education and Skills/Department for Culture, Media and Sport (DfES/DCMS) (2004) *Learning through physical education and sport: a guide to the school sport and club links strategy.* London: DfES.

Devon Local Education Authority (LEA) (2002) *A Devon approach to physical education: curriculum gymnastics.* Devon: Devon Curriculum Advice.

Fryer, M (1996) *Creative teaching and learning.* London: Paul Chapman Publishing.

Gower, K (2005) Planning in PE, in Capel, S (ed) *Learning to teach physical education in the secondary school.* Abingdon: RoutledgeFalmer.

Griggs, G (2007) Maximising creativity in primary physical education. Physical Education Matters, Winter ii-iii.

Griggs, G (2012) Getting athletics off the track, out the sack and 'back on track'. In Griggs, G (ed) *An Introduction to Primary Physical Education.* London: Routledge pps 151–159.

Hopper, B, Grey, J and Maude, T (2000) *Teaching physical education in the primary school.* Abingdon: RoutledgeFalmer.

Lavin, J (ed) (2008) *Creative approaches to physical education: helping children to achieve their true potential.* Abingdon: Routledge.

Lavin, J. (2012) Creative physical education. There is always another way ! in Griggs, G (ed) *An Introduction to Primary Physical Education.* London: Routledge. pp 221–231.

Martin, B (2000) Teaching outdoor and adventurous activities, in Bailey, R and Macfadyen, T (eds) *Teaching physical education 5–11.* London: Continuum.

McNeill, C, Marland, J and Palmer, F (1992) *Orienteering in the National Curriculum: a practical guide.* London: Harveys.

McNeill, C, Ramsden, J and Renfrew, T (1987) *Teaching orienteering.* London: Harveys.

Ministry of Education (1953a) *Planning the programme: physical education in the primary school.* London: HMSO.

Ministry of Education (1953b) *Moving and growing: physical education in the primary school.* London: HMSO.

Mosston, M and Ashworth, S (2010) *Teaching Physical Education.* Digitized. University of Michigan.

Murdock, E (2005) NCPE 2000 – where are we so far?, in Capel, S (ed) *Learning to teach physical education in the secondary school.* Abingdon: RoutledgeFalmer.

Pickup, I (2012) The importance of primary physical education, in Griggs, G (ed) *An Introduction to Primary Physical Education.* London: Routledge.pp13–24.

Price. L (2003) Primary school gymnastics – Teaching movement skills successfully. London: David Fulton Publishers.

Price.L (2012) Gymnastics in the primary years. The foundation of learning to move with enhanced confidence, competence and imagination. The importance of primary physical education in Griggs, G (ed) *An Introduction to Primary Physical Education*. London: Routledge pp108–134.

Reynolds, T (2000) Teaching gymnastics, in Bailey, R and Macfadyen, T (eds) *Teaching physical education 5–11*. London: Continuum.

Schools Council and Assessment Authority (SCAA) (1997) Expectations in physical education at Key Stages 1 and 2. London: SCAA.

Smith, P (2008) Creativity matters, in Lavin, J *Creative approaches to physical education: helping children to achieve their true potential.* Abingdon: Routledge.

Steinberg, H, Sykes, E, Moss, T, Lowery, S, Leboutillier, N and Dewey, A (1997) Exercise enhances creativity independently of mood. British Journal of Sports Medicine, 31, 2405.

Underwood, M (1991) *Agile.* Cheltenham: Nelson.

Williams, A (1997) *National Curriculum gymnastics.* London: Hodder and Stoughton.

Wainwright,N. (2012) Outdoor and adventurous activities. From desks to dens, in Griggs, G (ed) *An Introduction to Primary Physical Education.* London: Routledge. pp161–175.

Wait,S (2011) *Children learning outside the classroom: from birth to eleven.* London: Sage.